Deploying Cisco Unified Presence

Michael HouTong Luo, CCIE No. 6183

Copyrights

All rights reserved. No part of this book may be reproduced or transmitted in any form or by any means, electronic or mechanical, including photocopying, recording, or by any information storage and retrieval system, without written permission from the author, except for the inclusion of brief quotations in a review.

ISBN-13: 978-0-557-03953-1

Warning and Disclaimer

This book is designed to provide information about the Cisco Unified Presence. Every effort has been made to make this book as complete and as accurate as possible, but no warranty or fitness is implied.
The information is provided on an "as is" basis. The author shall have neither liability nor responsibility to any person or entity with respect to any loss or damages arising from the information contained in this book or from the use of the discs or programs that may accompany it.

Trademark Acknowledgments

All terms mentioned in this book that are known to be trademarks or service marks have been appropriately capitalized.
Author cannot attest to the accuracy of this information. Use of a term in this book should not be regarded as affecting the validity of any trademark or service mark.

About the author

Michael HouTong Luo, CCIE No. 6183, works for Cisco TAC (Technical Assistance Center) in the UCI (Unified Communication Infrastructure) team. Michael majorly supports voice appliances, such as CUCM (CallManager), CUPS (Presence), CER (Emergency Responder), etc. Michael has more than 15 years in IT industry and maintains many IT certifications, including CCIE, CCNP, CCDP, Certified UCCX and Presence Specialist, MCSE, OCP, VCP, MCNE, JNCIE, ACA, etc.

Author's Contact
houtong@gmail.com
http://htluo.blogspot.com/

What's New in this edition?

Revision date: Apr 18, 2010

Added: CUPS 8, Jabber/XMPP

Added: CUPC 8, CSF

Added: Message Archiving with external database (PostgreSQL)

Added: Message Auditing with 3rd-party compliance server (Facetime Vantage)

Added: Advanced Topic: Network Issue

Added: Outlook click-to-call troubleshooting

Updated: Exchange calendar integration

Updated: Customized LDAP search filter

Software versions:

CUPS 8.0.1
CUPC 8.0 (pre-release version)
Active Directory: Windows 2008 R2 Enterprise
PostgreSQL: 8.4.3 (Windows)
Facetime: Vantage 10.1 (Windows)
Microsoft SQL 2005 (to work with Facetime Vantage)

Note:
To get the latest version of this book, please order from author's publisher web site http://www.lulu.com/content/5552336. Because of distribution delay (usually 6-8 weeks), the content on resellers' site (such as Amazon, Barnes & Noble, etc.) might not be up-to-date.

Contents

CHAPTER 1. INTRODUCING CUPS 1
   PRESENCE OVERVIEW 1
      What is Presence? *1*
   CUCM (BLF) VS. CUPS 1
   CUPS FEATURES 2
      Instant Message *3*
      Presence - Availability *4*
      Presence – Phone *4*
      Presence – Calendar *4*
      Presence - Combination *5*
      Phone – Desk Phone *5*
      Phone – Soft Phone *6*
      Video Call *6*
      Voicemail *7*
      Web Conferencing *7*
      LDAP Integration *7*
      IP Phone Messenger *8*
      OCS/LCS integration *9*
      Sametime Plug-in *9*
      Outlook Plug-in *9*
   MAJOR CUPS COMPONENTS 10
      Sync Agent *10*
      SIP Proxy *10*
      Presence Engine *11*
   HOW THINGS WORK 11
      Instant Message *11*
      Presence – Availability *12*
      Presence – Phone Presence *13*
      Presence – Calendar *14*
      Phone – Desk Phone *15*
      Phone – Soft Phone *16*
      Voicemail *16*
      Web Conference *17*
      LDAP *18*
         Contact List 19
         Number Resolution 19
         Presence Mapping 20
      OCS/LCS integration *23*
      Sametime Plug-in *23*

CHAPTER 2. TESTING AND TROUBLESHOOTING TOOLS 25
   CISCO UNIFIED PERSONAL COMMUNICATOR (CUPC) 25
      Enabled Detailed Logging *25*
      Create Problem Report *26*

- *Show Server Health* 27
- REALTIME MONITORING TOOLS (RTMT) 28
  - *Login* 29
  - *Collect Files* 29
  - *Options* 31
- TEXT EDITOR 32
  - *Notepad* 32
  - *Wordpad* 33
  - *UltraEdit* 34
- KEYWORD SEARCHER 35
  - *Text Editor* 35
  - *Windows Search* 35
  - *WinGrep* 36
- SSH CLIENT 39
- SFTP SERVER 41
- PACKET SNIFFER 44
  - *Wireshark* 44
  - *Appliance built-in sniffer* 45
- SIP ANALYZER 46
  - *SIP Workbench* 46
- LOGS 48
  - *CUPC Logs* 48
  - *CUPS Logs* 48
  - *CUCM Logs* 48
- WEB INTERFACE 49
  - *CUPS Administration Page* 49
  - *CUPS User Option Page* 50

CHAPTER 3. INSTALLING CUPS 51

- PRE-INSTALLATION REQUIREMENTS 51
- INSTALLATION STEPS 51
  - *Step 1 Create an AXL user on CUCM* 51
  - *Step 2 Boot CUPS server from the installation DVD* 53
  - *Step 3 Auto Negotiation Configuration* 53
  - *Step 4 DHCP Configuration* 54
  - *Step 5 Static Network Configuration* 54
  - *Step 6 DNS Client Configuration* 55
  - *Step 7 Configure Platform Administrator Account* 55
  - *Step 8 First Node or Not* 56
  - *Step 9 NTP – Network Time Protocol* 57
  - *Step 10 Security Password* 57
  - *Step 11 SMTP Configuration* 58
  - *Step 12 Application User Configuration* 58
  - *Step 13 Complete* 59
- TROUBLESHOOTING INSTALLATION ISSUES 60
  - *Unsupported Platform* 60
  - *Trusted-peer Validation Error* 61

CHAPTER 4. INITIAL SETUP 63
POST INSTALL SETUP 63
SERVICE ACTIVATION 65
CONFIGURE SIP PROXY DOMAIN 65
CHANGE THE CUPS NODE NAME...66
SYNCHRONIZATION BETWEEN CUPS AND CUCM 67
TROUBLESHOOTING SYNCHRONIZATION ISSUES 68
Best practices..68
Initial Synchronization failed 69
CUCM updates not populated to CUPS immediately..............................69
Some data didn't synchronize from CUCM to CUPS 70
Everything's correct but SyncAgent won't start 70

CHAPTER 5. DEPLOYING AND TROUBLESHOOTING FEATURES 71
BEST PRACTICES 71
LICENSING 71
Server Licensing 71
Client Licensing 72
LOGON 75
Prerequisites 75
Step 1: CUCM: License the user 75
Test 76
Troubleshooting...77
    CUPC crashes on startup 78
    Unknown Login Failure 78
    Incorrect username/password 80
    Other logon issues 86
LDAP 86
Prerequisites 87
Step 1: CUPS: Set LDAP server type for CUPC 87
Step 2: LDAP: Create a Service Account in LDAP 88
Step 3: CUPS: Create a LDAP server in CUPS 88
Step 4: CUPS: Create a LDAP profile in CUPS and add users to it........89
Customized LDAP search base and filters..90
    Search Multiple OUs 90
    Filter unwanted data from search 91
Test 92
Troubleshooting...93
    CUPC failed to connect to LDAP... 94
    CUPC didn't return search results 96
    CUPC failed to add contacts.. 98
CLIENT STATUS...98
Prerequisites 99
Step 1: CUPS: Configure Proxy Domain 99
Step 3: Configure Digest Credential 100
    Option 1: CUCM: Digest Credential 101
    Option 2: CUPS: Incoming ACL 101
    Option 3: CUPS: Service Parameters 103

Test	*103*
Troubleshooting	*103*
Basic Concepts of SIP	104
Response	104
SIP messages between components	104
Best practices	106
Use SIP Workbench to isolate network issues	107
Self-status grey-out	109
Invalid Credentials	109
Proxy Domain not configured properly	110
Self-status not updated	110
Contact status not updated	111

PHONE STATUS 111

Prerequisites	*111*
Step 1: CUCM: Create SIP trunk	*112*
Step 2: CUPS: Create CUCM Presence Gateway	*113*
Step 3: CUPS: Confirm SIP publish mode and SIP publish trunk	*113*
Step 4: CUCM: Associate line appearance with to end user	*114*
Test	*115*
Troubleshooting	*116*
Best practices	117
Basic Configuration Error	117
CUCM-to-CUPS	118
CUPS – Presence Engine	120
CUPS – SIP Proxy	124

PHONE FEATURE 129

Soft Phone	*129*
Prerequisites	129
Naming Convention	130
Step 1: CUPS: Configure TFTP address	130
Step 2: CUCM: Add "Cisco Unified Personal Communicator" phone	130
Step 3: CUCM: Device Configuration	131
Step 4: CUCM: Configure Directory Number	131
Step 5: CUCM: User Configuration	132
Test	133
Troubleshooting	133
Phone Configuration – Download Failed	133
Failed to Connect – Server Connection Refused	135
Disconnecting (Pending Retry)…	138
Both Soft Phone and Desk Phone are "Not Active"	140
Desk Phone	*140*
Prerequisites	140
Step 1: CUCM: Associate device to end user	141
Step 2: CUCM: Specify Primary Extension for end user	141
Step 3: CUCM: Add end user to Standard CTI Enabled group	142
Step 4: CUPS: Assign user to CTI Gateway Profile	142
Test	143
Troubleshooting	144
Disconnecting (Pending Retry)…	144
Partial Connected – Cannot connect to phone	145
Not Connected – Stopped	146

   Not Connected – Invalid Credentials 147
   Both Soft Phone and Desk Phone are "Not Active" 149
 Application Dial Rules *150*
  Test 151
  Troubleshooting 151
   Verify CUCM database 152
   Verify CUPS database 152
   Verify CUPC 153
 Directory Lookup Rules *153*
  Name resolution for call information 153
  Name resolution for other features 154
  Test 156
  Troubleshooting 156
VOICEMAIL 157
 Retrieve Voicemail *157*
  Prerequisites 157
   Enable IMAP access on Unity Connection 157
   Enable IMAP access on Exchange 159
  Voicemail-related Menus on CUPS 161
  Step 1: CUPS: Configure "Mailstore" 161
  Step 2: CUPS: Configure Unity Server (optional) 162
  Step 3: CUPS: Create Unity Profile and assign users to it 163
  Step 4: CUPC: Configure user credential 163
  Troubleshooting 164
   Configuration issue 165
   IMAP connectivity/authentication issue 165
   IMAP referral issue 167
 Send Calls to Voicemail *167*
  Configuration 167
  Troubleshooting 168
   "Send to Voicemail" button grey out 168
   "Send to Voicemail" button clicked, but call was not sent to voicemail 168
   "Send to Voicemail" worked in Soft Phone mode but didn't work in Desk Phone mode 168
CALENDAR 169
 Prerequisites *169*
 Best practices *169*
 Introduction to certificates *170*
 Step 1: Exchange: Enable SSL for OWA *174*
  External CA 175
  Internal CA 175
  Self-signed certificate 175
   CN (Common Name) 176
   Expiration 177
   Certificate Authority Bit 177
   Steps to generate self-signed certificate and enable SSL 178
 Step 2: Exchange: Create Receive-As account *181*
  Create Account and Mailbox 182
  Assign "Receive-As" permission 182
  Exchange 2003 183
   Add "Receive As" permission to the account 183
  Exchange 2007 185
   Add "Receive As" permission to the account 185

- *Step 3: CUPS: Upload Certificates* 186
- *Step 4: CUPS: Configure Outlook Gateway* 188
- *Step 5: CUPC: Enable calendaring* 190
- *Test* 191
- *Troubleshooting* 192
  - FBA – Form Based Authentication 192
  - Configuration issues 194
    - You forgot to enable calendar integration from client side. 194
    - CUPS server time is different with Exchange time. 195
    - You uploaded the Exchange end entity certificate instead of its CA certificate. 195
    - You didn't upload all CA certificates in certificate chain. 196
    - You use IP address in presence gateway configuration while the Exchange certificate CN is FQDN 197
  - Typical log snippets 198
    - Starting up 198
    - Initial attempt 198
    - Loading certificates 199
    - Form Based Authentication 199
    - IIS redirect 200
    - Initial subscription response 200
    - Calendar search 200
    - Calendar Status 201
  - Certificate issues 202
    - Hostname does not match 202
    - CA not trusted 202
    - No CA bit in certificate 205
  - Permission issue 205
    - Use end user account in Outlook Gateway configuration. 206
    - Use service account to access end user's mailbox 206
  - Exchange interoperability issue 207
  - Exchange Hosted Solution 207
- **INSTANT MESSAGE** 208
  - *Prerequisites* 208
  - *Enable Instant Messaging* 209
  - *Test* 209
  - *Troubleshooting* 209
    - Best Practices 209
    - SIP domain issue 209
    - Logs 210
- **IP PHONE MESSENGER** 210
  - *Prerequisites* 210
  - *Step 1: Create IPPM application user* 211
  - *Step 2: Associate phones to IPPM application user* 211
  - *Step 3: Create IPPM phone service* 211
  - *Step 4: Subscribe phone to IPPM service* 212
  - *Step 5: Configure IPPM on CUPS* 213
  - *Test* 214
  - *Troubleshooting* 214
    - Best Practices 214
    - No visual or audio alerts on phone when message arrives 215
    - IPPM logs 215
- **WEB CONFERENCE** 215

Prerequisites *215*
Best Practices *215*
Step 1: CUPS: Configure Conferencing server *216*
Step 2: CUPS: Configure Conferencing Profile and assign users to it *216*
Step 3: CUPC: Configure MeetingPlace credential *216*
Test *217*
Troubleshooting *217*
    CUPC does not launch MP automatically 217
    Password issue 218

OCS/LCS/MOC INTEGRATION 219
Prerequisites *219*
Best Practices *219*
Step 1: CUCM: End User Provisioning *219*
Step 2: CUCM: Application User Provisioning *220*
Step 3: CUPS: Configure "Deskphone Control" *220*
Step 4: CUPS: User assignment *221*
Step 5: CUPS: Incoming and Outgoing ACLs *221*
Step 6: OCS: Static Route and Host Authorization *222*
Step 7: Active Directory: Server URI and Line URI *223*
    Scenario 1: Shared-line across multiple devices. 225
    Scenario 2: Shared-line across multiple partitions. 225
    Phone Selection Plug-in 225
Test *226*
Troubleshooting *226*
    Simplify the integration 227
    Divide and conquer 227
        MOC -> OCS 227
        OCS -> CUPS 228
        CUPS -> CUCM/Phone 230

SAMETIME INTEGRATION 231
Prerequisites *232*
Best Practices *233*
Configuration *233*
    Pre-Install Configuration 234
        Feature Control 234
        Control Desk Phone Settings 234
        LDAP Phone Attributes 235
        Phone Status Settings 235
        Sametime Client Version and Logging 237
        Directory Server Settings 237
        Directory Usage 238
        Dialing Rules Files 238
        Directory Type* 238
        User ID mapping 239
        ID Mapping Scenarios 241
    Post-Install Configuration 244
        Phone Control 245
        Phone Status 245
Installation *245*
    Troubleshooting 250

  Disable Sametime built-in telephony 250
 Troubleshooting *251*
  Logging settings 251
  Keywords in Logs 251
OUTLOOK CLICK-TO-CALL 253
 Overview *253*
 Searching Mechanism *255*
  1. Search for email address 255
  2. Search for display name 256
  3. Search for first name and last name 256
 Logs *257*

CHAPTER 6. OPERATION AND MAINTENANCE **259**

USER MANAGEMENT 259
 Add a user *259*
  Step 1: CUCM: Create End User 259
  Step 2: CUCM: Provision Desk Phone 259
  Step 3: CUCM: Provision Soft Phone 260
  Step 4: CUCM: Configure End User 260
  Step 5: CUCM: License End User 260
  Step 6: CUPS: Configure End User 261
 Delete a user *261*
  Remove a user from CUPS 261
  Remove CUPC soft phone from CUCM 261
  Remove a user from CUCM 261
 Change a user *262*
BULK ADMINISTRATION TOOL (BAT) 262
BACKUP AND RESTORE 264
PATCH AND UPGRADE 265

CHAPTER 7. ADVANCED TOPICS **267**

MULTI-NODE 267
 CUPC *267*
  Failover 267
   CUPC 1.2.x 267
   CUPC 7.0.x with CUPS 7.0.x 268
  Load-balancing 268
   CUPC 1.2.x 268
   CUPC 7.0.x with CUPS 7.0.x 269
 CUCM *269*
 OCS *270*
INTER-CLUSTER 271
 Steps to deploy inter-clustering *272*
  Step 1: CUPS: Configure same proxy domain for each cluster 272
  Step 2: CUPS: Create AXL group for each cluster 272
  Step 3: CUPS: Create AXL user for each cluster 273
  Step 4: CUPS: Configure Inter-cluster peers 274
  Step 5: CUPS: Activate AXL Service 274
  Step 6: CUPS: Verify Services 274
  Troubleshooting 275

NETWORK ISSUE	275
Typical traffic pattern for client/server	*276*
Typical firewall behavior	*276*
Traffic Pattern of CUPC/CUPS	*277*

CHAPTER 8. CUPS 8.0 AND CUPC 8.0 .... **279**

WHAT'S NEW	279
CUPS 8 ARCHITECTURE OVERVIEW	279
HISTORY OF JABBER/XMPP	280
JABBER/XMPP ON CUPS	282
HISTORY OF CUPC	283
CSF – CLIENT SERVICE FRAMEWORK	284
CSF ARCHITECTURE	285
WHAT'S NEW IN CONFIGURATION?	287
CUPS 8 NEW SERVICES	288
Network Services	*288*
Cisco UP XCP Router	288
Feature Services	*288*
XCP Connection Manager	289
XCP Authentication Service	289
XCP Text Conference Manager (TC)	289
XCP Message Archiver (MA)	289
XCP Web Connection Manager	290
XCP SIP/XMPP Federation Connection Manager	290
XCP Counter Aggregator	290
XCP Directory Service	290
CUPS 8 NEW FEATURES	290
Persistent Chat Room	*291*
Compliance	*291*
Message Archiving	291
3rd-Party Compliance	291
Dependencies	*291*
EXTERNAL DATABASE	292
Download PostgreSQL	*292*
Install PostgreSQL	*293*
Configure PostgreSQL	*295*
CONFIGURE CUPS TO USE EXTERNAL DB	298
PERSISTENT CHAT ROOM	300
Enable Persistent Chat	*300*
Test Persistent Chat	*301*
COMPLIANCE	302
Message Archiver	*303*
Configure Message Archiver	303
Test Message Archiver	304
3rd-Pary Compliance Server	*305*
FaceTime Vantage Configuration	306
CUPS Configuration	308
Test 3rd-Party Compliance	309
Compliance in Action	309

SERVER CONFIGURATION CHANGES FOR CUPC 8 310
   CUCM *310*
   CUPS *311*
CUPC 8 CHANGES 312
   Phone modes *312*
   Video Feature with Desk Phone *313*

CHAPTER 9. CUCIMOC 315

INTRODUCTION 315
COMPONENTS 316
   CSF – Client Service Framework *317*
      What is CSF? 317
      Stop and Start 318
      Configuration 318
      CSF – Softphone device 319
INSTALLATION 320
CONFIGURATION 321
   Registry Keys *321*
   CUCM *322*
      CUCIMOC Logon 322
      Soft phone 322
      Desk Phone Control 323
      Dial Rules 323
   Active Directory *324*
TROUBLESHOOTING 324

APPENDIX 327

Chapter 1. Introducing CUPS

Presence Overview

What is Presence?

Presence is a real-time indicator of a person's willingness and availability to communicate:
- Typically represented by status: Available, In Meeting, On Mobile, At Lunch, Be Back Shortly, etc.
- Includes details on user's preferred method to communicate: voice, video, or Instant Messaging.
- "Find-Me," "Follow-Me," or "Hide-Me."

Integration with calendaring, location, and workflow systems helps users automatically keep their presence status up to date and helps in the creation of streamlined business processes.

Instant Messaging (IM) is a very common example of the use of presence technology. Proprietary products such as IBM Lotus Sametime and free applications such as AOL Instant Messenger (AIM) can be used to add presence to any application. That faculty makes collaboration possible wherever and whenever users are online.

CUCM (BLF) vs. CUPS

In Cisco voice product family, "Presence" was first known as BLF (Busy Lamp Field) on CUCM. BLF is a CUCM feature that displays real-time status of another phone (off hook or on hook).

As seen from screen shot below, there's a BLF/Speed Dial button configured on button #8. This button serves two purposes:

1. Speed Dial.
   A user may press the button to dial extension 6001.

2. Presence
   We can see extension 6001's presence (on-hook or off-hook).

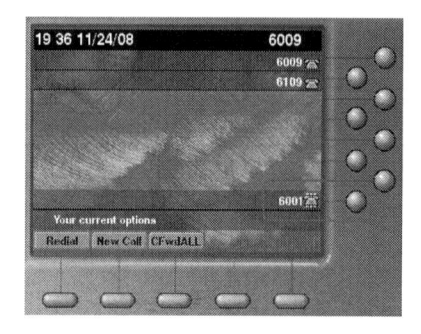

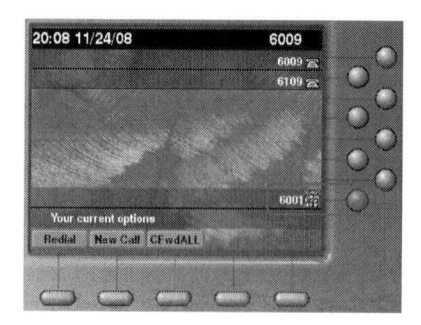

Left-hand side is when DN 6001 was on-hook (idle). Right-hand side is when DN 6001 was off-hook (in use)

Some customers still refer BLF as "presence". Be sure to ask what kind of "presence" they talk about.

Following is a comparison between BLF and CUPS features.

	BLF	CUPS
Where feature was built	CUCM server	CUPS server
Where we can see presence	On IP Phone	On client software (CUPC/MOC) or IP Phone (IPPM)
What kind of presence we can see	Phone presence	Phone, calendar, client availability.
Requires addition software/hardware	No (CUCM)	Yes (CUCM + CUPS/CUPC)
Additional features	N/A	Instant messaging, Voicemail/WebConf integration

CUPS features

As many other software, CUPS consists of many features. Since CUPS is pretty new on market, the most frequently asked question is: "What it can do for me?"

Before we discuss features, I'm going tell you something interesting about CUPS and CUPC.

CUPS stands for **C**isco **U**nified **P**resence **S**erver. CUPC stands for **C**isco **U**nified **P**ersonal **C**ommunicator. Many customers would treat CUPC as "Cisco Unified Presence Client". So it looked like a typical "Server/Client" model, just like Exchange/Outlook.

Actually, that was NOT the case.

First, CUPS and CUPC were designed and developed by two different, independent groups.

Second, CUPS was designed to be a "multi-purpose, open architecture" products, which serves many other products (like CVP – Cisco Voice Portal, MOC – Microsoft Office Communicator, etc.) other than just CUPC.

Third, CUPC was designed as multi-function communication software. It was never meant to be just a "client" for CUPS.

Because of the above, some CUPS features are not for CUPC. Some CUPC features don't depend on CUPS. Keep that in mind would help you understand the features better and isolate problems more quickly.

Instant Message

Above is what a CUPC looks like. The first impression would be – it's an IM (Instant Message) client, like MSN/Yahoo/AOL messenger.

That is right. IM (Instant Message) is one of the features of CUPC. You may send/receive IMs from/to CUPC users. In the latest version of CUPC/CUPS, you may also send/receive IMs to non-CUPC users (such as MOC user).

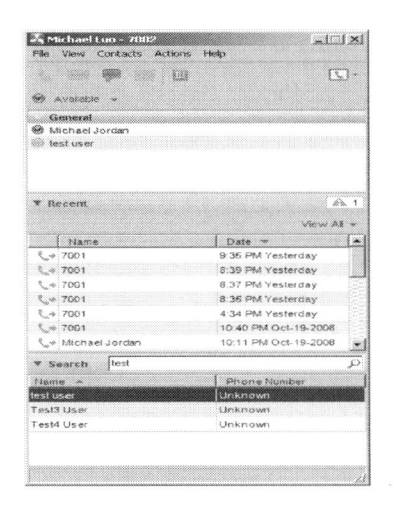

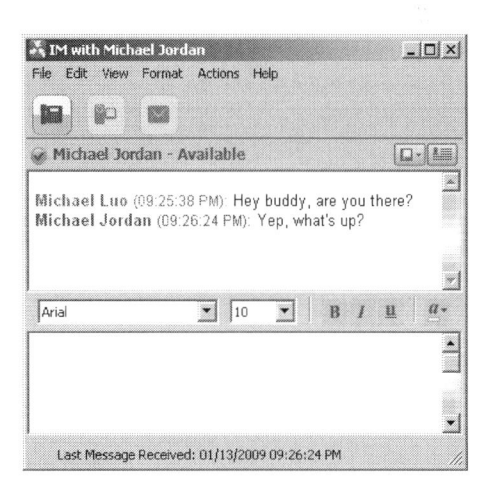

Presence - Availability

Like other IM clients, you may see your contact's status. For example, in the picture above, contact "Michael Jordan" is online/available. Contact "test user" is offline. Other statuses include "Away", "Idle", etc. You may also define your own status like "Out for lunch", "Leave for the day", etc. In our terms, those are called "availability" status.

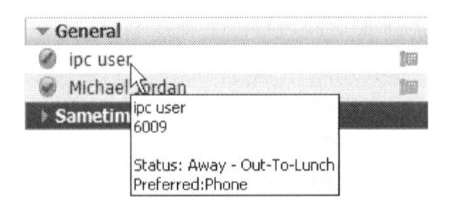

Presence – Phone

When integrating with CUCM, CUPC would be able to display another kind of presence information – phone presence, such as "On the phone", "Off the phone", "Do not disturb", etc. To distinguish from "Availability", we usually called this as "Phone Presence".

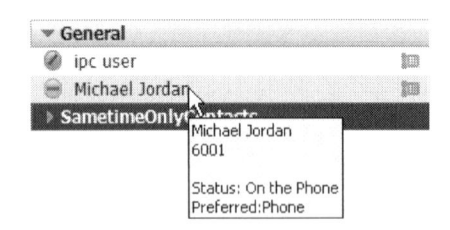

Presence – Calendar

A third kind of presence is called "Calendar Presence". When integrating with calendar system (e.g. Microsoft Exchange), CUPC would be able to display a contact as "In-a-meeting" if there's a "busy" event in his calendar. When the event is over, CUPC would change the status back to "available".

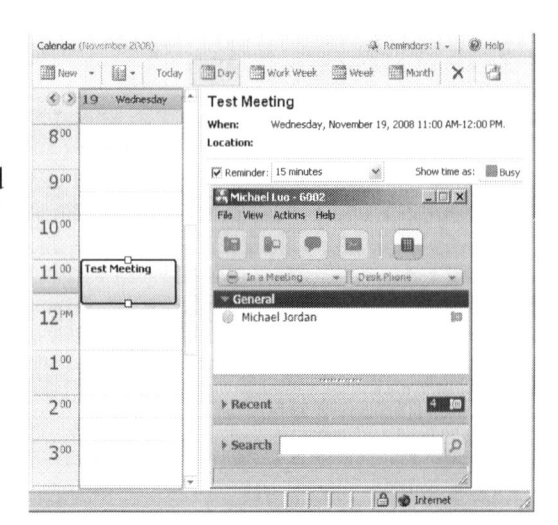

Presence - Combination

As discussed above, we have three kinds of presence for each contact. CUPC developers decided to use one single indicator to reflect three kinds of presence. Thus we need some kind of prioritization.

For example, a contact set his CUPC availability status to "Away". His Exchange calendar status is busy. He's also on the phone right now. How should CUPC display his presence? The rule is: Phone Presence > Calendar Presence > Availability.

In the scenario above, CUPC displays the user as "On-the-phone". If he puts the phone on hook, CUPC would display him as "In-a-meeting". If the meeting was over, CUPC would finally display him as "Away".

Understanding three kinds of presence will help us on troubleshooting. Because:
1. Each kind of presence is an independent feature. We'll need to troubleshoot different components for different presence issue.
2. Know the best way to test the feature. For example, if the user is on the phone, it's very difficult to test calendar presence feature, because "On-the-phone" status would override "In-a-meeting" status.

Phone – Desk Phone

CUPC can control your desk phone (e.g. Cisco 79xx IP phone). Which means, you may type the number you want to dial, and CUPC would make your desk phone dial that number for you. All the voice streams still go through your desk phone, which means, you still have to use you desk phone to hear and talk. The voice stream doesn't go through your computer.

If that's the case, why we want CUPC controls our desk phone? Why don't we just punch the keys on the phone?

The major reason to use desk phone control is the convenience of "click-to-dial".

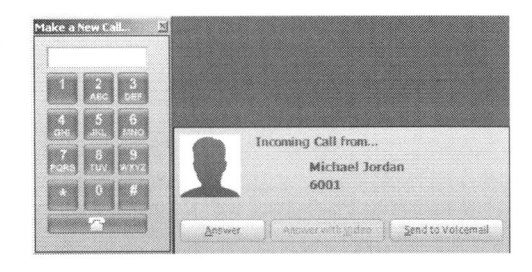

Imagine this – you are in IM session with somebody. You want to call him instead of typing. Instead of looking up his phone number and punch keys on the phone, you may just click a single icon on CUPC. CUPC then will dial out the number for you.

With application plug-ins, you may conveniently dial a contact within the application. For example, you received an email in Outlook. You want to call the sender. You may click the sender and let CUPC dial his number (if the number was in the address book).

For CUPC, the term "Desk Phone" refers to any other phones other than CUPC itself. So "Desk Phone" includes not only 79xx phones, but also IP Communicator. Don't confuse IP Communicator with CUPC "Soft Phone" below. IP Communicator is a "Desk Phone" from CUPC point of view.

Phone – Soft Phone

If you are on the road but still want to make/receive calls with your office phone. You may use the "Soft Phone" feature of CUPC.

Remember that in "Desk Phone" mode, voice stream still go through your desk phone. If you're away from your desk phone (office), there's pointless to use "Desk Phone" feature. Instead, you should change to "Soft Phone" mode in CUPC.

If configured properly, CUPC registers to CUCM as a soft phone (SIP). In soft phone mode, voice streams go to your computer. You may use computer's sound card and microphone to make/receive phone calls.

The cool things about CUPC soft phone mode are:
1. You don't need to install additional software. CUPC itself is a soft phone.
2. CUPC is a soft phone that can be run on MAC OS (which IP communicator can't do).

Video Call

You can make video calls if both parties have a camera plugged into the computer.

Based on CUPC phone modes (Soft Phone mode or Desk Phone mode), requirements are different.

In Soft Phone mode, video feature is built in CUPC. That means, CUPC needs to control the camera to establish video calls. If the camera was being used by other software, CUPC won't be able to do video call.

CUPS features 7

In Desk Phone mode, video feature is provided by Cisco Unified Video Advantage (CUVA) other than CUPC. If you can make a voice call but not video call in CUPC Desk Phone mode, you should troubleshoot CUVA instead of CUPC.

Voicemail

CUPC can notify you the arrival of new voicemail and allow you to retrieve and listen to voicemails from your computer. You may also divert the incoming call to voicemail (iDivert) with one-click on CUPC. Currently, CUPC only supports Unity with Exchange or Unity Connection.

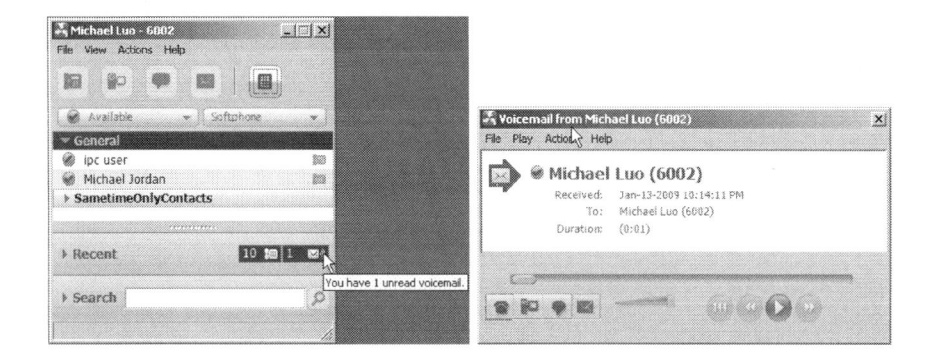

Web Conferencing

When integrating with Cisco MeetingPlace or Cisco MeetingPlace Express, CUPC can set up a web conference session and initiate the session on other party's computer (if you're on a call with him). This makes web conference integration more seamless.

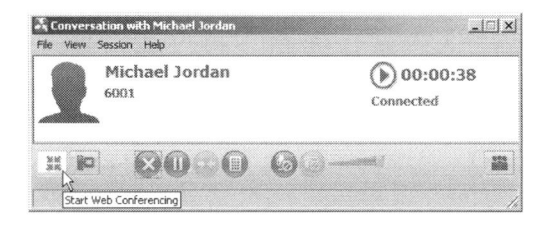

LDAP Integration

8 Chapter 1. Introducing CUPS

LDAP integration means you can search LDAP (Microsoft Active Directory, Netscape/Sun ONE LDAP) for contacts and add those contacts to CUPC contact list.

Even though it is listed as a "feature", it's actually more like a "requirement", because:
1. CUPC can only search users in LDAP. CUPC cannot search users in CUCM.
2. Without the search function, you'll have to add contacts manually. In pre-7.0 version of CUPC, you can only add contacts with user ID and display name, which means, you cannot click-to-dial or click-to-email on those contacts.
3. Some features are based on directory lookup (such as automatically launching web conference on remote end). Without LDAP, directory lookup would fail and those features won't work.

To make things more interesting, if CUCM was not integrated with LDAP but CUPC does, there might be a good chance you would be missing phone presence. We'll further discuss that in "components" and "troubleshooting" chapters.

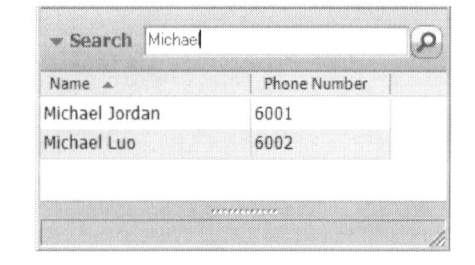

To make your life easier, please try you best to make both CUCM and CUPC integrated with LDAP.

IP Phone Messenger

IP Phone Messenger is also known as IPPM. It's a service running on Cisco IP Phone. With this service running, the IP Phone is capable of receiving/sending instant messages, either to an instant message client (such as CUPC) or to another IP Phone. It can also receive meeting notification.

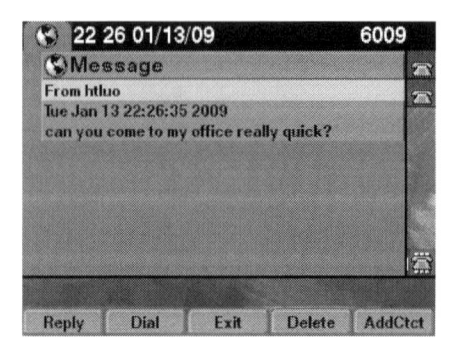

OCS/LCS integration

The feature does not require CUPC, because OCS/LCS has its own client (MOC). With OCS/LCS integration, MOC will be able to control a Cisco IP Phone.

Please note there are two kinds of integration: "Remote Call Control" (RCC) and "Inter-domain Federation". RCC provides phone control and phone presence. Inter-domain federation provides Instant Messaging and Availability status.

RCC is supported on CUPS version 6 and above. "Inter-domain Federation" is supported on CUPS version 7 and above.

Sametime Plug-in

Sametime plug-in allows you control IP phone and see phone presence.

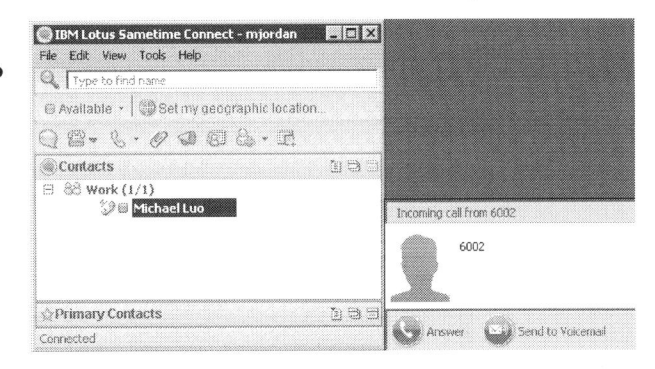

Outlook Plug-in

Outlook plug-in actually is part of CUPC installation. It allows you "click-to-dial" an Outlook contact.

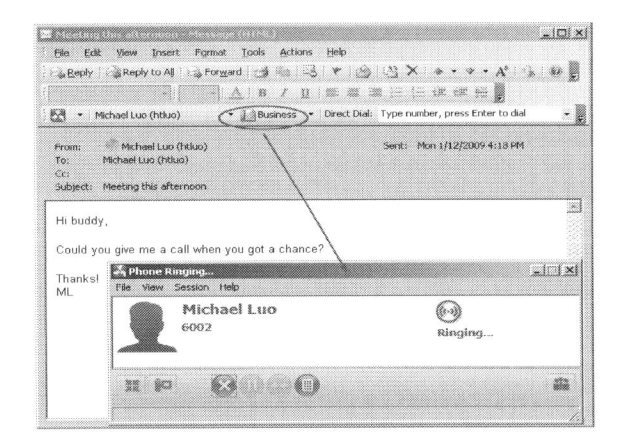

Major CUPS Components

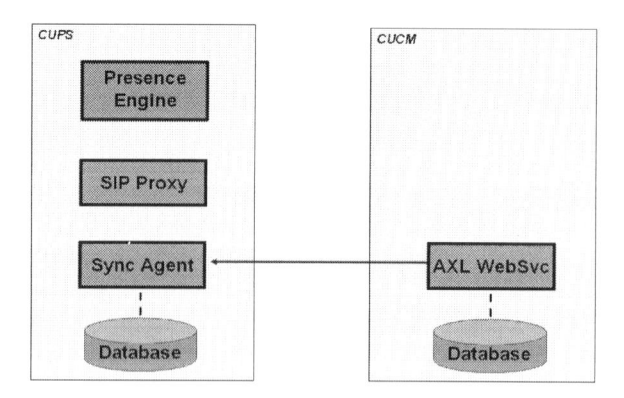

The picture above gives you a very high-level overview of CUPS and CUCM components. Please note that in order to give you a simple start, not all components are listed. We will add more components to the picture later.

Sync Agent

When you first integrate CUPS with CUCM, CUPS will try to do a full synchronization of CUCM database. This is a one-way synchronization, which means, CUCM data will flow to CUPS, but not vice versa. If synchronization is successful, CUPS would have the knowledge of CUCM, including users, devices, number plans, dial rules, etc.

In this synchronization, "Sync Agent" (on CUPS) is the client. "AXL Web Service" (on CUCM) is the server. The client needs a credential to access the server. This credential is an application user on CUCM that has "Standard AXL API Access" role.

Sync Agent will perform a full synchronization whenever it starts up (or restarts). After that, it will do partial synchronization whenever it receives a "Change Notification" from CUCM.

SIP Proxy

SIP Proxy is a CUP component. And its name indicates, it's a frontend interface to direct SIP traffic to different function components. For example, if SIP proxy receives a presence message from CUPC, it will forward it to Presence Engine for process. If SIP proxy receives a CSTA message from OCS, it will forward it to CTI Gateway to process.

Using proxy to route traffic has its pros and cons.

The pros are flexibility and scalability. Clients do not have to know the actual address of function components. Proxy would route the request to appropriate component based on configuration.

The cons are performance. Since proxy is a middle man, it adds costs to deliver time and CPU process.

To achieve both flexibility and performance, more and more developers tend to use such a mechanism – initial request goes through proxy, while subsequent requests go to functional components directly.

It is like 411 calls (directory service). You call 411 to find out what is the phone number of ABC airline. Once you have that number, subsequent calls to ABC airline do not have to go through 411. You may call the airline directly.

Presence Engine

Presence engine processes all presence-related messages, such as presence messages from CUPC (availability), from CUCM (phone presence) or from Exchange (calendar presence).

If presence engine dies, no presence information will be presented to user. Some features (such as IM) will be affected, some others won't.

How things work

Understand features dependencies will help you deploy or troubleshoot the product. For example, if feature B depends on feature A, you should deploy feature A before you deploy feature B. If feature B stopped working, you might want to check feature A to see if that's the cause.

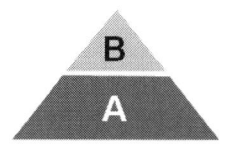

Instant Message

As demonstrated above, Instant Message (IM) traffic only occurs between CUPC and SIP Proxy (Proxy). IM traffic does NOT go through Presence Engine (PE).

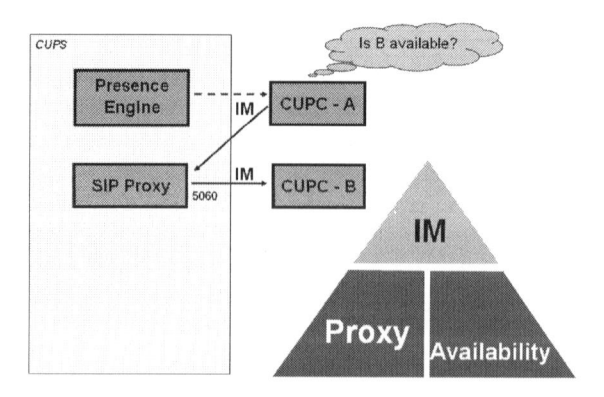

However, before CUPC actually send out IM, it will check recipient's availability status (online/offline). If recipient appears to be offline from sender's point of view, CUPC won't send IM.

IM feature depends on Presence-availability. That means, before troubleshooting IM feature, troubleshoot availability issue first.

Components:
1. CUPC – A
2. CUPC – B
3. Network path between CUPC – A and SIP Proxy
4. Network path between CUPC – B and SIP Proxy
5. SIP Proxy
6. Presence Engine

Presence – Availability

Availability refers to client status (Available, Away, Idle, Offline, etc.). Those statuses could be changed by user or by specific rules. For example, if the keyboard and mouse were inactive for a while, CUPC could change its status to 'Idle'. Once keyboard/mouse activity was detected, CUPC would change its status to 'Available'.

How things work 13

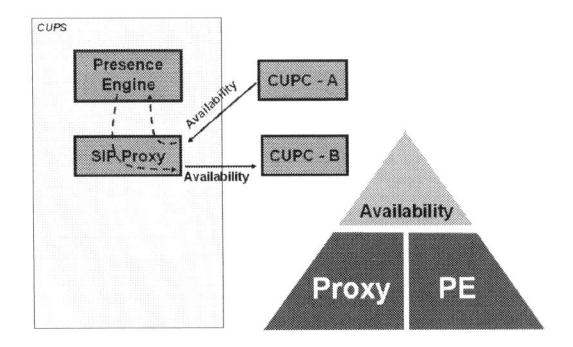

Availability information is initiated by CUPC, received by SIP Proxy, and processed by PE.

Components:
1. CUPC – A
2. CUPC – B
3. Network path between CUPC – A and SIP Proxy
4. Network path between CUPC – B and SIP Proxy
5. SIP Proxy
6. Presence Engine

Presence – Phone Presence

Phone presence refers to off-hook/on-hook/DND status. It was initiated by CUCM, processed by PE, delivered to CUPC via SIP Proxy.

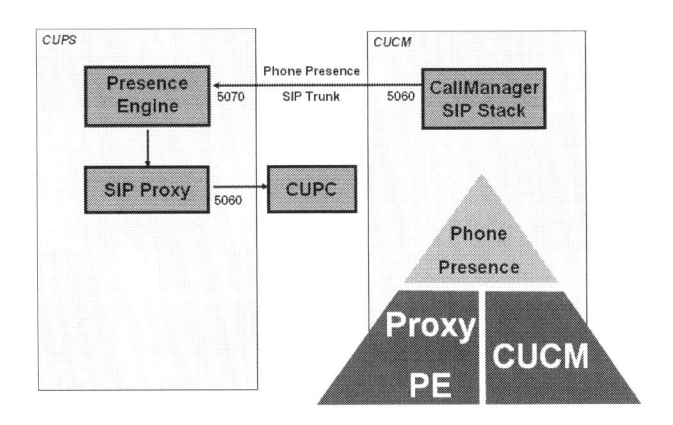

Please note the data flow was CUCM -> PE -> SIP Proxy -> CUPC.

14　Chapter 1. Introducing CUPS

When phone is off hook, phone sends an "offhook" signal to CUCM. If the line was a monitored line (see "deploying features" chapter for more details), CUCM sends PUBLISH SIP message to Presence Engine. Presence Engine sends NOTIFY SIP to CUPC via SIP Proxy.

Components:
1. CUCM (Callmanager)
2. SIP trunk
3. Presence Engine
4. SIP Proxy
5. CUPC

Presence – Calendar

In order for CUPS to "look" into users' calendar, a service account has to be created on Exchange. This service account has "Receive-As" permission on all mailboxes.

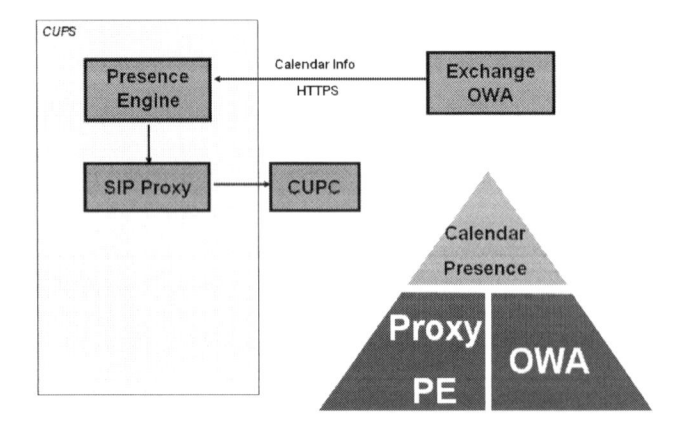

Because CUPS can view every user's mailbox (including the CEO's), security is a concern. To prevent hackers from intercepting the traffic between CUPS and Exchange, HTTPS is required.

In order to set up a HTTPS session, Presence Engine has to trust Exchange OWA certificate. That means:
1. Exchange OWA server has to enable HTTPS
2. A certificate has to be installed on Exchange OWA.

3. The CA certificate (not the OWA certificate) has to be installed on CUPS as "PE-trust".

I have to mention that though it looks like CUPS gets calendar information via OWA (Outlook Web Access), it actually gets it via WebDAV. WebDAV is a protocol that allow software query mailbox and calendar information. Keep that in mind might help you on in-depth troubleshoot. For example, on Exchange 2003, the OWA URL and WebDAV URL are the same as /exchange. But on Exchange 2007, OWA URL changed to /owa while WebDAV URL is /exchange.

Components:
1. Exchange OWA
2. HTTPS/Certificates
3. Presence Engine
4. SIP Proxy
5. CUPC

Phone – Desk Phone

CUPC utilizes CTI (Computer Telephony Interface) protocol to control desk phone. You should be familiar with this concept if you have experience with other CTI applications (such as Cisco Agent Desktop).

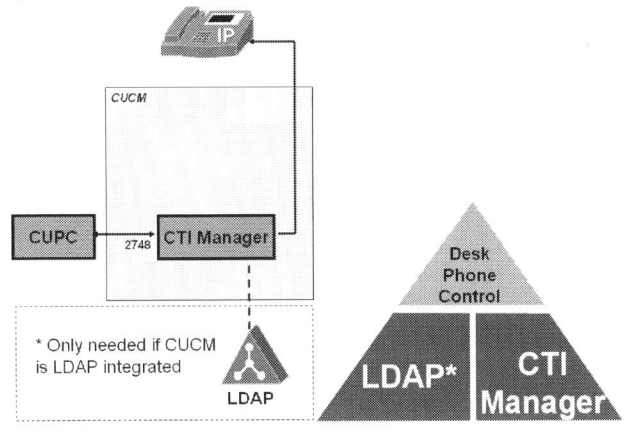

Along with the CTI request, CUPC will send end user credential for authentication purpose. Authentication may have to be done by LDAP if CUCM was using LDAP authentication.

If authentication was succeeded, CTI Manager will take action per request (get the phone off hook, dial out a number, etc.). CTI Manager will also send phone status back to CUPC (dial tone, call failed, etc.). Please note, the response sent by CTI Manager is NOT what we called "phone presence". Don't confuse CTI response with phone presence.

Components:
1. Desk phone
2. CTI Manager
3. LDAP (if CUCM was using LDAP authentication)
4. CUPC

Phone – Soft Phone

CUPC has a built-in phone. It's a SIP phone from CUCM point of view.

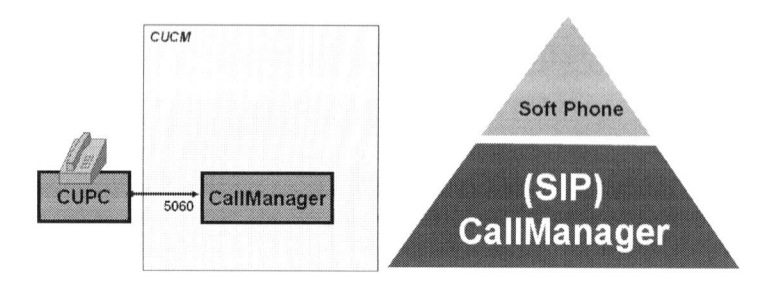

In order for this SIP phone to register with CUCM, a 'UPC' phone device has to be created on CUCM first.

UPC device name has to be in upper case and begins with UPC, followed by user ID. For example, if the user ID is "johndoe", the UPC device name has to be UPCJOHNDOE.

Each UPC device consumes 3 license DLUs. On CUCM 6.x or above, you may use "adjunct license", so it only consumes 1 DLU.

Components:
1. CallManager
2. CUPC

Voicemail

Currently, CUPC only support Unity with Exchange or Unity Connection. In order for CUPC to retrieve voicemail, IMAP service has to be enabled on the mail store.

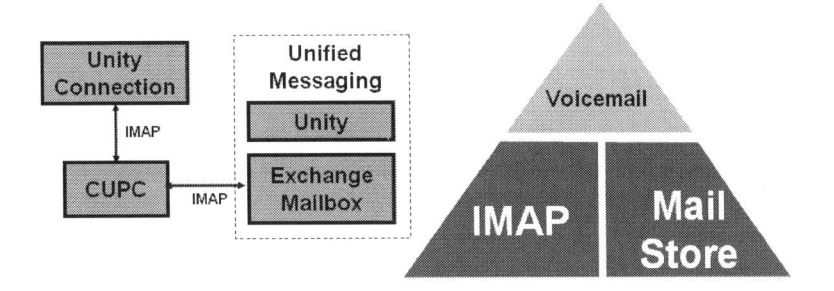

For Unity Connection, the mail store is the Unity Connection server itself.

For Unity (Unified Messaging), mail store is the Exchange mailbox server.

CUPC has to download every email in the INBOX to see which one is voicemail. If you have many emails in INBOX, it might take a long time for CUPC to display voicemail for the first time. After the initial scan, subsequent download would be faster. Because CUPC remember the last email it scanned and retrieve new emails only.

Components:
1. Mail store (Unity Connection or Exchange mailbox)
2. IMAP
3. CUPC

Web Conference

Web conference feature depends on MeetingPlace. CUPC is no more than software that launch MeetingPlace session for you (and for the other party if you are on the phone with him).

The "automation" feature on the other party depends on directory look up (LDAP). If LDAP feature was not configured properly, you may still launch web conference session from your end. But the "automation" won't work on the other party's computer. You'll have to send him the meeting invitation manually.

LDAP

LDAP is probably the most confusing part in CUPC features.

CUCM can be "LDAP-integrated", which means end users are synchronized from LDAP to CUCM user database.

CUCM can also be not integrated with LDAP, which means CUCM maintains its own user database.

For CUCM, LDAP integration is optional. It's up to CUCM administrator's decision to integrate with LDAP or not.

The confusing part is, on CUPS > Application > Cisco Unified Personal Communicator, there are some LDAP configuration menus. Many people would compare it with the LDAP menu on CUCM and think it's the LDAP integration part of CUPS.

For **CUPS**, there's no such a thing called "LDAP integration". CUPS just blindly copy the users from CUCM database to its own database. CUPS doesn't care if CUCM is LDAP integrated or not. (see path B in the diagram above).

On CUPC, LDAP was positioned by Cisco as "optional" feature. But for most of customers, it's a required feature. Why is that?

It takes a little bit to explain. But it's worth understanding the relationship behind the scene.

CUPC stands for "**C**isco **U**nified **P**ersonal **C**ommunicator". Per CUPC developers, it's not intended to be "Cisco Unified Presence Client".

CUPC has many features:
- Presence
- Instant Messaging
- Desk Phone Control
- Soft Phone
- Web Conference
- Voicemail
- Corporate Directory (LDAP) query

Among the features above, only Presence and Instant Messaging rely on CUPS. All other features do no rely on CUPS. (It's debatable though, because the configuration of those features is stored on CUPS).

Technically speaking, you may use other features without LDAP. Unfortunately, that's not the case because of CUPC developers' assumption.

Contact List

First of all, let's take a look at contact management. CUPC has a contact list, from which you may initiate instant messaging, phone calls, etc. Without a contact list, there's not too much you can do with CUPC.

How is the contact list constructed? The "regular" way is to do a LDAP query from CUPC, then add the search results to your contact list.

Without LDAP, you cannot query corporate directory. You'll have to add contacts to CUPC with other ways. Unfortunately, "other ways" do not do the same as the "regular" way.

"Other way" #1: You may create contacts from CUPC without querying LDAP. You'll have to manually enter information like first name, last name, phone number, etc. However, you cannot enter "UserID", which is the critical part for presence and instant messaging. If a contact was created in this way, you'll lose presence and instant messaging for this contact.

"Other way" #2: You may create contacts from CUPS user options page. You may enter UserID, first name, last name in this way. However, you cannot enter other information such as phone numbers. If a contact was created in this way, you'll lose "click-to-call" feature for this contact.

Number Resolution

Number resolution means look up the user by the phone number. This is useful in different scenarios.

Scenario 1: When you got incoming calls, missed calls or voicemails, you want to see the person's name instead of just a phone number. With LDAP, CUPC can look up the number in LDAP fields and try to correlate that to a person's name.

20   Chapter 1. Introducing CUPS

Scenario 2: When you try to escalate a voice call to a web conference call, CUPC needs to find out the other party's user ID in order to send him the meeting invitation. This is also done by number resolution.

Presence Mapping

As mentioned above, from CUPC developer point of view, all CUPC features are CUPC-centric (instead of CUPS-centric). Thus if presence was not working on CUPC, some other stuffs (such as LDAP, CUCM, CUPS) have to be reconfigured to meet CUPC's requirement. This is so different from the "server-centric" concept we're used to.
.
As mentioned above, the "regular" way to add a person to CUPC contact list is to do a LDAP query (search). Then you right-click on the search result and add that entry to contact list. A very important field is populated into database when you adding contacts in this way. This field is called "**User ID**", which is used to correlate a person on contact list to the presence information that received from CUPS server.

Let's see why this correlation is necessary. Take a look at the diagram below.

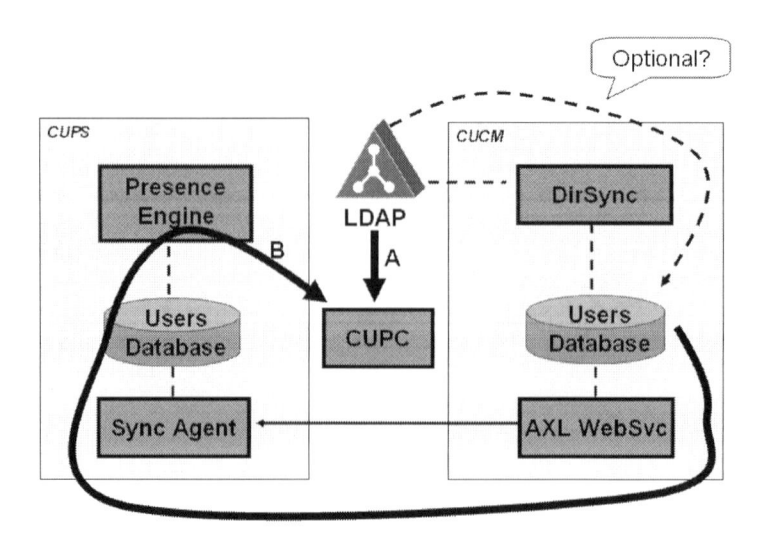

There are two paths in the diagram above – path A and path B.

Path A represents the message flow when CUPC add a contact from LDAP. When a LDAP entry was added to the contact list, a LDAP field is being used to populate the "**User ID**" field. For Active Directory, the default LDAP field being used is "sAMAccountName", which is the AD account name.

Path B represents the message flow of the "**Presence ID**", which is CUCM user ID. CUPS server uses this "Presence ID" to tag every presence message.

Now let's take a look at the dotted line in the diagram above. The dotted line represents the "optional" LDAP integration with CUCM.

If CUCM was integrated with LDAP, path A and path B start from the same source – LDAP. "User ID" and "Presence ID" are most likely to be the same. There will be no problem in this scenario.

If CUCM was NOT integrated with LDAP, path A and path B start from different sources – LDAP and CUCM database. "User ID" and "Presence ID" are most likely to be different. There will be problem in this scenario. See detailed workflow below.

CUPC:

Step 1	User searched for "John" in LDAP
Step 2	In search results, there's an entry called "John Doe"
Step 3	User right-clicked "John Doe" and added him to contact list
Step 4	CUPC populated database with LDAP attributes based on the configuration in "CUPS > Application > Cisco Unified Personal Communicator > Settings". For example, populate "UserID" in database with LDAP attribute "sAMAccountName". Let say, "sAMAccountName"="JohnDoe". Then "UserID"="**JohnDoe**"
Step 5	CUPC sent SUBSCRIBE message to CUPS to retrieve contact's status (**JohnDoe**'s status)

CUPC LDAP Attribute Mapping

Directory Server Type*: Microsoft Active Directory

UPC User Fields	LDAP User Fields
UserID	sAMAccountName
LastName	sn
Nickname	nickname

22   Chapter 1. Introducing CUPS

CUPS:

Step 1	CUPS synchronized user database from CUCM which is *NOT* integrated with LDAP. In CUCM database, there's an entry called "John Doe". User ID was "**JDoe**".
Step 2	CUPS tag presence information (such as availability, phone presence with user ID "**JDoe**".
Step 3	CUPS received a SUBSCRIBE message from CUPC for user "**JohnDoe**"
Step 4	CUPS looked up its database, but couldn't find a user with UserID="**JohnDoe**". CUPS sent "unavailable" status to CUPC.
Step 5	CUPC displayed the contact as "Offline" because CUPS said the contact (**JohnDoe**) status was unavailable. In fact, John's status was online in CUPS database with user ID "**JDoe**".

As described above, this usually happens when CUCM is not integrated with LDAP. Ideally, the solution is to integrate CUCM with LDAP. If that's not possible for whatever reason, you need to make sure the User ID in CUCM matches with the LDAP attribute CUPC was using.

In the example above, the easiest way is to change CUCM User ID to "JohnDoe" to match with sAMAccountName, which is the LDAP attribute CUPC using to form User ID.

Some people use extension numbers (IP phone numbers) on CUCM as User ID. For example, user John Doe's extension is 2001. John's User ID in CUCM was also set to 2001. People might want to keep their User ID in CUCM unchanged for whatever reasons. Changing sAMAccountName in AD is obviously not a viable option. In this case, you may update "ipPhone" attribute in LDAP and map that attribute to User ID. See screenshot below:

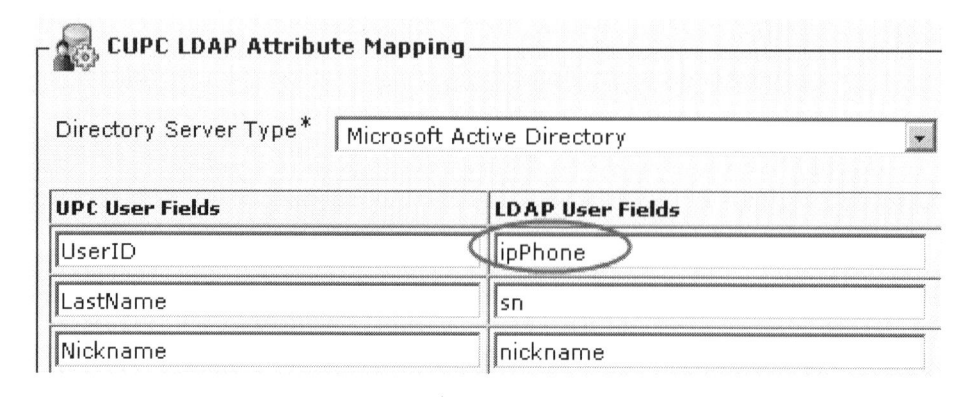

CUPC LDAP Attribute Mapping

Directory Server Type* : Microsoft Active Directory

UPC User Fields	LDAP User Fields
UserID	ipPhone
LastName	sn
Nickname	nickname

Please note:
1) The LDAP attribute name is case sensitive. "ipPhone" is different with "IPphone"
2) When you add LDAP search result to contact list, CUPC is using the value of "ipPhone" to form UserID. Please make sure you have everyone's ipPhone value updated in LDAP.

OCS/LCS integration

OCS/LCS integrates with CUPS to provide two features: phone control (or Remote Call Control / RCC) and phone presence.

The integration point is between OCS/LCS and CUPS. MOC interfaces with OCS/LCS instead of CUPS.

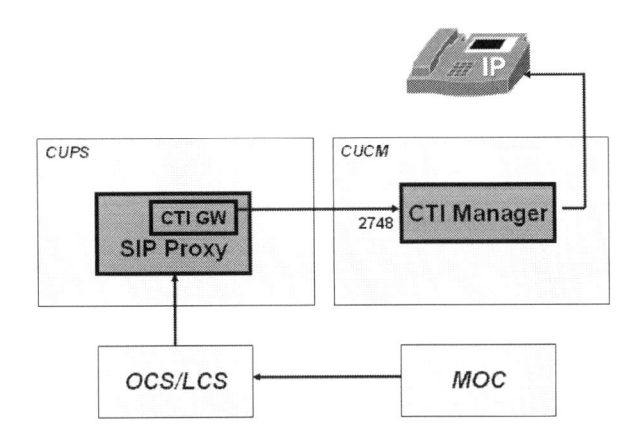

OCS/LCS communicates with CUPS with CSTA (Computer-supported telecommunications applications) protocol.

CSTA is independent of underlying protocols. On CUPS, CSTA runs on SIP protocol.

Once CSTA messages were received, SIP proxy will send CTI request to CTI Manager to control the phone. Actually CTI request was sent by a component called "CTI GW". But there are no separate logs for CTI GW. To debug CTI GW, you may turn on CTI GW option in SIP Proxy tracing.

Sametime Plug-in

Sametime plug-in is like a "mini-CUPC" resides in Sametime Connect (client). Since it's a "mini" version, it only contains the following features:

Chapter 1. Introducing CUPS

1) Phone Presence (ie. Off-hook/On-hook status)
2) Phone Control (ie. CTI control)
3) Voicemail (Unity or Unity Connection)
4) LDAP (for phone number lookup/reverse-lookup)

Contact management and instant messaging would rely on Sametime.

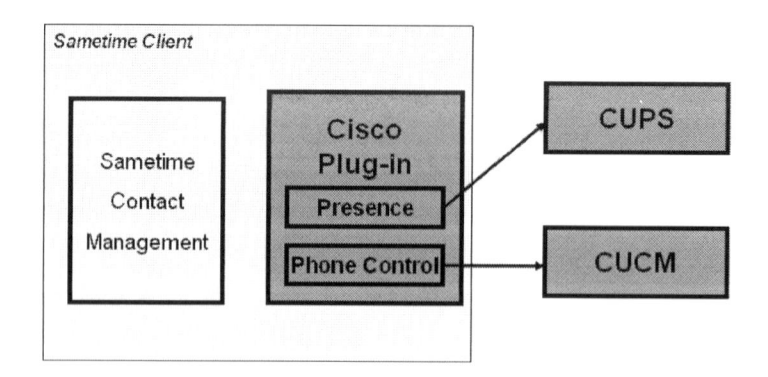

Before you deploying Sametime plug-in, you'd better test the following:

1) Make sure Sametime Connect (client) functions properly, including IM (Instant Messaging), Contact Lookup, Availability status, etc. If you need assistance, contact a Domino/Sametime engineer.
2) Make sure CUPC functions properly, including availability, phone presence, phone control, LDAP, etc. If you need assistance, refer to other chapters in this book or open a TAC case.

For "Phone Control" it's the same as CUPC desk phone control.

The mysterious part is "Presence". Even though it works the same as CUPC presence, we're facing another challenge – how to correlate the presence info from Cisco world to a contact in Domino world.

On Cisco side, all presence info was tagged with "User ID", which is the CUCM user ID. On Domino/Sametime, they use the concept called "Contact ID". The mapping logic has to be configured before you install the plug-in. If you want to change it, you'll have to reconfigure then reinstall. See "Deploying and Troubleshooting Features" chapter for details.

Chapter 2. Testing and Troubleshooting Tools

Good tools can help us test functionality of the product. They can also help us quickly narrow down and identify the problem.

Cisco Unified Personal Communicator (CUPC)

CUPC is one of the best tools in testing and troubleshooting.

- Most of people use CUPC as "CUPS client". Needless to say, their goal is to get features work on CUPC. Thus you need to test CUPC anyway.
- Even if you're not going to use CUPC (for example, you are going to use MOC instead), CUPC is still a good tool, because:
    a. If you can get CUPC worked, most of the CUPS components have been configured properly.
    b. Cisco TAC engineers are more familiar with CUPC than other 3rd-party software. It's easier for them to find the problem with CUPC then with other 3rd-party software.

You may download CUPC from www.cisco.com.

Enabled Detailed Logging

On CUPC "Help" menu, there's an option called "Enabled Detailed Logging". You should have this option turned on (checked) during testing and troubleshooting.

26   Chapter 2. Testing and Troubleshooting Tools

If for some reasons, you cannot get to CUPC GUI to enable "Detailed Logging" (e.g. CUPC crashed on startup), you may manually edit the configuration file:
1. Open C:\Documents and Settings\<*user_name*>\Application Data\Cisco\Unified Personal Communicator\uclocal.xml
2. Change the value after <property name="LastState.DetailedLogging"> to 5. So the line looks like below:
   <property name="LastState.DetailedLogging">5</property>
3. Save the file.

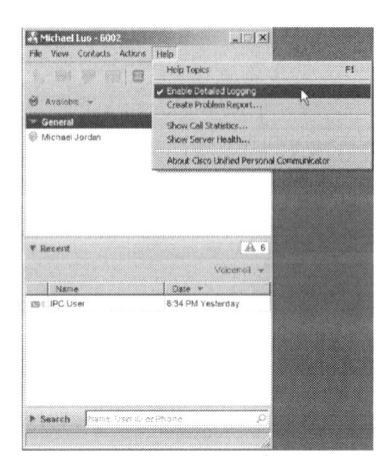

Create Problem Report

Whenever you have a problem with CUPC, you may generate a problem report. The problem report will contain CUPC logs and configuration files. You may send problem report to Cisco TAC for analysis or analyze it yourself.

There are two ways to generate problem report:
- Go to CUPC "Help" menu. Click "Create Problem Report"
- Go to Windows "Start" menu > Cisco Unified Personal Communicator > Create Problem Report.

"Create Problem Report" will create a zip file on your desktop. Sometimes, you want to take a quick look at the log files without creating a problem report. You may go to C:\Documents and Settings\<*user name*>\Local Settings\Application Data\Cisco\Unified Personal Communicator\Logs.

In the CUPC logs folder, UnifiedClientLog4CXX.txt is the latest log. UnifiedClientLog4CXX.txt.1 is the older one. UnifiedClientLog4CXX.txt.2 is even older, so on so forth.

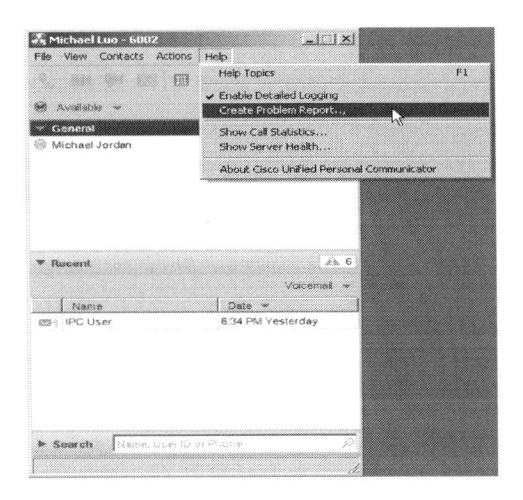

Show Server Health

Another useful menu on CUPC is "Help > Show Server Health". It will show you the status and configuration of each component.

There are two views for "Show Server Health" – Overall and Detailed view.

The overall view gives you an overview of all components.

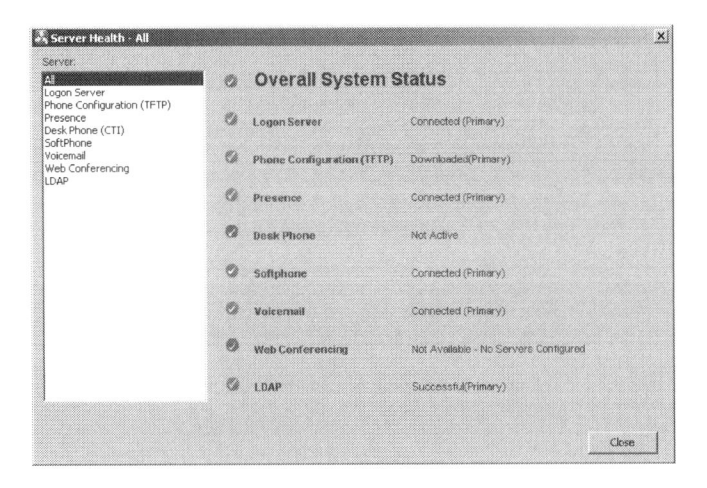

28   Chapter 2. Testing and Troubleshooting Tools

In the screenshot above, we can see that "Web Conferencing" is "Not Available". Reason is "No Servers Configured". It's probably a configuration issue.

On the left-hand side of "Server Health" window, you may highlight a specific item (e.g. LDAP) to see the detailed configuration and status of that item.

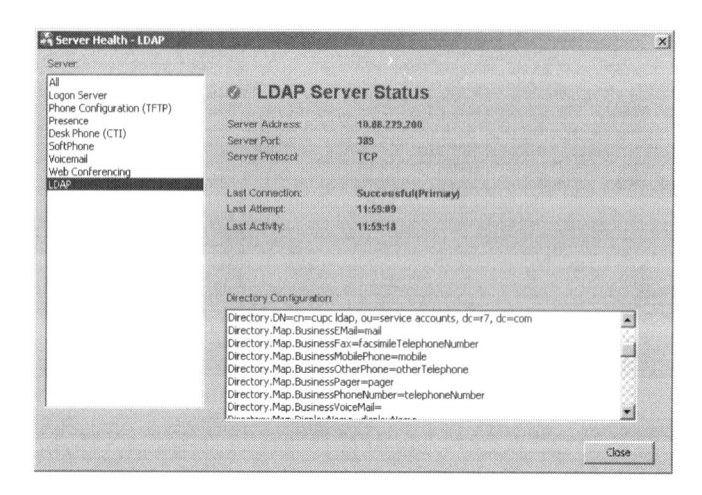

In the screenshot above, we can see that the Directory DN (Distinguished Name) is "cn=cupc ldap, ou=service accounts, dc=r7, dc=com" and some other information.

RealTime Monitoring Tools (RTMT)

RealTime Monitoring Tool (RTMT) is a Java-based tool provides real-time statistics of the appliances, such as CUP/Memory/Disk usage. Another important feature of RTMT is trace collection. It can collect trace files based on your selection.

RTMT can be downloaded from CUPS Administration web page > Application > Plug-in.

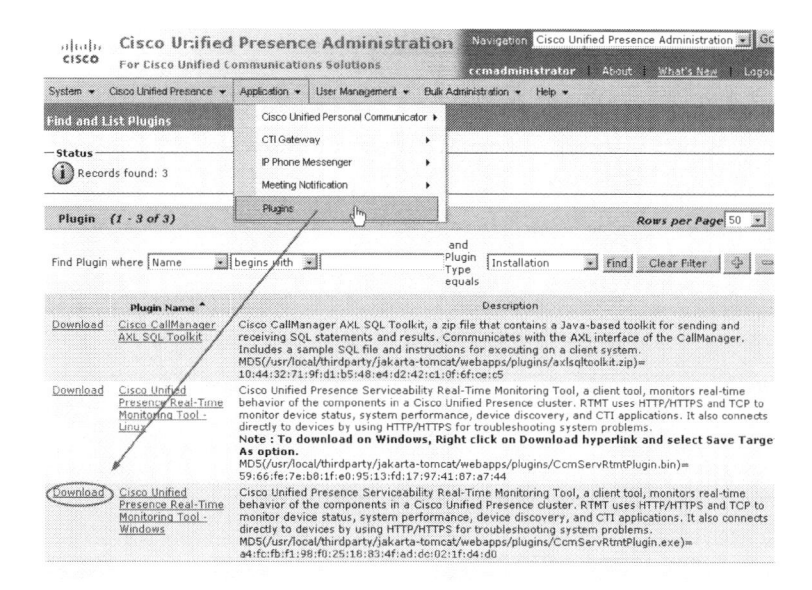

Login

RTMT communicate with CUPS server via HTTPS. You use the web administration username and password to login.

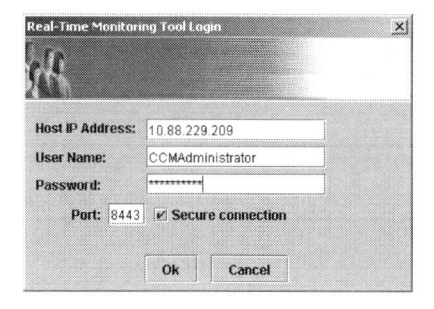

Collect Files

After logged in, go to "System > Trace & Log Central", then double-click "Collect Files".

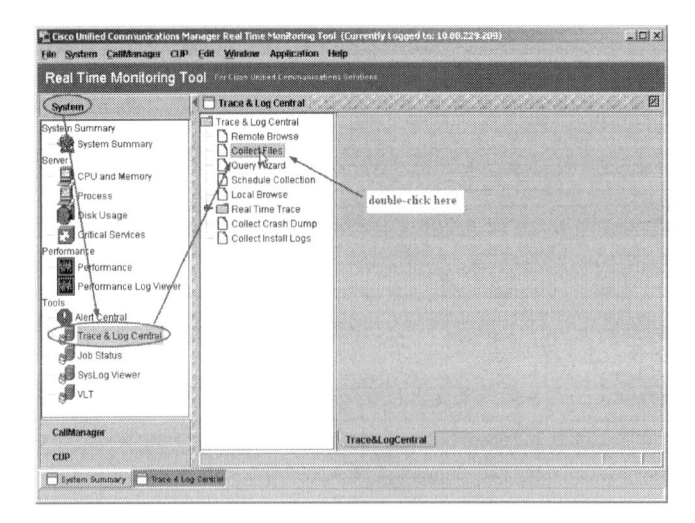

30   Chapter 2. Testing and Troubleshooting Tools

After double-click, it'll come up with a trace selection window.

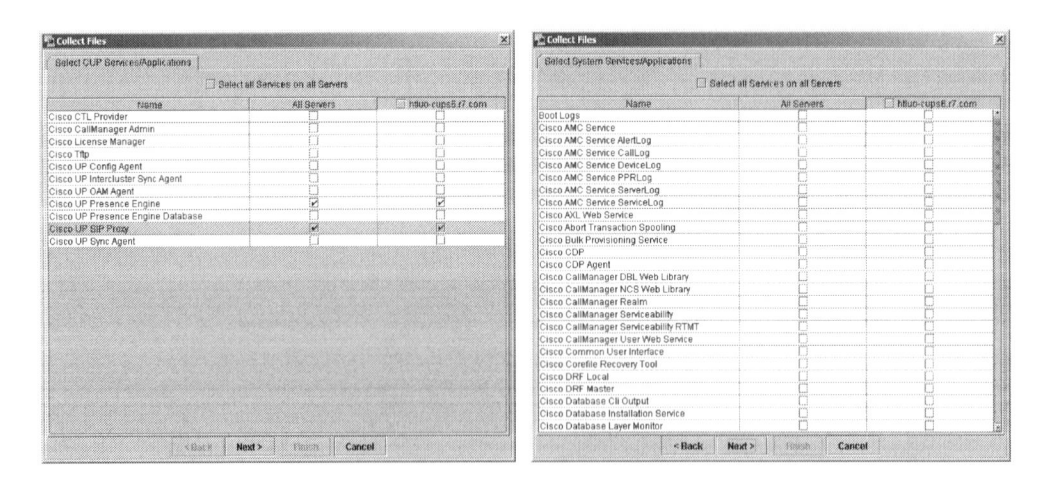

Select the traces you need, click 'Next'.

The next screen is actually a continuation of the previous screen. If you don't need any logs on the 2nd screen, just click 'Next' to skip it.

Finally, you'll come to the "Time and Location" screen. This screen allows you chose the time frame and the download location of trace files.

Options

![Collect Files dialog screenshot]

In time frame selection, you may either specify an absolute range or relative range.

If the problem happened quite a while ago and you know the exact time when the problem happened, you may choose "Absolute Range".

For example, a user reported an incident that happened yesterday at about 2:15pm. You want to specify an absolute rage from 2:00pm to 2:30pm to make sure the traces cover the problem.

Please make sure you select the correct time zone. Sometimes, the client computer running RTMT might be in a different time zone as the CUPS server.

If the problem just happened minutes ago (for example, you were reproducing the problem for troubleshooting purpose), you may choose "Relative Range".

Normally, you want to download trace files from "Active Partition". You don't choose "Inactive Partition" unless you know what that means (or told by Cisco TAC engineers).

You may click "Browse" button to choose a location (folder) where the traces files are to be downloaded to. If you don't choose a location, files will be downloaded to RTMT installation direction (C:\Program Files\Cisco\CallManager Serviceability\JRtmt).

I don't recommend you use the "Zip Files" option. This option will create multiple zip files for different kinds of traces hence make it more difficult for TAC engineer to process.

If you really want to zip the traces, you may use WinZip or WinRar to create a single zip after the files were downloaded. If you don't have WinZip or WinRar, you may right-click the download folder and "Send to > Compressed Folder" (Windows XP).

Do NOT choose "Delete Collected Log Files from Server".

Click "Finish" button to start download.

After trace files are downloaded, browse to the download folder and open those files with Notepad or Wordpad. Make sure the timestamps in the file content are actually in the time frame you wanted.

Text Editor

Every Windows comes with text editors such as Notepad or Wordpad.

Notepad

Notepad is probably the most popular one. We use it to open txt (text) files. However for the text files coming from Linux/Unix, things are a little bit different.

On Windows, each line in a text file ends with a carriage return (CR) and a line feed (LF). On Linux/Unix, each line ends with line feed (LF) only.

A text editor on Windows (such as Notepad) might not be able to display text files from Linux/Unix correctly.

Below is a trace file from CUCM 6.1.2 (Linux-based) displayed in Notepad: It's pretty hard to read because there's no line feed between lines.

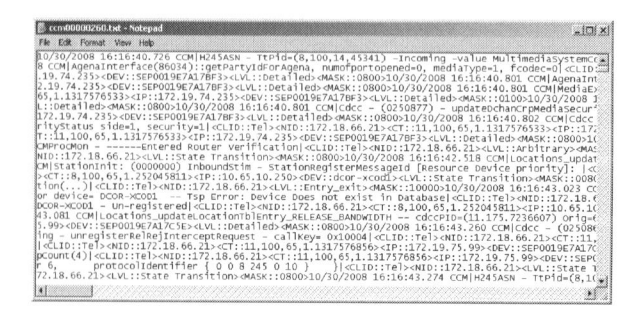

Wordpad

Strange enough, Wordpad has no problem display the LF-only text file. Below is the same trace file displayed in Wordpad. Please note that line feeds were displayed correctly.

Now things seem simple enough – we just use Wordpad to open trace files from Linux. However, to make our life so simple, Wordpad does not support search backward. See screenshot below. Notepad has a search "Up" option. Wordpad does not have. If you want to search a keyword back and forth in a file, Wordpad might not be the best choice.

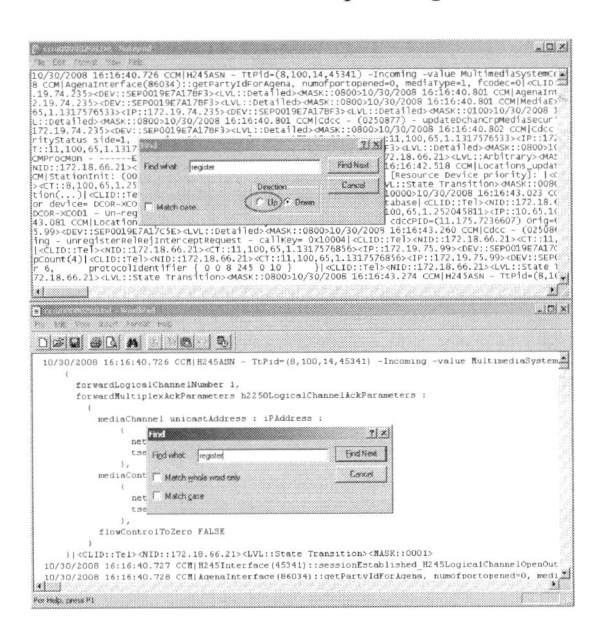

34   Chapter 2. Testing and Troubleshooting Tools

How do we deal with the dilemma? The cheap/easy way is to open the file in Wordpad, save it, open it with Notepad. Wordpad will convert the file to Windows format so Notepad can display line feed correctly.

Another option would be use a more powerful text editor which can handle Linux formats, such as UltraEdit.

UltraEdit

There are many powerful editors out there. I just happened to fall in love with UltraEdit for the following reasons:
1. It supports Linux file format (obviously).
2. It handles large files. (Notepad will freeze your computer if you try to open a large file).
3. It support command line parameters (which is a useful feature will talk about later).

Of course, you may find above features in other editors. It's just my personal preferences to use UltraEdit.

Following is the screenshot of UltraEdit.

You may find more information on http://www.ultraedit.com/.

Keyword Searcher

To analyze logs (traces), we usually need to search for some keywords. For example, search caller number in CUCM logs, search for a specific error "404 not found" in SIP proxy logs, etc.

There are many ways to search for keywords.

Text Editor

One of the ways is to open each log file and search the keyword in editor (such as notepad).

However, unless you know which file contains the information you need, it's impractical to open tens 100 files just to get "keyword not found" in 99 of them.

Windows Search

You may use Windows built-in search feature to search keywords in multiple files.

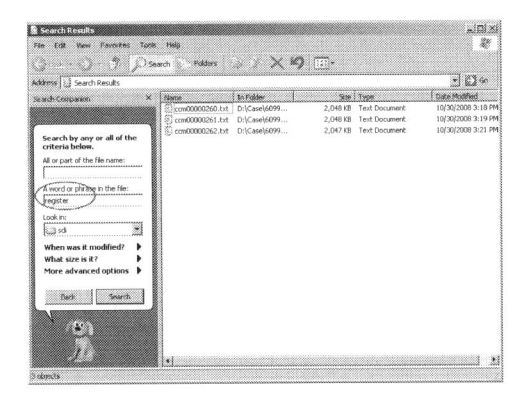

Windows search tells you which file contain the keyword. But sometimes, you'll get false positives because the keyword was too generic. It'll be great if we could preview the search results before we decide to open that file.

WinGrep

WinGrep is a powerful keyword searcher. The name comes from "Windows Grep". Grep is a command line text search utility originally written for Unix. The program's name derives from the Unix ed command, g/re/p which performs a similar operation.

After Wingrep was installed, you have a "Windows Grep" context menu when you right-click a folder.

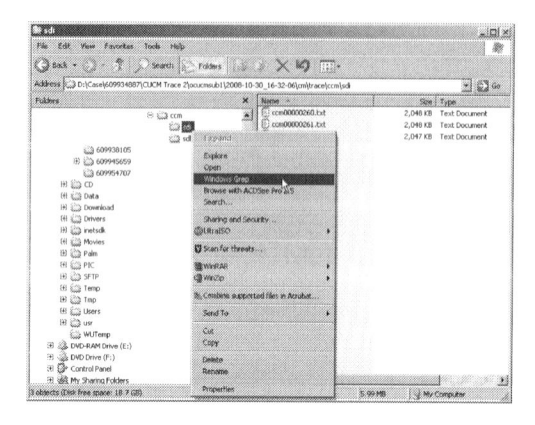

When you click "Windows Grep", it'll come up with a search option Window like below.

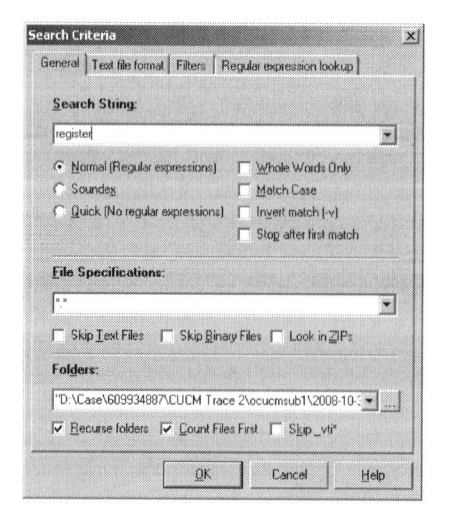

We're not going to explain every option (it deserves another book).

You put the keyword(s) in "Search String" box. For example put "register" to search for keyword "register".

You put file name wildcards in "File Specifications". For example, put *.* to search all files. Put *.log to search files with extension .log.

You may either choose "Normal (Regular expressions)" or "Quick (No regular expressions)".

If you don't know what "Regular express" is, I recommend you choose "Quick (No regular expressions)".

Below is a sample of search result.

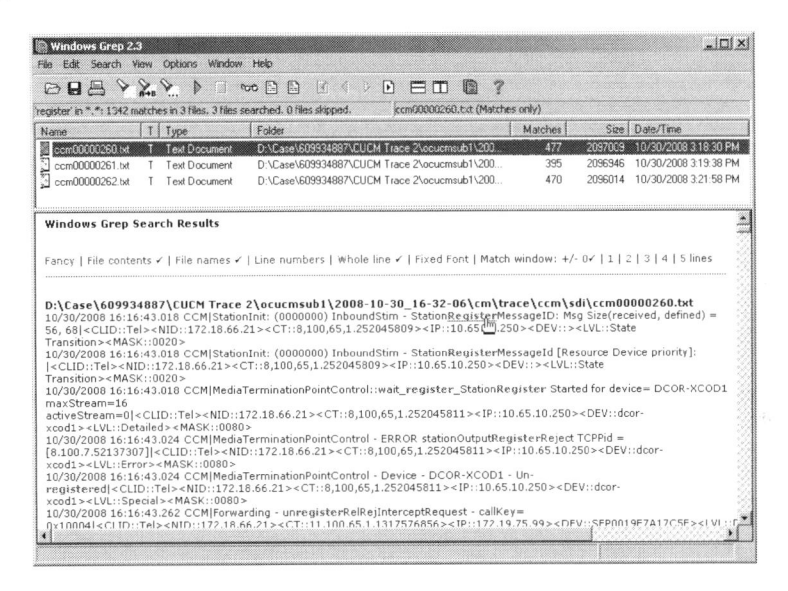

As you can see, WinGrep listed the files that contain the keyword.

When you highlight that file, WinGrep will display matching lines with keyword highlighted.

The "+/-" option controls how many lines being displayed before/after the matching line. Sometimes, you'll have to look couple lines above/below to determine if it's really the one you interested.

If you'd like to open the whole file for further analysis, you may click on the keyword. WinGrep will open the corresponding file in text editor. Even better, it will pose the cursor

38   Chapter 2. Testing and Troubleshooting Tools

at the right location (right line, right column), so you can start looking at the logs at the right spot.

To configure the text editor parameters, go to WinGrep menu "Options > Preferences > Editor".

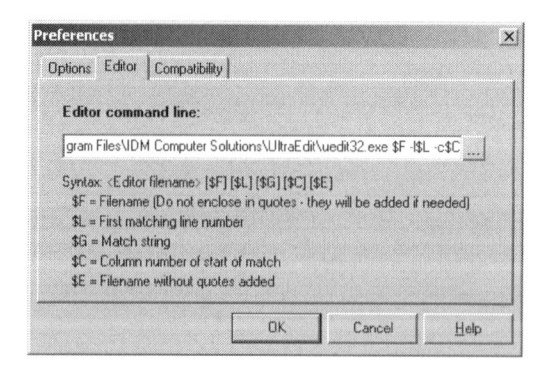

First part of the command is the text editor's location. In this example, that's C:\Program Files\IDM Computer Solutions\UltraEdit\uedit32.exe.

The first parameter is $F, which stands for the file name that contains the keyword you clicked in WinGrep. The name is delivered by WinGrep.

The second parameter is –l, which indicates the value followed is the line number. The $L variable will pass the actual line number where the keyword located at.

The third parameter is –c, which indicates the value followed is the column number. The $C variable will pass the actual line number where the keyword located at.

With above configured, whenever you click a keyword in WinGrep, it will open the corresponding file in UltraEdit, pose the cursor right at the keyword.

Please note that different editor has different parameters. Please check the user manual to put in the right parameter.

Another powerful feature of WinGrep is regular expression. In computing, regular expressions provide a concise and flexible means for identifying strings of text of interest, such as particular characters, words, or patterns of characters. See screenshot below for examples.

SSH Client   39

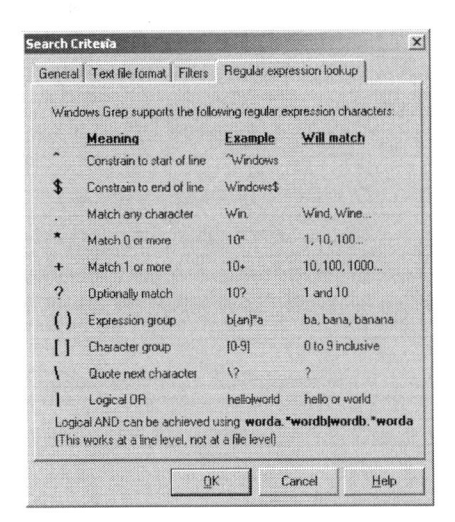

For more information regarding WinGrep, please see www.wingrep.com.

SSH Client

Sometimes, you need to access the command line interface (CLI) to admin or troubleshoot CUPS.

You may access CLI locally on the server console or remotely via SSH. CUPS does not support telnet for security consideration.

Putty is a free SSH client. It can be downloaded from http://www.chiark.greenend.org.uk/~sgtatham/putty/download.html.

Putty does not require installation. You may double-click and right it right away. Put in IP address (or DNS name) of CUPS and choose SSH. Click "Open" to connect.

40   Chapter 2. Testing and Troubleshooting Tools

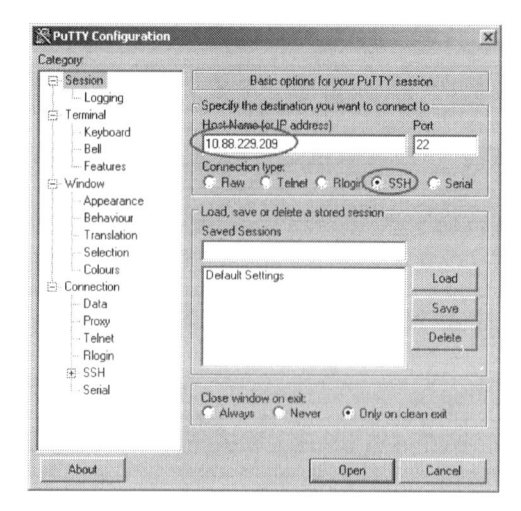

If this is the first time you connect to the CUPS server, you'll receive an alert message like below. Click "Yes" to continue.

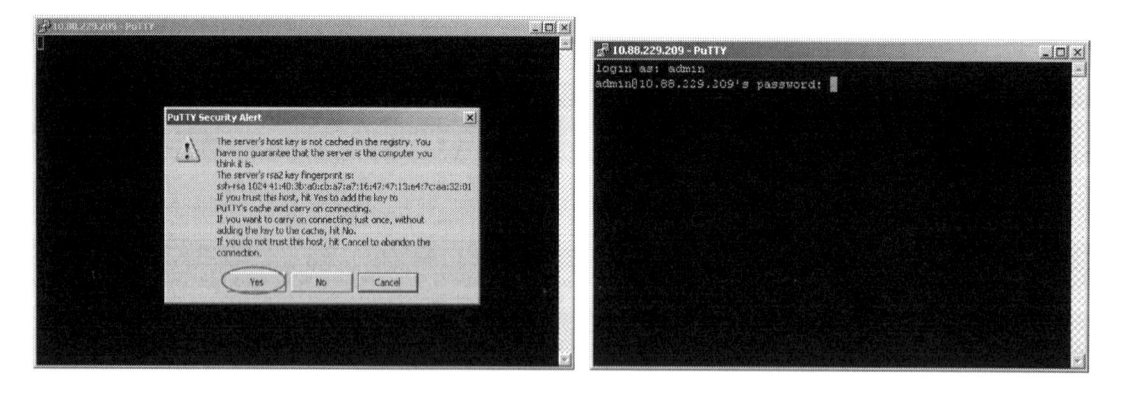

When got a login prompt, please use OS (Platform) Administrator user name and password to log in. Please note that OS Administrator and Application Administrator are two different accounts. You may make their username and password the same. But they are still two different accounts (one is in Linux user table - /etc/passwd, the other one is in appliance's database – Informix).

For more information regarding CLI commands, please refer to CUPS OS Administration Guide
(http://www.cisco.com/en/US/docs/voice_ip_comm/cups/6_0_1/op_system/administration/guide/iptpappa.html)

SFTP Server

A SFTP (Secure File Transfer Protocol) server is needed when you try to transfer files from/to a Cisco appliance (e.g. CUPS), such as:

1. Backup/Restore of the appliance configuration.
2. Install patches or upgrades for appliance.
3. Copy log files from appliance.

FreeFTPd is a free SFTP/FTP server. You may download the file from www.freeftpd.com.

Installation of FreeFTPd is pretty straight forward. You may accept the default settings and keep clicking "Next" until you finish. The only exception is the last dialog – "Do you want to run freeFTPd as a system service?"

I would recommend you answer "No" to this question unless you want to run freeFTPd 24x7. So you have better control on when it runs.

When you run freeFTPd the first time, SFTP is stopped by default. To start it, click "SFTP" on left. Click "Start" on right.

42 Chapter 2. Testing and Troubleshooting Tools

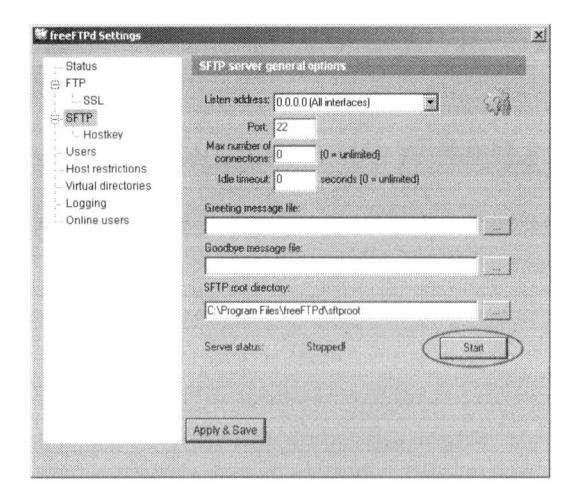

To add a user to freeFTPd, click "Users" on left, click "Add" to add user.

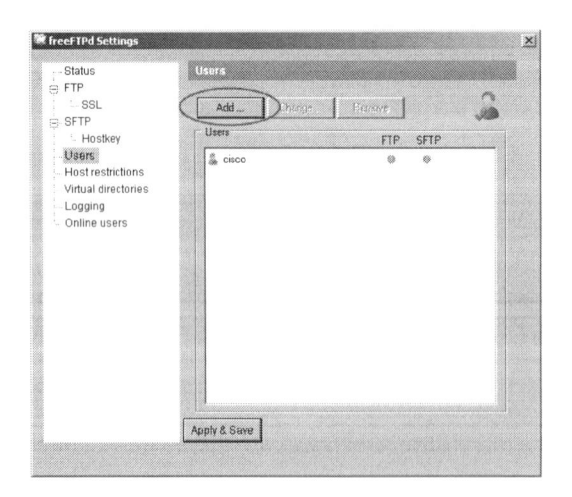

"Add User" window –

Login: Put in the user name. (e.g. cisco)
Authentication: Choose "Password stored as SHA1 hash".
Password: Put in the password (e.g. cisco)
Password (again): Put in the password again (e.g. cisco)
Home Directory: Put in the home directory for the user (or click browse button to browse to a directory).

SFTP Server 43

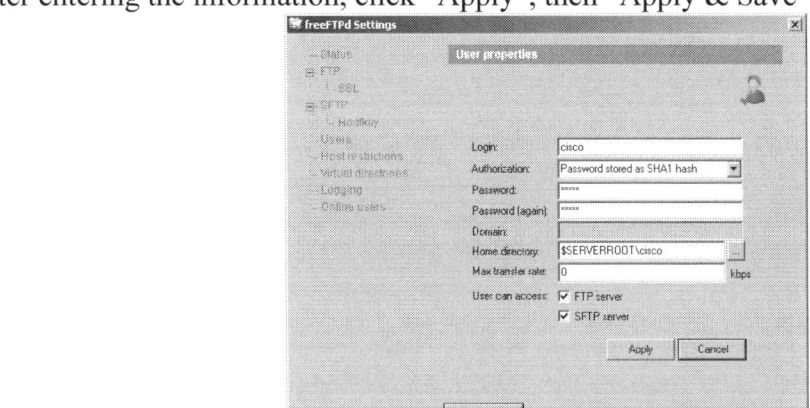

After entering the information, click "Apply", then "Apply & Save" button to save.

To test the installation/configuration, you need a SFTP client.

You may download PSFTP from
http://www.chiark.greenend.org.uk/~sgtatham/putty/download.html.

Download and save psftp.exe to your hard drive (e.g. C:\). Open a command prompt. Type "C:\psftp <ip-address>", where <ip-address> is the IP address of freeFTPd.

Type "y" to the host key warning. Log in with username and password. Use "mkdir test" command to create a test folder. Use "rmdir test" command to remove the folder.

44 Chapter 2. Testing and Troubleshooting Tools

If you got "OK" on both test commands, that means you have the right permission set up. Type "exit" to exit psftp.

Packet Sniffer

Wireshark

When troubleshoot network related issues, we usually need to use packet sniffer.

One of the most popular packet sniffer is Wireshark (www.wireshark.org).

How to use Wireshark is a big topic deserves its own book. We'll only cover the most frequently used options here.

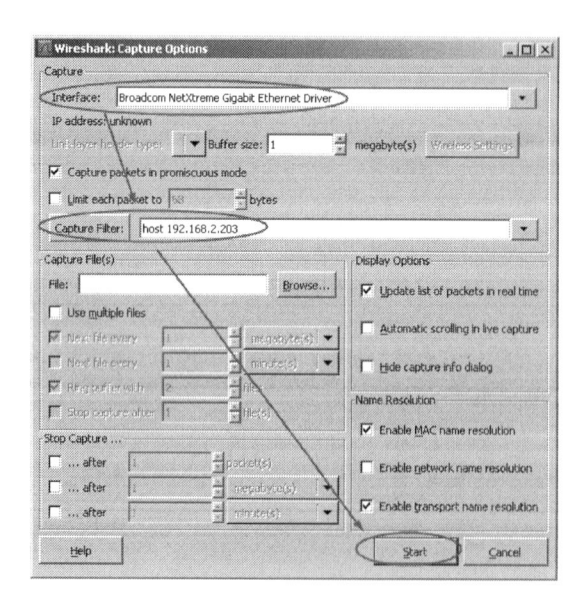

In the capture options window, the most important option is "Capture Filter". The reason to use a capture filter is to capture only the relevant traffic. You may filter by MAC address, protocol, port number, etc. The simplest way is to filter by IP address.

For example, you are troubleshooting a network issue between a CUPC computer and CUPS server. On CUPC computer, you want to set the filter to capture the traffic from/to CUPS server only. The syntax would be "host 192.168.2.203", where 192.168.2.203 is the IP address of CUPS server.

Appliance built-in sniffer

On Cisco appliance (such as CUPS), you cannot install any 3rd-party software. Fortunately, there's a built-in sniffer.

To use the built-in sniffer, you need to get to the command line. Please see "SSH Client" section before regarding remote access to command line.

The command syntax to initiate a network capture on CUPS server is as below:

```
utils network capture file cups count 100000 size ALL host all 192.168.2.100
```

For detailed explanation of each parameter, please refer to OS Administration Guide. The command above will capture up to 100,000 packets. Only packets between CUPS server and the computer with IP address 192.168.2.100 will be captured. The capture result will be put in a file named cups.cap (please note the system would automatically append extension .cap to the file name). The captured file is stored on CUPS server.

To get the file off CUPS server, you need a SFTP server. Please refer to "SFTP Server" section before for details.

The command to get the captured file off the box is as below:

```
file get activelog platform/cli/cups.cap
```

After you issued this command, system will ask you to input the IP address, port number, user ID, password and download directory of the SFTP server. After inputting those information, system will transfer the file to SFTP.

You may also get the packet capture with newer version of RTMT.

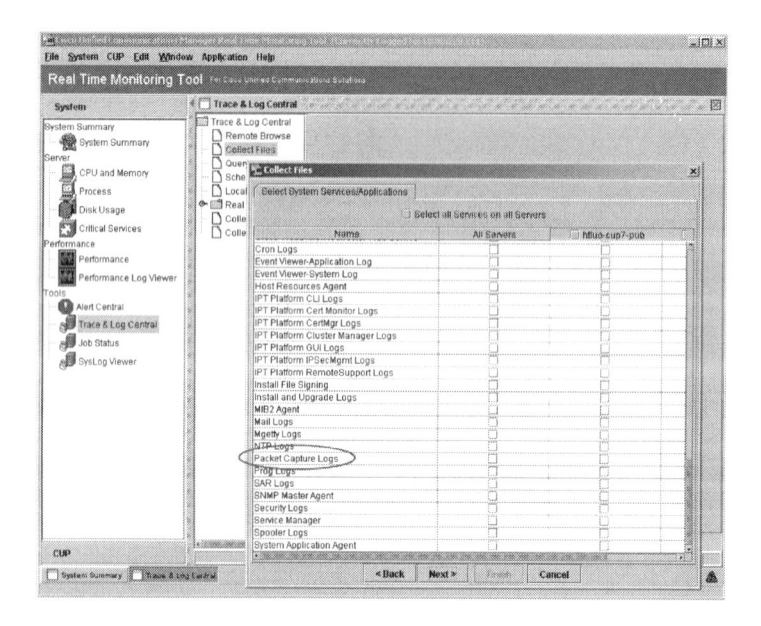

SIP Analyzer

SIP Workbench

SIP is a plain text protocol. You may trace a SIP conversation by looking through the logs (such as SIP proxy log on CUPS). However, it won't be a fun job if you have to trace a conversation in thousands (or tens of thousands) of lines.

With the help of a SIP analyzer, the job would be much easier.

SIP Workbench is one of the SIP analyzer. For more information, please see http://www.sipworkbench.com/.

SIP Workbench would take a sniffer capture file as input and give analysis like below:

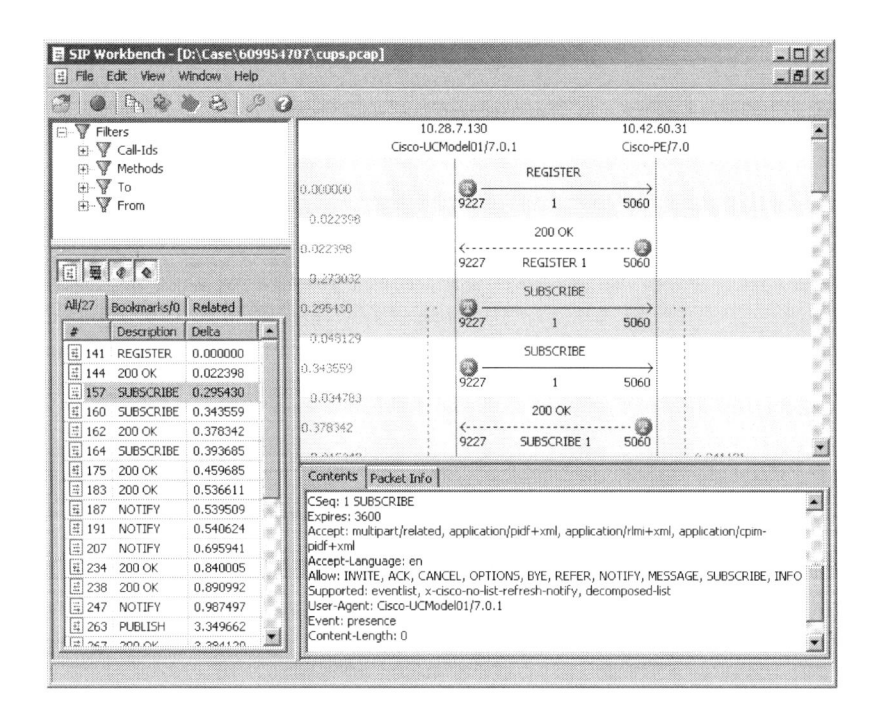

We'll further discuss how to use SIP Workbench to troubleshoot presence issue in later chapters.

Logs

CUPC Logs

CUPC 7.x traces are located at the following locations:

Windows XP:
C:\Documents and Settings\<userid>\Local Settings\Application Data\Cisco\Unified Personal Communicator\Logs

Windows Vista/Windows 7:
C:\Users\<userid>\AppData\Local\Cisco\Unified Personal Communicator\Logs

CUPC 8.x logs consist of CSF logs and CUPC logs. We'll cover that in "CUPS 8 and CUPC 8" chapter.

CUPS Logs

Three of the most important CUPS logs are: SyncAgent, SIP Proxy and Presence Engine.

Locations are as below:

SyncAgent Logs:
CLI: file list activelog epas/trace/epassa/log4j

SIP Proxy logs:
CLI: file list activelog epas/trace/esp/sdi

Presence Engine logs:
CLI: file list epas/trace/epe/sdi

CUCM Logs

Two of the most important CUCM logs are: CallManager, CTIManager.

Locations are as below:

CallManager:
CLI: file list activelog cm/trace/ccm

CTIManager:
CLI: file list activelog cm/trace/cti

Web Interface

You might not notice that the CUPS Admin page or CUPS user option page could be troubleshooting tools as well.

CUPS Administration Page

On CUPS Administration web page, you may go to Diagnostics > System Troubleshooter. The troubleshooter will check basic configuration of the system and give solutions on warnings or errors.

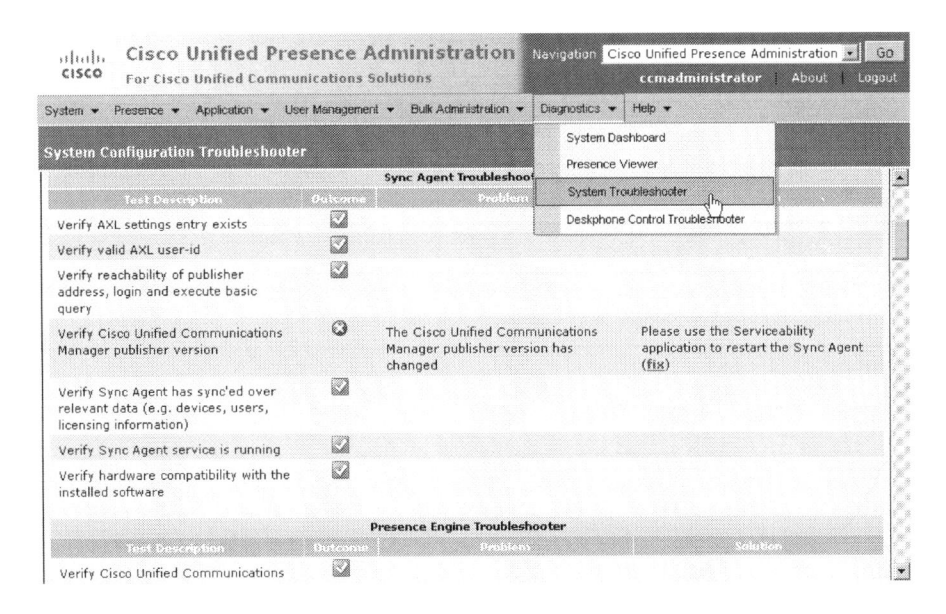

Please note that the troubleshooter only check basic configurations. It will not be able to detect all configuration issues.

CUPS User Option Page

CUPS user option page allows end user to set user preferences without administrator's intervention. It's also a useful tool to troubleshoot password/synchronization issue.

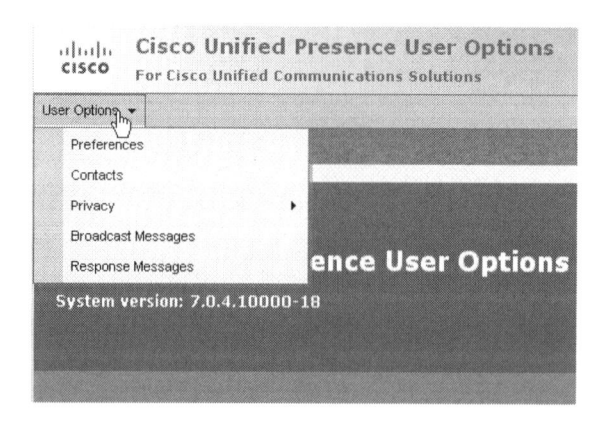

For example, you are troubleshooting CUPC login issue. You may troubleshoot in the following order:

1. Try to log in to CUCM user options page. If you can log in with the test account, that means the username and password are correct. If not, you should troubleshoot CUCM.
2. Try to log in to CUPS user options page. If you cannot log in with the same username/password in step 1, that's probably a synchronization issue. You should troubleshoot Sync Agent.
3. If you can log in to CUPS user option page, but not CUPC, it's probably a CUPC issue or SOAP issue.

Chapter 3. Installing CUPS

Pre-installation requirements

To install CUPS, you need the following material:

1. A supported server model. Please refer to CUPS release notes for all supported models.
2. A bootable CUPS DVD. You cannot download the bootable DVD online. You have to order the media.
3. A CUPS server license file.

And you also need the following information:

1. IP address and hostname that you're going to use for CUPS.
2. CUCM publisher IP address and hostname.
3. CUCM Application Administrator password.
4. CUCM Security Password.

Installation steps

Step 1 Create an AXL user on CUCM

AXL user account is used for data synchronization between CUCM and CUPS. It's an "application user" with "Standard AXL API Access" role.

1.1 Create a AXL group

On CUCM > User Management > Group, add a new group and give it a name (e.g. "AXL Group").

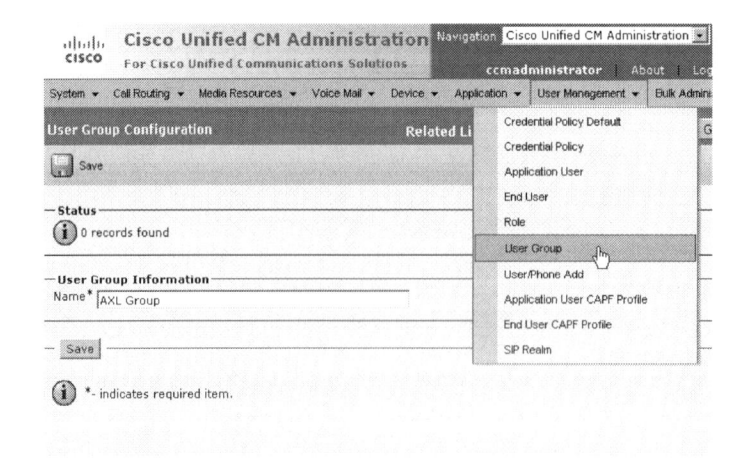

1.2 Add role to group

On the "Related Links" drop-down menu, choose "Assign Role to User Group" and click "Go".

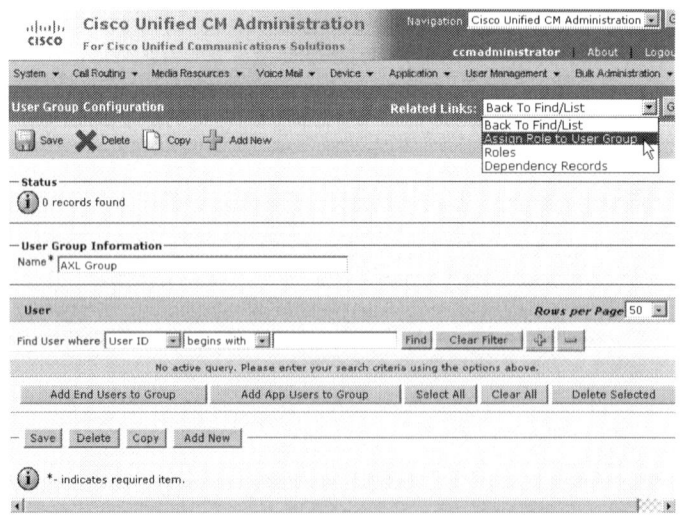

1.3 Assign role to group

Click "Assign Role to Group" > "Find" > Choose "Standard AXL API Access" > "Add Selected" > "Save"

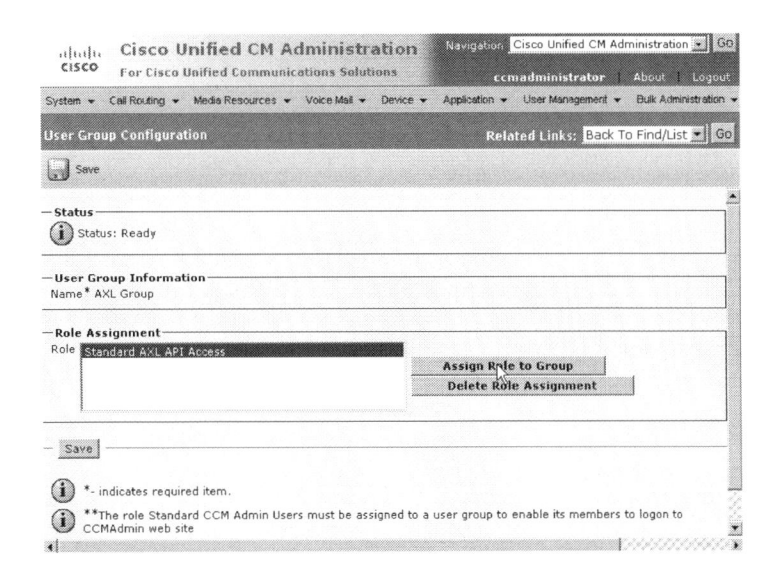

1.4 Create an application user and add the user to AXL group

Go to CUCM Admin > User Management > Application User. Add a new user. Add this user to AXL Group.

As a good practice, use simple password (no special characters) as initial password.

Step 2 Boot CUPS server from the installation DVD.

Follow the screen instructions to continue. To save some trees on the planet, we'll only cover some of the most important steps of installation.

Step 3 Auto Negotiation Configuration

You would choose "Yes" in most of the cases. If your LAN switch cannot do auto negotiation, choose "No" here and manually configure speed and duplex.

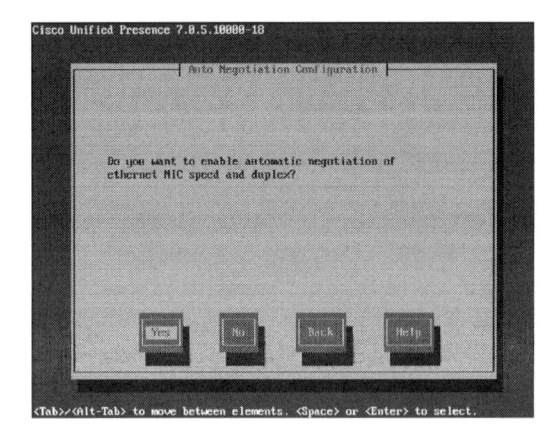

Step 4 DHCP Configuration

You would choose "No" in most of the cases. Usually, a server will use static IP address instead of DHCP dynamic IP.

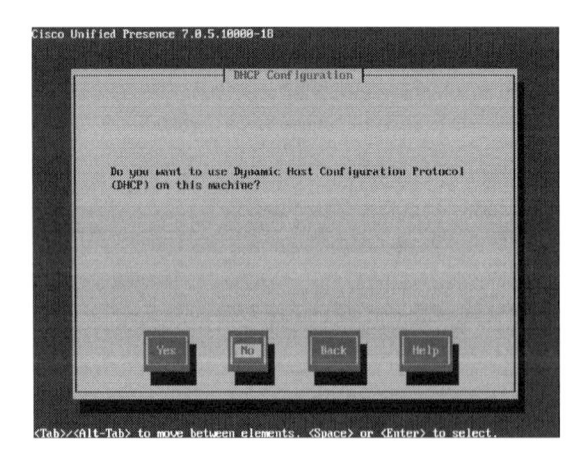

Step 5 Static Network Configuration

Enter host name for CUPS. Please note the hostname enter here must match with the host name you configure in step 1.4. I would recommend you use lower case in both places to avoid potential issues (remember Linux is case sensitive)

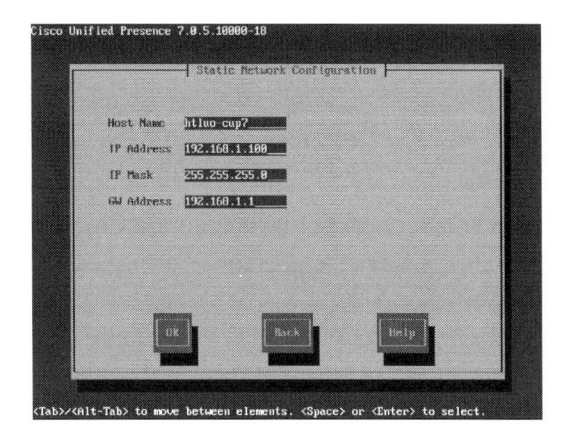

Step 6 DNS Client Configuration

As a best practice, I would recommend you choose "No" here, even if you intend to use DNS.

The reasons are:
1. You may always configure/change DNS afterwards.
2. Less dependencies in installation, less likely you would run into problem.

However, if you intend to use the "Calendar" feature (Exchange integration), you usually need a DNS (will explain later). So it's your choice to configure DNS now or later.

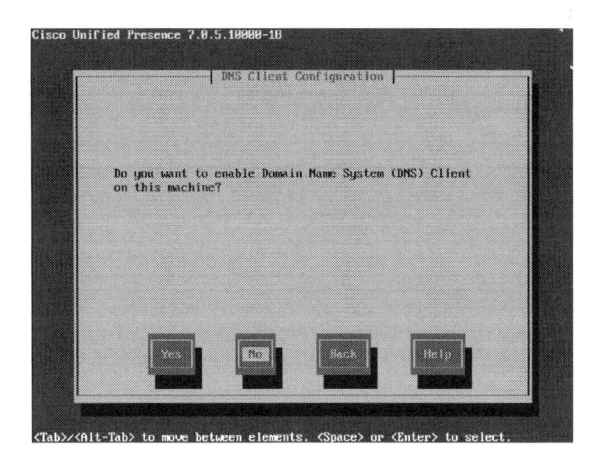

Step 7 Configure Platform Administrator Account

On this screen, we configure "Platform Administration" account and password. Please note on Cisco appliance (CUCM, CUPS, etc.), there are two kinds of accounts need to be configured during installation – platform admin account and application admin account.

The account configured in this step would be used in the following places:
1. "Cisco Unified OS Administration" web page
2. Command Line Interface (CLI)
3. "Disaster Recovery System" web page

Technically, you could make platform administrator and application administrator use same username. I don't recommend this, because:

1. They are actually two different accounts even with the same user name.
2. If you change one of their passwords and forgot to change the other one, you might got confused which one is which.

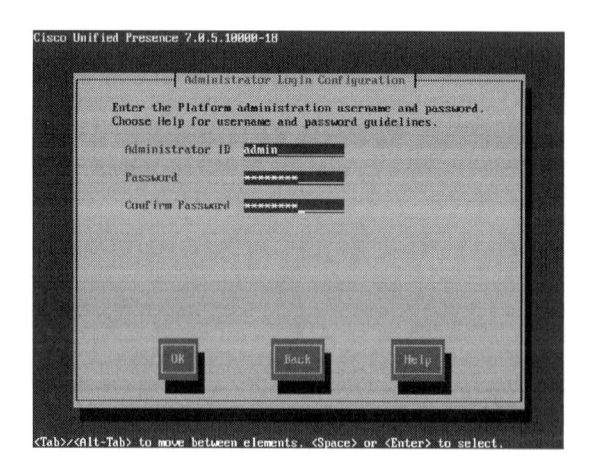

Step 8 First Node or Not

This screen asks you if the CUPS server you're installing is the first CUPS server in the cluster. Usually, the answer is yes, unless you're installing the 2nd CUPS server in the cluster (for High Availability).

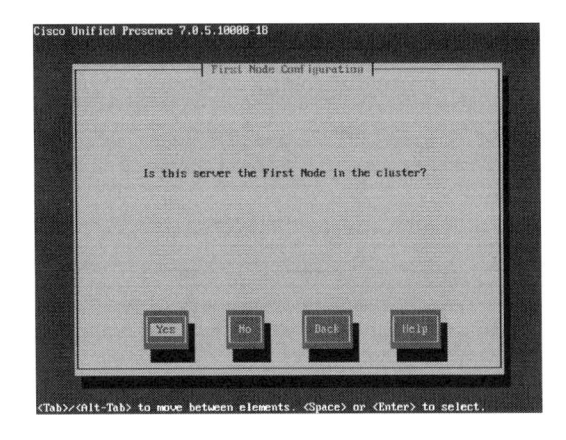

Step 9 NTP – Network Time Protocol

This screen is to configure a time source for CUPS. It is recommended that you point it to the CUCM publisher. You may also point it to any reliable NTP source. But CUPS will change it to CUCM publisher after install and make it not editable.

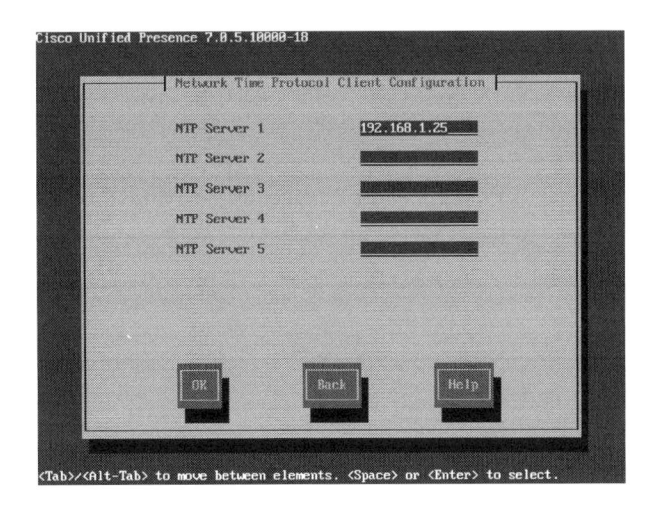

Step 10 Security Password

This screen is to enter the security password of the CUCM cluster. This password is used to set up a trust (IP-SEC) connection between CUPS and CUCM. This password is only used for server installation. So it's not uncommon that people forgot this password. If you forgot it, you may reset it from CUCM publisher (see CUCM documents about "password recovery"). If you reset it, you'll have to reset it on every server in the cluster.

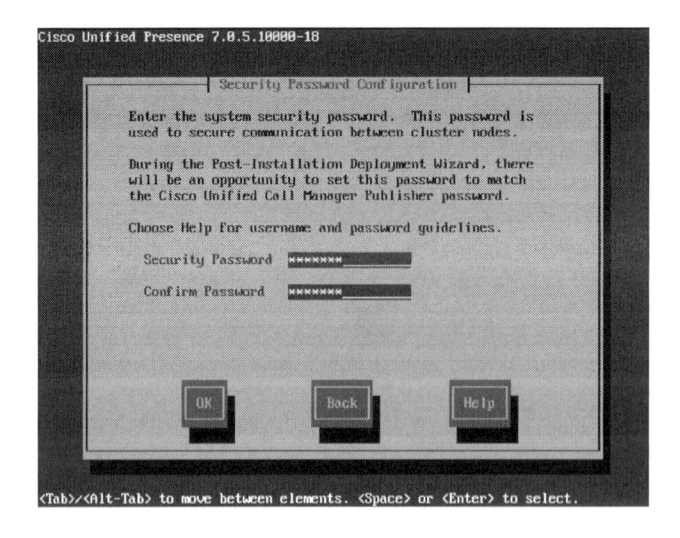

Step 11 SMTP Configuration

Choose "No" on this screen.

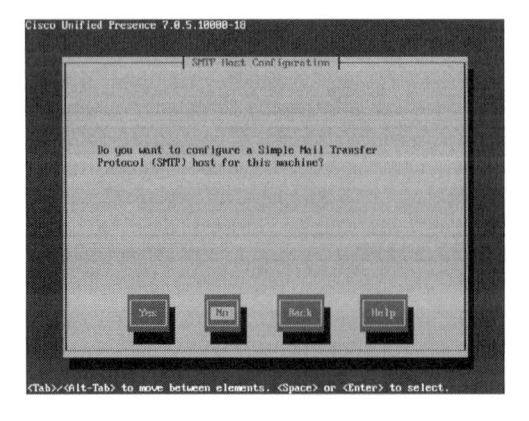

Step 12 Application User Configuration

On this screen, you configure the Application Administrator account for CUPS. This is the account you use to manage the CUPS server. It would be used in the following places:

1. "Cisco Unified Presence Administration" web page
2. "Cisco Unified Serviceability" web page

Please don't confuse "application administrator" with "platform administrator". Write down username and password for both accounts and put it in a safe place.

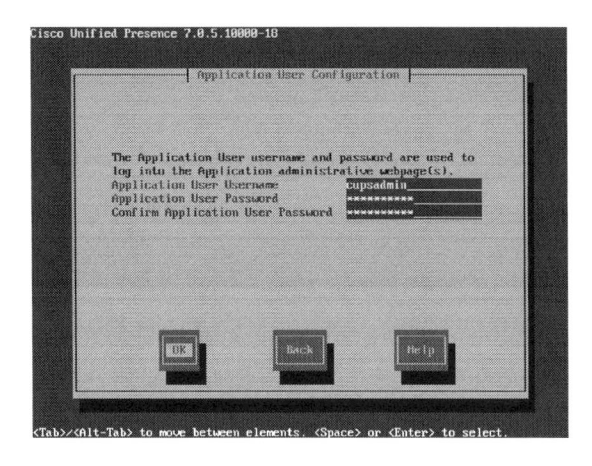

Step 13 Complete

The following screen will come up if the installation was completed.

Troubleshooting installation issues

Unsupported Platform

If you got "Unsupported Platform" error, please refer to CUPS release note to see if the server model is supported or not.

Usually, this kind of problem was caused by Non-Cisco servers.

Cisco OEM servers from HP and IBM and named them "MCS" server (such as MCS 7845, MCS 7835, etc.). For supportability consideration, Cisco only tested a limited number of models (a combination of CPU, memory, hard drive, disk controller, etc.).

If a customer purchased a server form HP/IBM instead of Cisco, the hardware specification could be different. If the software couldn't find the hardware specification on its "support list", it will refuse to install.

If you believe your model should be supported but still getting "unsupported model" error, please collect installation logs and open a TAC case.

To get installation logs, you have to get to console command line. Try to hit ALT-F2 during installation. If you couldn't get to command line, you need a "Recovery CD". You may download the "Recovery CD" from www.cisco.com.

Boot from Recovery CD. The system boots into Linux with a little menu of options:

```
[W] [w] Windows pre-installation setup.
[F] [f] Check and automatically correct disk file systems.
[M] [m] Check and manually correct disk file systems.
[V] [v] Verify the disk partitioning layout.
[Q] [q] Quit
```

Press ALT-F2 to get a root shell prompt.

Installation logs are in /tmp directory. Files you might be interested include:

hw_validation_err
installation.log
anaconda.log

hw_info

Trusted-peer Validation Error

Trusted-peer validation error looks like below:

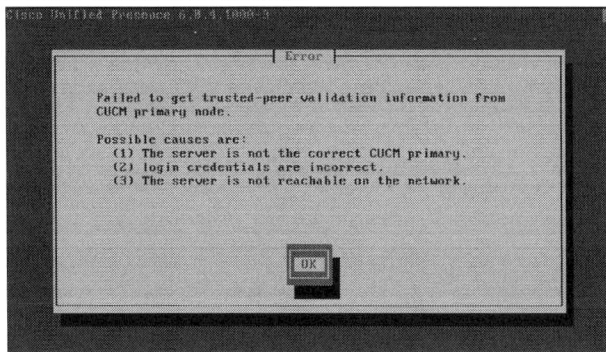

[Error dialog: "Failed to get trusted-peer validation information from CUCM primary node. Possible causes are: (1) The server is not the correct CUCM primary. (2) login credentials are incorrect. (3) The server is not reachable on the network."]

The most confusing part is #2 – "login credentials are incorrect".

#2 is actually referring to "security password" of CUCM cluster. Unlike application admin or OS admin password, we rarely use the "security password" and there's no tool to verify it.

As a TAC engineer, I've seen many cases that customer claimed they entered the right password but still not work.

The only way to tell is to look at CUCM publisher's syslog. You may either get it via RTMT or with CLI command "file get activelog syslog/CiscoSyslog".

In CiscoSyslog, search for keyword "integrity". If you saw messages like below, it's a "security password" issue.

```
CiscoSyslog:Aug 28 11:15:54 bldr-ccm99-a local7 3 : 64: Aug 28
17:15:54.745 UTC : %CCM_CLUSTERMANAGER-CLUSTERMANAGER-3-
CLM_MsgIntChkError: ClusterMgr message integrity check error.  Sender's IP
address:10.94.150.97 App ID:Cisco Cluster Manager Cluster ID: Node
ID:bldr-ccm99-a
```

Chapter 4. Initial Setup

Post Install Setup

The first time you log into CUPS Administration web page, you'll see a screen like above. Here you enter the hostname and IP address of the CUCM Publisher.

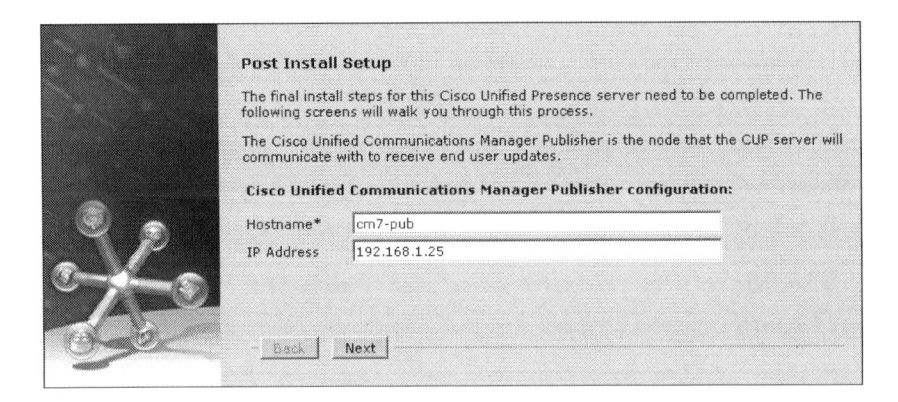

The next screen will ask you to enter the AXL user information of CUCM. This is the user you created prior the installation.

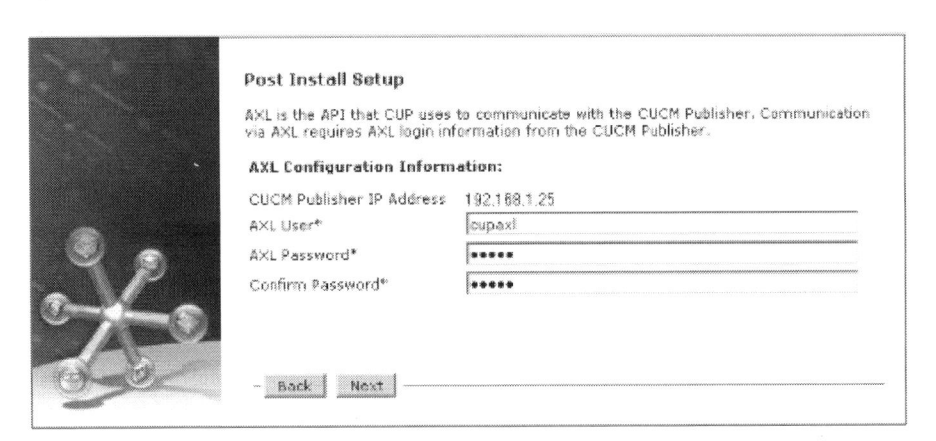

The next screen will ask you enter the CUCM cluster password ("Security Password"). This is not the CUCM Admin password. This password is only used when you add new servers to the cluster.

Chapter 4. Initial Setup

Next is the confirmation screen.

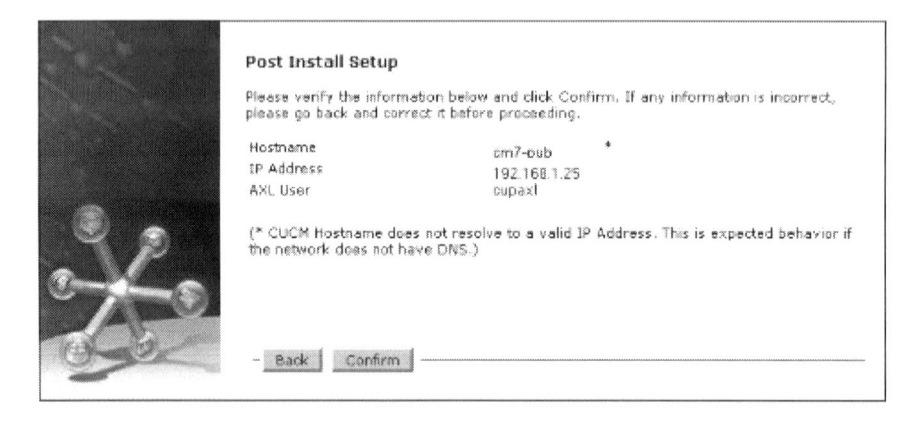

Finally, the post install is completed. You may click home to go to the administration home page.

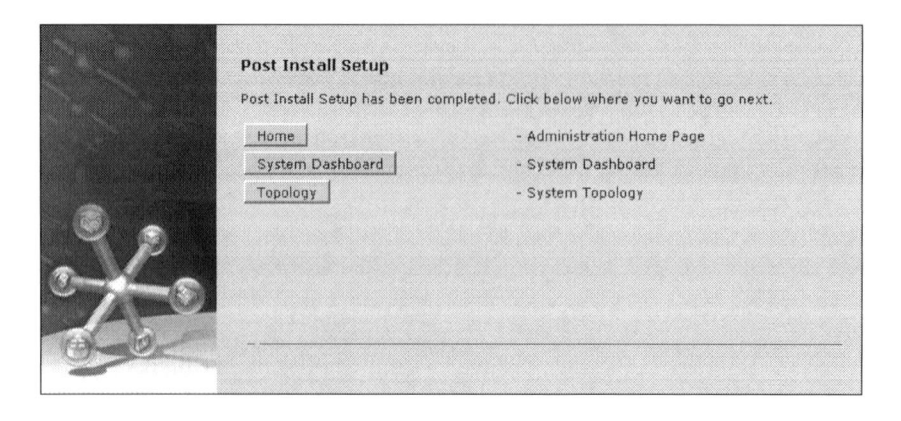

Service Activation

There are some key services on CUPS:

Cisco UP SyncAgent - to synchronize database between CUCM and CUPS
Cisco UP SIP Proxy - to handle the SIP traffic from clients
Cisco UP Presence Engine - to receive and digest presence information

Those services are deactivated by default. Before you can use CUPS, you need to activate them from "Cisco Unified Serviceability > Tools > Service Activation".

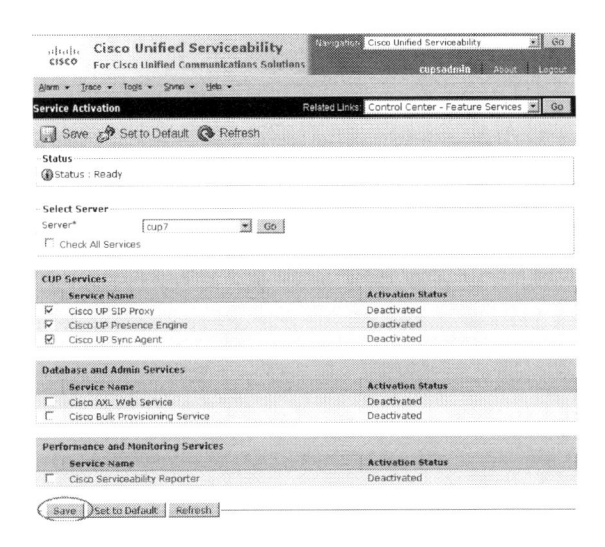

Other services are optional.

Configure SIP Proxy Domain

After service activation, the next thing to do is to configure a SIP Proxy Domain. Though SIP Proxy Domain looks like a DNS domain, they have different purposes. Even if you're not going to use DNS in your environment, you should still configure a SIP Proxy Domain (and give it a bogus name like "acme.com").

To configure SIP Proxy Domain, go to CUPS Administration web page > System > Service Parameters > Cisco UP SIP Proxy, then enter the value into "Proxy Domain".

66   Chapter 4. Initial Setup

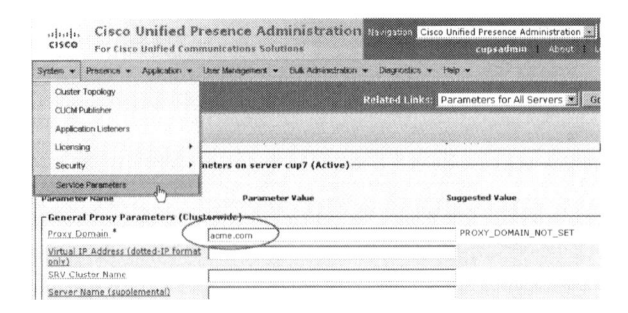

[screenshot: Cisco Unified Presence Administration — Service Parameters menu, showing General Proxy Parameters (Clusterwide) with Proxy Domain set to "acme.com"]

At the bottom of the page, there's another parameter called "Federation Routing CUP FQDN". It'll be the "CUPS hostname + SIP Proxy Domain".

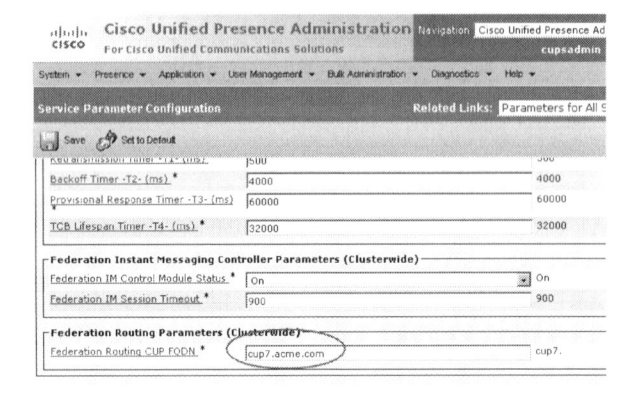

[screenshot: Service Parameter Configuration page showing Federation Routing Parameters (Clusterwide) with Federation Routing CUP FQDN set to "cup7.acme.com"]

Again, even if you're not going to use DNS, you still need to configure those parameters.

Best practice:
Make sure DNS domain matches with SIP Proxy Domain. Make sure you have a DNS entry that resolves "CUPS hostname + SIP Proxy Domain" to the IP address of the CUPS server.

Change the CUPS node name

This step is optional. It is only needed if client computers cannot resolve **hostname** of the CUPS.

To change the CUPS node name, go to CUPS Administration > System > Cluster Topology, click the "Edit" hyperlink below the hostname.

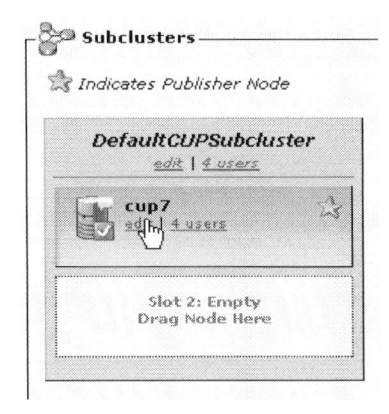

On the next page, you may change the "Name" filed from host name to IP address or FQDN (Fully Qualified DNS Name) of the CUPS server.

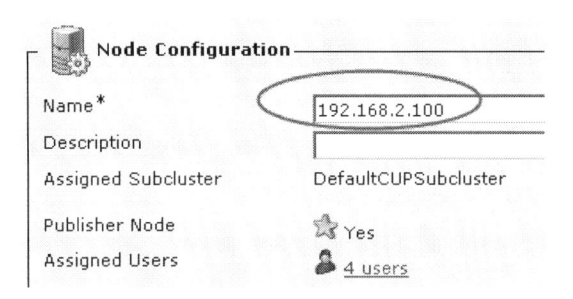

Synchronization between CUPS and CUCM

After installation, CUPS will try to copy the whole database from CUCM. This is a one-way synchronization.

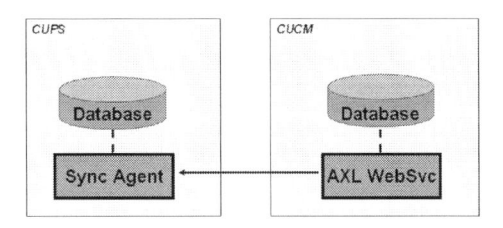

SyncAgent is a service on CUPS. It uses AXL protocol to pull information from CUCM. In order to get access to CUCM, SyncAgent need a CUCM credential (AXL credential).

Chapter 4. Initial Setup

When SyncAgent starts (or restarted), it will try to synchronize the whole database from CUCM. If CUCM has lots of phones or users, it will take a long time to finish synchronization. To see if synchronization has completed or not, you may go to CUPS Admin > System > CUCM Publisher.

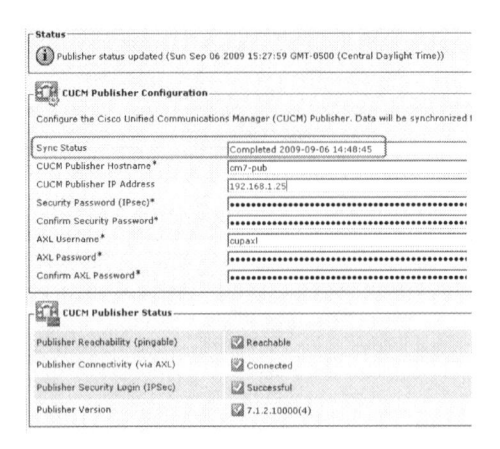

See the timestamp after "Completed".

After the initial synchronization was completed, subsequent updates will be "incremental updates". Whenever configuration was changed on CUCM, CUCM cluster manager will send change notification to CUPS cluster manager. CUPS cluster manager will call SyncAgent to pull the updates. Under normal circumstance, all changes on CUCM should reflect to CUPS immediately.

Troubleshooting synchronization issues

Best practices

1. Run "Troubleshooter" to identify problems.
2. Use simple username/password for initial setup. You may change it to complex password later.
3. Username and password are case-sensitive.
4. Sync Agent won't be able to start until username/password is configured properly.

Initial Synchronization failed

AXL credential was entered during installation. However software installer doesn't verify the AXL credential (username, password, permission). So there's a possibility synchronization doesn't work right after installation.

The easiest way to check SycnAgent status is to run System Troubleshooter.

Test Description	Outcome	Problem	Solution
Verify AXL settings entry exists	✓		
Verify valid AXL user-id	✓		
Verify reachability of publisher address, login and execute basic query	✗	Unable to connect to Cisco Unified Communications Manager publisher node with address 192.168.1.25	Please verify the publisher address, AXL user-id, and AXL password on the CUCM Publisher page (fix)
Verify Sync Agent service is running	✓		
Verify hardware compatibility with the installed software	✓		

Suggestions:

1. On CUCM Admin > User Management > Application User, check AXL user. Make sure it has "Standard AXL API Access" role. Re-type password and avoid special characters in password.
2. On CUCM Serviceability > Tools > Control Center – Feature Services, make sure "Cisco AXL Web Service" is running.
3. On CUPS > Cisco Unified Presence > Security > AXL Configuration, make sure username and password match step 1 above. Please note username is case-sensitive.
4. On CUPS Serviceability > Tools > Control Center – Network Services, make sure "Cisco UP Sync Agent" is running.

CUCM updates not populated to CUPS immediately

If initial synchronization succeeded but subsequent update didn't populate to CUPS from CUCM, it's most likely a cluster manager issue (change notification failed).

The workaround is to manually restart "Cisco UP Sync Agent" service.

Usually, the problem was because IP address/hostname or security password was changed on CUPS or CUCM. You may verify this from CUPS Admin > System > CUCM Publisher.

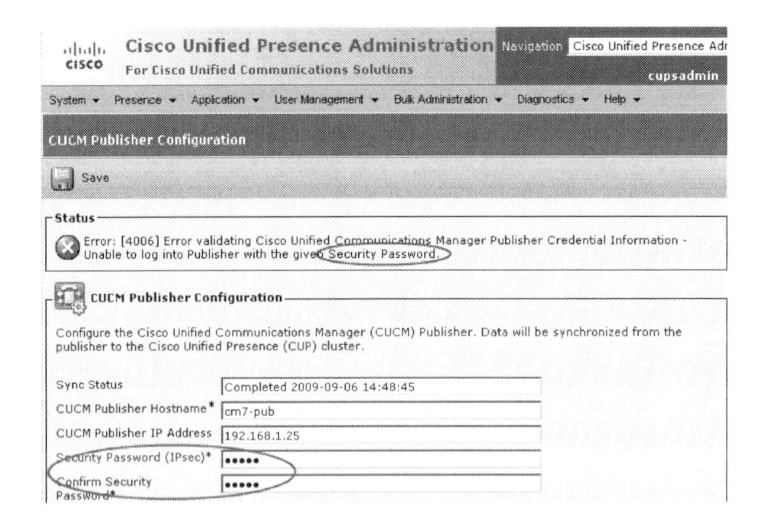

Some data didn't synchronize from CUCM to CUPS

Usually, this kind of problem is a bug of CUPS. CUPS copy all data from CUCM. But CUPS also have its own rules for database tables. If rules were violated, CUPS won't insert it into its database. Please collect SyncAgent logs and open a TAC case.

Everything's correct but SyncAgent won't start

If everything (AXL credential, connectivity) checked out, but SyncAgent still won't start, it's probably the source data (CUCM data) contains some special characters (non-English characters and causes SyncAgent malfunctioning. If that's the case, you need to open a ticket with Cisco TAC.

Chapter 5. Deploying and Troubleshooting Features

Before deploying CUPS/CUPC features, I recommend you read "how things work" chapter. So you understand the dependencies between features/components.

Best practices

1. Deploy features one by one
2. Always run CUPS Troubleshooter. It won't fix all problems, but would find basic configuration errors.
3. If you're having difficulty, **don't** "play around" with server parameters (such as application listeners, routing methods, etc.). It'll make the problem more difficult to troubleshoot. You should either read documentations or open a TAC case.
4. Always use "switch and test" to isolate client problems. For example, a user cannot get online in CUPC. Try another account on the same computer. Then try the same account on a different computer.
5. Keep it simple. Test from LAN (local network) first. Then move to WAN. Then move to VPN.

Licensing

Since CUPS/CUPC is a server/client model, we have server licensing and client licensing.

Server Licensing

In order to activate the services on CUPS server, you need CUPS server license file and install it on CUPS.

A CUPS server license looks like this:

UPS20070910074310599.lic
```
INCREMENT ENT_PE_NODE cisco 1.0 permanent uncounted \
     VENDOR_STRING=<Count>2</Count><OrigMacId>0014C2C3C601</OrigMacId><Li
cFileVersion>1.0</LicFileVersion> \
     HOSTID=0014c2c3c601 \
     NOTICE="<LicFileID>20070910074310599</LicFileID><LicLineID>1</LicLin
eID> \
```

72   Chapter 5. Deploying and Troubleshooting Features

```
        <PAK></PAK>" SIGN="176F 0F31 F8FB BEB6 98D2 28FF F2A8 D2F7 \
    660A 146A 48B9 3047 7E9D E388 ABC2 180E 30AE 9F8D 1B75 366E \
    6703 03EE 2194 AF85 03FB 1289 5A36 AAB4 1D16 E298"
INCREMENT ENT_PROXY_NODE cisco 1.0 permanent uncounted \
    VENDOR_STRING=<Count>2</Count><OrigMacId>0014C2C3C601</OrigMacId><Li
cFileVersion>1.0</LicFileVersion> \
    HOSTID=0014c2c3c601 \
    NOTICE="<LicFileID>20070910074310599</LicFileID><LicLineID>2</LicLin
eID> \
    <PAK></PAK>" SIGN="05A4 83C3 DF43 19F7 691E 740D 3FD8 DBED \
    80F1 E4A3 FDE6 B42E 2E32 D753 406F 1617 9CEA 257D 6063 1F61 \
    4904 11CE 8566 C442 2076 3220 A669 7588 701E 4D09"
```

In the license file above, we have 2 units for PE (Presence Engine) and 2 units for PROXY (SIP Proxy). That means we can install a two-node CUPS cluster with this license.

"HostID" field indicates the MAC address of CUPS server.

To install server license, you log into CUPS Admin web page > System > Licensing > License File Upload.

Client Licensing

Client licensing is controlled on CUCM other than CUPS.

A UPC client license file is no different than a CUCM DLU (Device License Unit) file. It looks like this:

`UPC20070920064210697.lic`

```
INCREMENT PHONE_UNIT cisco 5.0 permanent uncounted \
    VENDOR_STRING=<Count>10</Count><OrigMacId>0015600B65BD</OrigMacId><L
icFileVersion>1.0</LicFileVersion> \
    HOSTID=00145e41f6e3 \
    NOTICE="<LicFileID>20060925060658438</LicFileID><LicLineID>1</LicLin
eID> \
    <PAK></PAK>" SIGN=195CDA5807EC
```

In the license file above, we have 10 units. These units are no different than regular CUCM DLUs, which means, you may use these units for regular IP phone use. Or you may use regular IP phone DLUs for CUPC.

"HostID" field indicates the MAC address of **CUCM** server. It's a common error that people register their CUP "user license" with the MAC address of CUPS server.

Licensing

Different client features consume different number of DLUs (or units).

Feature	DLUs consumed	Acronym in Licensing
Phone Presence	1	CUP
Log in to CUPC	1	CUPC
Soft Phone feature of CUPC	3 (or 1 with adjunct licensing*)	UPC

* Adjunct licensing is supported on CUCM 6.x and above.

Let take a look at some scenarios, so you can understand the licensing model better.

Scenario 1: Use CUPC and all its features
DLUs needed: 1 (CUP) + 1 (CUPC) + 3 (UPC) = 5

Scenario 2: Use CUPC but NOT using Soft Phone feature
DLUs needed: 1 (CUP) + 1 (CUPC) = 2

Scenario 3: Use Soft Phone only
DLUs needed: 1 (CUPC) + 3 (UPC) = 4

Scenario 4: Use MOC (Microsoft Office Communicator) instead of CUPC
DLUs needed: 1 (CUP)

Adjunct licensing is a new feature on CUCM 6.x and above. It allows you "associate" a soft phone (such as IP Communicator or Personal Communicator) to a desk phone (79xx). By doing this, the soft phone will consume one DLU instead of three DLUs.

To license CUP or CUPC, you go to CUCM Admin > System > Licensing > Capabilities Assignment. Once you have the options checked, CUCM will deduct DLUs from license pool.

Chapter 5. Deploying and Troubleshooting Features

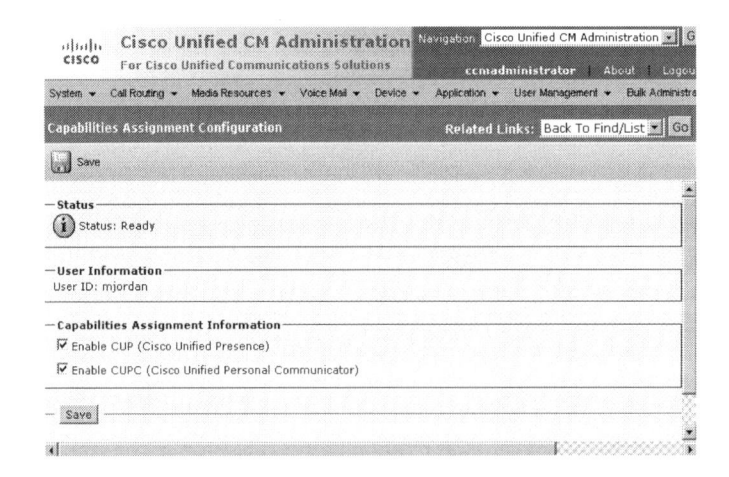

There's no explicit way to license the Soft Phone feature. To use the Soft Phone feature, you need to create a device on CUCM Admin > Device > Phone with the type "Cisco Unified Personal Communicator". Once the device is created, CUCM will deduct DLUs from license pool.

To configure Adjunct Licensing, go to CUCM Admin > Device > Phone. Click on the soft phone device (such as UPC device). On the device configuration page, there's a parameter called "Primary Phone". If a "Primary Phone" was chosen, CUCM will deduct one DLU for the soft phone (instead of three DLUs).

Notes:

1. The "Primary Phone" parameter on this page is for licensing purpose only. Technically, you may choose any phone as the primary phone and achieve the same result. It will not affect any function or feature of the phone.
2. Each Desk Phone can have maximum of two Soft Phones associated to it.

Logon

If you are going to use CUPC (Personal Communicator), the first "feature" you need to deploy is "logon".

"Logon" isn't really a feature. But in order to use CUPC features, you have to log onto CUPC first.

Prerequisites

1. You have a CUCM end user ready (CUCM Admin > User Management > End User)
2. You have CUPC installed on client computer

Steps to deploy feature:

Step 1: CUCM: License the user

1. Go to CUCM Admin > System > Licensing > Capabilities Assignment.
2. Search for the user you want to deploy.
3. Click on the user.
4. Check "Enable CUP (Cisco Unified Presence)" and "Enable CUPC (Cisco Unified Personal Communicator)" checkboxes.
5. Click "Save"

Notes:
1. "Enable CUP (Cisco Unified Presence)" is for Phone Presence feature.
2. "Enable CUPC (Cisco Unified Personal Communicator)" is for CUPC login feature.
3. You may enable Phone Presence without enabling CUPC login. For example, you're using a 3rd-party client (such as Sametime client) instead of CUPC.
4. If you enable CUPC, you have to enable Phone Presence.

5. If you have more than one user in search result, you may choose multiple user and click "Bulk Assignment"

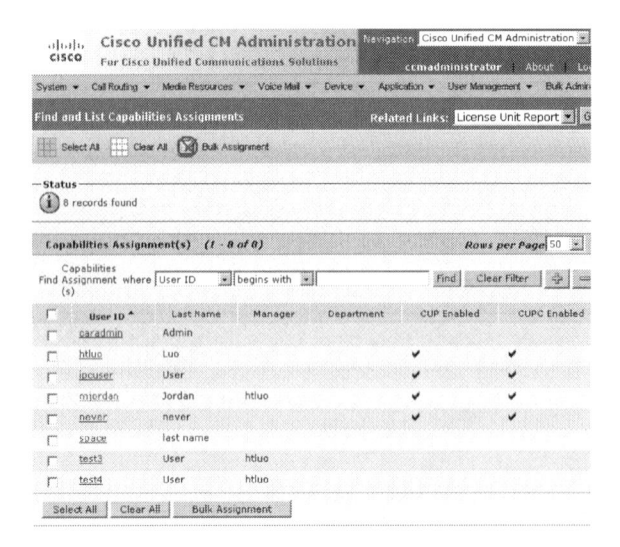

Now we licensed the user. What next?

In an ideal world, that's it. That's the only step you need to deploy "logon" feature.

Test

To test the feature, you may try to log on to CUPC. Username/password is your CUCM end username/password. Logon server is the CUPS server.

Logon 77

If you can get passed this logon window, it means the logon feature has been deployed successfully. After logon, CUPC looks like this:

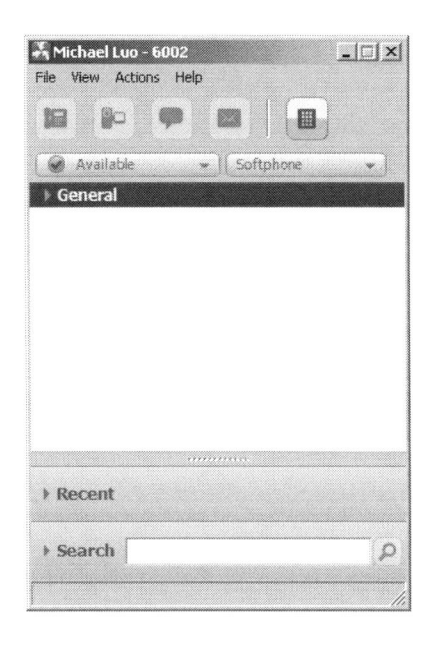

Note: Don't panic if you see every menu grey out. That is because we haven't deployed any other feature yet. (Again, "login" is the first feature we deploy)

Troubleshooting

Most frequently seen problems:

1. CUPC crashes during (or before) login
   This was usually caused by unfriendly security software.

2. Unknown login failure
   This is probably because user was not licensed to use CUPC. It could be:
      a. The user was not licensed on CUCM.
      b. The user was licensed on CUCM but information failed to synchronize to CUPS.

3. CUPC says username/password is incorrect
   This could be caused by:
      a. User mistyped the username/password

78   Chapter 5. Deploying and Troubleshooting Features

      b. CUCM authentication issue (verify from CUCM first)
      c. Synchronization issue (password on CUCM was not synchronized to CUPS)
      d. Synchronization issue (authentication method on CUCM was not synchronized to CUPS)
      e. LDAP server certificate was not installed on CUPS (only applicable when CUCM is using secure LDAP authentication)
      f. CUCM credential policy issue

CUPC crashes on startup

Possible cause: Incompatible security software, especially one called "EMBASSY Trust Suite"

Suggestion: Uninstall security software.

Go to Windows Control Panel and look for software called "EMBASSY Trust Suite". If it exists, uninstall it and try CUPC again.

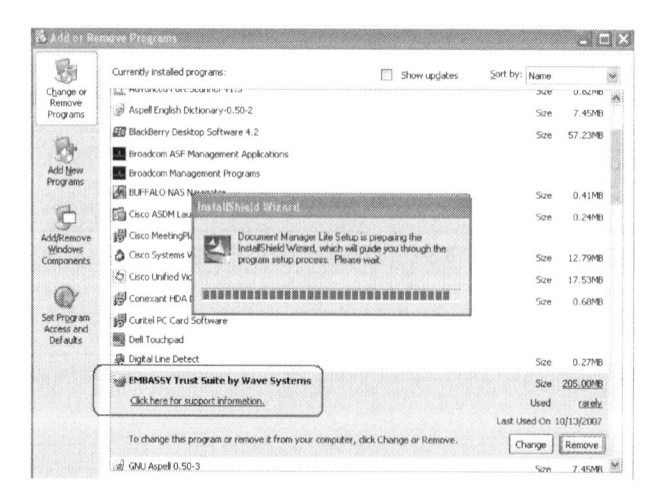

Note: "EMBASSY Trust Suite" is known to cause many software issues not just with Cisco, but also with IBM and Oracle. This issue is documented in CUPC release notes.

Unknown Login Failure

Possible Cause: user was not licensed to use CUPC

Suggestion: License user to use CUPC

For detailed information regarding licensing, see "Licensing" section before.

To verify licensing information was synchronized properly, go to CUPS Admin > System > Status. Search for the user. See if the user was licensed for CUPC. If it does not match what you configured on CUCM, it's possibly a Sync Agent issue. Follow instructions in "synchronization" section to troubleshoot.

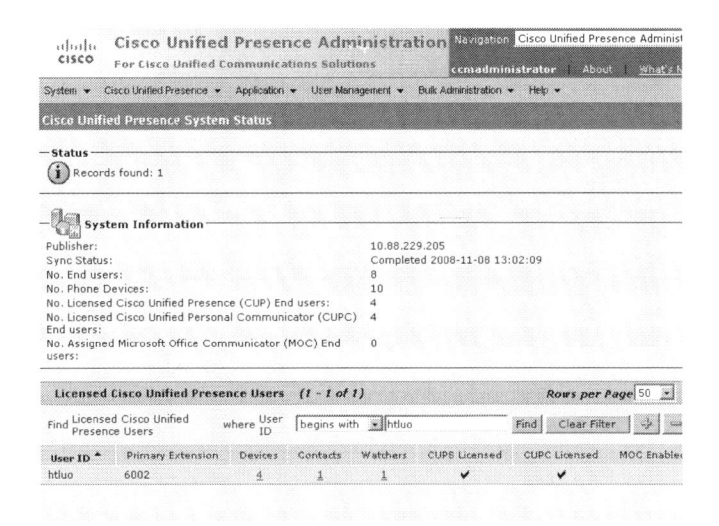

Incorrect username/password

To troubleshoot authentication issues, we need to understand how authentication was done.

On Cisco appliance (CUCM, CUPS, etc.), there are two authentication methods:

1. Native Authentication (or Local Authentication)
   Appliance authenticates end user with its local database.

2. LDAP Authentication
   Appliance authenticates end user with LDAP (Active Directory or Netscape LDAP).

Note: Don't confuse LDAP Authentication with LDAP Synchronization, though in most of the cases, they are enabled together. For more information, please refer to CUCM design guide (http://www.cisco.com/en/US/docs/voice_ip_comm/cucm/srnd/6x/directry.html).

Following are the data flow of Native Authentication and LDAP Authentication.

Native Authentication

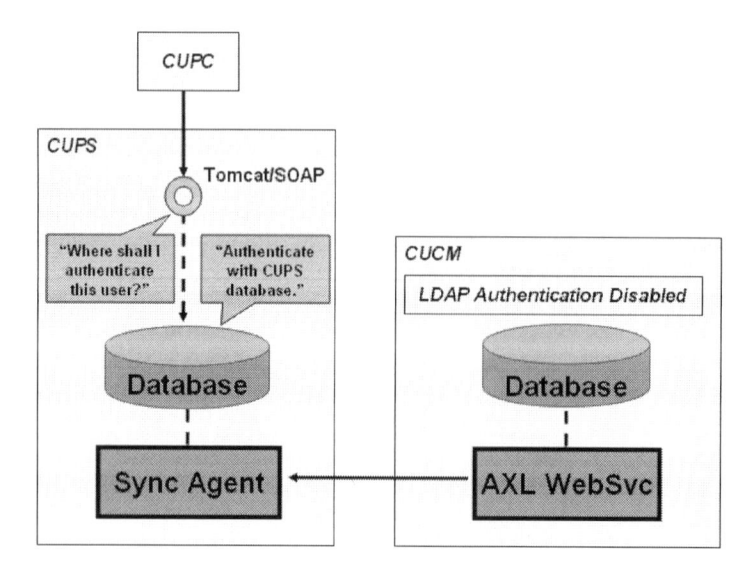

LDAP Authentication

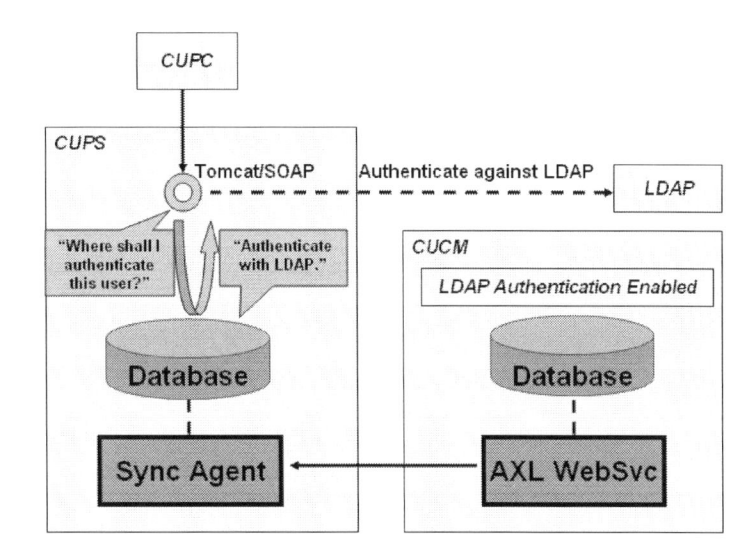

Possible cause #1: username/password was incorrect

Suggestion: Verify username/password.

The most effective way to verify username/password is to use User Option page.

Open a web browser. Go to https://ip-address-of-CUCM/ccmuser (where ip-address-of-CUCM is the actual IP address of your CUCM server). Try to log in with the end user's username and password. If you failed to log in, the problem is on CUCM. Please troubleshoot CUCM authentication first.

Note: On CUCM, the end user ID needs to be in "Standard CCM End Users" group to log in. Please refer to CUCM documentation regarding user groups (http://www.cisco.com/en/US/docs/voice_ip_comm/cucm/admin/6_1_1/ccmcfg/b08usgrp.html).

Logs: Cisco Tomcat Security Logs from CUCM.

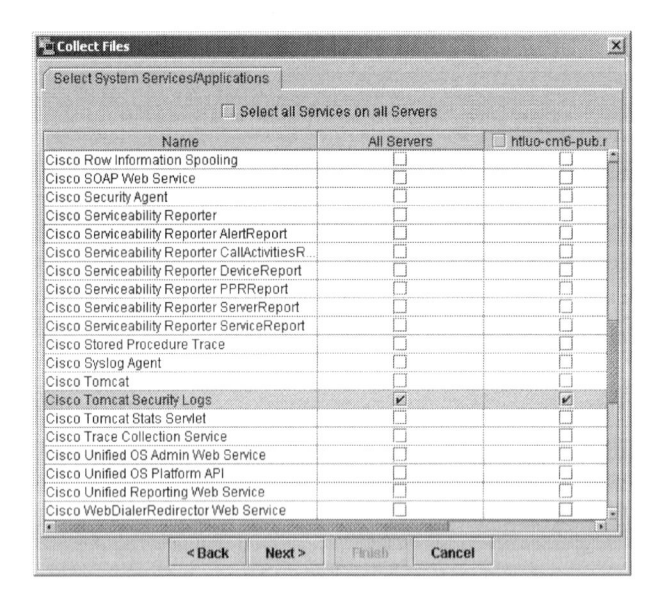

Chapter 5. Deploying and Troubleshooting Features

In Tomcat Security logs, you may search for the user ID. From there, you may see what authentication method CUCM was using and why the authentication was failed.

Logs snippets:
```
2008-11-09 08:49:00,540 DEBUG [http-8443-Processor25]
impl.AuthenticationDB - authenticateUser: userId=htluo isLogin true
2008-11-09 08:49:00,541 INFO   [http-8443-Processor25]
security.Log4jEncLogger - Log4jEncLogger: Constructor
2008-11-09 08:49:00,541 INFO   [http-8443-Processor25]
security.Log4jEncLogger - CCMEncryption: Constructor
2008-11-09 08:49:00,541 INFO   [http-8443-Processor25]
security.Log4jEncLogger - Exiting CCMEncryption()
2008-11-09 08:49:00,658 DEBUG [http-8443-Processor25]
impl.AuthenticationDB - authenticateUser: ImsReadCredentials result
userOID_ =16e2e7f4-bdf3-41d5-a67a-0aa633b81728 credentialOID_=f8ef2ad0-
0889-4906-aa0b-10dfd675a4a4 encryptedCredential_
=52df4a645faddf43341446492bfb222c3260437b userCantChange_=false
userMustChange_ =false doesNotExpire_=true isInactive_ =false
daysToExpiry_=0 needWarning_ =0 timeLastAccessed_=1226242140 hackCount_ =0
timeHackedLockout_=0 timeOfLockout_ =0 timeLastChanged_=1226171030
timeLastHacked_ =0 userType_=1 endUserStatus_ =1
2008-11-09 08:49:00,659 DEBUG [http-8443-Processor25]
impl.LDAPConfiguration - getLDAPObject:
2008-11-09 08:49:00,659 DEBUG [http-8443-Processor25]
impl.LDAPConfiguration - returning singleton object =
com.cisco.security.ims.impl.LDAPConfiguration@c37ace
2008-11-09 08:49:00,660 DEBUG [http-8443-Processor25]
impl.AuthenticationDB - authenticateUserWithPassword:
isAuthenticateWCorpDirectory flag is = TRUE
```

In the log snippets above, we can see that CUCM was trying to authenticate user "htluo" with LDAP ("`isAuthenticateWCorpDirectory flag is = TRUE`").

```
2008-11-09 08:49:00,663 DEBUG [http-8443-Processor25]
impl.AuthenticationLDAP - makeConnection:
ldapURL[0]=ldap://10.88.229.200:3268
```

Now we see the LDAP server was 10.88.229.200. Port number is 3268 (Active Directory Global Catalog).

```
2008-11-09 08:49:00,680 DEBUG [http-8443-Processor25]
impl.AuthenticationLDAP - authenticateUserWithPassword: dn=CN=Michael Luo,
OU=People,DC=r7,DC=com
```

By looking up the user ID "htluo", a DN (Distinguished Name) was found in LDAP ("`dn=CN=Michael Luo, OU=People,DC=r7,DC=com`")

```
2008-11-09 08:49:00,701 DEBUG [http-8443-Processor25]
authentication.AuthenticationImpl - loginUtil: Authentication complete
with result=1
```

"`result=1`" means authentication failed. "`result=0`" means success.

Possible cause #2: CUPS and CUCM out of synchronization

If you were able to log in to CUCM User Option page, you may continue troubleshoot CUPS.

Open a web browser. Go to https://ip-address-of-CUPS/ccmuser (where ip-address-of-CUPS is the actual IP address of your CUPS server). Try to log in with the end user's username and password. If you were able to log in to CUCM but failed to log in to CUPS, it's probably CUPS and CUCM are out-of-sync.

Out-of-sync could mean two things:

1. Password is out-of-sync (Native Authentication)
2. Authentication Method is out-of-sync

Suggestions:
1. Restart Sync Agent service on CUPS.
2. Restart Cisco Tomcat on CUPS

Note: To restart Tomcat, issue this command on CLI: `utils service restart Cisco Tomcat`

Logs: Cisco Tomcat Security Logs from CUPS.

Possible cause #3: LDAP Certificate was not installed on CUPS

This only happens when "LDAP Authentication with SSL" was enabled on CUCM.

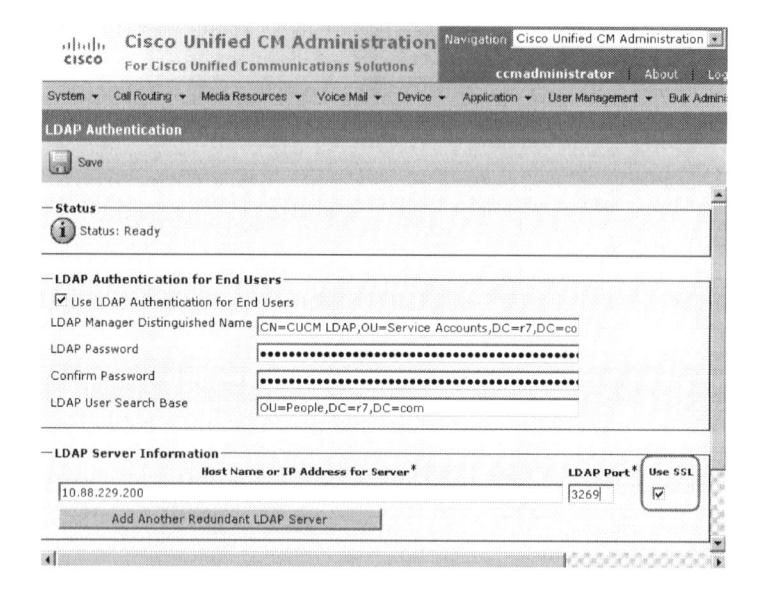

When SSL was enabled for LDAP, a LDAP certificate is required on the appliance. If you installed the certificate on CUCM but forgot to install it on CUPS, authentication request initiated from CUPS will fail.

Logs: Cisco Tomcat Security Logs from CUPS.

Possible cause #4: Credential Policy on CUCM

Suggestion: Uncheck "User Must Change at Next Login"

If CUCM is using native authentication (not LDAP authentication), there's a "credential policy" for each end user account (CUCM Admin > User Management > End User > End User Configuration).

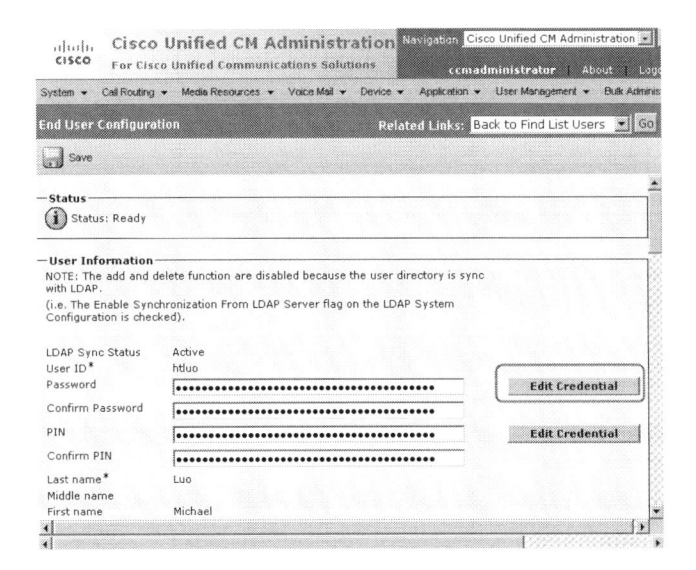

On "End User Configuration" page, click "Edit Credential" next to the password field. On "Credential Configuration" page, there's an option called "User Must Change at Next Login". This option must be unchecked.

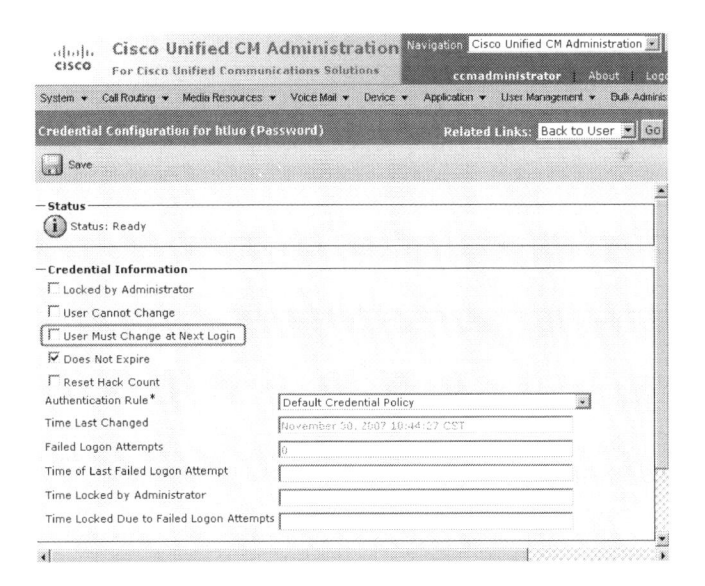

If the "User Must Change at Next Login" option was checked, you will fail to log on to CUPC. But you can log on to CUPS user option page without problem.

Other logon issues

If you have other logon issues not listed here, please collect the following logs:

From CUPS:

1. Cisco UP Client Profile Agent
2. Cisco Tomcat Security Logs

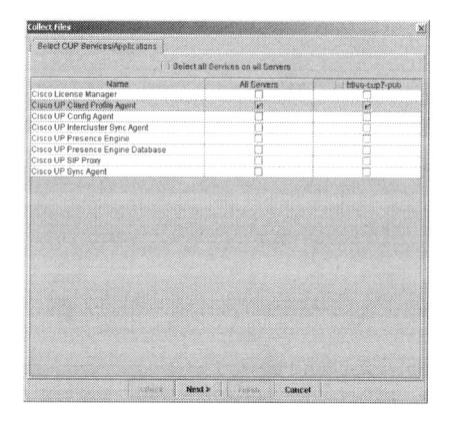

From CUPC:

Create Problem Report.

LDAP

LDAP is probably the most confusing part in CUPS/CUPC deployment.

Frequently asked questions are:

1. Do I need a LDAP?
2. Do I need to integrate LDAP with CUCM?
3. Do I need to integrate LDAP with CUPS?

Short answers:

1. Yes, you need a LDAP (Active Directory or Netscape LDAP)

LDAP

2. It is not required, but strongly recommended. If your CUCM is not LDAP integrated, make sure the user IDs in CUCM are the same as in LDAP.
3. There's no such a thing called "integrate LDAP with CUPS". Instead, you need to integrate LDAP with CUPC. Otherwise, some features won't work.

I recommend you review the "how things work" section for better understanding of CUCM/CUPS/LDAP.

Prerequisites

1. A LDAP server (Active Directory or Netscape LDAP)
2. User IDs in CUCM are the same as in LDAP (case sensitive). You may achieve this by one of the following methods:
    a. Integrate CUCM with LDAP.
    b. Manually make the user IDs in CUCM the same as in LDAP.

Steps to deploy feature:

Step 1: CUPS: Set LDAP server type for CUPC

1.1 Go to CUPS Admin > Application > Cisco Unified Personal Communicator > Settings
1.2 In "Directory Server Type", choose your LDAP server type.
1.3 Click "Save"

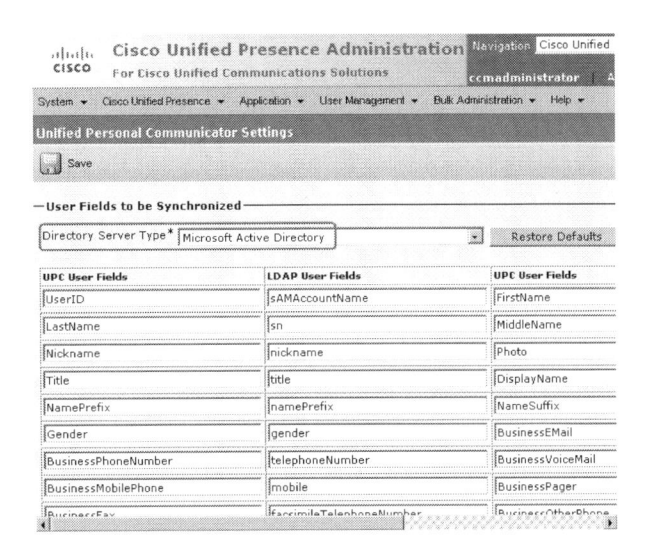

Note:
> The fields below "Directory Server Type" are used for attribute mapping. The default setting should work. You may customize it if you'd like. For example, you might want to map the "UserID" to "ipPhone" instead of "sAMAccountName". See chapter "How things work" for more details.

Step 2: LDAP: Create a Service Account in LDAP

2.1 Create a regular account in LDAP (does not require any special permission)
2.2 Clear the option "User must change password at next logon"
2.3 Choose the option "User cannot change password"
2.4 Choose the option "Password never expires"
2.5 After creating the account, get the fully qualified distinguished name (DN) of the account. This information is required in the steps later. For Active Directory, the easiest way to get the DN is to use "dsquery" command. Below are the command syntax and the command output.

```
C:\>dsquery user -samid cupcldap
"CN=CUPC LDAP,OU=Service Accounts,DC=r7,DC=com"
```

The command is "`dsquery user -samid cupsldap`". "cupsldap" is the account name.

The output of this command is `"CN=CUPC LDAP,OU=Service Accounts,DC=r7,DC=com"`. We'll use this as the "Bind Distinguished Name" later.

Notes:
1. It is recommended that you create a dedicated account for this purpose only. It is NOT recommended to share the account with another application (such CUCM, Unity, etc.). During the integration/test, the service account might be locked up. If you used a shared account, it will lock up other applications as well.
2. Due to the current limitation of CUPS, please create the account in a container/OU that the container/OU or any upper container/OU does NOT have special characters like quote ("), close angle bracket (>), open angle bracket (<), backslash (\), ampersand (&), percent (%).

Step 3: CUPS: Create a LDAP server in CUPS

1.1 Go to CUPS Admin > Application > Cisco Unified Personal Communicator > LDAP Server
3.2 Click "Add New"
3.3 In "Name" filed, enter a name you like
3.4 In "Hostname/IP Address" field, enter IP address of the LDAP server. If you're using Active Directory, it's recommended to use global catalog server.
3.5 In "Port" field, enter the LDAP port. Please verify the port number with your LDAP administrator.
3.6 In "Protocol Type", choose a protocol. Please verify the protocol with your LDAP administrator.
3.7 Click "Save"

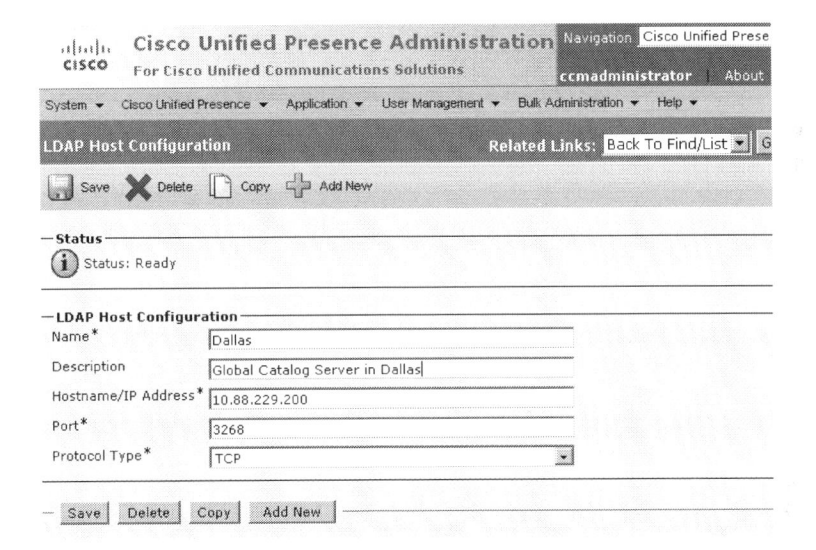

Step 4: CUPS: Create a LDAP profile in CUPS and add users to it

4.1 Go to CUPS Admin > Application > Cisco Unified Personal Communicator > LDAP Profile.
4.2 Click "Add New"
4.3 Uncheck "Anonymous Bind" (because most of LDAP servers won't allow anonymous bind)
4.4 Check "Recursive Search". (because you usually want to search all sub-containers instead of just the current container)
4.5 In "Name" filed, enter a name you like.
4.6 In "Bind Distinguished Name (DN)", enter the DN we got from step 1.5
4.7 In "Password" and "Confirm Password" fields, enter the password for the account

Chapter 5. Deploying and Troubleshooting Features

4.8 In "Search Context" field, enter the search context. If you're not sure what to enter, please contact the LDAP administrator or refer to CUCM LDAP authentication.
4.9 In "Primary LDAP Server", choose the LDAP server you configured in step 2.
4.10 Click "Add Users to Profile"
4.11 Select users and click "add selected"

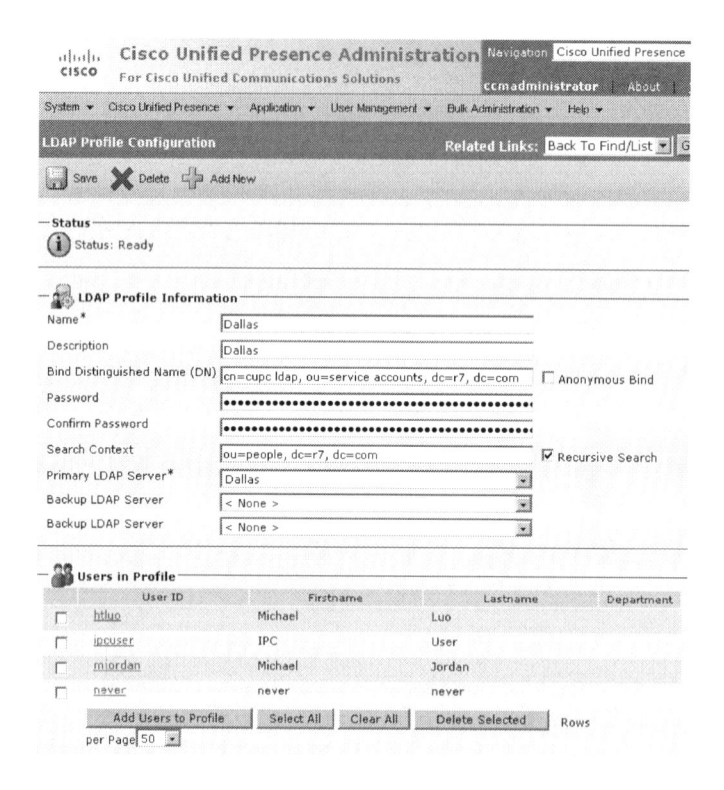

Notes:
Even though we configure LDAP information on CUPS server, this information is used by CUPC *directory lookup* only. CUPS/CUPC does not use this information for user synchronization or authentication.

Customized LDAP search base and filters

Search Multiple OUs

LDAP 91

There will be a time that you want to search multiple OUs and for whatever reason, you can't point the search base to their mutual parent. In this case you may use # sign to separate multiple OUs in search base.

For example, you'd like to have CUPC searched for the following two OU.

OU1: ou=sales, dc=acme, dc=com
OU2: ou=support, dc=acme, dc=com
The "simplest" way would be point the search base to "dc=acme, dc=com". You may also configure the search base like this:

```
ou=sales,dc=acme,dc=com#ou=support,dc=acme,dc=com
```

Filter unwanted data from search

Usually, people want to the LDAP search return results on persons only. Unfortunately, LDAP usually returns "non-person" data, such as computers, application data, etc.

You may apply LDAP filter to filter out the data you want.

For example, if you don't want computer objects to be returned by LDAP, you may set the search base as below:

```
ou=employees,dc=acme,dc=com;&(!objectClass=computer)
```

"!" means "not" in the filter syntax.

Please note that the syntax below might not generate result you expected:

```
ou=employees,dc=acme,dc=com;&(objectClass=user)
```

At first glance, it should return user objects only (not computer objects). That's a reasonable assumption. However, some LDAP vendors (such as Microsoft) think otherwise. Take a look at the screenshot below:

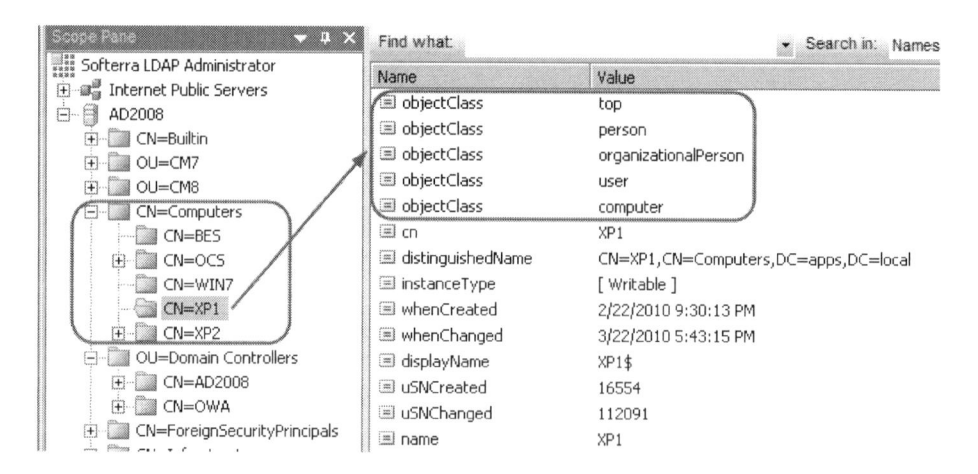

92 Chapter 5. Deploying and Troubleshooting Features

You'll notice that the computer object "XP1" has multiple objectClasses associated. "User" and "person" are two of them. Thus "objectClass=user" or "objectClass=person" will contain computer objects also. That's probably not what you want. So to filter out computer objects, you need to use (!objectClass=computer).

Test

1. Log in to CUPC.
2. Go to CUPC Help menu > Show Server Health > Highlight "LDAP" on the left.
3. On the right hand side, you will be able to see the LDAP connection status and the configuration details (such as Directory DN). If connection status is "Successful", that means CUPC connects to LDAP successfully.

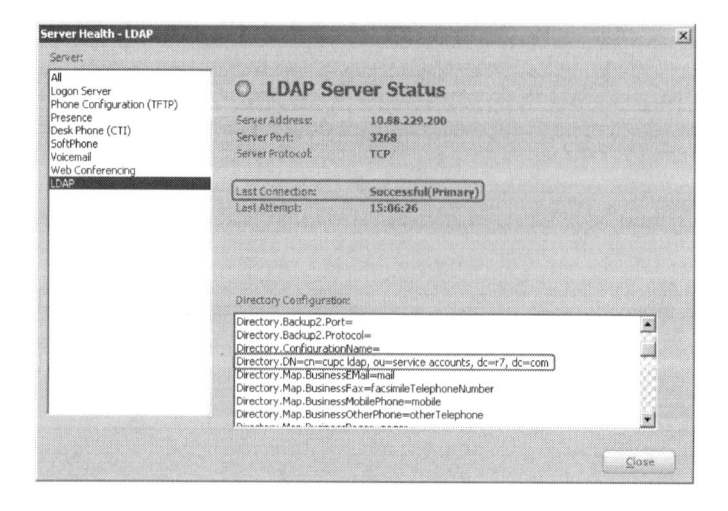

4. Close "Show Server Health" window.
5. In CUPC search box, type a contact's name in LDAP (e.g. Michael). Hit "Enter" to search.
6. If the name was in LDAP, CUPC should display search results.
7. Right-click one of the search results > Add Contact to Group > General. The contact should be added to "General" group.

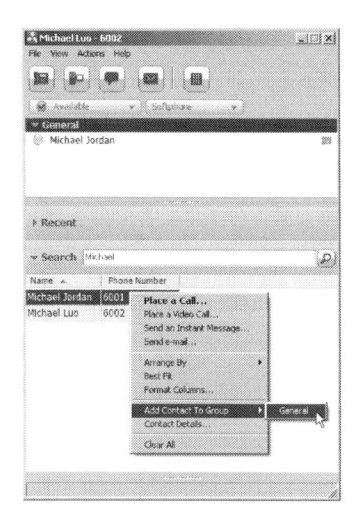

Troubleshooting

Frequently seen problems:

1. CUPC failed to connect to LDAP
   This could be caused by:
   a. Incorrect LDAP server address, port number in LDAP server
   b. Incorrect distinguished name (or wrong format) in LDAP profile
   c. Incorrect password in LDAP profile (or the account has been locked out)

2. CUPC connected to LDAP, but didn't return any search results
   This could be caused by:
   a. "Recursive Search" was unchecked in LDAP profile
   b. Incorrect "Search Context" in LDAP profile
   c. Slow response from LDAP

3. CUPC returned search results, but failed to add the search result to contact list. This could be caused by:
    a. Incorrect "Directory Server Type"
    b. Incorrect LDAP attribute mapping

CUPC failed to connect to LDAP

Possible cause #1: Incorrect LDAP server address, port number in LDAP server

Suggestions:
1. Verify LDAP address and port number with LDAP administrator.
2. Verify connection by telneting to LDAP address and port number.

On Windows machine, open a command prompt. Type the command below:

```
telnet 192.168.1.10 3268
```

192.168.1.10 is the IP address of LDAP. 3268 is the port number.

If you got a blinking cursor, it means the connection was established.

If you got a message like below, it means the connection couldn't be established.

```
Connecting To 192.168.1.10...Could not open connection to the host, on port 3268: Connect failed
```

Possible cause #2 Incorrect distinguished name (or wrong format) in LDAP profile

Suggestion: Verify distinguished name with "dsquery" command.

Example:
```
C:\>dsquery user -samid cupcldap
"CN=CUPC LDAP,OU=Service Accounts,DC=r7,DC=com"
```

Possible cause #3 Incorrect password in LDAP profile (or the account has been locked out)

LDAP

This one is very difficult to verify and fix unless you know how things work.

1. When CUPC logs in, it downloads configuration from CUPS server, including LDAP DN and password.
2. CUPC will use the downloaded DN/password to authenticate with LDAP to do binding.
3. CUPC will not get any updated configuration until next logon.

If for whatever reason, CUPC got the wrong LDAP information, it would lock out the LDAP account in three strikes. In order to fix this, you have to do the following in the right order:

1. Update the LDAP configuration in CUPS Admin > Application > Cisco Unified Personal Communicator > LDAP Profile.
2. Log off and log on CUPC.

Simple enough? Not necessarily. It would be simple if you have only one computer running CUPC.

If you have 50 computers running CUPC, things wouldn't be that simple. You'll have to make sure all those 50 computers got the updated configuration. The only way to do that is to get all CUPC logged out. This won't be an easy job because there's no centralized force logout feature on CUPS. You have to find the CUPC one by one and manually exit them. Sometimes, this would be as difficult as impossible.

If you failed to exit all the CUPC, they will keep striking LDAP with the wrong password and keep locking the account no matter how many times you unlock it. When the LDAP account was locked, all CUPC will lose the feature to search LDAP. If your CUCM was using the same account, congratulations, you break the CUCM as well.

Before an enhancement can be made to the product, here's a workaround.

1. Once the LDAP account was locked by CUPC, create another LDAP account (you may create it in advance as a contingency plan).
2. On CUPS Admin > Application > Cisco Unified Personal Communicator > LDAP Profile, carefully enter the new account's information.
3. For those CUPC log off and log on after the change, they will get new information and would be able to search LDAP.
4. For those CUPC didn't log out, they will keep striking the old account and lock it up. But it doesn't matter because we are using a new account on LDAP.

96   Chapter 5. Deploying and Troubleshooting Features

If you believe that all CUPC have been logged out, but the account is still getting locked, here's the way to track it down:

Go to your Active Directory server (domain controller) > Event Viewer > Security log. Look at the audit failure events. You would find some events like below.

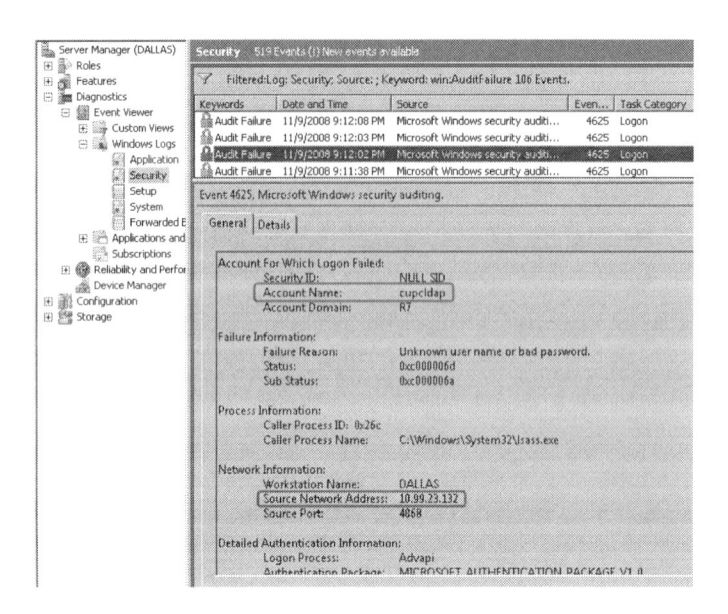

In the event above, "Account Name" is "cupcldap", which is the service account used by all CUPC. "Source Network Address" is "10.99.23.132", which is the IP address of the computer that attempted the failed logon.

How to track that IP address down to a physical location is beyond the discussion of this book. But at least you know which computer was locking out the account.

CUPC didn't return search results

Possible cause #1   "Recursive Search" was unchecked in LDAP profile

Suggestion: Make sure "Recursive Search" was checked in LDAP profile

If "Recursive Search" was not checked, CUPC will not search any sub-containers.

Look at the example below:

LDAP 97

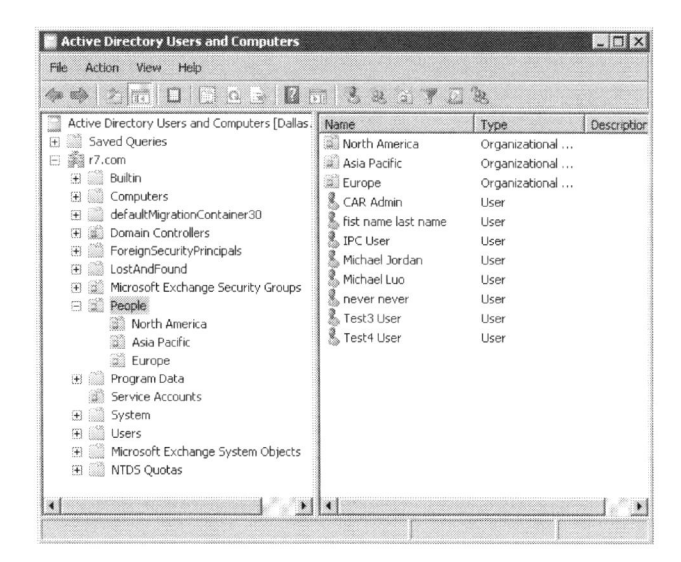

![Active Directory Users and Computers screenshot showing r7.com tree with People container expanded to show North America, Asia Pacific, and Europe sub-containers. Right pane lists users including CAR Admin, IPC User, Michael Jordan, Michael Luo, Test3 User, Test4 User, etc.]

In LDAP profile, search context was set to "OU= People, DC=r7, DC=com" and "Recursive Search" was not checked. In this case, CUPC will search "People" container only. It will not search "North America", "Asia Pacific" or "Europe". If the contacts you tried to find was in one of those containers, CUPC won't find them.

Possible cause #2 Incorrect "Search Context" in LDAP profile

Suggestion: Double-check "Search Context" in LDAP profile

In LDAP profile, if the "Search Context" was misconfigured (or not configured), CUPC won't be able to search LDAP. Thus no result would be returned.

Possible cause #3 Slow response from LDAP

Suggestion: Use global catalog server as LDAP server.

If you have a large corporate directory and the search context was pointed to the root of directory, it will take a long time to find a contact. And it seems like CUPC didn't return anything.

To speed up the search, go to CUPS Admin > Application > Cisco Unified Personal Communicator > LDAP Server. Use global catalog server in LDAP server configuration. Make sure you use the global catalog port as well.

98   Chapter 5. Deploying and Troubleshooting Features

If you still have problem on LDAP search, do a sniffer capture from CUPC computer and open a TAC case.

CUPC failed to add contacts

Possible cause #1 Incorrect "Directory Server Type"

Suggestion: Double-check "Directory Server Type" in CUPS > Application > Cisco Unified Personal Communicator > Settings.

If the "Directory Server Type" was set to a wrong type, you won't be able to add contacts. This is because CUPC has to map the correct attributes to database.

Possible cause #2 Incorrect LDAP attribute mappings

Suggestions:
1. In CUPS > Application > Cisco Unified Personal Communicator > Settings, select correct "Directory Server Type".
2. In CUPS > Application > Cisco Unified Personal Communicator > Settings, click "Restore Defaults".

Again, incorrect attribute will cause CUPC failed to add contacts to database. "Restore Defaults" would put all mappings to a "base working configuration".

For more information, refer to CUPC troubleshooting guide:
http://www.cisco.com/en/US/docs/voice_ip_comm/cupc/7_0/english/troubleshooting/guide/trouble.html#wp1043195

Client Status

"Client Status" refers to CUPC status such as "Available", "Away", "Offline", etc.

Client status is a very fundamental and important feature. If client status was not functioning properly, you may see symptoms including but not limited to the following:

1. You CUPC status is offline
2. You cannot change your own status (e.g. change from "Available" to "Away")
3. You are not able to see other people's status
4. You changed phone mode (e.g. from Soft Phone to Desk Phone), but it didn't reflect on GUI
5. You cannot send instant message
6. You can send instant message but the recipient cannot reply to you

Prerequisites

1. SIP Proxy and Presence Engine services are running on CUPS
2. The user has been licensed to use CUP and CUPC
3. You are able to log in to CUPC

Steps to deploy feature:

Step 1: CUPS: Configure Proxy Domain

Proxy domain is used for SIP message routing. Technically, proxy domain should match DNS domain.

It's not uncommon that DNS is not available (or DNS entries have not added to DNS server) at the time you deploying CUPS. What should we enter as the proxy domain?

You should still enter the DNS domain name. You should not enter IP address. Because:

a. IP address can substitute a FQDN or hostname, but it cannot substitute a domain name.
b. If you're like 99.99% of other people, you probably have only one domain and only need to deal with one domain. If that's the case, it doesn't matter what you put in the proxy domain. You may put ANYTHING there and CUPS would still work like a champ. Since you could put in anything, why not put in the DNS domain name?

1.1 Go to CUPS Admin > System > Service Parameters
1.2 Choose a server in "Server"
1.3 Choose "Cisco UP SIP Proxy" from "Service"
1.4 Enter your DNS domain name in "Proxy Domain" field

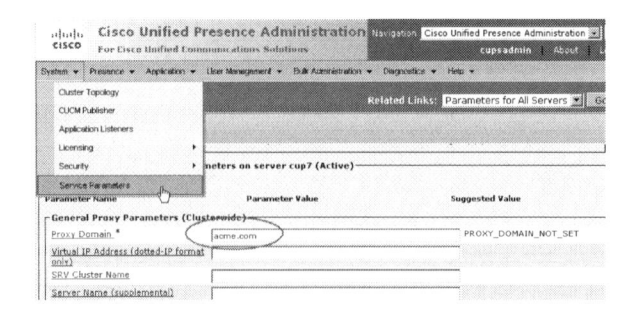

100 Chapter 5. Deploying and Troubleshooting Features

Notes: Please use lower case in domain name. Capital case would cause problems in some CUPS versions.

At the bottom of the page, there's another parameter called "Federation Routing CUP FQDN". It'll be the "CUPS hostname + SIP Proxy Domain".

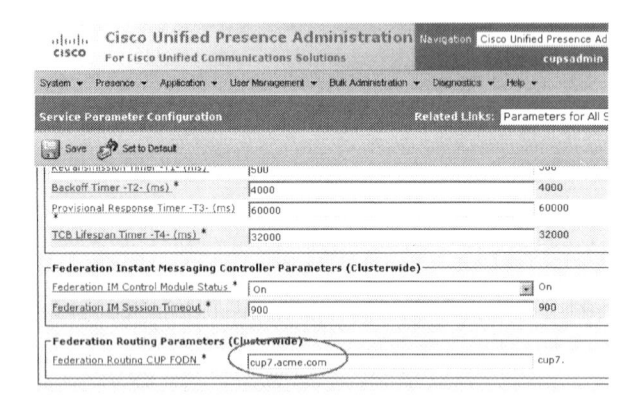

Step 3: Configure Digest Credential

"Digest Credential" is an authentication mechanism of SIP protocol. In order for CUPC to connect to SIP proxy, you need to configure Digest Credential for end user, or bypass/disable it. Each option has its pros and cons.

Options	Control Level	Security Level	Amount of work
Digest Credential	User	Most secure	Most
Incoming ACL	Subnet	Somehow secure	Medium
Service Parameter	System-wide	Not secure	Least

Option 1: CUCM: Digest Credential

Use this option if you need highest security. When this option is used, only CUCM users can connect to CUPS server SIP proxy.

To configure digest credential, do the following:

- 3.1 Go to CUCM Admin > User Management > End User > search for an end user.
- 3.2 Click the end user.
- 3.3 On the "End User Configuration" page, enter some text in the "Associated PC Digest Credential". Enter the same text in "Confirm Digest Credential"

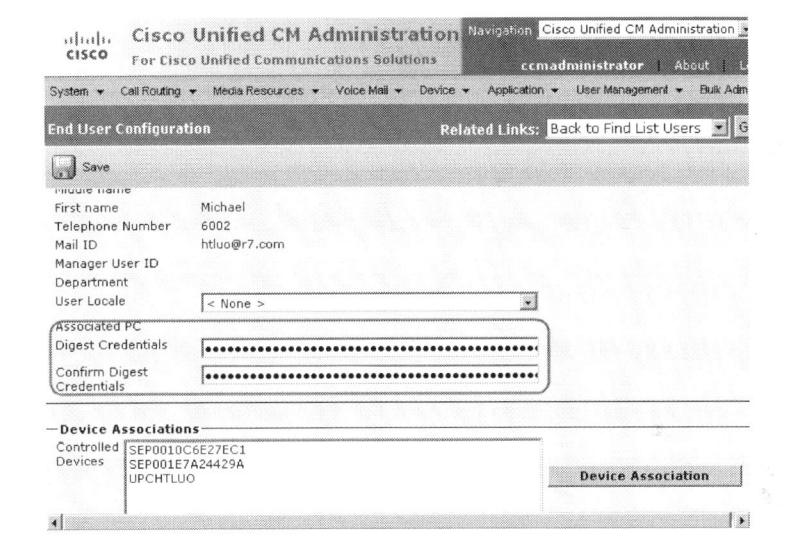

Note: The digest credential could be anything, but cannot be blank.

Option 2: CUPS: Incoming ACL

Use this option when you want to bypass the digest credential check for a specific IP address or subnet.

Example 1: You trust all the computers on your local subnet. You may configure an incoming ACL to allow your local subnet. Then you don't have to configure digest credential for each CUCM user.

Example 2: You are integrating CUPS with OCS. There's no way to configure digest credential for OCS on CUCM or CUPS. The only way to work around this is to configure an incoming ACL with the OCS' IP address. Hence CUPS will bypass the digest credential check for that IP.

To configure incoming ACL, do the following:

    3.1 Go to CUPS Admin > System > Security > Incoming ACL.
    3.2 Click "Add New"
    3.3 Put in the description and address pattern

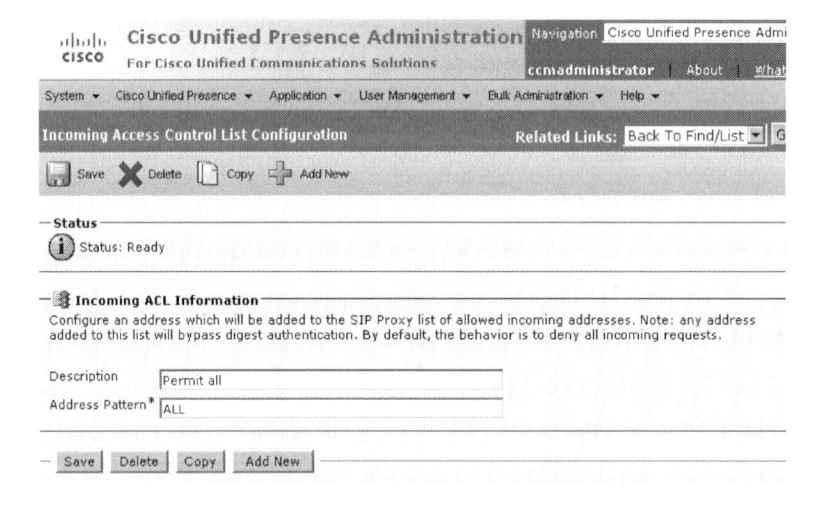

Examples of ACLs:

Host Address Description	Configuration Example
All hosts	• Allow from all
A partial domain namje	• Allow from company.com
A full IP address	• Allow from 10.1.2.3
A partial IP address	• Allow from 10.1
A network/netmask pair	• Allow from 10.1.0.0/255.255.0.0
A network/nnn CIDR specification	• Allow from 10.1.0.0/16

Note: You may ignore "Allow from". For example "All" equals to "Allow from all".

Option 3: CUPS: Service Parameters

Use this option if you want to turn off the authentication at all. This is usually not recommended because of security concerns.

To turn off authentication totally, do the following:

    3.1 Go to CUPS Admin > System > Service Parameters
    3.2 Select a server > select "Cisco UP SIP Proxy"
    3.3 Set "Authentication Module Status" to "Off"
    3.4 Save configuration
    3.5 Restart "Cisco SIP Proxy" service

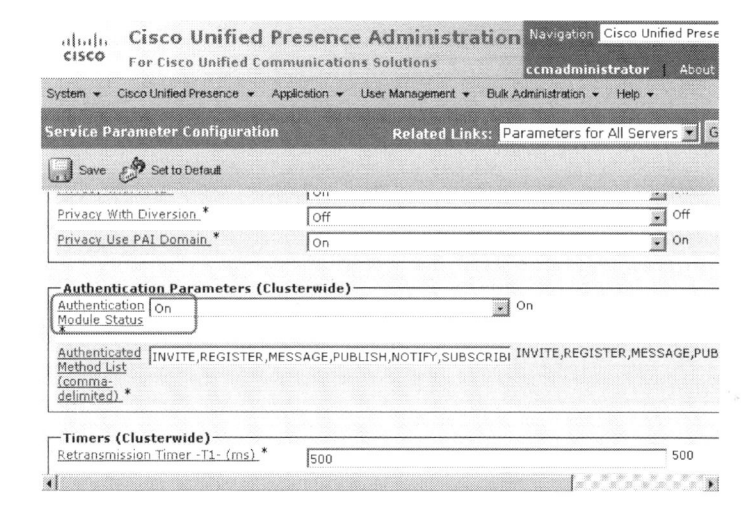

Test

1. Log in to CUPC
2. Observe CUPC status changes to 'Available'
3. Try to change CUPC status to 'Away'. Status should change to 'Away' immediately.
4. Try to change CUPC status to 'Available'. Status should change to 'Available' immediately.

Troubleshooting

Have some basic ideas of SIP would help us read SIP messages. Knowing what SIP messages each component sends would help us track the dialog.

Basic Concepts of SIP

For detailed information regarding SIP, please refer to IETF website: http://www.ietf.org/html.charters/sip-charter.html.

We'll only cover some basic concepts here.

Response (a.k.a. Acknowledgement)

Each SIP message sent will have a response from the other end. For example, CUPC sends a REGISTER SIP message to CUPS. If the REGISTER was successful, CUPS would respond a "200 OK" to CUPC.

SIP response codes are very similar to HTTP response.

- 1xx: Provisional — request received, continuing to process the request;
- 2xx: Success — the action was successfully received, understood, and accepted;
- 3xx: Redirection — further action needs to be taken in order to complete the request;
- 4xx: Client Error — the request contains bad syntax or cannot be fulfilled at this server;
- 5xx: Server Error — the server failed to fulfill an apparently valid request;
- 6xx: Global Failure — the request cannot be fulfilled at any server

SIP messages between components

During CUPC logon

- REGISTER
  After CUPC logged in, it will send REGISTER message to SIP Proxy to claim its existence. If CUPS respond a "200 OK", CUPS will light up the self-status menu.

- SUBSCRIBE (self status)
  CUPC then subscribes it self status. A 'subscribe', as indicated by the word itself, is a request to the CUPS. It's like "Hey, CUPS, I'd like to be notified of any status change on this user".

Someone might ask – "Why does CUPC need to subscribe its own status? Shouldn't it know its own status locally?" The answer is, we have many different kinds of presence – availability, phone presence, and calendar presence. CUPC might be aware of its self-status locally, which is availability information. But CUPC won't be able to know phone presence and calendar presence unless it 'subscribes' those information.

- SUBSCRIBE (contacts)
  This one is very obvious. To receive presence updates of your contacts, you have to subscribe their presence information.

  If you add yourself to your contact list, CUPC will not send subscribe for self-status (because yourself is on the contact-list already).

- PUBLISH
  After CUPC logged in, it will send its last known status to CUPS in PUBLISH message. Last known status means the last status when CUPC last logged off. If CUPC never logged on before, it will try to publish "Available" status.

- NOTIFY
  When CUPS receives the initial PUBLISH from CUPC, it will send out NOTIFY to subscribers (also known as "Watchers").

When CUPC change its own status

- PUBLISH
  Whenever CUPC changes its own status(availability), it will send PUBLISH message to CUPS. CUPS will send NOTIFY to all subscribers (also known as "Watchers").

- NOTIFY
  When CUPS receives the a PUBLISH message from CUPC, it will send out NOTIFY to subscribers (also known as "Watchers").

When phone status changes

- PUBLISH
  When the phone on-hook/off-hook status changes, CUCM will send PUBLISH message to CUPS. CUPS will send out NOTIFY to subscribers (also known as "Watchers").

- NOTIFY
  When CUPS receives the a PUBLISH message from CUPC, it will send out NOTIFY to subscribers (also known as "Watchers").

Best practices

Lots of client status issues are caused by network issue. Because of that, it's recommended to rule out network issues first, before you dive into logs and traces.

Many people didn't believe the problem was caused by network because they could send emails and copy files without any issue. Since "all other applications" worked fine, they thought it was CUPS/CUPC issue.

Well, the answer is "Yes" and "No".

Yes. The problem seems to happen on CUPS/CUPC only. But the solution is not on CUPS/CUPC.

CUPS/CUPC use SIP protocol to fulfill lots of functions. SIP protocol has two unique characters that might be vulnerable to network limitations:

1. SIP message could be very huge in size.
   This means those messages could fail to traverse the network if defragment/reassemble was not set up properly on network equipments (routers, VPN, etc.)

2. SIP is "content aware"
   This means, when NAT (Network Address Translation) happens, not just the header, but also the content needs to be translated properly.

During the test, the CUPC computer would be better connecting to the same local network (LAN) as the CUPS server. You'd better turn off all firewall software on the CUPC computer. It didn't mean that you cannot use firewall with CUPC/CUPS. But to make our test and troubleshooting more efficient, we want to make the picture as simple as possible.

Sometimes, the firewall was hiding in a place that you would probably never think about.

Example #1: A customer was having client status issue with CUPC. He uninstalled all firewall software from CUPC computer. He connected CUPC computer to the same LAN switch with the CUPS server. Problem still persisted. Finally, he found out that on the LAN switch (Cisco Catalyst 6509), there's a FWSM (Firewall Switching Module). Once appropriate rules were configured on the FWSM, problem was resolved.

Example #2: In order to get firewall out of picture, customer stopped "Windows Firewall" service. He uninstalled McAfee desktop firewall. He looked everywhere he could think about, except "Cisco VPN Client". There's a "Stateful Firewall" option in Cisco VPN Client. Needless to say, uncheck that option fixed the problem.

Sometimes, it might be very difficult to get CUPC on to the same network as CUPS. For example, you're deploying/troubleshooting the feature remotely, which is 3000 miles away from the CUPS server. In this case, you should try to RDP (remote desktop) or VNC into a computer that is local to the CUPS and test from there.

Use SIP Workbench to isolate network issues

Lots of people know sniffer is a good tool to troubleshoot network issues. It's a good tool as long as you know how to use it. Unfortunately, most of the sniffer software (such as Wireshark) only gives you the "raw packets". Assembling raw packets into SIP messages won't be a fun job. Not even mention tracing a SIP dialog in thousands of packets.

SIP Workbench will make this formidable job a piece of cake.

SIP Workbench will take sniffer capture file as input. Please refer to chapter 2 regarding how to get sniffer capture from CUPC and CUPS side.

Once you got the sniffer capture, you may open it in SIP Workbench. SIP Workbench will show you all the SIP dialogs.

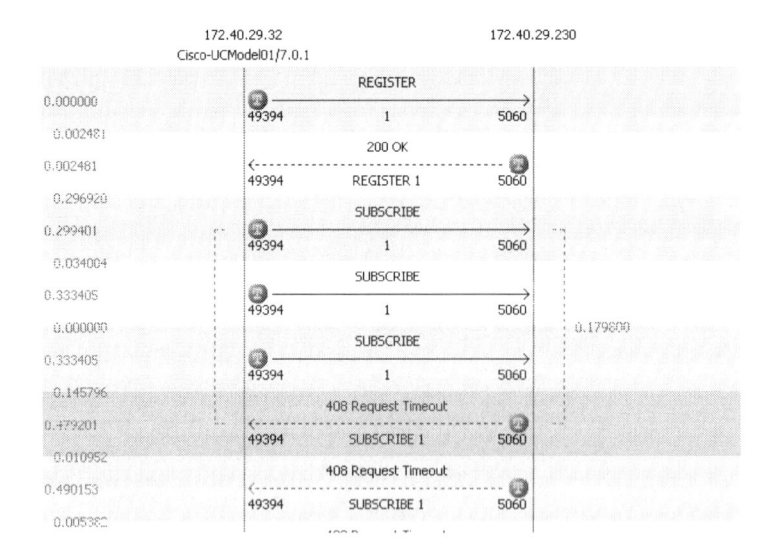

108 Chapter 5. Deploying and Troubleshooting Features

[SIP Workbench diagram showing message flow between 172.40.29.32 (Cisco-UCModel01/7.0.1) port 49394 and 172.40.29.230 port 5060: REGISTER → 200 OK (REGISTER 1) → SUBSCRIBE → SUBSCRIBE → SUBSCRIBE → 408 Request Timeout (SUBSCRIBE 1) → 408 Request Timeout (SUBSCRIBE 1), with timing annotations.]

Look at the SIP Workbench output above. You don't have to be a SIP expert to tell the following:

1. SIP REGISTER worked fine. Because we see "200 OK" for that REGISTER
2. SIP SUBSCRIBE seemed to have problem. Because we got "408 Request Timeout"

Isn't this much easier than reading raw packets or traces/logs?

Most frequently seen issues on Client status:

1. CUPC status menu was grey out. You cannot click the status menu.
   This usually means CUPC failed to connect to PE (Presence Engine). It could be caused by:
   a. Digest Credential or Incoming ACL was not configured.
   b. Proxy domain was not configured properly.
   c. Network issue

2. CUPC status menu was lit up. But it stays "offline". You can click the menu. But you cannot change the status to "Available".
   This could be caused by:
   a. Presence Engine service parameter
   b. Transport Listeners
   c. Method Event Routing.
   d. Network issue

3. CUPC self-status works fine. But you cannot see other contacts' status
   This could be caused by:
   a. User ID mapping issue (LDAP not integrated)
   b. Privacy Policy
   c. Network issue

Self-status grey-out

When CUPC self-status is grey out, it usually means CUPC failed to connect to PE (a.k.a. Presence Engine or Presence). The first place to look at is CUPC > Help > Show Server Health. The "Presence" item would tell you what the problem might be.

After CUPC logon, it will send "REGISTER SIP" message to CUPS (SIP Proxy), trying to register itself. CUPC won't light up the self-status menu until it receives a "200 OK" for its registration attempt. If CUPC self-status was grey out, you should look at logs or sniffer captures to see why "200 OK" was not received for the registration attempt.

Invalid Credentials

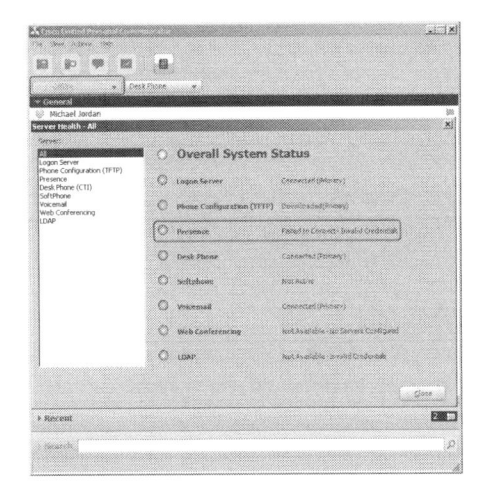

This usually means no digest credential or incoming ACLs configured. Hence CUPC cannot authenticate with SIP Proxy and not able to pass SIP messages to Presence Engine.

110 Chapter 5. Deploying and Troubleshooting Features

Suggestion: Please refer to "Digest Credential" section to configure digest credential or incoming ACL.

Proxy Domain not configured properly

If proxy domain was not configured or configured as IP address, you'll see the presence item in CUPC "Show Server Health" keep bouncing between "Connecting" and "Disconnecting (Pending Retry)".

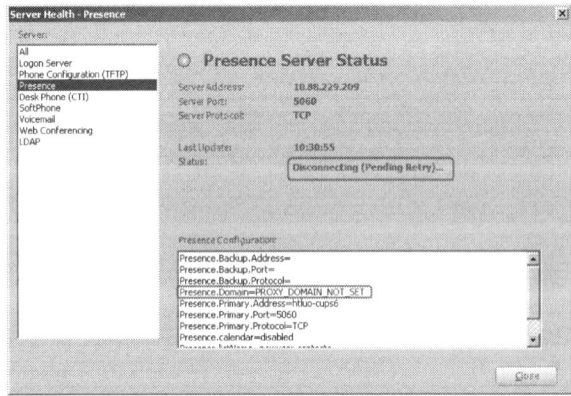

Suggestion: Please refer to "Proxy Domain" section for configuring proxy domain.

Self-status not updated

Take a look at the screenshots below. Can you tell the difference?

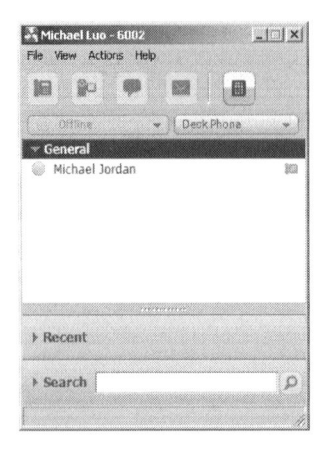

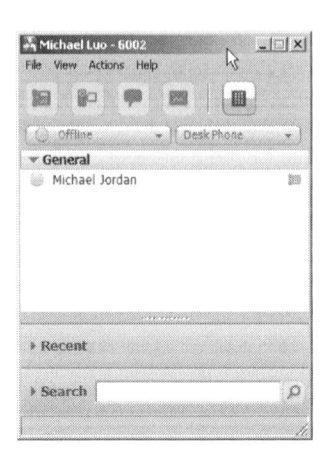

On the left-hand side, self-status menu is grey out. It means CUPC didn't receive a "200" response for its REGISTER attempt.

On the right-hand side, self-status is lit up, but its status is offline and you can't change it to anything else. The status could be Available or Away, but you won't be able to change the status. You won't be able to change the phone mode either. In fact, if you log off and log on again, you'll see the changes.

This is called "self-status issue". Either SUBSCRIBE (self) or PUBLISH was failed.

Suggestions: Look at traces and sniffer captures. See if you got "200" response for SUBSCRIBE or PUBLISH messages.

Contact status not updated

This issue is very similar to "self-status" issue. Either the contact failed to send PUBLISH, or you failed to SUBSCRIBE the contact.

The difference is: the publisher (your contacts) and subscriber (you) are on two different computers. The problem could be on publisher, subscriber, or network.

Suggestion: Use "swap test" to narrow down the problem. (Swap accounts, swap computers, etc.)

For more information, refer to CUPC troubleshooting guide:
http://www.cisco.com/en/US/docs/voice_ip_comm/cupc/7_0/english/troubleshooting/guide/trouble.html#wp1194705

Phone Status

Phone status (or phone presence) refers to the on-hook/off-hook status of the phone. When the status changes on the phone, CUCM will send (PUBLISH) presence information to CUPS. CUPS will send (NOTIFY) presence information to CUPC.

Prerequisites

1. SIP Proxy and Presence Engine services are running on CUPS
2. The user has been licensed to use CUP and CUPC*
3. You are able to log in to CUPC*
4. CUPC client status feature has been deployed and tested*

Note: CUPC is not required if you use MOC (Microsoft Office Communicator). But as mentioned before, CUPC is a very good testing tool. I would recommend you use CUPC for testing purpose even if you plan to use MOC.

Step 1: CUCM: Create SIP trunk

1.1 Log in to CUCM Admin web page
1.2 Go to Device > Trunk. Click "Add New"
1.3 All fields with asterisk are required fields. But the most two important ones are "Destination Address" and "Destination Port". In "Destination Address", enter the IP address of CUPS. In "Destination Port" enter 5060. (Note: On CUPS 6.x, the Destination Port is 5070)

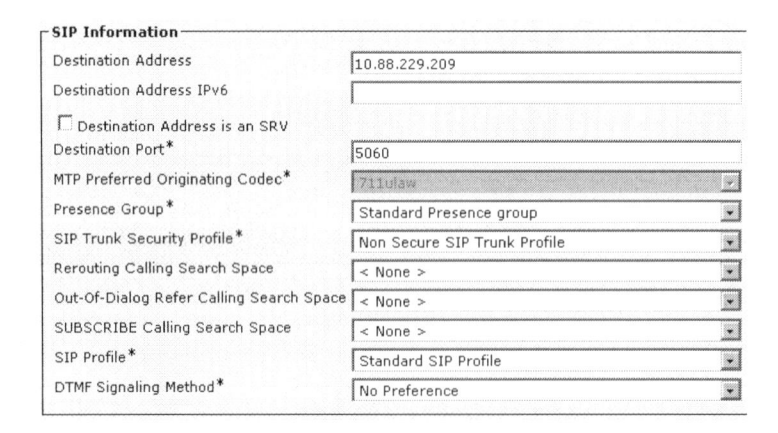

1.4 If you have more than one SIP trunk, you need to specify a "CUP PUBLISH trunk"
   a. Go to CUCM Admin > System > Service Parameters
   b. From the "Server" drop-down menu, select a server that running CallManager service
   c. From the "Service" drop-down menu, select "Cisco CallManager"
   d. Look for the filed "CUP PUBLISH Trunk"
   e. Select the SIP trunk you created in step 3 and save.
   f. Save

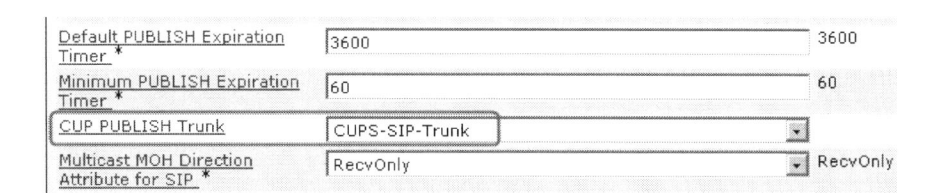

Step 2: CUPS: Create CUCM Presence Gateway

2.1 Log in to CUPS Admin web page
2.2 Go to Cisco Unified Presence > Presence Engine > Gateways. Click "Add New"
2.3 In "Presence Gateway Type" field, choose "CUCM"
2.4 In "Description" field, enter some description
2.5 In "Presence Gateway" field, enter IP address of CUCM.
   Note: You just need to create one presence gateway for the whole CUCM cluster.
   The presence gateway has to be the CUCM that running "Cisco CallManager" service.

Step 3: CUPS: Confirm SIP publish mode and SIP publish trunk

3.1 Log in to CUPS Admin web page
3.2 Go to Cisco Unified Presence > Settings
3.3 Make sure "Enable SIP Publish on Cisco Unified Communications Manager" was checked.
3.4 Make sure the correct SIP trunk was selected as the SIP publish trunk.

114 Chapter 5. Deploying and Troubleshooting Features

[Screenshot of Cisco Unified Presence Administration - Cisco Unified Presence Settings page showing Status: Ready, and Settings with "Enable Instant Messaging (cluster-wide)" and "Enable SIP Publish on Cisco Unified Communications Manager" checked, with Cisco Unified Communications Manager SIP Publish Trunk set to CUPS-SIP-Trunk]

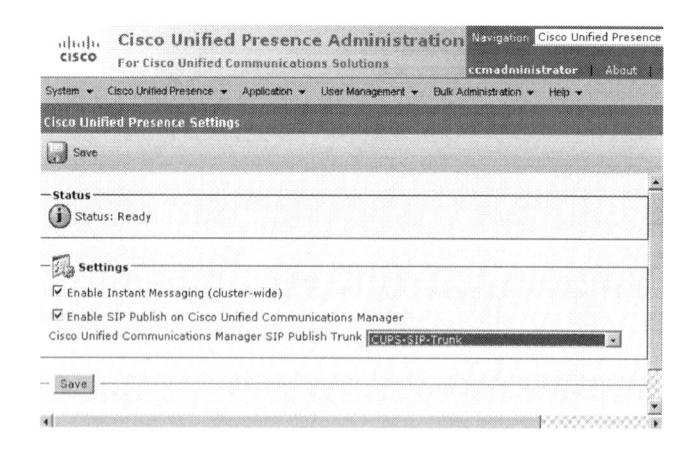

Step 4: CUCM: Associate line appearance with to end user

In order to see contacts' phone presence, your CUPC actually subscribe their presence from CUPS. CUPS, in turn will subscribe phone presence from CUCM.

All "subscriptions" are based on user ID. There needs to be a mechanism to map those user IDs to a phone line, so the line status could reflect to a user's presence. This mapping mechanism is called "Line Appearance Association".

Do not confuse "line appearance association" with "device association".

Association Type	Configured On	Purpose
Line Appearance Association	Device > Phone > DN	Phone Presence
Device Association	User Management > End User	Device Control (such as CTI)

4.1 Log in to CUCM Admin web page
4.2 Go to Device > Phone
4.3 Search for phones. Click on one of the search results
4.4 On the device configuration page, click Directory Number on left. You will go to "Directory Number Configuration" page.

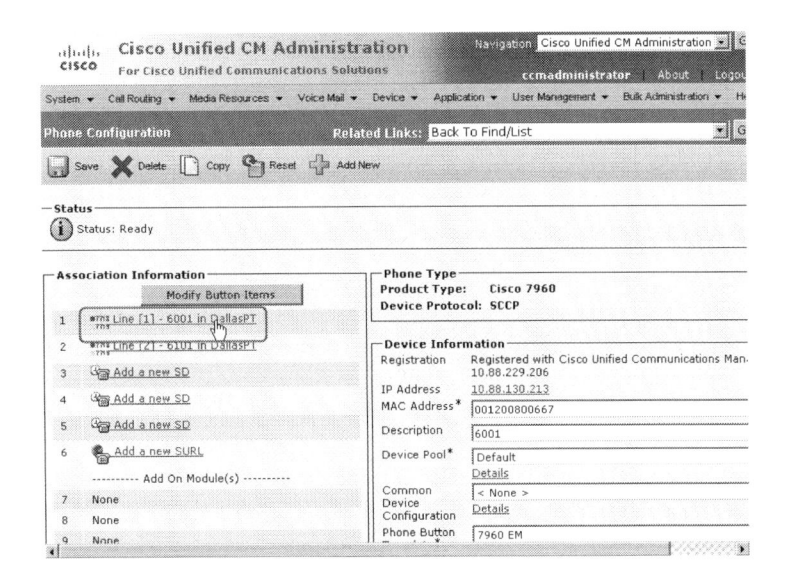

4.5 On the "Directory Number Configuration" page, go to the bottom of the page. You'll see "Users Associated with line".
4.6 Click "Associate End User"
4.7 On the popup windows, find and select user(s). Click "Add Selected"
4.8 Now this line is associated with the end user(s) you selected.

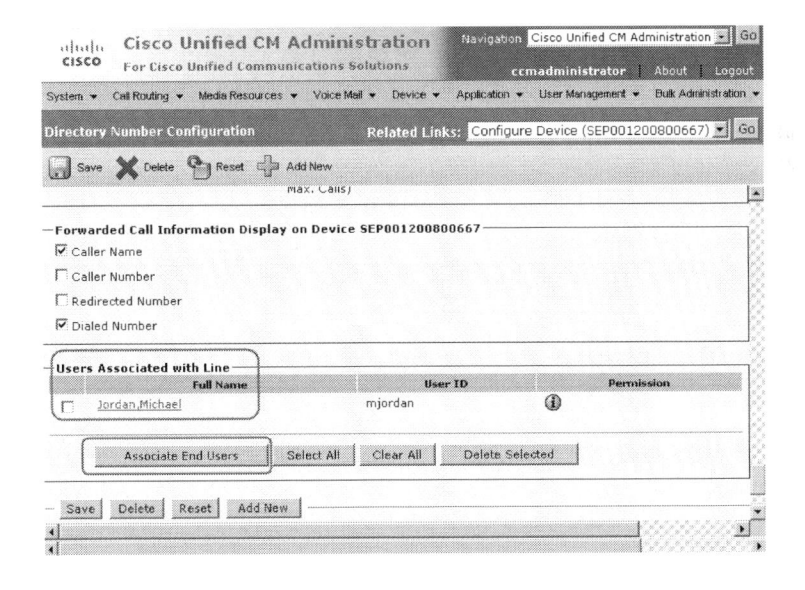

Test

116 Chapter 5. Deploying and Troubleshooting Features

1. Log in to CUPC
2. Watch CUPC self-status go to Available (or Away).
3. Get the phone off-hook (pick up the handset, or put the phone on speaker). Make sure you hear dial tone.
4. Watch CUPC status changes to "On the Phone"

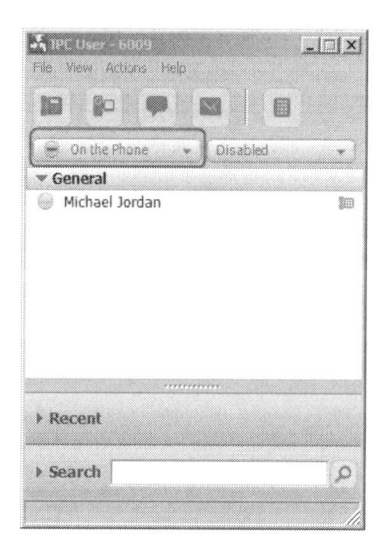

Please don't confuse phone presence with phone control. They are two independent features and NOT related to each other. From the screenshot above, you can see that we have phone presence ("On the Phone"). But the phone mode is "Disabled".

On the other hand, a phone control function doesn't guarantee phone presence. As you can see from screenshot below, the "Dialtone" window was because CUPC receive a signal from CTI. It has nothing to do with phone presence.

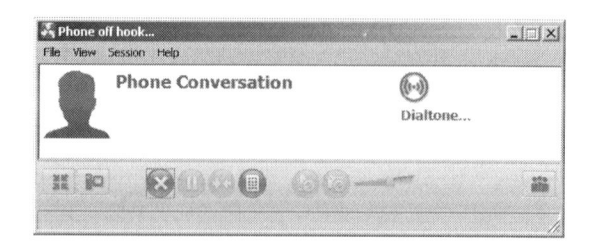

Troubleshooting

Best practices

1. Make sure "client status" feature is working before you test "phone presence". If "client status" was not working properly, "phone presence" might be affected as well. Here's why:
    a. All presence information (availability, phone presence, calendar presence) is delivered from CUPS to CUPC by NOTIFY message.
    b. If CUPC client status didn't update properly, it could be NOTIFY issue.
    c. If NOTIFY has issue, phone presence might not be delivered either.
2. Run troubleshooter to eliminate basic configuration errors.
3. Troubleshoot problem from source. Source is CUCM.
4. Troubleshoot problem segment by segment. From CUCM to CUPS. From CUPS to CUPC.

Basic Configuration Error

CUPS Troubleshooter should be able to find basic configuration errors.

Frequently seen errors are:

1. On CUCM, SIP trunk was configured with wrong destination IP address or destination port number.
2. On CUCM, SIP trunk security profile was misconfigured. Usually, the default "Non Secure SIP Trunk Profile" would work. Unfortunately some people modify the configuration on this profile. So it's not "default" anymore. Below is what a "Non Secure SIP Trunk Profile" should look like.

SIP Trunk Security Profile Information	
Name*	Non Secure SIP Trunk Profile
Description	Non Secure SIP Trunk Profile authenticated by null Str
Device Security Mode	Non Secure
Incoming Transport Type*	TCP+UDP
Outgoing Transport Type	TCP
☐ Enable Digest Authentication	
Nonce Validity Time (mins)*	600
X.509 Subject Name	
Incoming Port*	5060
☐ Enable Application Level Authorization	
☑ Accept Presence Subscription	
☑ Accept Out-of-Dialog REFER	
☑ Accept Unsolicited Notification	
☑ Accept Replaces Header	

118 Chapter 5. Deploying and Troubleshooting Features

3. On CUCM, CUP PUBLISH SIP trunk was misconfigured
4. On CUPS, CUCM presence gateway was misconfigured. (e.g. you point to a CUCM server that "Cisco CallManager" service is NOT running)
5. On CUPS, PUBLISH mode or PUBLISH trunk was misconfigured.

Suggestion:
1. Run CUPS Troubleshooter
2. Following deployment steps to check configuration.

CUCM-to-CUPS

Rule of thumb: Whenever the phone status was changed, CUCM should send PUBLISH SIP message to CUPS.

When troubleshoot phone presence issue, we want to troubleshoot from CUCM, because it's the source of information. If CUCM didn't send out phone presence, there's nothing CUPS could do.

To see if CUCM sends out phone presence or not, we need "Cisco CallManager" logs. We need them from the CUCM server where phones registered with. (This CUCM server may or may not be the presence gateway you configured on CUPS).

A simple test would be get the phone off-hook and see if presence information got sent out.

When the phone was off-hook, CUCM should have "offhook" message in CallManager logs. I would use WinGrep to search for this: `StationInit.*OffHook.*SEP0010C6E27EC1`.

The regular expression above would search for the off-hook event in CallManager logs.

StationInit: Means the message was initiated by a station (phone).
Offhook: Off-hook event.
SEP0010C6E27EC1: device name of the phone.

Below is an example line in CallManager log:

```
11/13/2008 22:58:48.653 CCM|StationInit: (0000014)
OffHook.|<CLID::StandAloneCluster><NID::10.88.229.206><CT::2,100,65,1.1421
718><IP::10.99.23.132><DEV::SEP0010C6E27EC1><LVL::State
Transition><MASK::0020>
```

Please make sure the timestamp matches the time you did the off-hook test.

Usually in the same second, CUCM would send out a PUBLISH SIP message to CUPS.

```
11/13/2008 22:58:48.662 CCM|//SIP/SIPTcp/wait_SdlSPISignal: Outgoing SIP
TCP message to 10.88.229.209 on port 5070 index 2320
PUBLISH sip:ipcuser@10.88.229.209:5070 SIP/2.0
Date: Fri, 14 Nov 2008 04:58:48 GMT
From: <sip:ipcuser@10.88.229.206>;tag=113187399
Event: presence
Content-Length: 894
User-Agent: Cisco-CUCM6.1
To: <sip:ipcuser@10.88.229.209>
Expires: 3600
Content-Type: application/pidf+xml
Call-ID: eac9b980-91d10588-10f5-cee5580a@10.88.229.206
Via: SIP/2.0/TCP 10.88.229.206:5060;branch=z9hG4bKdd3120bf7bd
CSeq: 101 PUBLISH
Max-Forwards: 70
SIP-If-Match: 5920d9b3

<?xml version="1.0" encoding="UTF-8" standalone="no" ?>
<presence xmlns="urn:ietf:params:xml:ns:pidf"
entity="ipcuser@10.88.229.206"
xmlns:r="urn:ietf:params:xml:ns:pidf:status:rpid"
xmlns:ce="urn:cisco:params:xml:ns:pidf:rpid"
xmlns:dm="urn:ietf:params:xml:ns:pidf:data-model"
xmlns:so="urn:cisco:params:xml:ns:pidf:source"
xmlns:sc="urn:ietf:params:xml:ns:pidf:servcaps">
   <tuple id="81264399-01e5-05f7-1b3a-7e6db8053650-85dba09d-efa6-0541-3174-
16806e09605b">
     <status>
     <basic>closed</basic>
     </status>
     <r:activities><r:busy/></r:activities>
     <sc:servcaps>
       <sc:audio>true</sc:audio>
     </sc:servcaps>
     <contact priority="0.8">sip:6009@10.88.229.206:5060;dpkid=85dba09d-
efa6-0541-3174-16806e09605b;npkid=81264399-01e5-05f7-1b3a-
7e6db8053650</contact>
     <model>Cisco IP Communicator</model>
     <timestamp>2008-11-14T04:58:48Z</timestamp>
   </tuple>
</presence>
```

In the log snippets above:

Outgoing SIP TCP message to 10.88.229.209 on port 5070 means the message was sent to CUPS (10.88.229.209) on presence engine port (5070).

`PUBLISH sip:ipcuser@10.88.229.209` means this message is to publish a phone status for user "ipcuser" on 10.88.229.209 (CUPS).

`closed` means the phone is off-hook (busy/not available).

We also see the phone's DN (6009) and phone type (IP Communicator).

If you could find the "offhook" but couldn't find "PUBLISH SIP", follow suggestions below:

Suggestions:
1. Run CUPS Troubleshooter to rule out basic configuration errors
2. On CUCM Device > Trunk, check SIP trunk configuration (and security profile)
3. On CUCM Device > Trunk, reset SIP trunk
4. On CUCM System > Service Parameters, check PUBLISH SIP Trunk
5. On CUCM Device > Phone, check line appearance association
6. On CUCM System > Licensing > Capabilities Assignment, check end users licensing
7. On CUPS Cisco Unified Presence > Presence Engine > Presence Gateway, check presence gateway configuration
8. On CUPS Cisco Unified Presence > Settings, check PUBLISH mode
9. On CUPS, restart Presence Engine

Until you can see "PUBLISH SIP" message, you should stick on CUCM traces. Focus on "Cisco CallManager" logs to investigate why PUBLISH was not sent.

CUPS – Presence Engine

If PUBLISH was sent from CUCM, you may continue troubleshooting on CUPS.

Please remember, PUBLISH is sent from CUCM to Presence Engine (PE). After "digesting" the message, PE sent NOTIFY to CUPC via SIP Proxy. The data flow is as below:

CUCM -> Presence Engine -> SIP Proxy -> CUPC

Let's assume there are no network issues in the picture (you should have eliminated this per "Best practices" before).

When PUBLISH message arrives at CUPS, the first stop is Presence Engine. We should try to find the message in Presence Engine logs. The identifier is "Call-ID".

Let's take a look at the PUBLISH message in previous section ("CUCM-to-CUPS"). The "Call-ID" is "eac9b980-91d10588-10f5-cee5580a@10.88.229.206". Search this Call-ID in Presence Engine logs, we got following:

```
11/13/2008 22:58:48.666 EPE|traffic.tcp.receive 376318 DEBUG  ==== receive
SIP msg from 10.88.229.206:55754 on 10.88.229.209:5070 over TCP ======
PUBLISH sip:ipcuser@10.88.229.209:5070 SIP/2.0
Date: Fri, 14 Nov 2008 04:58:48 GMT
From: <sip:ipcuser@10.88.229.206>;tag=113187399
Event: presence
Content-Length: 894
User-Agent: Cisco-CUCM6.1
To: <sip:ipcuser@10.88.229.209>
Expires: 3600
Content-Type: application/pidf+xml
Call-ID: eac9b980-91d10588-10f5-cee5580a@10.88.229.206
Via: SIP/2.0/TCP 10.88.229.206:5060;branch=z9hG4bKdd3120bf7bd
CSeq: 101 PUBLISH
Max-Forwards: 70
SIP-If-Match: 5920d9b3

<?xml version="1.0" encoding="UTF-8" standalone="no" ?>
<presence xmlns="urn:ietf:params:xml:ns:pidf"
entity="ipcuser@10.88.229.206"
xmlns:r="urn:ietf:params:xml:ns:pidf:status:rpid"
xmlns:ce="urn:cisco:params:xml:ns:pidf:rpid"
xmlns:dm="urn:ietf:params:xml:ns:pidf:data-model"
xmlns:so="urn:cisco:params:xml:ns:pidf:source"
xmlns:sc="urn:ietf:params:xml:ns:pidf:servcaps">
   <tuple id="81264399-01e5-05f7-1b3a-7e6db8053650-85dba09d-efa6-0541-3174-
16806e09605b">
     <status>
     <basic>closed</basic>
     </status>
     <r:activities><r:busy/></r:activities>
     <sc:servcaps>
       <sc:audio>true</sc:audio>
     </sc:servcaps>
     <contact priority="0.8">sip:6009@10.88.229.206:5060;dpkid=85dba09d-
efa6-0541-3174-16806e09605b;npkid=81264399-01e5-05f7-1b3a-
7e6db8053650</contact>
     <model>Cisco IP Communicator</model>
     <timestamp>2008-11-14T04:58:48Z</timestamp>
   </tuple>
</presence>
```

122 Chapter 5. Deploying and Troubleshooting Features

"`receive SIP msg from 10.88.229.206`" means this is a SIP message received from CUCM (10.88.229.206).

"`Call-ID: eac9b980-91d10588-10f5-cee5580a@10.88.229.206`" correlate this message with the message in CallManager logs.

Rest of the message is pretty much the same as the one in CallManager logs.

After receiving the PUBLISH message, Presence Engine has to "digest" it before sending out NOTIFY to subscribers. This digest process will take all factors into consideration; such has different types of presence information (availability, phone, calendar), user's privacy settings, etc.

After processing, you'll see a message in the log like this

```
11/13/2008 22:58:48.689 EPE|traffic.sip.send 372190 INFO   ==== send SIP
msg to 10.88.229.209:5060 over UDP ======
NOTIFY sip:ipcuser@10.99.23.132:50001;transport=TCP SIP/2.0
From: <sip:ipcuser@r7.com>;tag=c0b3949b
To: <sip:ipcuser@r7.com>;tag=2676d805
CSeq: 1073741838 NOTIFY
Call-ID: 59133e5551358e44NjRmNzBmNGIxOGU1OGMxNjJmZTkwZGFjZDMzZWVlMzE.
Event: presence
User-Agent: Cisco-PE/6.0
Contact: <sip:10.88.229.209:5070;transport=udp>
Route: <sip:.c91cfda4-f05adc16-6c7f811-
32d4d1d7@10.88.229.209:5060;maddr=10.88.229.209;transport=udp;lr>
Content-Length: 1632
Content-Type: application/pidf+xml
Subscription-State: active;expires=2305
Via: SIP/2.0/UDP 10.88.229.209:5070;branch=z9hG4bK2c422f0f-1964-4f48-b5bc-
d5d84a77ede0
Max-Forwards: 69

<?xml version="1.0" encoding="UTF-8"?>
<presence entity="sip:ipcuser@r7.com"
xmlns="urn:ietf:params:xml:ns:pidf">
<dm:person xmlns:dm="urn:ietf:params:xml:ns:pidf:data-model" id="ipcuser">

  <cupc:preferredcomm
xmlns:cupc="urn:cisco:params:xml:ns:pidf:cupc">3</cupc:preferredcomm>

  <activities xmlns="urn:ietf:params:xml:ns:pidf:rpid">
    <busy/>
  </activities>

</dm:person>

    <tuple xmlns="urn:ietf:params:xml:ns:pidf" id="cisco-upc">
```

```
        <contact priority="0.6">sip:ipcuser@r7.com</contact>
        <note xml:lang="en"/>
        <sc:servcaps xmlns:sc="urn:ietf:params:xml:ns:pidf:servcaps">
           <sc:video>false</sc:video>
           <sc:audio>false</sc:audio>
           <sc:text>true</sc:text>
           <sc:type>text/plain</sc:type>
           <sc:type>application/x-cisco-cupc+xml</sc:type>
     </sc:servcaps>
        <user-input>active</user-input>
        <status>
           <basic>open</basic>
        </status>
   </tuple>

     <tuple xmlns="urn:ietf:params:xml:ns:pidf" id="81264399-01e5-05f7-
1b3a-7e6db8053650-85dba09d-efa6-0541-3174-16806e09605b">
        <status>
           <basic>closed</basic>
     </status>
        <r:activities xmlns:r="urn:ietf:params:xml:ns:pidf:status:rpid">
           <r:busy/>
        </r:activities>
        <sc:servcaps xmlns:sc="urn:ietf:params:xml:ns:pidf:servcaps">
           <sc:audio>true</sc:audio>
     </sc:servcaps>
        <contact priority="0.8">sip:6009@10.88.229.206:5060;dpkid=85dba09d-
efa6-0541-3174-16806e09605b;npkid=81264399-01e5-05f7-1b3a-
7e6db8053650</contact>
        <model>Cisco IP Communicator</model>
        <timestamp>2008-11-14T04:58:48Z</timestamp>
     </tuple>
</presence>.
```

This message is to NOTIFY the subscriber of new presence information. In this case, subscriber is the CUPC at IP address of 10.99.23.132.

For flexibility and scalability, Presence Engine sends it to SIP Proxy instead of sending it to subscriber directly.

"`send SIP msg to 10.88.229.209:5060`" means this message is sent to CUPS SIP Proxy (10.88.229.209:5060).

"`NOTIFY sip:ipcuser@10.99.23.132:50001`" means this is a NOTIFY message attention to the user "ipcuser" at 10.99.23.132 (CUPC). Port 50001 is the listening port of CUPC.

Please note the Call-ID has changed, because it's a new message initiated by Presence Engine.

124 Chapter 5. Deploying and Troubleshooting Features

You might wonder, since Presence Engine (PE) and SIP Proxy are on the same box, why PE has to send message through proxy.

Again, this is for flexibility and scalability. In our case, it PE just happened to be on the same box as Proxy. In large-scale network, PE and Proxy could be on two different boxes.

CUPS – SIP Proxy

In previous step, Presence Engine sends NOTIFY to SIP Proxy. Now, we are going to look at SIP Proxy log. Similarly, by searching for the Call-ID in NOTIFY message, we found this in proxy log:

```
11/13/2008 22:58:48.690 ESP|[Thu Nov 13 22:58:45 2008] PID(6967)
sip_tcp.c(2983) sip_tcp received auth state as: 0 for connid: 1 from
sip_sm
[Thu Nov 13 22:58:45 2008] PID(6967) sip_tcp.c(495) sip_tcp is now sending
ok pdu 10.88.229.205 connid 1, sock_fd 29 1 msgs
[Thu Nov 13 22:58:45 2008] PID(7011) mod_sip.c(375) ipc handler 1 msgs
PID(7011) sip_protocol.c(5663) Received 2274 bytes UDP packet from
10.88.229.209:32877
NOTIFY sip:ipcuser@10.99.23.132:50001;transport=TCP SIP/2.0
From: <sip:ipcuser@r7.com>;tag=c0b3949b
To: <sip:ipcuser@r7.com>;tag=2676d805
CSeq: 1073741838 NOTIFY
Call-ID: 59133e5551358e44NjRmNzBmNGIxOGU1OGMxNjJmZTkwZGFjZDMzZWVlMzE.
Event: presence
User-Agent: Cisco-PE/6.0
Contact: <sip:10.88.229.209:5070;transport=udp>
Route: <sip:.c91cfda4-f05adc16-6c7f811-
32d4d1d7@10.88.229.209:5060;maddr=10.88.229.209;transport=udp;lr>
Content-Length: 1632
Content-Type: application/pidf+xml
Subscription-State: active;expires=2305
Via: SIP/2.0/UDP 10.88.229.209:5070;branch=z9hG4bK2c422f0f-1964-4f48-b5bc-
d5d84a77ede0
Max-Forwards: 69

<?xml version="1.0" encoding="UTF-8"?>
<presence entity="sip:ipcuser@r7.com"
xmlns="urn:ietf:params:xml:ns:pidf">
<dm:person xmlns:dm="urn:ietf:params:xml:ns:pidf:data-model" id="ipcuser">

  <cupc:preferredcomm
xmlns:cupc="urn:cisco:params:xml:ns:pidf:cupc">3</cupc:preferredcomm>

  <activities xmlns="urn:ietf:params:xml:ns:pidf:rpid">
    <busy/>
  </activities>
```

```
</dm:person>
    <tuple xmlns="urn:ietf:params:xml:ns:pidf" id="cisco-upc">
      <contact priority="0.6">sip:ipcuser@r7.com</contact>
      <note xml:lang="en"/>
      <sc:servcaps xmlns:sc="urn:ietf:params:xml:ns:pidf:servcaps">
        <sc:video>false</sc:video>
        <sc:audio>false</sc:audio>
        <sc:text>true</sc:text>
        <sc:type>text/plain</sc:type>
        <sc:type>application/x-cisco-cupc+xml</sc:type>
    </sc:servcaps>
      <user-input>active</user-input>
      <status>
        <basic>open</basic>
      </status>
  </tuple>

    <tuple xmlns="urn:ietf:params:xml:ns:pidf" id="81264399-01e5-05f7-
1b3a-7e6db8053650-85dba09d-efa6-0541-3174-16806e09605b">
      <status>
        <basic>closed</basic>
    </status>
      <r:activities xmlns:r="urn:ietf:params:xml:ns:pidf:status:rpid">
        <r:busy/>
      </r:activities>
      <sc:servcaps xmlns:sc="urn:ietf:params:xml:ns:pidf:servcaps">
        <sc:audio>true</sc:audio>
    </sc:servcaps>
      <contact priority="0.8">sip:6009@10.88.229.206:5060;dpkid=85dba09d-
efa6-0541-3174-16806e09605b;npkid=81264399-01e5-05f7-1b3a-
7e6db8053650</contact>
      <model>Cisco IP Communicator</model>
      <timestamp>2008-11-14T04:58:48Z</timestamp>
    </tuple>
</presence>
```

This means SIP Proxy has received the NOTIFY message from Presence Engine.

SIP Proxy then send this NOTIFY message to CUPC:

```
11/13/2008 22:58:48.692 ESP|PID(7011) sip_sm.c(1100) Sent 2279 bytes TCP
packet to 10.99.23.132:50001
NOTIFY sip:ipcuser@10.99.23.132:50001;transport=tcp SIP/2.0
Via: SIP/2.0/TCP 10.88.229.209:5060;branch=z9hG4bKcab2a00d-920d229a-
d0b7480-9138e986-1
From: <sip:ipcuser@r7.com>;tag=c0b3949b
To: <sip:ipcuser@r7.com>;tag=2676d805
CSeq: 1073741838 NOTIFY
Call-ID: 59133e5551358e44NjRmNzBmNGIxOGU1OGMxNjJmZTkwZGFjZDMzZWVlMzE.
```

Chapter 5. Deploying and Troubleshooting Features

```
Event: presence
User-Agent: Cisco-PE/6.0
Contact: <sip:10.88.229.209:5070;transport=udp>
Content-Length: 1632
Content-Type: application/pidf+xml
Subscription-State: active;expires=2305
Via: SIP/2.0/UDP
10.88.229.209:5070;received=10.88.229.209;branch=z9hG4bK2c422f0f-1964-
4f48-b5bc-d5d84a77ede0
Max-Forwards: 68

<?xml version="1.0" encoding="UTF-8"?>
<presence entity="sip:ipcuser@r7.com"
xmlns="urn:ietf:params:xml:ns:pidf">
<dm:person xmlns:dm="urn:ietf:params:xml:ns:pidf:data-model" id="ipcuser">

  <cupc:preferredcomm
xmlns:cupc="urn:cisco:params:xml:ns:pidf:cupc">3</cupc:preferredcomm>

  <activities xmlns="urn:ietf:params:xml:ns:pidf:rpid">
    <busy/>
  </activities>

</dm:person>

    <tuple xmlns="urn:ietf:params:xml:ns:pidf" id="cisco-upc">
      <contact priority="0.6">sip:ipcuser@r7.com</contact>
      <note xml:lang="en"/>
      <sc:servcaps xmlns:sc="urn:ietf:params:xml:ns:pidf:servcaps">
        <sc:video>false</sc:video>
        <sc:audio>false</sc:audio>
        <sc:text>true</sc:text>
        <sc:type>text/plain</sc:type>
        <sc:type>application/x-cisco-cupc+xml</sc:type>
    </sc:servcaps>
      <user-input>active</user-input>
      <status>
        <basic>open</basic>
      </status>
  </tuple>

    <tuple xmlns="urn:ietf:params:xml:ns:pidf" id="81264399-01e5-05f7-
1b3a-7e6db8053650-85dba09d-efa6-0541-3174-16806e09605b">
      <status>
        <basic>closed</basic>
    </status>
      <r:activities xmlns:r="urn:ietf:params:xml:ns:pidf:status:rpid">
        <r:busy/>
      </r:activities>
      <sc:servcaps xmlns:sc="urn:ietf:params:xml:ns:pidf:servcaps">
        <sc:audio>true</sc:audio>
    </sc:servcaps>
      <contact priority="0.8">sip:6009@10.88.229.206:5060;dpkid=85dba09d-
efa6-0541-3174-16806e09605b;npkid=81264399-01e5-05f7-1b3a-
7e6db8053650</contact>
```

```
        <model>Cisco IP Communicator</model>
        <timestamp>2008-11-14T04:58:48Z</timestamp>
    </tuple>
</presence>
```

In CUPC resiplog.txt, search for the same Call-ID:

```
DEBUG | 20081113-225848.531 |    | RESIP:TRANSPORT | 3976 |
ConnectionBase.cxx:251 | ##ConnectionBase: CONN_BASE: 04872E5C [ V4
10.88.229.209:43086 TCP target domain=unspecified received on: Transport:
[ V4 0.0.0.0:50001 TCP target domain=unspecified connectionId=0 ]
connectionId=3 ] received: NOTIFY
sip:ipcuser@10.99.23.133:50001;transport=tcp SIP/2.0
Via: SIP/2.0/TCP 10.88.229.209:5060;branch=z9hG4bKcab2a00d-920d229a-
d0b7480-9138e986-1
Via: SIP/2.0/TCP
10.88.229.209:5070;received=10.88.229.209;branch=z9hG4bK2c422f0f-1964-
4f48-b5bc-d5d84a77ede0
Max-Forwards: 68
Contact: <sip:10.88.229.209:5070;transport=udp>
To: <sip:ipcuser@r7.com>;tag=2676d805
From: <sip:ipcuser@r7.com>;tag=c0b3949b
Call-ID: 59133e5551358e44NjRmNzBmNGIxOGU1OGMxNjJmZTkwZGFjZDMzZWVlMzE.
CSeq: 1073741838 NOTIFY
Content-Type: application/pidf+xml
User-Agent: Cisco-PE/6.0
Subscription-State: active;expires=3595
Event: presence
Content-Length: 1632

<?xml version="1.0" encoding="UTF-8"?>
<presence entity="sip:ipcuser@r7.com"
xmlns="urn:ietf:params:xml:ns:pidf">
<dm:person xmlns:dm="urn:ietf:params:xml:ns:pidf:data-model" id="ipcuser">

  <cupc:preferredcomm
xmlns:cupc="urn:cisco:params:xml:ns:pidf:cupc">3</cupc:preferredcomm>

  <activities xmlns="urn:ietf:params:xml:ns:pidf:rpid">
    <busy/>
  </activities>

</dm:person>

    <tuple xmlns="urn:ietf:params:xml:ns:pidf" id="cisco-upc">
      <contact priority="0.6">sip:ipcuser@r7.com</contact>
      <note xml:lang="en"/>
      <sc:servcaps xmlns:sc="urn:ietf:params:xml:ns:pidf:servcaps">
        <sc:video>false</sc:video>
        <sc:audio>false</sc:audio>
        <sc:text>true</sc:text>
        <sc:type>text/plain</sc:type>
```

128 Chapter 5. Deploying and Troubleshooting Features

```
        <sc:type>application/x-cisco-cupc+xml</sc:type>
      </sc:servcaps>
        <user-input>active</user-input>
        <status>
          <basic>open</basic>
        </status>
    </tuple>

      <tuple xmlns="urn:ietf:params:xml:ns:pidf" id="81264399-01e5-05f7-
  1b3a-7e6db8053650-85dba09d-efa6-0541-3174-16806e09605b">
        <status>
          <basic>closed</basic>
        </status>
        <r:activities xmlns:r="urn:ietf:params:xml:ns:pidf:status:rpid">
          <r:busy/>
        </r:activities>
        <sc:servcaps xmlns:sc="urn:ietf:params:xml:ns:pidf:servcaps">
          <sc:audio>true</sc:audio>
        </sc:servcaps>
        <contact priority="0.8">sip:6009@10.88.229.206:5060;dpkid=85dba09d-
  efa6-0541-3174-16806e09605b;npkid=81264399-01e5-05f7-1b3a-
  7e6db8053650</contact>
        <model>Cisco IP Communicator</model>
        <timestamp>2008-11-14T04:58:48Z</timestamp>
      </tuple>

  </presence>
```

Please note the tuple ID for the phone presence ("closed"). Search this tuple ID in CUPC logs (UnifiedClientLog4CXX.txt), we'll find this:

```
2008-11-13 22:58:48,546 [0x504] DEBUG LCPresent - (MWMSG_PRESENCE_OFFHOOK)
sip:ipcuser@r7.com: Off-hook 81264399-01e5-05f7-1b3a-7e6db8053650-
85dba09d-efa6-0541-3174-16806e09605b
2008-11-15 14:51:12,546 [0x598] DEBUG LCIsuaLog - (WABIMSG_SDKMSG)
CSuaCallControlManager.Singleton.Asynchronous::CSuaSIPEventClientSubscript
ion::RequestSendSIPNotifyResponse[343] - Found dialog. true|200
[URI:ipcuser@r7.com] (presence)
2008-11-15 14:51:12,546 [0x504] DEBUG LCPresent - User:sip:ipcuser@r7.com
Rpid status:, UC status:4  BUSY, DeviceStatus 53
```

At this point, the trace is completed. We see the message flew through logs as below:

CallManager logs (CUCM) > Proxy logs (CUPS) > PE logs (CUPS) > resiplog (CUPC) > UnifiedClientLog (CUPC).

Notes:
1. Every SIP message should have a "200 OK" response. If you couldn't find the response or the response code is not 200, something was wrong.

2. Track phone presence from source (CUCM). Then trace it segment by segment until you get to CUPC.

For more information, refer to CUPC troubleshooting guide:

http://www.cisco.com/en/US/docs/voice_ip_comm/cupc/7_0/english/troubleshooting/guide/trouble.html#wp1179506

Phone Feature

Phone feature allows you make calls with mouse clicks from computer instead of punching keys on telephone. This feature is more useful when you use it along with contact management software such as Outlook contacts or CUPC LDAP.

There are two phone modes in CUPC – soft phone mode and desk phone mode.

In soft phone mode, CUPC uses your computer's microphone and speaker to emulate a telephone (SIP phone). You don't need other "soft phone" (such as Cisco IP Communicator) to use this feature.

In desk phone mode, CUPC controls an external phone via CTI protocol. The interesting thing is: "external phone" could be a hard phone (Cisco 79xx series) or a soft phone (Cisco IP Communicator).

Soft Phone

Prerequisites
1. You can log in to CUPC
2. You have enough DLU license available
3. CUPC self-status works fine*

Note:
1. Soft phone feature might use 3 or 1 DLU. Please refer to "licensing" section for details.
2. Phone feature does not depend on CUPC self-status. However, if self-status was not updated properly, CUPC would have problem identify its phone mode.

130 Chapter 5. Deploying and Troubleshooting Features

Like many other phones (Cisco 79xx series, CIPC, etc.), we have to register the phone to CUCM before we can use it. Before a phone can register to CUCM, a corresponding device has to be created on CUCM first. The configuration page is on CUCM Admin > Device > Phone.

Naming Convention

Each phone in CUCM has a device name. Device name for CUPC needs to follow some rules:

1. All letters have to be in upper case (capital case)
2. Device name has to begin with UPC
3. Device name has to match CUCM end user ID
4. Device name cannot be longer than 15 characters, which means corresponding end user ID cannot be longer than 12 characters.

For example, if end user ID is "johndoe", CUPC device name has to be "UPCJOHNDOE".

Step 1: CUPS: Configure TFTP address

1.1 Go to CUPS Admin > Application > Cisco Unified Personal Communicator > Settings.
1.2 In "Primary TFTP Server" field, enter the IP address of TFTP server (usually CUCM server)
1.3 Optionally, in "Backup TFTP Server" fields, enter the IP address of other TFTP servers for backup purpose.

Step 2: CUCM: Add "Cisco Unified Personal Communicator" phone

2.1 Go to CUCM Admin > Device > Phone
2.2 Click "Add New"

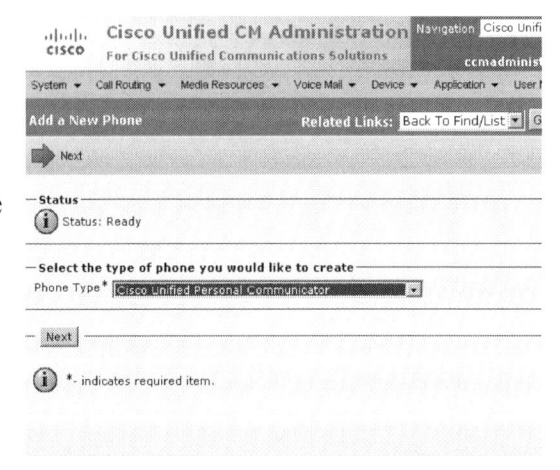

2.3 From drop-down menu, choose "Cisco Unified Personal Communicator"
2.4 Click "Next"

Step 3: CUCM: Device Configuration

3.1 In "Device Name" field, enter the device name. Please refer to "naming convention" for the correct format.
3.2 Configure all other parameters like you configure a regular phone.
3.3 Click "Save" when you finish configuration

Step 4: CUCM: Configure Directory Number

4.1 On the left-hand side of the device configuration page, click "Add a new DN"
4.2 If you have a desk phone, use the same DN on the desk phone.
4.3 If you do not have a desk phone, enter an available DN you want to use
4.4 Configure other parameters
4.5 Click "Save" when you finish configuration

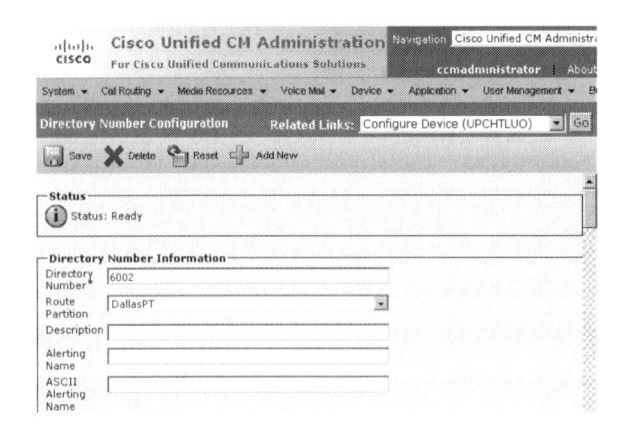

Step 5: CUCM: User Configuration

5.1 Go to CUCM Admin > User Management > End User
5.2 Find the user you want to configure. Click on search result. You will go to the user configuration page.
5.3 Click "Device Association". Find the CUPC device you just created. Choose it and click "Save selected". You'll see the CUPC device shows up on "Controlled Devices" list.

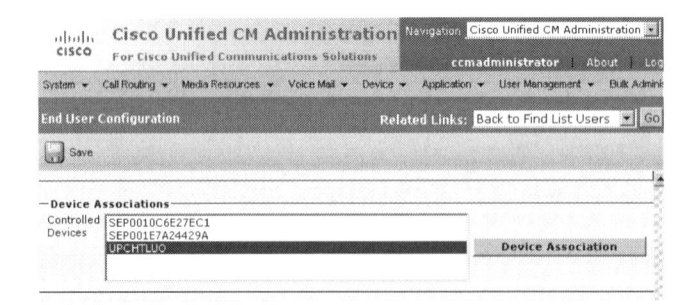

5.4 Scroll down the page until you can see "Directory Number Associations". From the "Primary Extension" drop-down menu, choose a primary extension number.

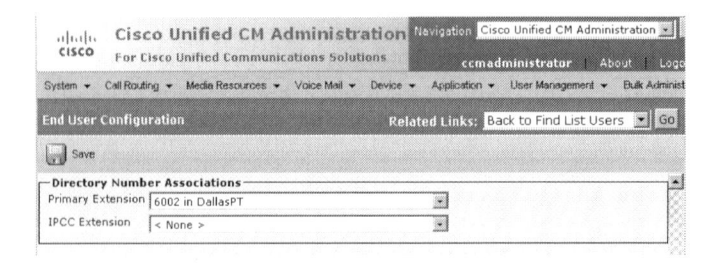

Test

1. Log in to CUPC
2. Click phone mode menu. Choose Soft Phone.
3. Click dial pad. Enter an internal extension number. Press Enter.
4. Call should proceed as expected

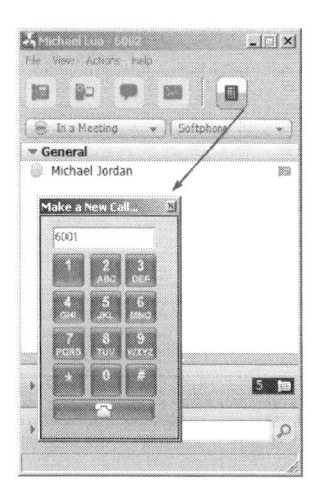

Troubleshooting

Phone Configuration – Download Failed

Symptom:
- When you tried to change to Soft Phone mode, it goes to "disabled" state.
- "CUPC > Help > Show Server Health" shows "Phone Configuration – Download Failed"

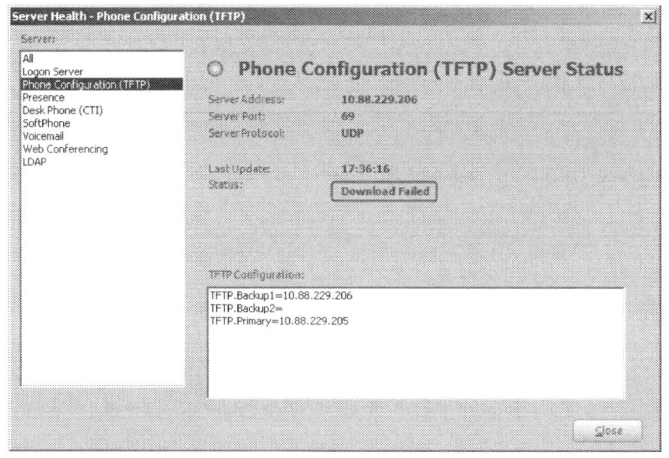

This problem could be caused by:
1. CUPC could not connect to TFTP server.

134 Chapter 5. Deploying and Troubleshooting Features

2. CUPC connected to TFTP, but the CUPC configuration file does not exist.

There's a tftp command on Windows XP you may use to test the TFTP download.

```
C:\test>tftp -i 10.88.229.205 get UPCHTLUO.CNF.XML
Timeout occurred

C:\test>
```

10.88.229.205 is the IP address of TFTP server. UPCHTLUO.CNF.XML is the configuration file name. Phone configuration file name is in the format of *Devicename*.CNF.XML.

From the screen output above, we got a timeout message while trying to download from TFTP. Please check your firewall or network connectivity.

If download was successful, you'll see a screen output like below:

```
C:\test>tftp -i 10.88.229.205 get UPCHTLUO.CNF.XML
Transfer successful: 7487 bytes in 5 seconds, 1497 bytes/s

C:\test>
```

If the requested file does not exist on TFTP, you'll get a screen output like below:

```
C:\test>tftp -i 10.88.229.205 get NOTEXIST.CNF.XML
Error on server : File not found

C:\test>
```

Suggestions:

1. If you got timeout in tftp command test, check firewall and network connectivity.
2. If you got "File no found" in tftp command test, check if the CUPC device name complies to naming convention.

Failed to Connect – Server Connection Refused

From CUPC > Show Server Health, you may see the "Phone Configuration" item is green (configuration downloaded). But the soft phone failed to connect. Phone mode menu was disabled.

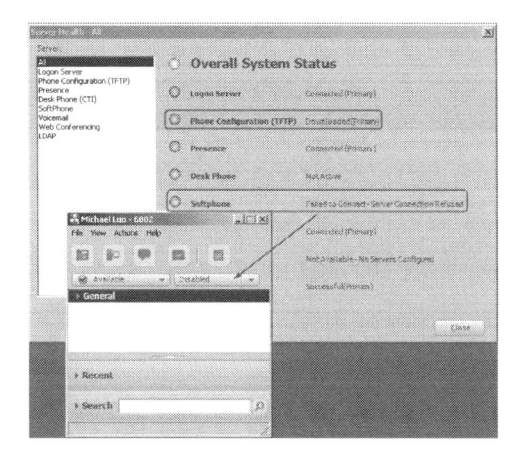

This usually means the soft phone configuration was incorrect on CUCM.

Keep in mind that CUPC soft phone is a SIP phone. To troubleshoot SIP phone problem, we should look at SIP message in client logs and Cisco CallManager logs.

Here are log snippets from CUPC log:

```
2008-11-16 11:30:11,953 [0x598] DEBUG LCIsuaLog - (WABIMSG_SDKMSG) [0] -
SENDING TO 10.88.229.206:5060 via UDP
REGISTER sip:10.88.229.206 SIP/2.0
Via: SIP/2.0/UDP 10.99.23.133:50000;branch=z9hG4bK-d87543-
bb639306f7623d33-1--d87543-;rport
Max-Forwards: 70
Contact:
<sip:6002@10.99.23.133:50000;rinstance=bccd0e37721d40c1>;+sip.instance="<u
rn:uuid:00000000-0000-0000-0000-
000000006002>";+u.sip!devicename.ccm.cisco.com="UPCHTLUO";+u.sip!model.ccm
.cisco.com="358"
To: "Michael Luo"<sip:6002@10.88.229.206>
```

136 Chapter 5. Deploying and Troubleshooting Features

```
From: "Michael Luo"<sip:6002@10.88.229.206>;tag=f23a7d49
Call-ID: 3e119a18d165693bNjRmNzBmNGIxOGU1OGMxNjJmZTkwZGFjZDMzZWVlMzE.
CSeq: 1 REGISTER
Expires: 3600
Allow: INVITE, ACK, CANCEL, OPTIONS, BYE, REFER, NOTIFY, MESSAGE,
SUBSCRIBE, INFO
Supported: eventlist, norefersub, X-cisco-callinfo, extended-refer
User-Agent: Cisco-UCModel01/1.2.2
Content-Length: 0
.
.
.
2008-11-16 11:30:12,140 [0x598] DEBUG LCIsuaLog - (WABIMSG_SDKMSG) [0] -
RECEIVING from 10.88.229.206:5060 via UDP
SIP/2.0 404 Not Found
Date: Sun, 16 Nov 2008 17:30:14 GMT
Warning: 399 htluo-cm6-sub "Line not configured"
From: "Michael Luo"<sip:6002@10.88.229.206>;tag=f23a7d49
Content-Length: 0
To: "Michael Luo"<sip:6002@10.88.229.206>;tag=2098130573
Call-ID: 3e119a18d165693bNjRmNzBmNGIxOGU1OGMxNjJmZTkwZGFjZDMzZWVlMzE.
Via: SIP/2.0/UDP 10.99.23.133:50000;branch=z9hG4bK-d87543-
bb639306f7623d33-1--d87543-;rport
CSeq: 1 REGISTER
```

"`sip:6002@10.88.229.206`" means CUPC tries to register line (directory number) 6002 with 10.88.229.206 (CUCM).

"`SIP/2.0 404 Not Found`" means CUCM couldn't find the line 6002 on device UPCHTLUO.

By reviewing the configuration of UPCHTLUO, we found that the only DN configured on this device is 6005. Of course CUPC won't be able to register line 6002 on this device.

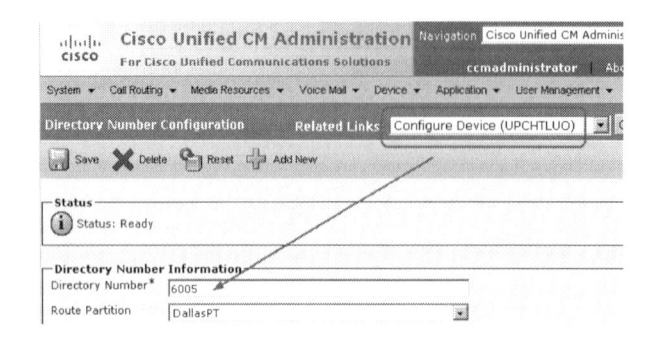

You might ask the question "since DN 6005 was configured on CUPC, why it would try to register with line 6002?"

Let's look at the CUPC log again:

```
2008-11-16 11:30:05,640 [0x3b8] INFO   LCMiddleware -
(MWMSG_CFGMGR_USERCONFIG) ConfigurationManager: per-user configuration =
    Directory.MaxResults = 1000
    Directory.MaxTime = 30
    CallControl.provider = WABI
    Presence.inPersistentState = false
    VoiceMail.password = ***************
    VoiceMail.userName = [[USER:htluo]]
    Presence.displayName = Michael Luo
    Presence.persistAwayWhenOfflineFlag = false
    Availability.idleAfterElapsed = 20
    VoiceMail.password.encrypted = ***************
    CallControl.Lineid = 6002
    CallControl.Devicename = SEP001E7A24429A
    Credentials.Digest = ***************
    Presence.userName = [[USER:htluo]]
    Presence.listName = htluo-contacts
Presence.calendar = enabled
```

Notice the "`CallControl.Lineid = 6002`". This is from the CUCM > User Management > End User configuration.

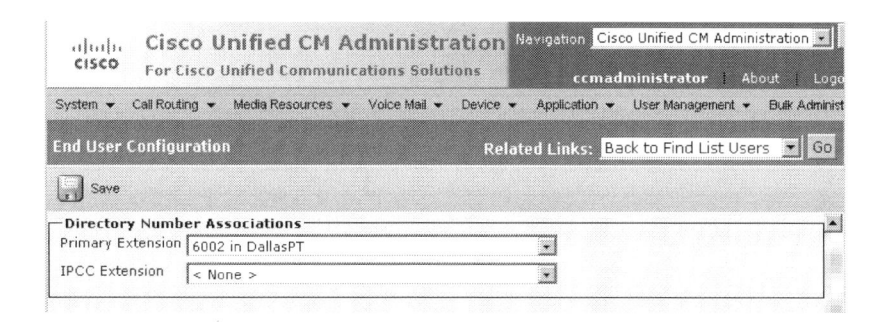

Since 6002 was chosen here, CUPC would try to register with DN 6002.

The next question would be: "Why 6002 would show up here, if 6005 is the only DN configured on UPCHTLUO?"

The answer is: there must be more than one device associated with user HTLUO. "Primary Extension" drop-down menu would list all DNs on all associated devices.

Suggestion: Choose the correct DN as "Primary Extension".

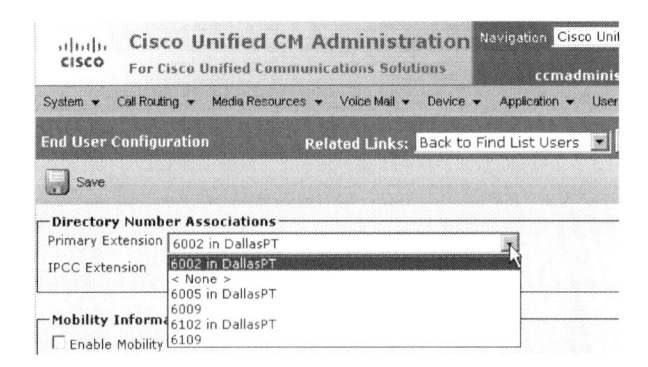

138 Chapter 5. Deploying and Troubleshooting Features

Please note the DN chosen here would also be used for Desk Phone control (CTI). That's why you want to use the same DN on both soft phone and desk phone.

Disconnecting (Pending Retry)...

From CUPC > Show Server Health, you may see the "Phone Configuration" item is green (configuration downloaded). But the soft phone item shows "Disconnecting (Pending Retry)...". Phone mode menu was grey out.

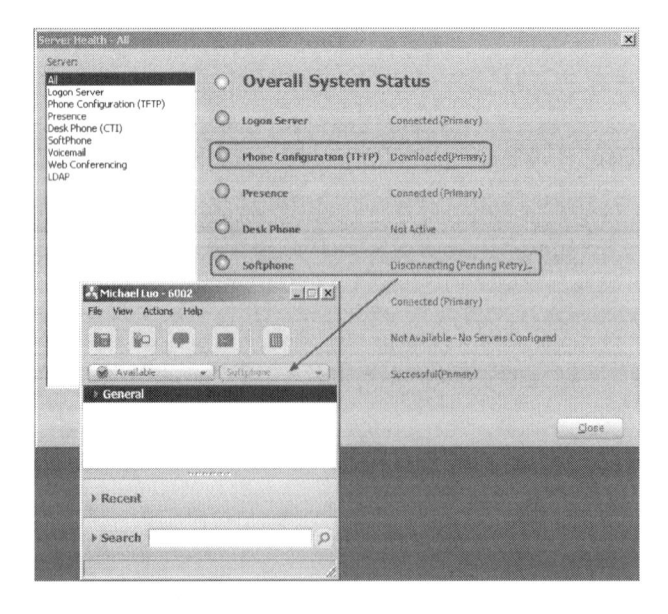

Looking at CUPC log:

```
2008-11-16 12:25:43,906 [0x58c] DEBUG LCIsuaLog - (WABIMSG_SDKMSG) [0] -
RECEIVING from 10.88.229.206:5060 via UDP
SIP/2.0 485 Ambiguous
Date: Sun, 16 Nov 2008 18:25:46 GMT
Warning: 399 htluo-cm6-sub "Transport protocol mismatch (config=TCP,
rcvd=UDP)"
From: "Michael Luo"<sip:6002@10.88.229.206>;tag=86451803
Content-Length: 0
To: "Michael Luo"<sip:6002@10.88.229.206>;tag=662293484
Call-ID: 7f12cc040d7e4329NjRmNzBmNGIxOGU1OGMxNjJmZTkwZGFjZDMzZWVlMzE.
Via: SIP/2.0/UDP 10.99.23.133:50000;branch=z9hG4bK-d87543-
c93cd22a9e5cd12d-1--d87543-;rport
CSeq: 1 REGISTER
```

"`RECEIVING from 10.88.229.205:5060 via UDP`" means this is a message from 10.88.229.206 (CUCM). Protocol is UDP.

"`Transport protocol mismatch (config=TCP, rcvd=UDP)`" means there's a protocol mismatch. Protocol configured on CUCM was TCP. But the SIP message received by CUCM was UDP.

Looking at the CUPC phone security profile on CUCM, we notice the "Transport Type" was set to "TCP". However, CUPC would only use UDP to register soft phone (not configurable). That's why there's a "protocol mismatch".

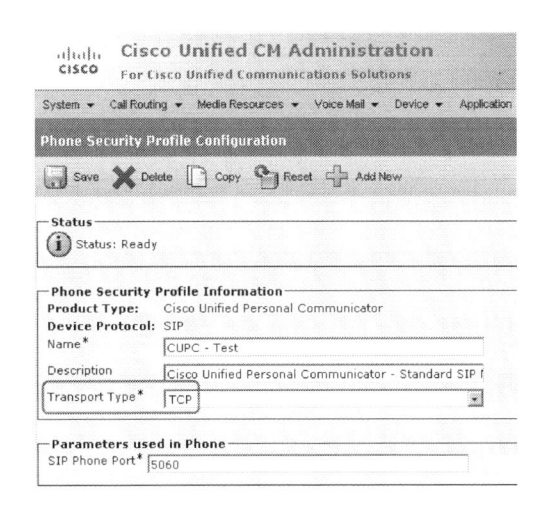

Suggestion: On CUCM > System > Security Profile > Phone Security Profile; find the profile being used by CUPC. Change the "Transport Type" to "TCP+UDP" or "UDP".

140 Chapter 5. Deploying and Troubleshooting Features

Both Soft Phone and Desk Phone are "Not Active"

Phone configuration was downloaded. But you cannot switch to soft phone or desk phone. In CUPC > Show Server Health, both Soft phone and Desk Phone are "Not Active".

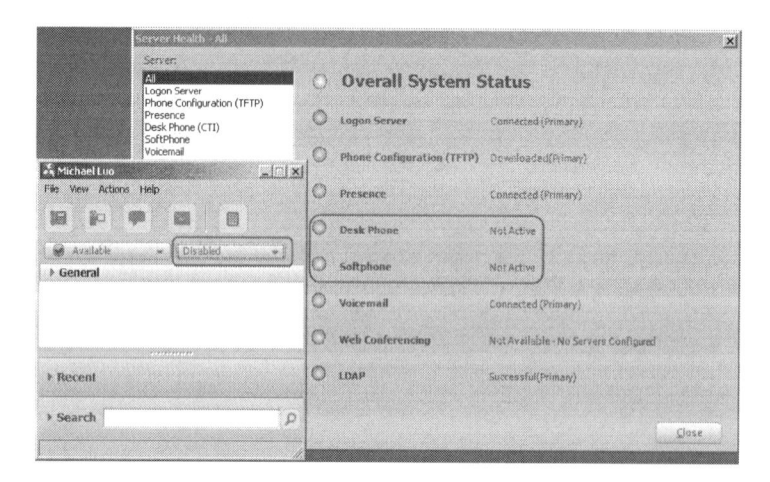

Usually, this is because no primary extension was configured on end user configuration page.

CUPC log confirms this:

```
2008-11-16 17:36:28,203 [0x678] WARN    LCSessionManager -
(MWMSG_SMI_NOLINECONFIGURED) SessionManagerImpl::Start() No Primary
Extension configured!
```

Suggestion: Go to CUCM Admin > User Management > End User. Configure primary extension for the user.

Desk Phone

In Desk Phone mode, CUPC uses CTI protocol to control a phone device. Please note that CUPC just controls the phone. To hear and speak, you still need to use the physical phone's handset (or speaker phone).

Prerequisites

1. The phone device (desk phone) is registered and functioning properly.
2. CTIManager service is running on CUCM servers.
3. You can log in to CUPC

4. CUPC self-status works fine*

Note:
Phone feature does not depend on CUPC self-status. However, if self-status was not updated properly, CUPC would have problem identify its phone mode.

Step 1: CUCM: Associate device to end user

Device association would tell CUCM which user is in control of which device(s).

1.1 Go to CUCM Admin > User Management > End User.
1.2 Find a user and click on the search result. You will go to user configuration page.
1.3 Click "Device Association". Find the phone device (desk phone) you want CUPC control. Choose it and click "Save selected". You'll see the phone device shows up on "Controlled Devices" list.

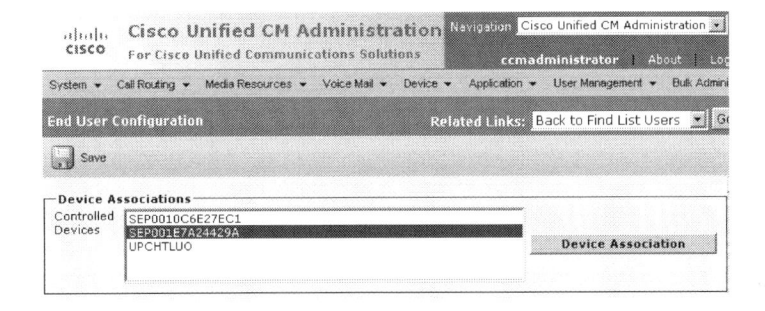

Step 2: CUCM: Specify Primary Extension for end user

Primary Extension designation tells CUPC which line to control.

On the user configuration page, look for "Directory Number Associations". From the "Primary Extension" drop-down menu, choose a primary extension number.

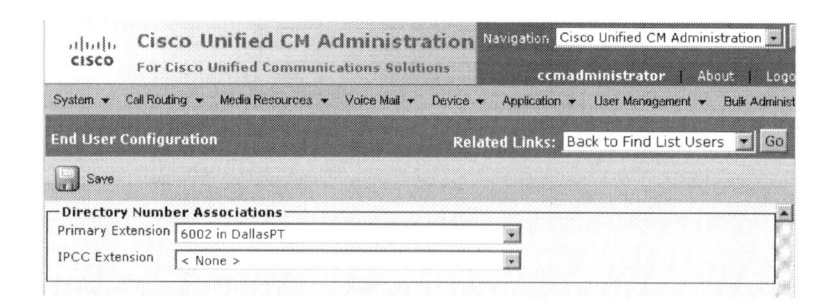

Step 3: CUCM: Add end user to Standard CTI Enabled group

CUPC uses end user credential on CTI. The end user needs to be in "Standard CTI Enabled" group. Otherwise, he can't use CTI.

3.1 On the end user configuration page, look for "Permission Information"
3.2 Click "Add to User Group"
3.3 Find "Standard CTI Enabled" group. Choose it and click "Save Selected". You'll see "Standard CTI Enabled" group shows up on the groups list

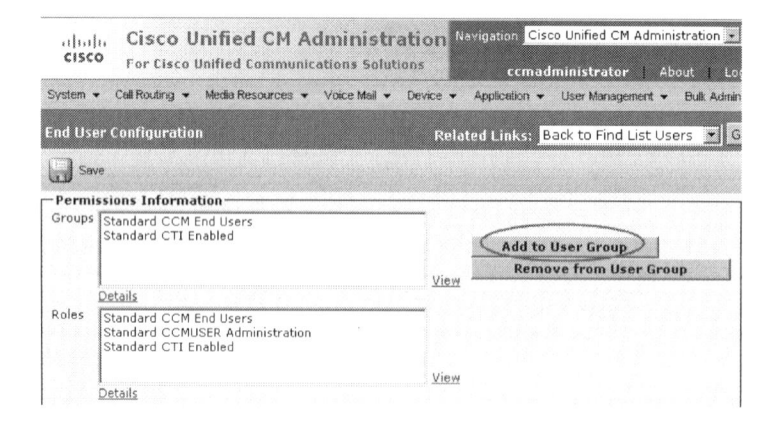

Step 4: CUPS: Assign user to CTI Gateway Profile

Each CUPC user is assigned to a CTI profile. CTI profile tells CUPC which CTIManager server(s) to contact for desk phone control.

When CUPS synchronizes database from CUCM, CUPS automatically creates two profiles for each CUCM device pool - one for TCP, one for TLS. Usually we'll use the TCP one, unless you environment requires you use TLS.

The automatically created profiles will have names in the format below:

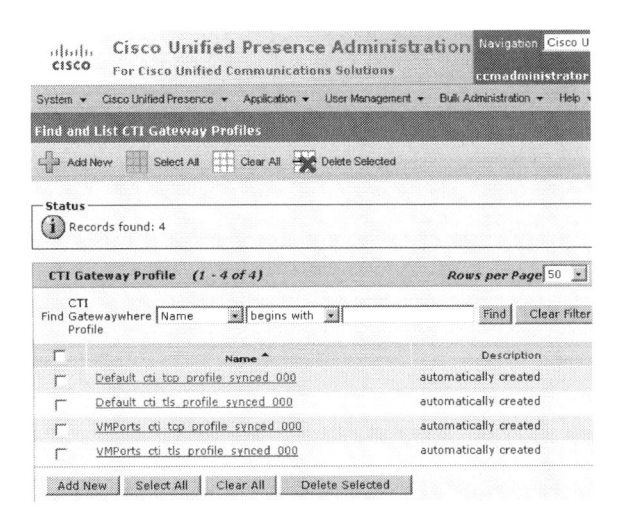

```
Name_of_DevicePool_cti_tcp_profile_synced_000
Name_of_DevicePool_cti_tls_profile_synced_000
```

For example, for the "mainoffice" device pool, CUPS will create two profiles named "mainoffice_cti_tcp_profile_synced_000" and "mainoffice_tls_tcp_profile_synced_000".

1.1 Go to CUPS Admin > Application > CTI Gateway Profile. Click "Find".
1.2 Select the profile that matches your desk phone's device pool.
1.3 On the "CTI Gateway Profile Configuration" page, make sure the CTI Gateway servers are the ones you want to use.
1.4 Click "Add Users to Profile". Find and selected the user you want to add. Click "Add Selected". Now the user is added to profile.

Test

1. Log in to CUPC.
2. From the phone mode menu, choose "Desk Phone". Observe the phone mode changes to Desk Phone.
3. Click Dial Pad button. Enter an internal extension number and press Enter.
4. Call should proceed as expected. You'll notice your desk phone is on speaker phone mode. Ring tone is being played on the desk phone.

Troubleshooting

Disconnecting (Pending Retry)...

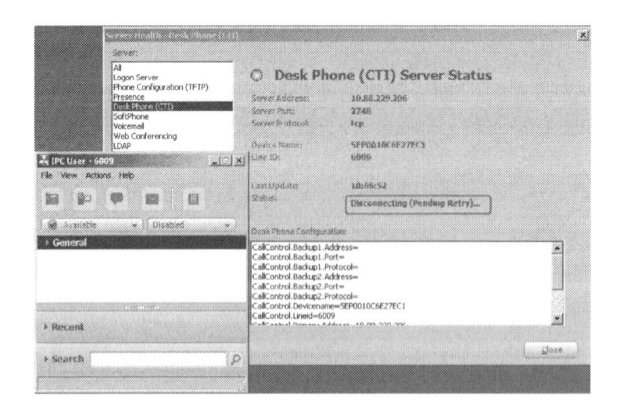

This is an indication of connectivity issue.

CUPC logs:

```
2008-11-16 18:06:18,015 [0x66c] DEBUG LCConnection - CALLMANAGER_CTI
startConnection(): 10.88.229.206:2748(tcp)
.
.
.
2008-11-16 18:06:18,093 [0x6fc] WARN  LCCallControl -
(CCMSG_QBE_CCMCONNECTFAILED) Failed to connect to CTI Manager,
PR_GetError() = -5928
.
.
.
2008-11-16 18:06:18,093 [0x6fc] DEBUG LCConnection - CALLMANAGER_CTI
reportResult(DISCONNECTED): reason=UNREACHABLE, functionality=NONE
```

You may use Windows telnet command to further confirm

Suggestions:
1. Check if CTIManager service is running on CUCM server
2. Check firewall and network connectivity

Partial Connected – Cannot connect to phone

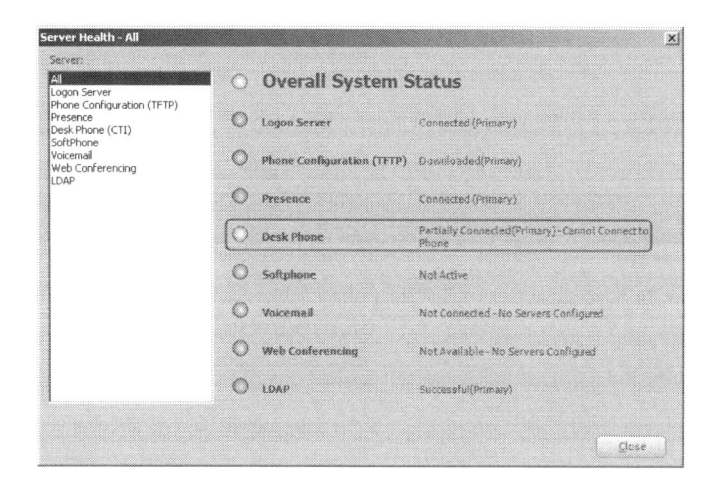

This means CUPC was able to connect to CTIManager. But CTIManager was not able to control the phone. Either the phone was not registered or the phone is not associated with the user or the phone is not CTI enabled.

CUPC log:

```
2008-11-16 18:46:17,750 [0x704] DEBUG LCConnection - CALLMANAGER_CTI
reportResult(CONNECTED): reason=NO_PHONE,
functionality=FULL_WITH_EXCEPTION
2008-11-16 18:46:17,750 [0x704] DEBUG LCConnection - CALLMANAGER_CTI
setFunctionality(): [NONE] --> [FULL_WITH_EXCEPTION]
```

Suggestions:
1. Check if the phone is registered.
2. Check if the phone is associated on "End User Configuration" page.
3. Check if the phone has "Allow Control of Device from CTI" enabled.

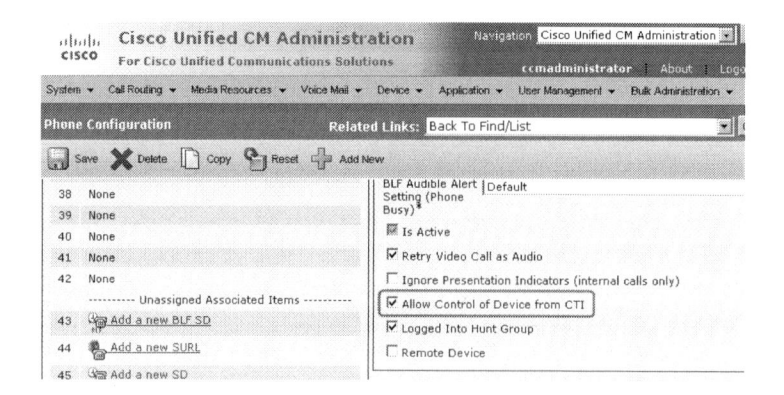

146 Chapter 5. Deploying and Troubleshooting Features

Not Connected – Stopped

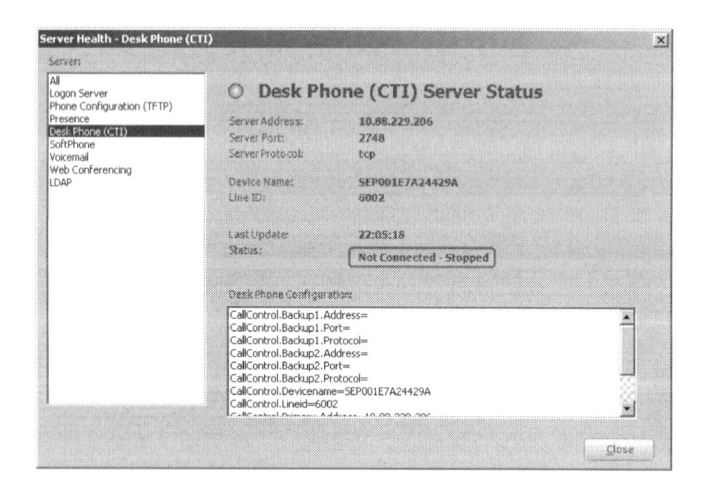

This usually means CTIManager authentication failed.

CUPC authenticates CTIManager with end user credential. Authentication failure could be caused by:

1. The end user was not in "Standard CTI Enabled" group
2. LDAP authentication failed

If the end user was not in "Standard CTI Enabled" group, he cannot use CTI at all. You'll see the following message in CUPC log:

```
2008-11-16 22:21:26,968 [0x704] WARN   LCCallControl -
(CCMSG_QBE_PROVIDEROPENFAILED) ProviderOpen failed: Directory login failed
- User not present in Standard CTI Users group.
```

Suggestion: On CUCM > User Management > End User configuration page, add the user to "Standard CTI Enabled" group.

For LDAP authentication problem, you'll see the following message in CUPC log:

```
2008-11-16 22:05:18,781 [0x714] WARN   LCCallControl -
(CCMSG_QBE_PROVIDEROPENFAILED) ProviderOpen failed: Directory login failed
- timeout
```

We'll discuss LDAP authentication issue in the following section.

Not Connected – Invalid Credentials

Sometimes, LDAP authentication issue would present itself in a different message – "Invalid Credentials" (see screenshot below).

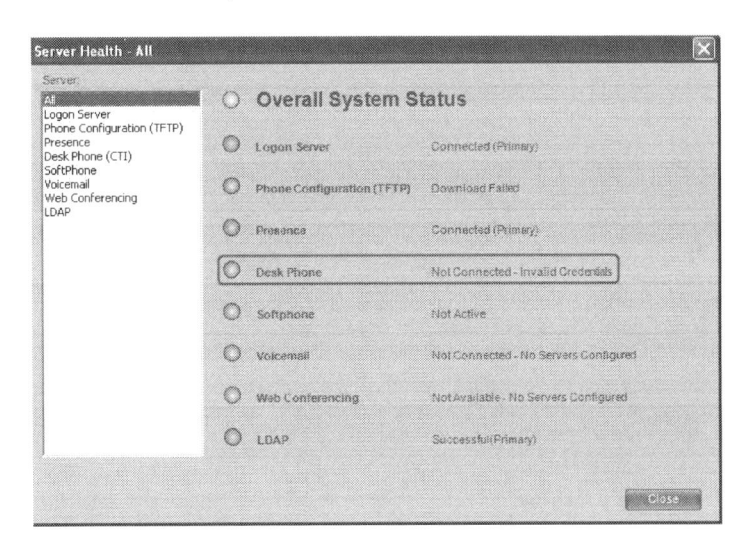

CUPC log:
```
2008-11-16 22:57:28,876 [0x910] WARN   LCCallControl -
(CCMSG_QBE_PROVIDEROPENFAILED) ProviderOpen failed: Directory login failed
- invalid user credentials.
```

This LDAP authentication issue is very confusing, because you didn't have LDAP authentication issue on other applications (including some Cisco applications).

148 Chapter 5. Deploying and Troubleshooting Features

In short, this is a defect (bug) in CUCM. CUCM 7.x should fix this bug.

However, understanding how the bug happens and how the workaround works will help us see under the hood of the system. This may help us solve other problems as well.

Let's take a look at how CTI call control interacts with LDAP authentication.

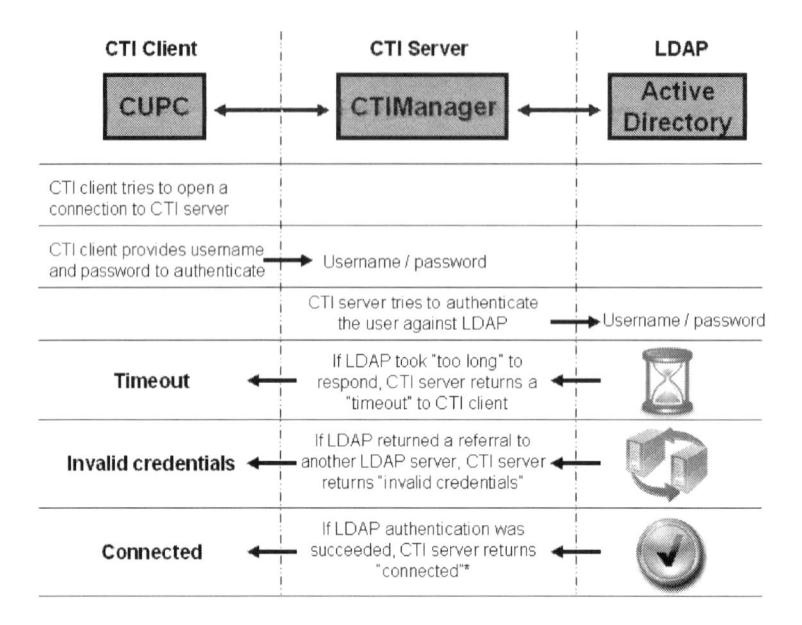

	CTI Client	CTI Server	LDAP
	CUPC	CTIManager	Active Directory
	CTI client tries to open a connection to CTI server		
	CTI client provides username and password to authenticate	Username / password	
		CTI server tries to authenticate the user against LDAP	Username / password
Timeout		If LDAP took "too long" to respond, CTI server returns a "timeout" to CTI client	
Invalid credentials		If LDAP returned a referral to another LDAP server, CTI server returns "invalid credentials"	
Connected		If LDAP authentication was succeeded, CTI server returns "connected"	

Note:
The user has also to be in "Standard CTI Enabled" group in CUCM. But that's not relevant with LDAP authentication.

"Referral" means the authentication server does not have the information (or updated information) for the user and refer the client to authenticate with another server that holds the information. This happens when you have more than one domain controllers.

As seen from the diagram above, slow response and referral from LDAP could cause problem for CUPC desk phone feature.

A solution to solve both problems is to use Global Catalog (GC) for authentication. Global Catalog is a service running on Active Directory domain controllers. Global Catalog server holds all account information and responds more quickly. Cisco has more information regarding this on design guide:
http://www.cisco.com/en/US/docs/voice_ip_comm/cucm/srnd/6x/directry.html#wp1045381

Phone Feature 149

To configure CUCM use Global Catalog for authentication, do the following.

Suggestions:
1. Go to CUCM Admin > LDAP > LDAP Authentication.
2. Make sure the server you configured is Global Catalog server.
3. Make sure the LDAP port is the Global Catalog port. By default it's 3268.
4. Restart CTIManager service on CUCM.

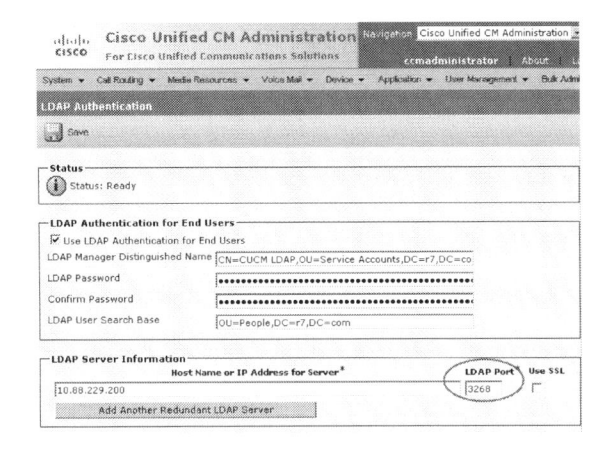

Note:
CTIManager won't take the change until restart. Since CUPC uses CTI for desk phone control, you won't see the fix until you restart CTIManager.

Both Soft Phone and Desk Phone are "Not Active"

Phone configuration was downloaded. But you cannot switch to soft phone or desk phone. In CUPC > Show Server Health, both Soft phone and Desk Phone are "Not Active".

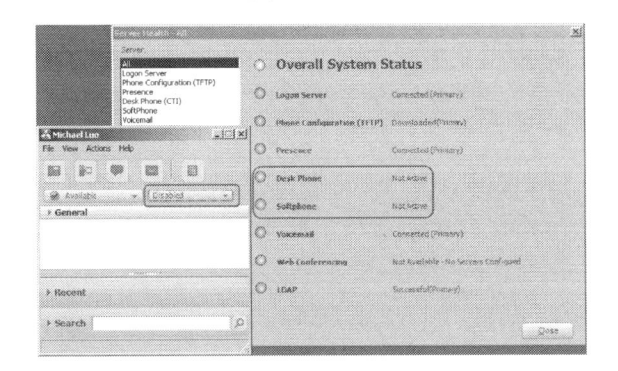

Usually, this is because no primary extension was configured on end user configuration page.

CUPC log confirms this:

```
2008-11-16 17:36:28,203 [0x678] WARN   LCSessionManager -
(MWMSG_SMI_NOLINECONFIGURED) SessionManagerImpl::Start() No Primary
Extension configured!
```

Suggestion: Go to CUCM Admin > User Management > End User. Configure primary extension for the user.

Application Dial Rules

One of the useful features of CUPC is "click-to-dial". You may click a contact in CUPC or Outlook and dial his phone number.

Usually, PBX (including CUCM) requires you dial a digit before you can make external calls (for example, dial 9 to get external dial tone). Unfortunately, people usually do not put the prefix 9 in their address book. When you try to do click-to-dial, CUPC dials whatever number stored in the address book. And the call would fail without the prefix.

An easy solution is to use CUCM Application Dial Rules. Application Dial Rules (or ADRs) will apply to Cisco applications (such as CUPC, Attendant Console, etc.) for digit manipulation.

Please note Application Dial Rules are different with translation patterns on CUCM. Application Rules take effect on client side. When the digits are sent to CUCM, they have already been manipulated. Following is the workflow of application dial rules.

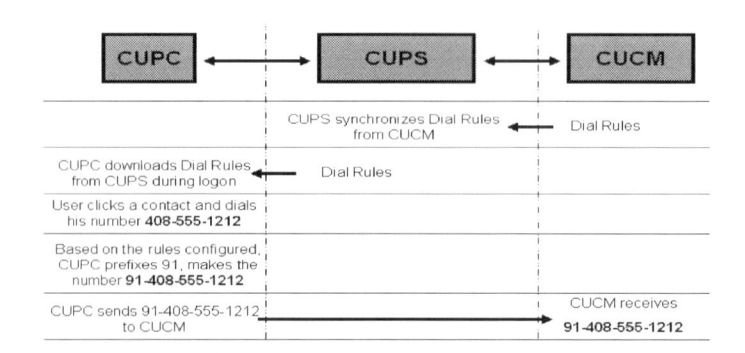

To configure application dial rules, follow steps below:

1. Go to CUCM Admin > Call Routing > Dial Rules > Application Dial Rules
2. Click "Add New"
3. Enter any name you like in "Name" field
4. Enter the number of digits you want to match in "Number of Digits" field.
5. Enter the number of digits you want to remove in "Total Digits to be Removed" field.
6. Enter the number you want to prefix in "Prefix With Pattern" field.

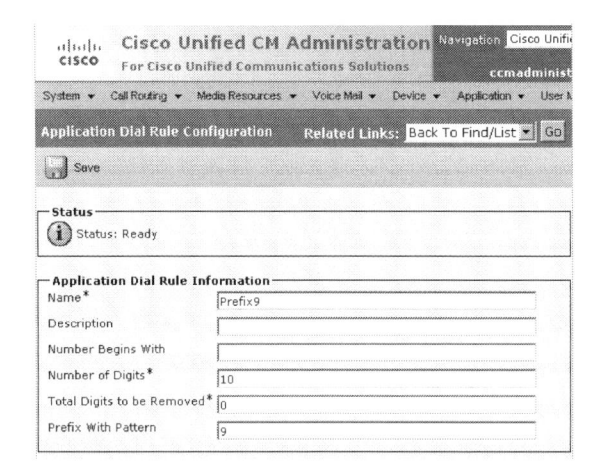

Test

1. Log off and log in to CUPC. So CUPC can download the updated dial rules.
2. On CUPC or Outlook, right-click a contact with a 10 digit number and dial it.
3. Observe the call proceeds as expected and ring the destination number.

In this test, we're assuming all 10 digit numbers need to be prefixed with 9 to dial out.

Troubleshooting

The most common problem on dial rules is: "it didn't take effect."

As explained before, dial rules flows from CUCM to CUPS, then from CUPS to CUPC.

152 Chapter 5. Deploying and Troubleshooting Features

Verify CUCM database

The most efficient way to verify is to look into CUCM database. SSH to the CUCM and run the command below:

```
run sql select * from applicationdialrule
```

Here's the screen output.

```
admin:run sql select * from applicationdialrule
pkid                                   name    description numbeginwith numofdigit
s digitsremoved prefix priority tkapplicationdialrule
======================================== ======= =========== ============ ==========
= ============== ====== ======== ====================
76843890-829f-fe36-237c-90e0c3642299 Prefix9                               10
 0               9       1        1
admin:
```

You can easily correlate that with the configuration on CUCM web interface.

If this matches what you have configured on CUCM web interface that means the CUCM database is good.

Verify CUPS database

We SSH to the CUPS and run the same command:

```
run sql select * from applicationdialrule
```

Here's the screen output.

```
admin:run sql select * from applicationdialrule
pkid                                   name    description numbeginwith numofdigit
s digitsremoved prefix priority tkapplicationdialrule
======================================== ======= =========== ============ ==========
= ============== ====== ======== ====================
76843890-829f-fe36-237c-90e0c3642299 Prefix9                               10
 0               9       1        1
admin:
```

That means CUPS has the same data as CUCM (which it should). If it doesn't contain the same data as CUCM, you have to troubleshoot synchronization issues. See corresponding sections before for details.

Phone Feature 153

Verify CUPC

Make sure you log off and log on CUPC to get the updated configuration.

In CUPC log, you'll find the following:

```
2008-11-18 16:59:26,625 [0x3b4] INFO   LCMiddleware -
(MWMSG_CFGMGR_SYSCONFIG) ConfigurationManager: system dial rules =
    Inbound rules
         Prio Length        Begins With Remove      Prefix With
    Outbound rules
         Prio Length        Begins With Remove      Prefix With
           1    10                         0                  9
```

At this point, we verified that the dial rules got populated to CUPC.

Directory Lookup Rules

Directory lookup is a very important in CUPC. It might be more important than you have thought.

Whenever CUPC tries to look up the name by a telephone number, it will search the LDAP for the phone number. If LDAP feature was not configured for CUPC, or the number cannot be found in LDAP, CUPC won't be able to display the name.

Name resolution for call information

Directory lookup configured and working properly:

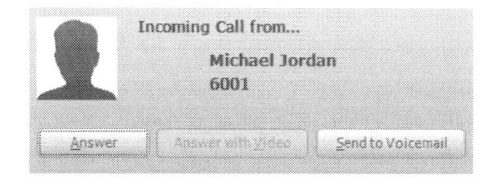

Incoming Call from...
Michael Jordan
6001
Answer   Answer with Video   Send to Voicemail

Directory lookup was not configured properly:

154 Chapter 5. Deploying and Troubleshooting Features

Without directory lookup, all we can see is the number. The name would be "Unknown".

Similarly, on the "Recent Call" window, we'll see numbers instead of names if directory lookup was not configured properly.

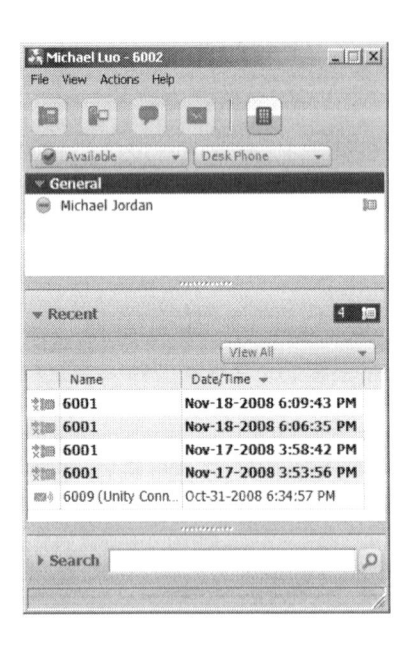

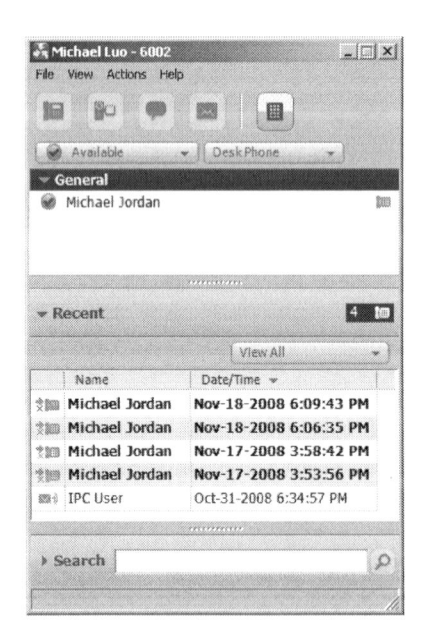

Name resolution for other features

Name resolution is not just for cosmetic effects. It will also affect other features.

When you on the phone with somebody, you may escalate the voice call to a web conference call. Upon request, CUPC will set up the web conference and launch it on the other party's computer.

The key component in this "automation" is name resolution. CUPC has to find the user ID for the other party by looking up the phone number. If the user ID cannot be found, automation cannot be done.

What could possibly break the name resolution?

Possible cause #1, LDAP feature has not been set up properly.

Suggestion: Follow deployment guide to set up LDAP feature.

Possible cause #2, the phone number in LDAP does not match the phone number CUCM passes over.

In LDAP, the phone number configured might be the full number (e.g. 408-555-1212). The phone number passed by CUCM usually would be the extension number configured on the phone (e.g. 1212). This causes mismatch.

Directory lookup rules can solve this problem.

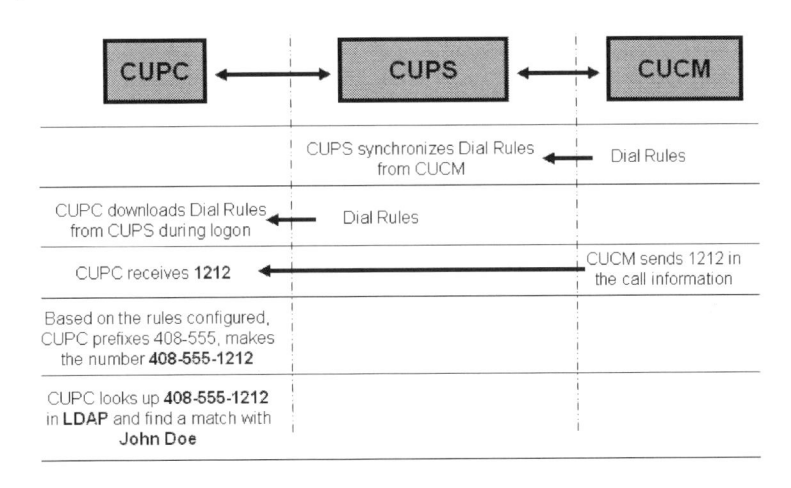

```
        CUPC  ←→       CUPS       ←→    CUCM

                       CUPS synchronizes Dial Rules  ← Dial Rules
                              from CUCM

        CUPC downloads Dial Rules  ← Dial Rules
          from CUPS during logon

        CUPC receives 1212  ←                CUCM sends 1212 in
                                             the call information

        Based on the rules configured,
        CUPC prefixes 408-555, makes
           the number 408-555-1212

        CUPC looks up 408-555-1212
        in LDAP and find a match with
                  John Doe
```

To configure Directory lookup dial rules, follow the steps below:

1. Go to CUCM > Call Routing > Dial Rules > Directory Lookup Dial Rules
2. Click "Add New"
3. Enter any name you like in "Name" field
4. Enter the number of digits you want to match in "Number of Digits" field.
5. Enter the number of digits you want to remove in "Total Digits to be Removed" field.
6. Enter the number you want to prefix in "Prefix With Pattern" field.

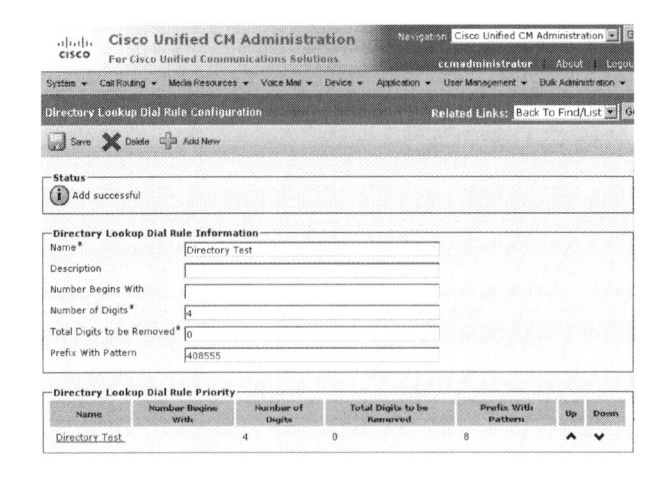

Chapter 5. Deploying and Troubleshooting Features

[Screenshot: Cisco Unified CM Administration — Directory Lookup Dial Rule Configuration page showing Name: Directory Test, Number of Digits: 4, Total Digits to be Removed: 0, Prefix With Pattern: 408555]

In CUPC log:

```
2008-11-18 20:48:14,281 [0x424] INFO   LCMiddleware -
(MWMSG_CFGMGR_SYSCONFIG) ConfigurationManager: system dial rules =
    Inbound rules
        Prio Length       Begins With Remove       Prefix With
          1    4                         0                4085555
    Outbound rules
        Prio Length       Begins With Remove       Prefix With
          1    10                        0                9
```

"Inbound rules" in CUPC log refers to "Directory Lookup Dial Rules" in CUCM.

Test

1. Make a test to or from CUPC.
2. Observe the called-party or calling-party's name displayed on call alerting window

Troubleshooting

Troubleshooting "Directory Lookup Dial Rules" is pretty much the same as "Application Dial Rules".

1. Verify CUCM database
2. Verify CUPS database
3. Verify CUPC

VoiceMail 157

Don't for get "Directory Lookup Dial Rules" depends on LDAP. Make sure LDAP feature was configured properly on CUPC.

VoiceMail

Retrieve Voicemail

You may use CUPC to retrieve your voicemails from Unity. Whenever there's a new voicemail comes in, CUPC will notify you. You may download the voicemail and play it with CUPC.

Prerequisites
1. You have Cisco Unity up and running.
2. CUPC only supports Unity with Exchange or Unity Connection (Does not support Unity with Domino).
3. IMAP was enabled on Exchange *mailbox* server or Unity Connection.
4. You can log in to CUPC.

Enable IMAP access on Unity Connection

1. Enable IMAP on a Class of Service (COS)

    1.1 Go to Unity Connection Admin > Class of Service > Class of Service
    1.2 Click the Class of Service you'd like to configure
    1.3 Enable "Allow Users to Access Voice Mail Using an IMAP Client". Choose option "Allow Users to Access Message Bodies"

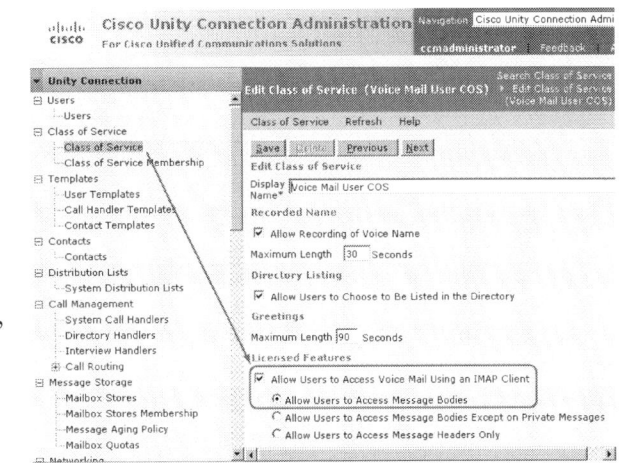

2. Assign users to the Class of Service (COS)

158 Chapter 5. Deploying and Troubleshooting Features

2.1 Go to Unity Connection Admin > Users > Users
2.2 Click the user you'd like to configure
2.3 From "Class of Service" menu, choose the Class of Service you configured in step 1

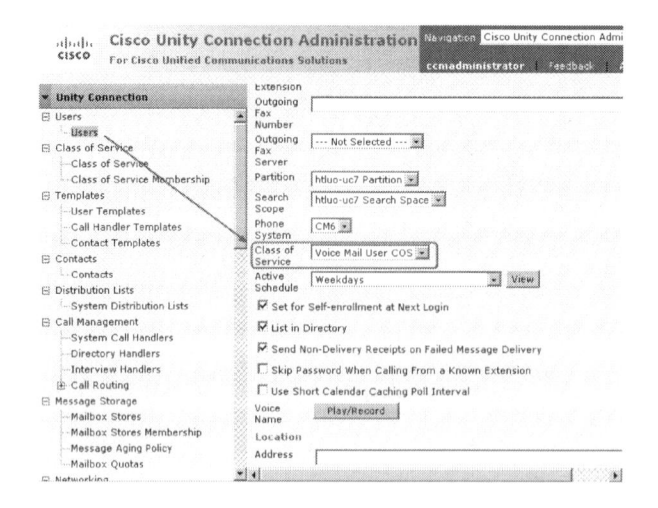

3. Change IMAP password for user

Don't confused IMAP password with voicemail password. Voicemail password is the PIN number you use to access voicemail from IP phone. IMAP password is the password you use to access voicemail from web applications. Those are two different/separate passwords.

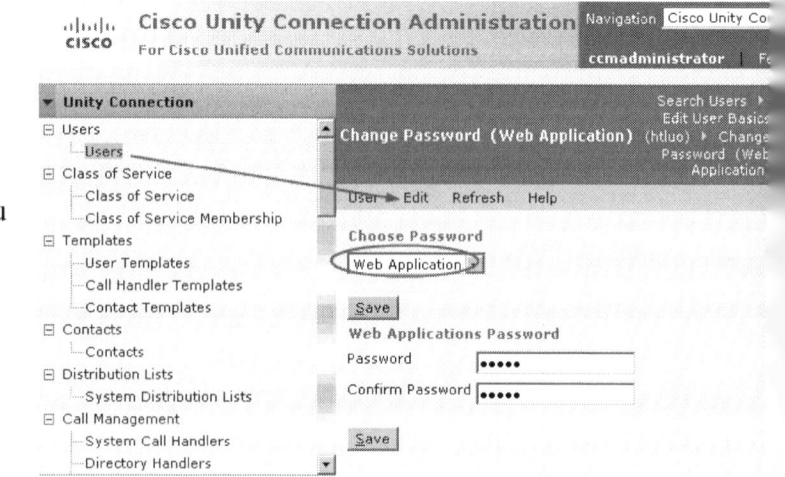

3.1 Go to Unity Connection Admin > Users > Users
3.2 Click the user you'd like to configure
3.3 From menu on the top, click "Edit > Change Password"
3.4 From the "Choose Password" drop-down menu, choose "Web Application"
3.5 Enter password in "Password" and "Confirm Password" fields. Save.

Enable IMAP access on Exchange

When you have a Unity/Exchange integration, voicemails are actually stored on Exchange mailbox server. For CUPC to access the mailbox server, IMAP service has to be enabled.

IMAP service is disabled on Exchange server by default. To enable it follow the steps below:

1. Enable and start "Microsoft Exchange IMAP4" service.

   1.1 Go to Windows Services.
   1.2 Double-click "Microsoft Exchange IMAP4"
   1.3 Set "Startup Type" to "Automatic". Click "Apply"
   1.4 Click "Start" to start the service

Note:
Due to the current limitation of CUPC, you have to enable IMAP service on mailbox servers. We'll further explain this later in configuration steps.

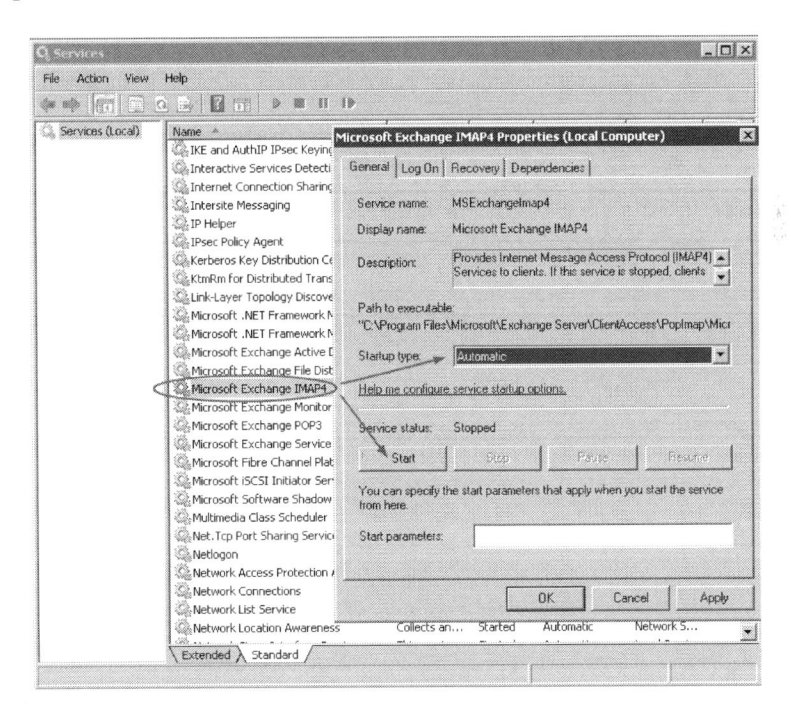

2. (Optional) Set SSL options.

On Exchange 2003, SSL option is disabled by default. When SSL is disabled, IMAP service is listening on TCP port 143. I would recommend you NOT to use SSL during initial setup and testing. You may enable SSL after the initial test was succeeded.

To enable SSL, follow steps below:

2.1 Open Exchange System Manager
2.2 Go to "Administrative Groups > First Administrative Group > Servers"
2.3 Expand the mailbox server you want to configure
2.4 Go to "Protocols > IMAP4"
2.5 Right-click "Default IMA4 Virtual Server" > "Properties"
2.6 Click "Access" > "Authentication"
2.7 By default, "Requires SSL/TLS encryption" is unchecked.
2.8 To enable SSL, check this option.

Note: When "Require SSL/TLS encryption" is checked, you can only access the IMAP via SSL. Default port is TCP port 993.

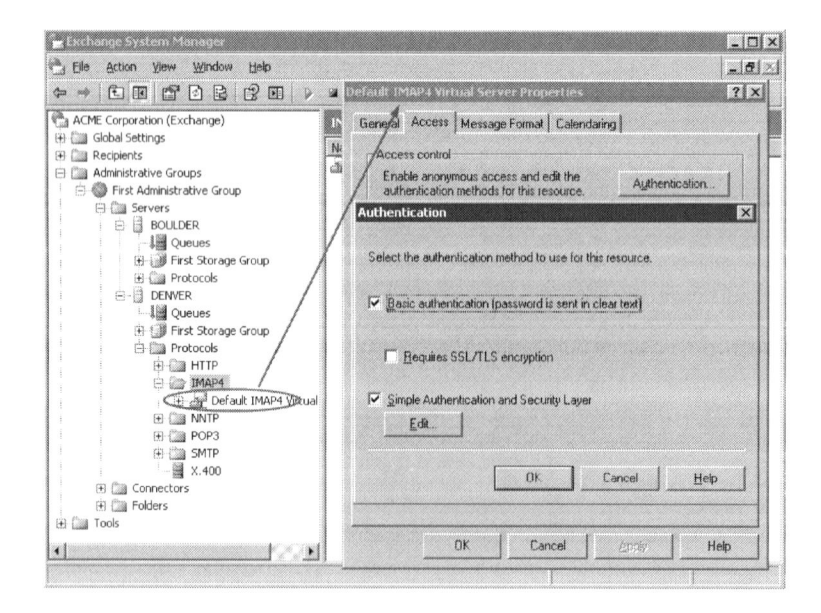

On Exchange 2007, SSL option is enabled for IMAP by default. To disable SSL and use plain text password (recommended for testing purpose), type the command below in Exchange Management Shell:

```
Set-IMAPSettings -LoginType 1
```

You need to restart "Microsoft Exchange IMAP4" service to take effect.

Voicemail-related Menus on CUPS

On CUPS Admin, there are three menus that are voicemail related – Voicemail Server, Voicemail Profile and Mailstore.

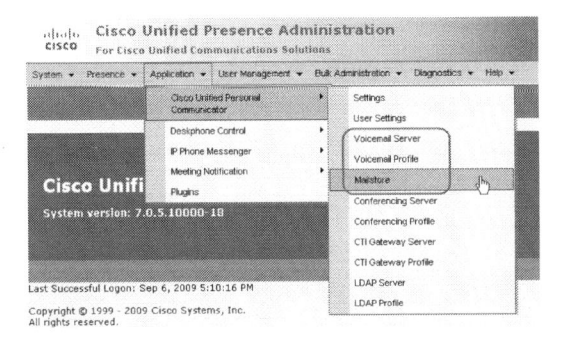

Surprisingly, "Voicemail Server" is optional (it's used for "secure messaging"). "Mailstore" and "Voicemail Profile" are required.

Step 1: CUPS: Configure "Mailstore"

"Mailstore" refers to the actual storage location of voicemails. For Unity, it's the Exchange mailbox server that stores voicemails. For Unity Connection, it's the Unity Connection server itself.

Mailstore configuration is required if you want to use voicemail feature of CUPC.

1.1 Go to CUPS Admin > Application > Cisco Unified Personal Communicator > Mailstore.
1.2 Click "Add New"
1.3 In "Name" field, enter a name you'd like to use.
1.4 In "Hostname/IP address" field, enter the address of Exchange mailbox server (if you're using Unity with Exchange) or Unity Connection (if you are using Unity Connection).
1.5 In "Port" and "Protocol Type", enter the correct IMAP port number and protocol. Default TCP port for Exchange and Unity Connection is 143. Default SSL port for Exchange is 993. Default TLS port for Unity Connection is 7993. If you're not sure, consult your Unity engineer.

If you have voicemails on multiple servers (mailstores), you need to create multiple stores and profiles. For example, if you have user A's voicemail on server A and user B's voicemail on server B, you need to create two mailstores and two voicemail profiles. Then assign user A and user B to different profiles.

Step 2: CUPS: Configure Unity Server (optional)

At the time this book was written, this step is only required if you're using "Secure Messaging" feature with Unity (not Unity Connection). If you're not using this feature with Unity, you may skip this step and go to step 3.

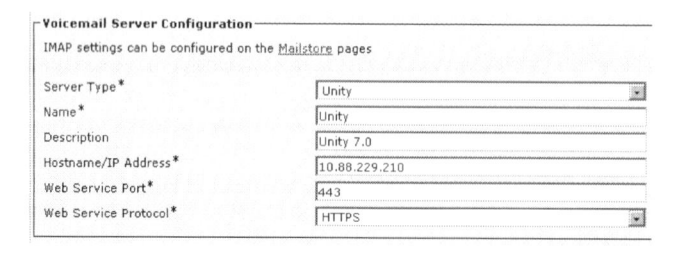

2.1 Go to CUPS Admin > Application > Cisco Unified Personal Communicator > Unity Server
2.2 In "Server Type", choose "Unity". (Though "Unity Connection" is an option here, it is not used on this version)
2.3 In "Name", enter a name you like.
2.4 In "Hostname/IP Address", enter the IP address of the Unity server.

2.5 In "Web Service Port" and "Web Service Protocol", enter the port and protocol that you use to access the Unity web admin. Default HTTPS port is 443. Default HTTP port is 80. For security, it's recommended to use HTTPS.

Again, at this moment, only Unity secure messaging use this configuration. Unity Connection does not use this configuration.

Step 3: CUPS: Create Unity Profile and assign users to it

Voicemail Profile Configuration	
Name*	NewYork VM Profile
Description	NewYork VM
Voice Messaging Pilot	7990
Primary Voicemail Server	Unity
Backup Voicemail Server	< None >
Backup Voicemail Server	< None >
Primary Mailstore	Ex07MBX01
Backup Mailstore	< None >
Backup Mailstore	< None >

☑ Make this the default Voicemail Profile for the system.

3.1 Go to CUPS Admin > Application > Cisco Unified Personal Communicator > Unity Profile
3.2 Click "Add New"
3.3 In "Name" field, enter a name you'd like to use.
3.4 In "Voice Messaging Pilot" drop-down menu, choose the pilot number for Unity voicemail.*
3.5 In "Primary Mailstore", choose the mailstore you configured in step 1.
3.6 (Optionally) If you're using "Secure Messaging" feature with Unity, in "Primary Unity Server" field, choose the Unity server you configured in step 2.
3.7 Click "Add Users to Profile". Find the user you want to add. Select the user and click "Add Selected"

Note: the "Voice Messaging Pilot" configuration is for "Send to Voicemail" feature, which we'll cover later.

Step 4: CUPC: Configure user credential

164 Chapter 5. Deploying and Troubleshooting Features

Depending on your Unity configuration, IMAP password may or may not be the same as LDAP or CUCM password. Hence CUPC allows you to configure the Unity credential from client side.

To configure Unity credential, follow steps below:

    4.1 Log in to CUPC.
    4.2 Go to File > Preferences > Accounts
    4.3 Configure username and password under "Cisco Unity"

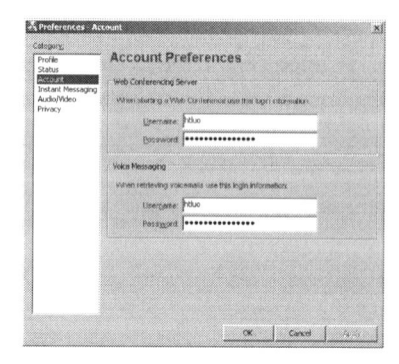

This is another confusing part – "What credential/password I should use here?"

For Unity, this should be the mailbox name/password, ie. Active Directory username/password.

For Unity Connection, this is the "Web Application" password, not the "PIN number".

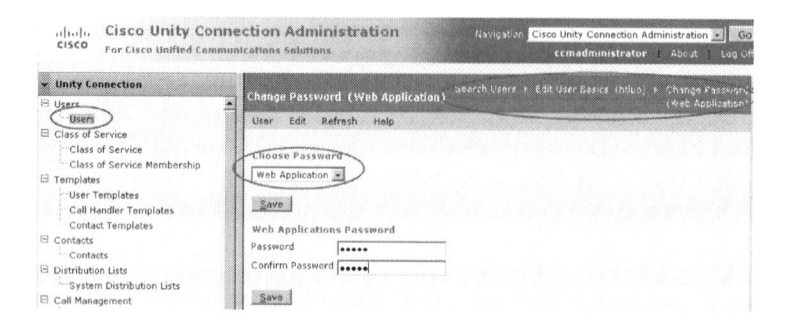

Troubleshooting

Configuration issue

One of the frequently seen problems is configuration issue. In a "Unified Messaging" Unity deployment, Unity server and Exchange mailbox server are on two different boxes. On CUPS Admin > Application > Cisco Unified Personal Communicator > Unity Server, you should enter the address of the Exchange mailbox server, not the Unity server.

IMAP connectivity/authentication issue

The easiest way to test IMAP is to use Windows telnet command. However, to test IMAP with telnet, you cannot use SSL option on IMAP server. This is why I recommended you NOT to use SSL during initial setup and testing.

To test connectivity use command below:

```
telnet 10.88.229.190 143
```

In the command above, 10.88.229.190 is the IP address of IMAP server. 143 is the port number.

If you got screen output like below, connection is failed. Either IMAP service is not running on the server, or IMAP service was configured on a different port. Or traffic was blocked by firewall.

```
C:\>telnet 10.88.229.200 143
Connecting To 10.88.229.200...Could not open connection to the host, on port 143
: Connect failed

C:\>
```

If you can connect to IMAP server, type the command below:

```
1 capability
```

Each IMAP command begins with a number as the sequence number. IMAP server will respond with the corresponding sequence number.

166 Chapter 5. Deploying and Troubleshooting Features

This command will give you the capability of the IMAP service on this port. Please note the "LOGINDISABLED" in the screen blow. That means login has been disabled on the port we telnet to (143). Usually, this is an indication that the "Require SSL" option was enabled on Exchange.

```
Telnet 10.88.229.190
* OK The Microsoft Exchange IMAP4 service is ready.
1 capability
* CAPABILITY IMAP4 IMAP4rev1 LOGINDISABLED STARTTLS IDLE NAMESPACE LITERAL+
1 OK CAPABILITY completed.
```

Please refer to instructions before to disable the SSL option.

If IMAP LOGIN was allowed on port 143, we may continue testing with username and password:

```
Command Prompt
* OK The Microsoft Exchange IMAP4 service is ready.
1 capability
* CAPABILITY IMAP4 IMAP4rev1 AUTH=NTLM AUTH=GSSAPI STARTTLS IDLE NAMESPACE LITER
AL+
1 OK CAPABILITY completed.
2 login htluo cisco
2 OK LOGIN completed.
3 logout
* BYE Microsoft Exchange Server 2007 IMAP4 server signing off.
3 OK LOGOUT completed.

Connection to host lost.

C:\>
```

First command is to display IMAP server's capability.

Second command is to test IMAP credential. The syntax is "`2 login <username> <password>`", where <username> is the actual username and <password> is the actual password.

If the username/password is correct, you'll get "OK LOGIN completed".

You may use "`logout`" command to close the connection.

The username/password we test here should be used in CUPC > File > Preference > Accounts > Cisco Unity.

IMAP referral issue

In some Exchange deployments, there might be more than one mailbox server. If the mailbox requested is on a different server other than the IMAP server, IMAP server will send a referral message to IMAP client (CUPC), asks IMAP client to talk to another server.

Unfortunately, CUPC does not support IMAP referral right now. If you have multiple users on different mailbox servers, you have to do the following:

1. Enable IMAP service on all Exchange mailbox servers.
2. On CUPS, configure different "Unity Server" and "Unity Profile" for different users.

In CUPC log, you will see messages like below:

```
2008-11-03 11:30:54,794 [0x914] ERROR LCVoiceMail -
(MWMSG_VOICEMAIL_LOGERROR) ?[REFERRAL
imap://int%2Fmail01;AUTH=*@mail02.abc.com/INBOX] There is no replica for
that mailbox on this server.
```

Send Calls to Voicemail

Configuration

When you have an incoming call, CUPC will display a call alert window. You may send the call to voicemail without answering it. This is very similar to "iDivert" function on IP phones.

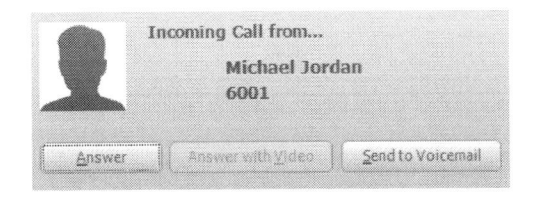

Prerequisites and deployment steps are exactly the same as deploying "retrieve voicemail" feature. The key point is to choose a "Voice Messaging Pilot" number. Please refer to step 2.6 in previous section ("retrieve voicemail").

Troubleshooting

"Send to Voicemail" button grey out

If "Send to Voicemail" button was grey out on incoming call alert window, there's no VM pilot number configured in CUPS Voicemail Profile. Please note, you need to configure a VM pilot number in profile explicitly. You cannot just choose "Default".

"Send to Voicemail" button clicked, but call was not sent to voicemail

"Send to Voicemail" button was enabled (lit), you clicked on it, but nothing seemed to happen. The incoming call is still ringing your phone.

This is usually caused by call routing issue, including:

- Calling Search Space

    When you click "Send to Voicemail" button, it's the caller's CSS (Calling Search Space) that matters. If it's an external (PSTN) call, you might want to check the CSS on incoming gateways and see if they can reach the voicemail pilot.

    "Cisco Callmanager" traces will be able to tell you what happened on the failed call.

- Application Dial Rules

    Application Dial Rules also affect call routing. Since it works silently in the background, something you might not notice it. See below for details.

"Send to Voicemail" worked in Soft Phone mode but didn't work in Desk Phone mode

In rare occasions, you'll find the "Send to Voicemail" button works fine in CUPC Soft Phone mode, but not in Desk Phone mode.

You checked the Calling Search Space. They are the same on Soft Phone and Desk Phone

You wouldn't believe it "Application Dial Rules", because rules should apply to both phone modes. Well, yes and no.

In regular outbound calls (such as you dial from dial pad, click-to-dial), rules apply regardless of the phone mode.

When you click "Send to Voicemail", things are a little bit different.

In Soft Phone mode, it utilizes "iDivert" function of the phone to divert the call to voicemail. No digit was sent. Hence no rules would apply.

In Desk Phone mode, it uses CTI protocol. To divert the call, CUPC has to send a CTI redirect message with the voicemail pilot number. Once there were digits involved, application dial rules kicked in.

If "Send to Voicemail" works in Soft Phone mode but doesn't work in Desk Phone mode, make sure the VM pilot number didn't fall into dial rules. You may make exclusion in the rules. Or make the rules more specific, so the VM pilot number doesn't match them.

Calendar

Prerequisites

1. Exchange 2003 SP1 (or above). Or Exchange 2007.
2. SSL (https) was enabled on Outlook Web Access (OWA)
3. You can log in to CUPC
4. CUPC client status was working fine

Best practices

1. If you don't want to deal with CA, you may use makecert.exe to generate self-singed certificate for Exchange OWA server.
2. During troubleshooting, you might want to disable FBA on WebDAV directory (default is /exchange). Changing authentication method on WebDAV will not change the feel and look of OWA. It will not affect OWA user authentication.

Introduction to certificates

A certificate is like an identification card for a person (e.g. a driver license). A person may use ID card to identify himself. Analogously, a computer may use certificate to identify itself.

When looking at a person's ID card, we usually ask ourselves these questions:

1. Does the person look like the photo on the ID card?
2. Do I trust the issuer of the card?
3. Is the card really from the issuer (is it a fake one)?

To answer those questions, we usually take the following actions:

1. Compare the person with the photo.
2. Ask yourself if you trust the issuer of the card. If you trust the issuer, you should trust the card they issued.
3. Find a way to verify the authenticity of the card (e.g. watermark, laser mark or other anti-forgery technology).

Analogously, a computer uses the same way to validate a certificate:

1. Look at the Common Name (CN) of the certificate. Is that the same name I tried to communicate with (e.g. mail.acme.com)?
2. Find out the issuer of the certificate (e.g. Verisign). Do I trust this issuer? i.e. Is the issuer in my trust certificate store?
3. Decrypt the certificate with issuer's public key. If the certificate can be decrypted successfully, the authenticity is validated. (public key / private key algorithm)

Usually, every **end entity** certificate would have an issuer. For example, your Exchange OWA server is an end entity. Its issuer is Verisign. The issuer is usually referred as CA (Certificate Authority). CA has a certificate to identify itself. We called it a CA certificate.

Take a look at the certificate below:

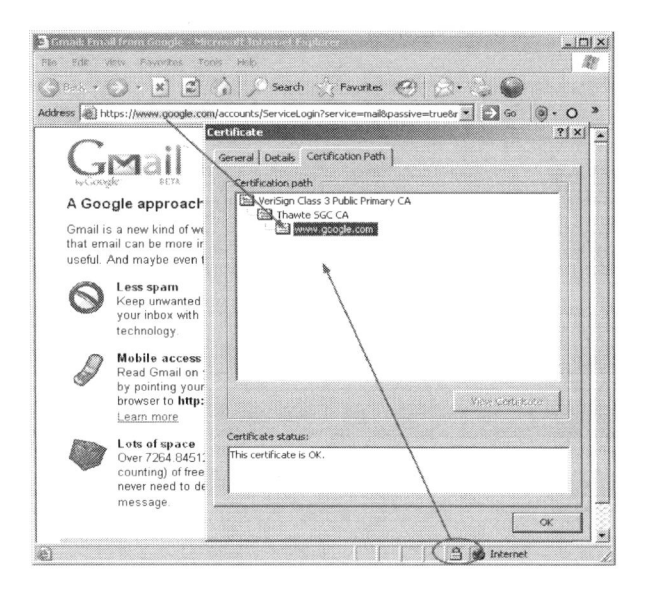

We opened a web page to https://www.google.com. Double-click the lock icon on web browser brings up the certificate details. It tells us the following:

- The Common Name (CN) of this certificate is www.google.com.
- The issuer of this certificate is "Thawte SGC CA".
- The issuer of "Thawte SGC CA" is "VeriSign Class 3 Public Primary CA"

The certificate of www.google.com is an **end entity certificate**.
The other two certificates are called **CA certificates**.
The certificate "Thawte SGC CA" is called **intermediate certificate**.
The certificate "Verisign Class 3 Public Primary CA" is called **root certificate**.

For a computer to trust www.google.com, what needs to be done?

Many people were under the impression that the computer needs to trust the certificate of www.google.com, more specifically, to put the certificate www.google.com into the computer's certificate trust store. This is not true.

In fact, the computer needs to trust the issuer of www.google.com, which is "Thawte SGC CA" in this case. More specifically, the computer needs to have the certificate "Thawte SGC CA" in its certificate trust store.

172 Chapter 5. Deploying and Troubleshooting Features

In order to trust "Thawte SGC CA", the computer needs to trust the issuer, which is "Verisign Class 3 Public Primary CA" in this case. More specifically, the computer needs to have the certificate "Verisign Class 3 Public Primary CA" in its certificate trust store.

"Verisign Class 3 Public Primary CA" is the top (root) CA in the chain. Its certificate was issued by itself. This is called "self-signed" or "self-issued" certificate. Root CA certificate is always a self-signed certificate.

In summary:
For computer A to trust computer B,
1. Computer A needs to have all **CA certificates** of computer B. (All CA certificates in the certificate chain).
2. Computer A does NOT need the **end entity** certificate of computer B.

In our example above, our computer needs to have "Thawte" certificate and "Verisign" certificate. It does NOT need to have "google" certificate.

Now we need "Thawte" and "Verisign" certificates. How do we extract them from the "google" certificate?

1. In "Certification Path" window, highlight the CA certificate you want to extract (for example "Thawte SGC CA"). Click "View Certificate". It will display "Thawte SGC CA" certificate in another window.

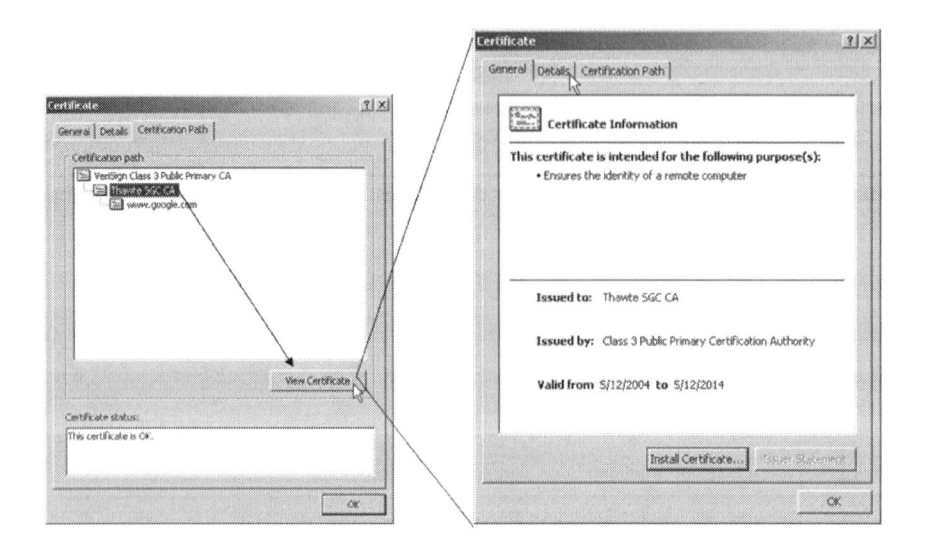

2. On the new window, go to "Details" tab. Click "Copy to File". It will bring up "Certificate Export Wizard" window. Click "Next" to go to next windows.

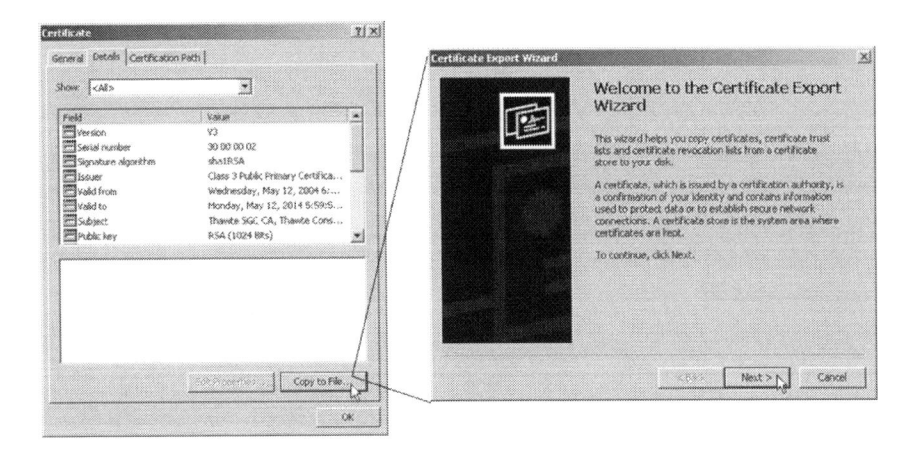

3. Choose "Base-64" as the file format. Click "Next".

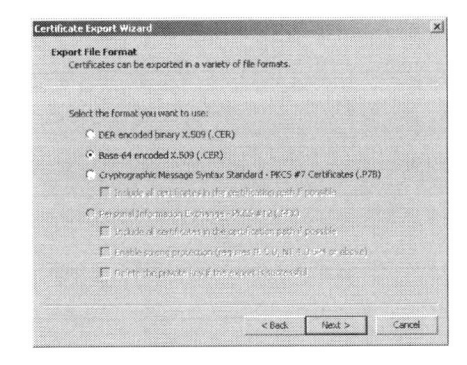

4. Enter a file name. Click "Browse" to choose a location you want to store the file (e.g. C:\). Click "Next".

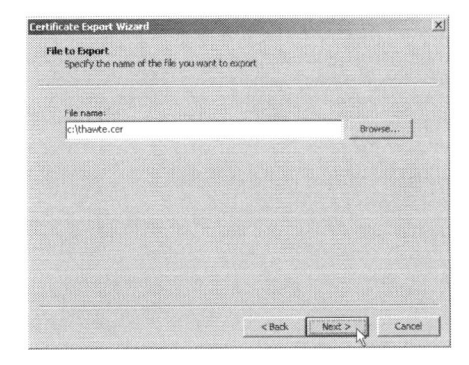

5. Click "Finish" on the "Completing" window.

6. You'll find the certificate file in the location you chose.

Repeat steps above to extract another CA certificate until all certificates in the chain have been exported.

Now you know how certificate works in SSL. You know some terminologies of certificates. You know how to extract CA certificates from an end entity certificate. In the following section, we're going to discuss the steps to deploy calendar feature on CUPS.

Step 1: Exchange: Enable SSL for OWA

Enabling SSL for OWA (Outlook Web Access) server should be a job of Exchange engineer (unless you're the Exchange engineer him/herself). OWA runs on IIS (Internet Information Server)

Please refer to Microsoft documentations for enabling SSL on IIS (http://support.microsoft.com/kb/324069)

To enable SSL, you need to have a certificate for Exchange.

Here are the three options for certificates:

- Get the certificate from an external CA (Certificate Authority), such as VeriSign, GoDaddy, Thawte, etc.
- Get the certificate from an internal CA server, such as Microsoft Certificate Server.

- Use a self-signed/self-issued certificate

External CA

Getting certificate from external CA is a common practice, especially when the company already using the external CA for other applications.

Internal CA

Internal CA means the company has a CA server running internally. Microsoft has the CA service built in on all Windows server systems.

Cisco has a document regarding using the internal CA to issue certificates: http://www.cisco.com/en/US/docs/voice_ip_comm/cups/6_0_1/install_upgrade/deployment/guide/dgmsint.html#wp1051620

In my opinion, I don't recommend you refer to the document above. Because:

- If you are experienced enough to handle a CA server and certificates, the above document won't do much help for you.
- If you depend on that document to install your CA server, I would strongly recommend you NOT to do so. You might not understand the ramification of having a CA in the Active Directory environment.

If you really want to use internal CA, please get a certified CA engineer do it.

Self-signed certificate

This is my favorite one. It does not require a CA server. It does not require an external certificate.

There are many ways to create **self-signed** certificate on OWA (IIS). I would recommend you use a Microsoft utility called "makecert.exe". (You may go to www.microsoft.com and search for "makecert")

The advantages of using "makecert.exe" (versus GUI) are:

176 Chapter 5. Deploying and Troubleshooting Features

	GUI	makecert.exe
Common Name in certificate	Hostname of the OWA	Any name you specify
Expiration	One year	Any time you specify
Certificate Authority Bit	Cannot be set	Can be set

CN (Common Name)

Common name is a very important part in certificates. Examples below show you the common name of a certificate:

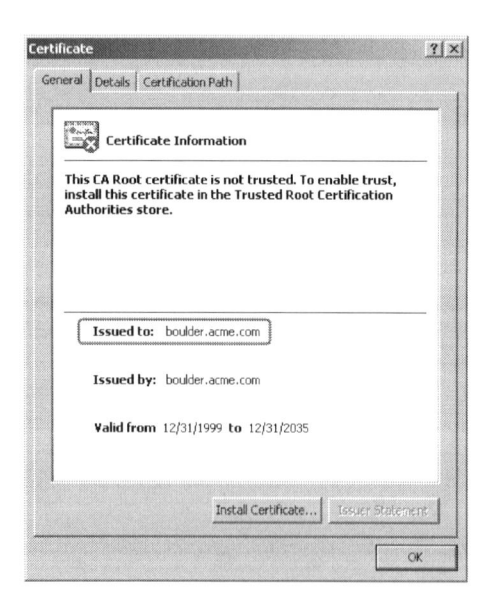

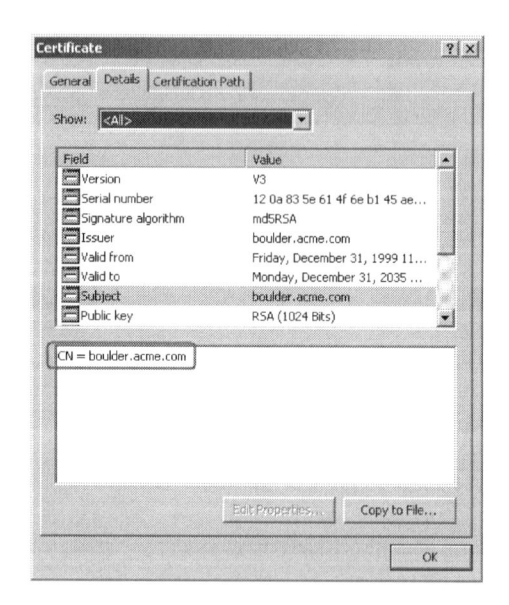

In TCP/IP network, DNS is usually optional. If we cannot get to a host by DNS name, we can always use IP address as alternatives.

In SSL/HTTPS, this is totally different.

https://boulder.acme.com or https://10.88.229.196 would be totally different even though they are actually the same box. For security reason, SSL requires the server name in the client request match the CN (common name) in the certificate. (please reference "introduction to certificates" – item #1)

When using Windows GUI to generate the self-signed certificate, it will set the hostname (computer name) as the CN. The CN would be "boulder", instead of "boulder.acme.com".

In that case, you need to use the name "boulder" to initiate SSL connection. This requires the initiator to be able to resolve the name "boulder". If you CUPS server can resolve FQDN only (e.g. boulder.acme.com), you'd better make sure CN in certificate is FQDN.

With makecert.exe, you may specify any name as the CN in certificate. In a non-DNS environment, you can even specify an IP address as the CN. So you can set up the SSL connection with IP address.

Expiration

If you generate the certificate from GUI, it will expire in one year. If you generate certificate with makecert.exe, you may specify when you want the certificate to expire.

Certificate Authority Bit

This is another important piece of certificate. The "Certificate Authority Bit" (or "CA bit") would indicate if the certificate was issued by a CA or not. Some applications (including CUPS) won't trust a certificate without CA bit.

Below are two certificates. The left one has CA bit. The right one does not have CA bit.

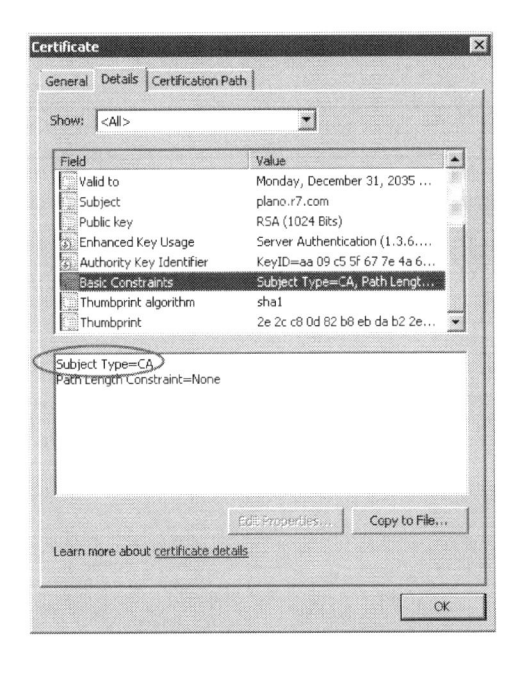

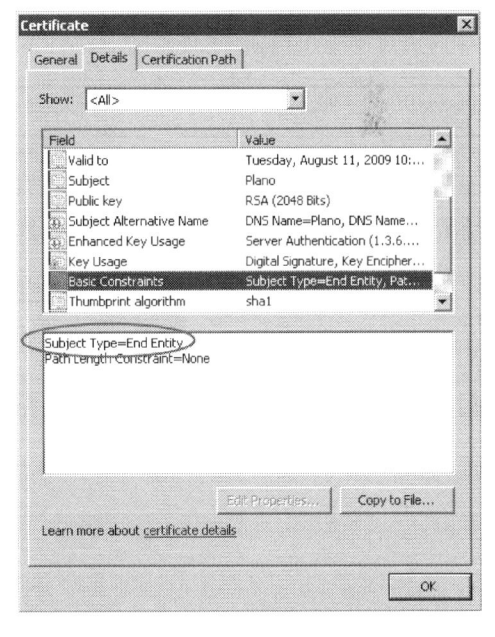

178 Chapter 5. Deploying and Troubleshooting Features

The ***command syntax*** of makecert.exe would be like below:

```
makecert -r -pe -n "CN=www.yourserver.com" -b 01/01/2000 -e 01/01/2036 -
eku 1.3.6.1.5.5.7.3.1 -ss my -sr localMachine -sky exchange -sp "Microsoft
RSA SChannel Cryptographic Provider" -sy 12 -cy authority
```

Notes:
1. Copy makecert.exe to the OWA server and run it from command prompt.
2. Substitute www.yourserver.com with the actually FQDN (fully qualified domain name) or IP address of your OWA server. This will be the CN (Common Name) in the certificate.
3. The only options you may change is the name of the server, the beginning time (-b) and the ending time (-e). Other parameters should be entered as is.

Steps to generate self-signed certificate and enable SSL

Here we are going to discuss self-signed certificate installation procedure only. For external CA or internal CA, please refer to Cisco documentation:
http://www.cisco.com/en/US/docs/voice_ip_comm/cups/6_0_1/install_upgrade/deployment/guide/dgmsint.html#wp1051620

1. Download makecert.exe from Microsoft.
2. Copy makecert.exe to OWA server. You may put it on C:\.
3. On OWA server, open a command prompt and type the command below

```
makecert -r -pe -n "CN=www.yourserver.com" -b 01/01/2000 -e 01/01/2036
-eku 1.3.6.1.5.5.7.3.1 -ss my -sr localMachine -sky exchange -sp
"Microsoft RSA SChannel Cryptographic Provider" -sy 12 -cy authority
```

Substitute www.yourserver.com with the FQDN of your OWA server, for example "denver.acme.com". This command will generate a certificate and put it into Windows registry of the OWA server.

4. Open Internet Information Services Manager, or the custom MMC containing the Internet Information Services snap-in.

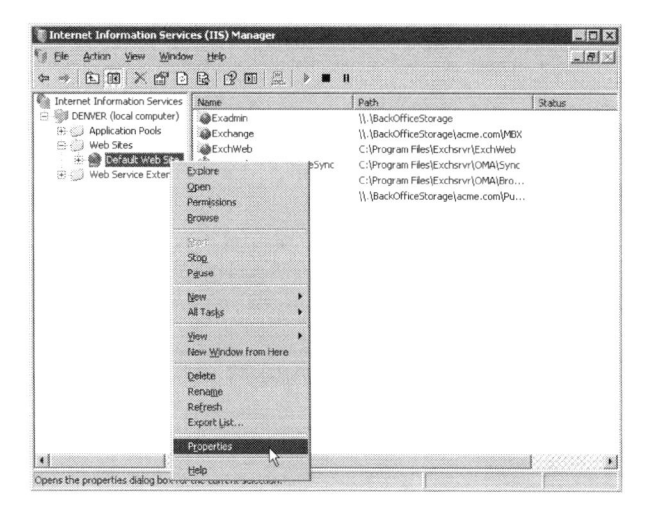

5. Expand Internet Information Services (if needed) and browse to the Web site that hosts the OWA (usually Default Web Site).
6. Right-click on the site and then click Properties.
7. Click the Directory Security tab.

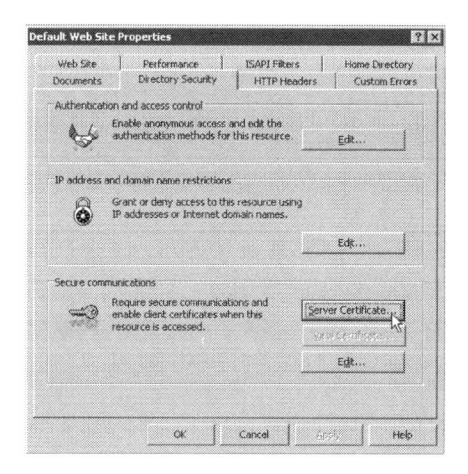

8. Under the Secure Communications section, click Server Certificate.
9. On the Web Server Certificate Wizard, click Next.

Chapter 5. Deploying and Troubleshooting Features

10. Choose "Assign an existing certificate". Click "Next".

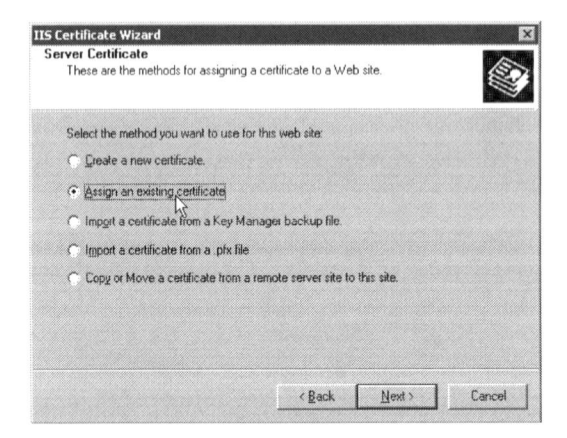

11. Highlight the certificate you want to install and click "Next".

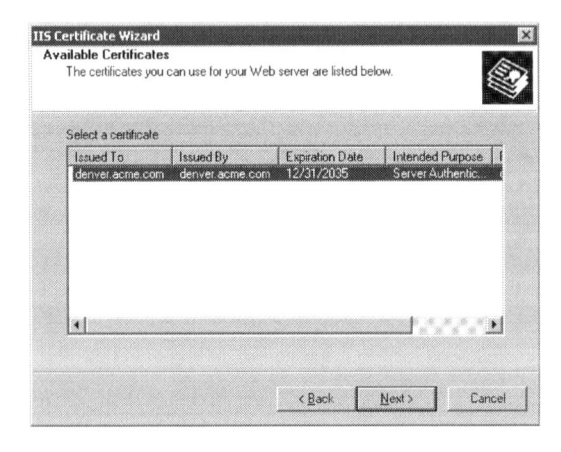

12. Review the "Certificate Summary" screen and click "Next".

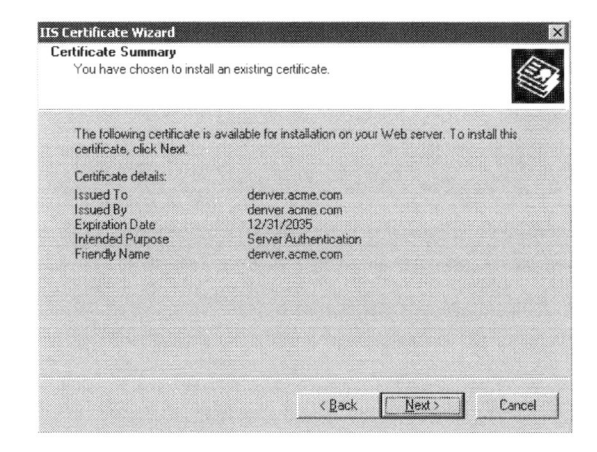

13. Click "Finish" on the "Completing" screen.

14. Restart IIS (Internet Information Server) to take effect.

Step 2: Exchange: Create Receive-As account

For CUPS to see every user's calendar, a special account has to be created in Exchange. We call this "Receive-As" account. This account will be able to view everybody's calendar.

Please note this step actually consists of two steps:
- Create the account and mailbox
- Assign "Receive-As" permission to the account

Create Account and Mailbox

Create account and mailbox should be straight forward. So we're not going to cover the details here. But there's one catch on "Creating Mailbox".

Thought you "created" the mailbox for the account, the mailbox didn't actually get created until the account logs onto Exchange (either via Outlook or OWA).

If the account never logged on to Exchange, the mailbox would never get created. Without the mailbox, you cannot assign permissions to the account.

It is recommended that you log onto OWA with the newly created account before you assign permissions. The first time you logon, you'll see a screen like this. This is called "First Time Logon" screen.

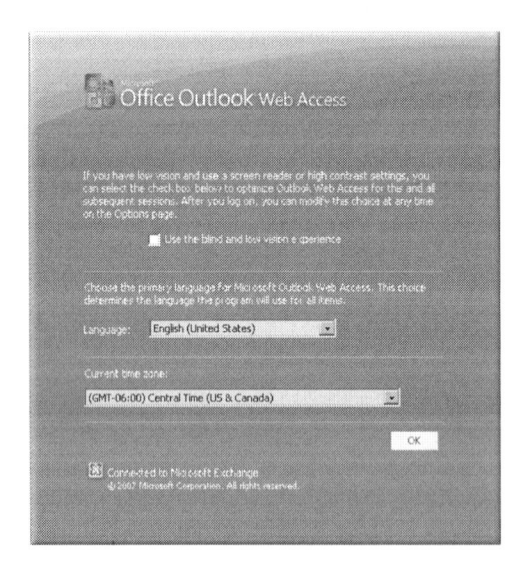

Assign "Receive-As" permission

On Exchange, if account A has "Receive-As" permission on account B's mailbox, A can read B's email and calendar. In order for CUPS to read everyone's calendar, we need to give CUPS account "Receive-As" permission on everyone's mailbox.

On Exchange, "mailboxes" are contained in "database". "Databases" are contained in "Storage Groups".

Instead of assigning permission to individual mailboxes, we usually assign permission on containers (Storage Groups). Child objects will inherit permissions assigned to parent containers.

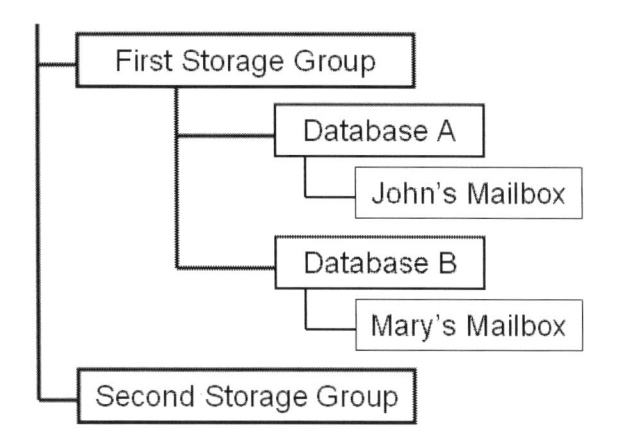

```
├── First Storage Group
│       ├── Database A
│       │       └── John's Mailbox
│       └── Database B
│               └── Mary's Mailbox
└── Second Storage Group
```

Prerequisites:
1. You already have an Exchange account created for the CUPS integration.
2. There's no special permission required for this account at this point.
3. The account needs to have an Exchange mailbox. And the mailbox has been opened for at least once (from Outlook or Outlook Web Access).

It is recommended that you create a dedicated account for this integration. It is NOT recommended that you use an existing account that is being used by another service or application (such as "Administrator" or "UnityInstall" etc.).

Cisco documents said that you need "View-Only Administrator" and "Receive-As" permission on the account. In fact, you just need "Receive-As".

Exchange 2003

Add "Receive As" permission to the account

2.1 Open "Exchange System Manager"
2.2 Expand "Administrative Group > First Administrative Group > Servers > your mailbox server > First Storage Group".

184 Chapter 5. Deploying and Troubleshooting Features

2.3 Open the "Mailbox Store" properties.

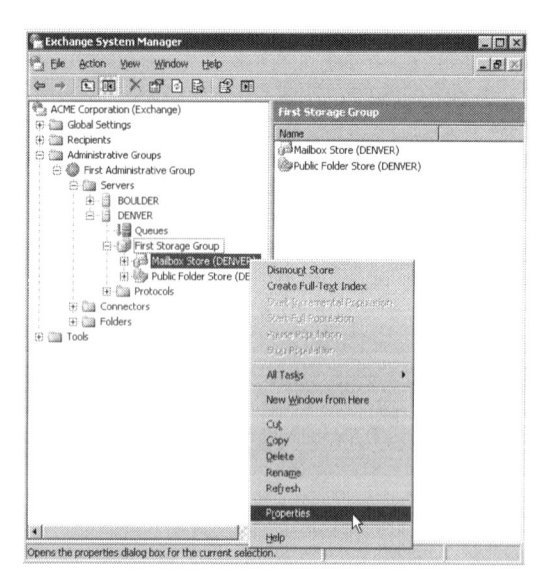

2.4 Go to "Security" tab. Add the service account and make sure it has "Receive As" permission. Click "OK".

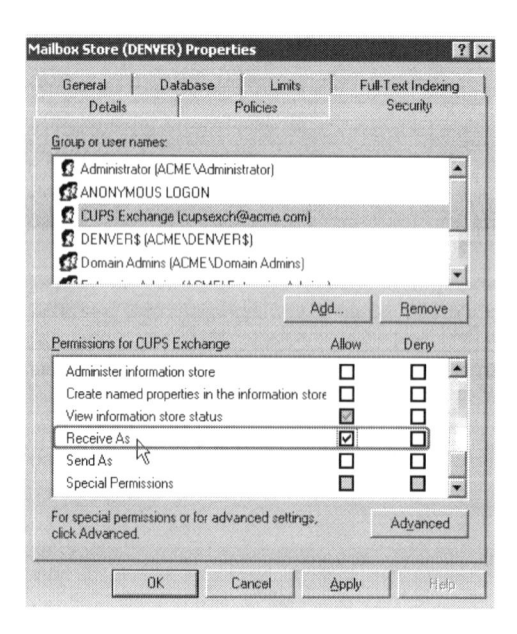

Exchange 2007

In Exchange 2007, lots of work has to be done in "Exchange Management Shell" instead of GUI.

Before you run the following command, please make sure the service account has a mailbox. And the service account has logged into Outlook or Outlook Web Access at least once (the mailbox won't get created until the account actually logged in).

Add "Receive As" permission to the account

If you want to give "Receive-As" permission to the account for everybody (usually you do), use the command below. This command assigns permission to all storage groups.

```
Get-StorageGroup | add-ADPermission -user cupsexch -ExtendedRights Receive-As
```

"cupsexch" is the account used for CUPS integration.

If you just want to assign permission to a specific storage group, you may use the command below:

```
Add-ADPermission -Identity "First Storage Group" -User cupsexch -ExtendedRights Receive-As
```

"cupsexch" is the integration account. "First Storage Group" is the storage group we want "cupsexch" have permission on.

Similarly, if you want to assign the permission to specific end user (for testing purpose), you may use the command below:

```
Add-ADPermission -Identity "r7.com/People/Michael Luo" -User cupsexch -ExtendedRights Receive-As
```

"cupsexch" is the integration account. "r7.com/People/Michael Luo" is the end user we want "cupsexch" have permission on.

If you assigned permission at storage group level, it would take some time to populate to mailbox level (usually 3-4 hours). To verify the permission has been populated to mailbox level, use command below:

186 Chapter 5. Deploying and Troubleshooting Features

```
Get-MailboxPermission htluo -user cupsexch | Format-Table -autosize
```

Where 'htluo' is the end user's mailbox, "cupsexch" is the service account. If the permission has been populated to the mailbox level, you'll see screen output like below:

```
Machine: Plano | Scope: r7.com
[PS] C:\>Get-MailboxPermission htluo -user cupsexch | Format-Table -autosize

Identity                     User            AccessRights IsInherited Deny

r7.com/People/Michael Luo    R7\cupsexch     {FullAccess} True        False


[PS] C:\>_
```

"`AccessRights = {FullAccess}`" means the account "cupsexch" has full access on mailbox "htluo" (full name is "Michael Luo").
"`IsInherited = True`" means this permission was inherited from higher level ("Storage Group" level).

If you see this, you may move on. Otherwise, wait until you got similar output.

Step 3: CUPS: Upload Certificates

For CUPS to set up SSL connection with Exchange, we need to upload Exchange's CA certificates to CUPS. If there is more than one CA in the certificate chain, we need to upload all of them.

    3.1 Go to CUPS OS Administration web page
    3.2 Click "Security > Certificate Management"

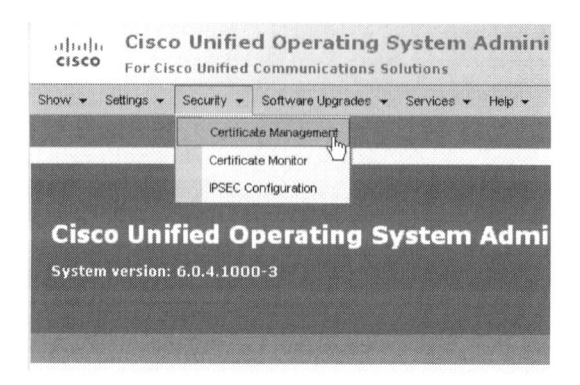

3.3 Click "Upload Certificate"

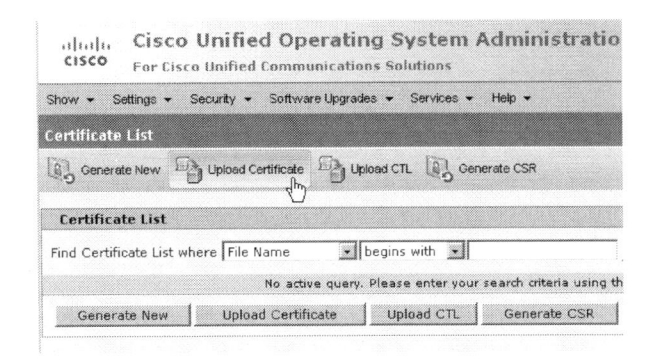

3.4 From "Certificate Name", choose "PresenceEngine-trust" (On CUPS 8.x choose "cup-trust"). Click "Browse" to locate the certificate you want to upload.

3.5 Click "Upload File". Notice the screen says "Success: Certificate Uploaded".

188 Chapter 5. Deploying and Troubleshooting Features

3.6 Click "Close".
3.7 Click "Find" on the "Certificate List" window. You should see the newly uploaded certificate showing on the list. Please note the certificate would be shown as "sipproxy-trust". This is by designed.

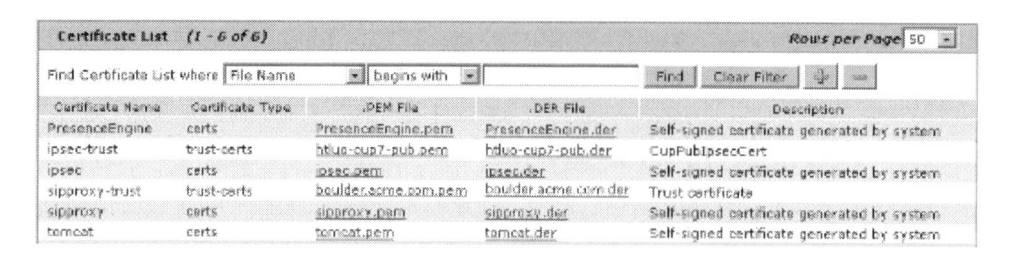

3.8 If you have more than one CA certificate in the certificate chain, repeat steps above to upload them.

Step 4: CUPS: Configure Outlook Gateway

4.1 Go to CUPS Admin > Cisco Unified Presence > Presence Gateways.
4.2 Click "Add New". You'll come to the "Presence Gateway Configuration" page.
4.3 From "Presence Gateway Type", choose "Outlook".
4.4 In "Description" filed, enter any description you like.

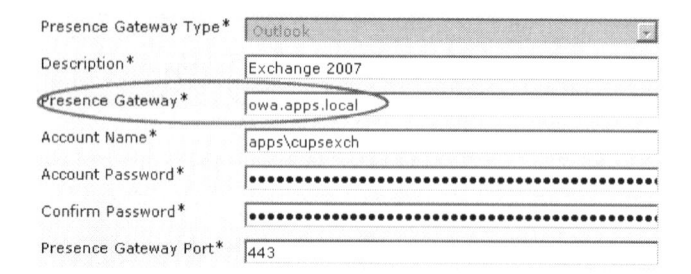

4.5 In "Presence Gateway", enter the Common Name of the Exchange certificate. For example, in the OWA certificate is as below. The name we use in "Presence Gateway" *must* be owa.apps.local. You cannot use a different name or IP address even if it is resolved to the same destination. If the common name is not resolvable from CUPS, you'll have to configure DNS.

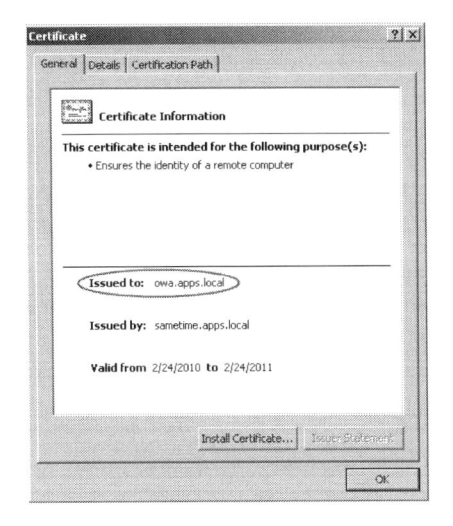

4.6 In "Account Name", enter the "Receive-As" account you created in step 2. It is recommended to enter the account in "***Domain\Account***" format. (e.g. "acme\cupsexch".
4.7 Enter account password.
4.8 Save the configuration.
4.9 Go to CUPS Serviceability web page and restart "Cisco UP Presence Engine" service.

If you have not uploaded certificate(s) per "Step 3: CUPS: Upload Certificates", you'll see "Missing Certificate" and a "Configure" button on the configuration page (as below).

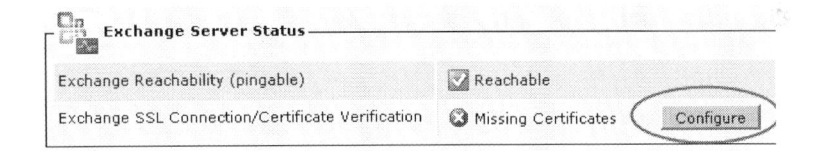

You may click "Configure" button to configure certificate. The purpose of this button is to provide a "convenient" way to upload certificates. In ideal situations, this will retrieve CA certificates from the certificate chain presented by OWA and install it on CUPS.

I don't recommend use this button. It doesn't work when a CA certificate was missing from the certificate chain presented by OWA (which is technically possible and normal). Instead, you should follow "Step 3: CUPS: Upload Certificates" to upload certificates.

190 Chapter 5. Deploying and Troubleshooting Features

Below is the screen when certificate was missing from chain. If you saw this screen, you should follow "Step 3: CUPS: Upload Certificates" to upload certificates.

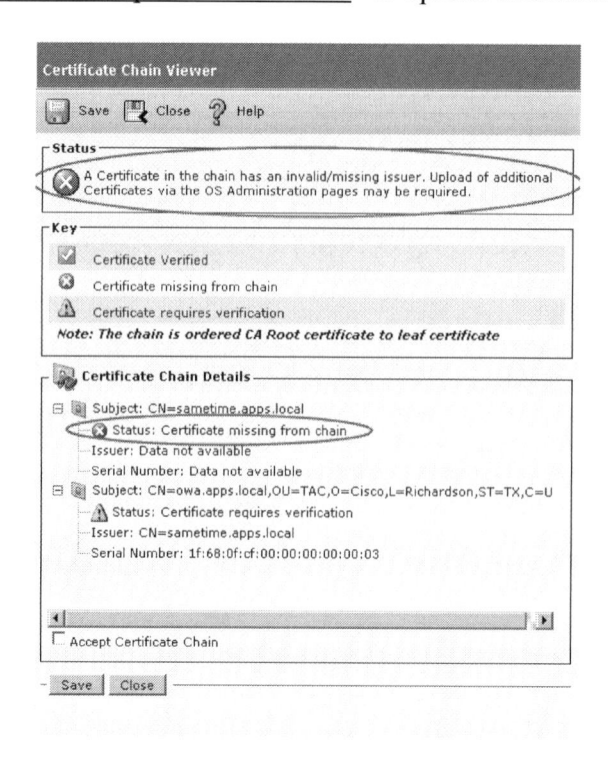

Step 5: CUPC: Enable calendaring

Not everybody wants to expose their calendar status. Hence you have the option to turn it on or off. You may either do it from your CUPS user options page or from CUPC.

From **User Options page**

User Options > Preferences, set "Include Calendar information in my Presence Status" to "On".

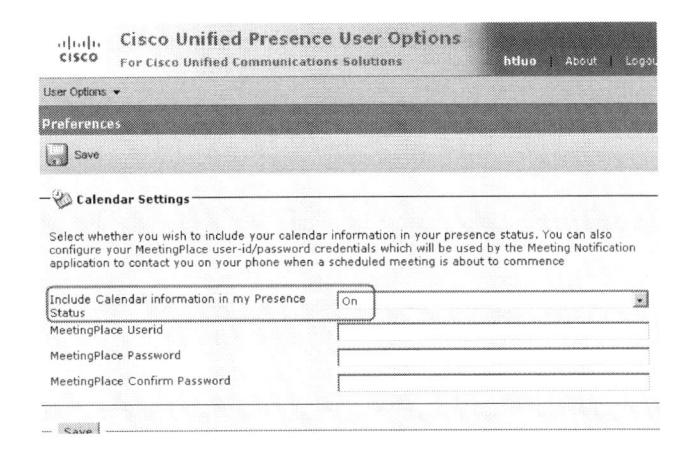

From **CUPC**

1. Log in to CUPC
2. Go to File > Preferences > Status
3. Enable "Show me as In-a-Meeting whenever my Outlook calendar shows me as busy".

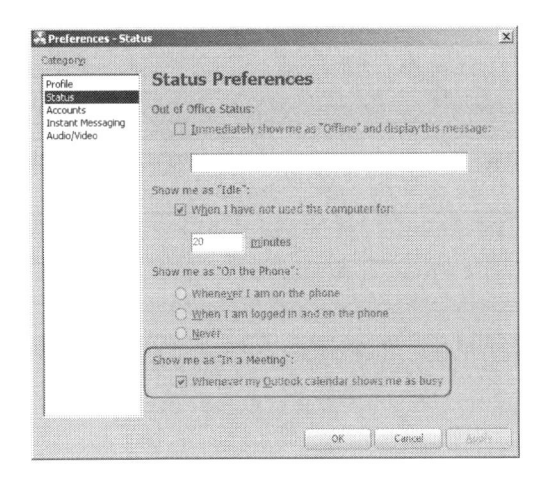

Test

While doing this test, you cannot be on the phone, because "on-the-phone" status would override "in-a-meeting" status.

1. Log in to CUPC.

2. Observe its status goes to "Available"
3. Create an appointment in Outlook. Make sure you set its status to "Busy". Make sure the appointment time cover the current time.
4. Observe CUPC status goes to "In a Meeting"
5. Delete the appointment from Outlook.
6. Observe CUPC status goes to "Available"

Troubleshooting

FBA – Form Based Authentication

During troubleshooting, you may encounter the term "FBA". What is FBA? Why it matters?

FBA is an Exchange terminology. It stands for Form Based Authentication. For OWA (Outlook Web Access), you may configure "Standard Authentication" or "Form Based Authentication" (either one).

When end users need to access OWA server from external network (through firewall), FBA is needed, because "Standard Authentication" only works inside firewall.

CUPS supports both authentication methods. There's no difference in CUPS configuration. It's your choice to use FBA or standard authentication. However, if you enabled FBA in the wrong place, it could add complexity to troubleshooting.

What does mean "wrong place"? FBA should be enabled on OWA virtual directory only. It is not required (and not recommended) to enable FBA on other virtual directories.

To understand virtual directories, please see Microsoft document at
http://technet.microsoft.com/en-us/library/bb885041(EXCHG.80).aspx

How to you tell if an OWA is using FBA or standard authentication? How to configure FBA or standard authentication? Try to open a web page to OWA.

If you got the authentication screen on a web form, OWA is using Form Based Authentication.

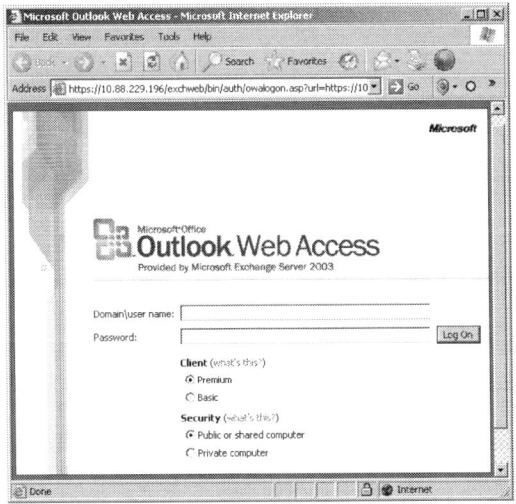

Form Based Authentication 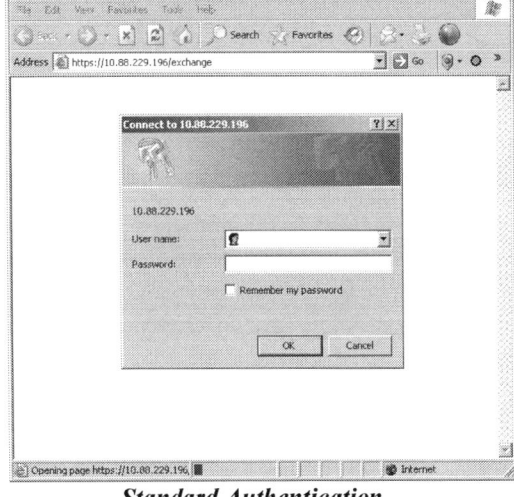   *Standard Authentication*

If you got the authentication screen on a popup window, OWA is using standard authentication.

FBA settings on Exchange 2003

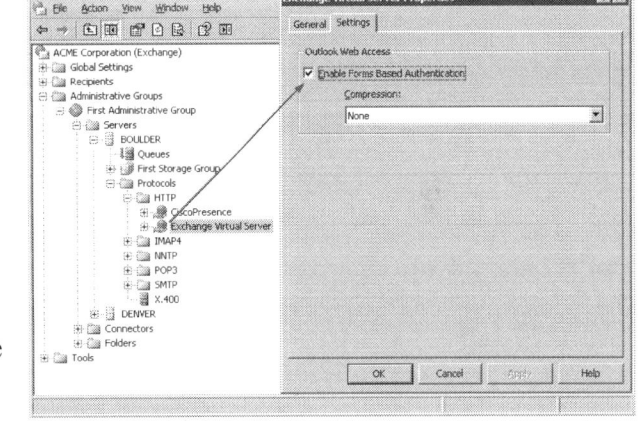

1. Launch Exchange 2003 System Manager
2. Expand "Administrative Group > First Administrative Group > Servers > your OWA server > Protocols > HTTP"
3. Right-click "Exchange Virtual Server", go to "Properties"
4. On "Settings" tab, you may enable or disable Form Based Authentication
5. Restart IIS Admin and World Wide Web service to take effect

FBA settings on Exchange 2007

1. Launch "Exchange Management Console".
2. Expand "Server Configuration > Client Access".
3. Highlight a CAS (Client Access Server)

194 Chapter 5. Deploying and Troubleshooting Features

4. Go to "Outlook Web Access" tab.
5. Double-click "owa (Default Website)"
6. Go to "Authentication" tab.
7. You may choose "Forms-Based Authentication" or "Standard Authentication".
8. Restart IIS Admin and World Wide Web service to take effect.

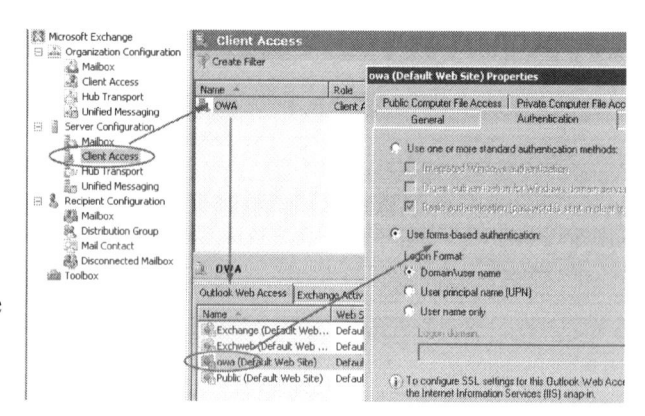

In Exchange 2007 environment, you may have different role servers – CAS, Mailbox, Hub Transportation, etc. Authentication settings on CAS will affect end user logon (as described above). Authentication settings on Mailbox server will affect CUPS.

On Mailbox "/exchange" virtual directory, use "Standard Authentication" instead of FBA.

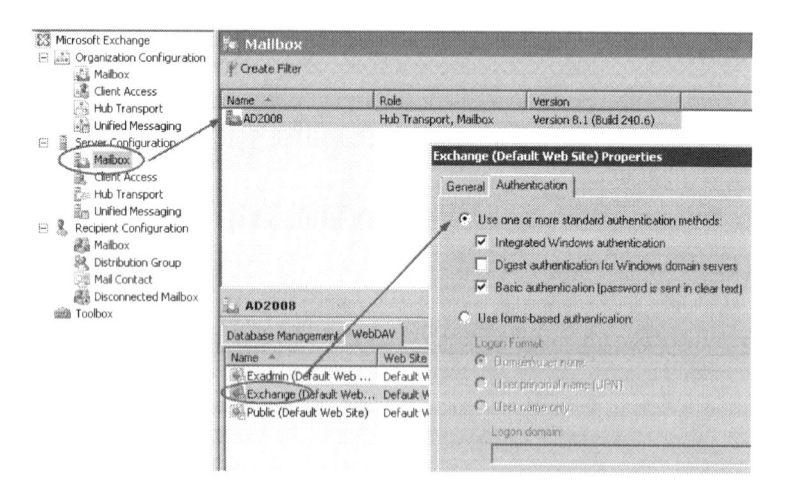

Configuration issues

Basically, this kind of issue was caused by NOT following the deployment documentations. We'll list some frequently seen problems here.

You forgot to enable calendar integration from client side.

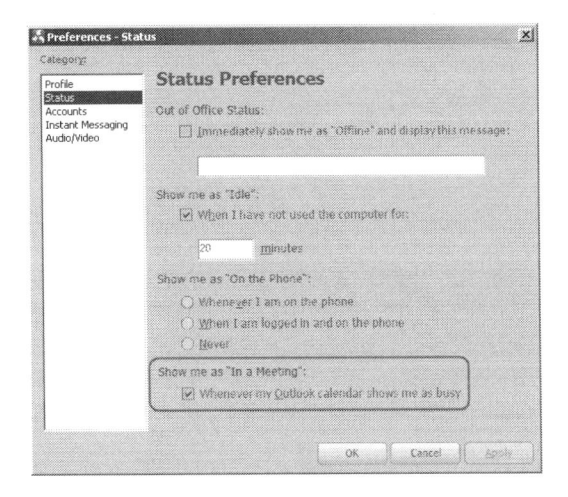

Suggestion: Use CUPC or CUPS user options page to turn on calendar integration.

CUPS server time is different with Exchange time.

For example, CUPS server was set to GMT time while Exchange server was local time. CUPC didn't show you as "In a Meeting" because CUPS was looking at the wrong times slot in your calendar.

Use "show status" command to see the current time on CUPS:

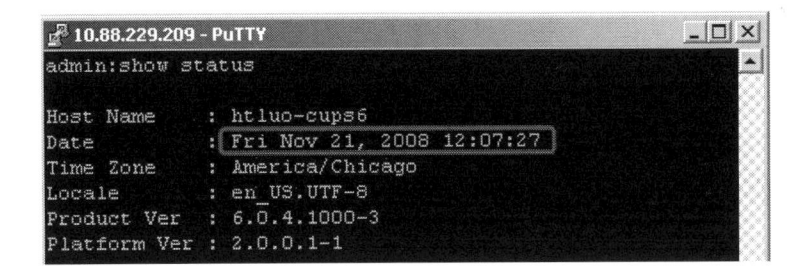

Suggestion: Set CUPS to the same time as Exchange server.

You uploaded the Exchange end entity certificate instead of its CA certificate.

We need to upload Exchange's CA certificate to CUPS. We don't upload Exchange (end entity) certificate itself. One exception would be self-signed Exchange certificate. In this case, the Exchange certificate is also the CA certificate.

For example, in the screen below, we don't upload www.google.com (end entity certificate) to CUPS. We upload "Thawte SGC CA" (CA certificate) to CUPS.

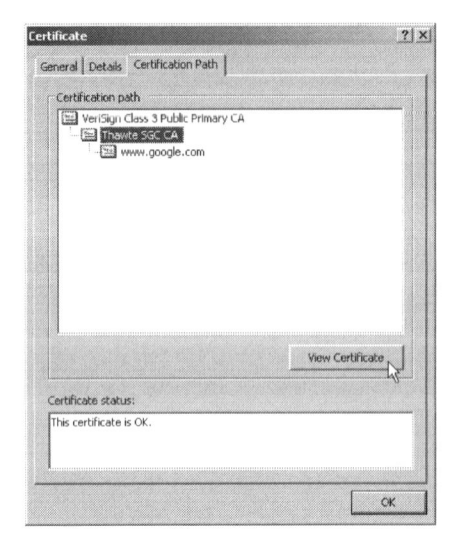

Suggestion: Upload CA certificate instead of end entity certificate.

Note: If you used self-signed certificate on Exchange OWA, there wouldn't be this problem. Because the OWA certificate itself is a CA certificate.

You didn't upload all CA certificates in certificate chain.

There was more than one CA in the certificate chain. You uploaded the direct CA certificate, but didn't upload all of them.

For example, in the screen below, we need to upload "Thawte SGC CA" and "VeriSign Class 3 Public Primary CA" certificates to CUPS. If you forgot one of them, CUPS won't trust www.google.com.

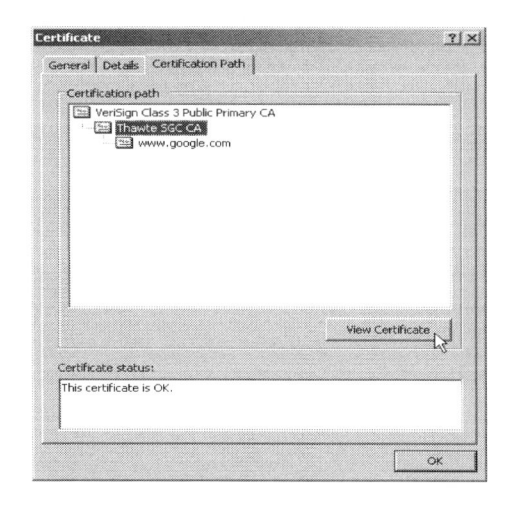

Suggestion: Upload all CA certificates in the certificate chain.

Note: If you used self-signed certificate on Exchange OWA, there wouldn't be this problem. Because the OWA certificate itself is a CA certificate and there's only one CA certificate in this scenario.

You use IP address in presence gateway configuration while the Exchange certificate CN is FQDN

Look at the screens below. You put IP address in "Presence Gateway". This will not work unless you have the IP address as CN (Common Name) in the certificate (which is very rare). Due to the design of SSL, the requesting address should match the CN in certificate (letter to letter match).

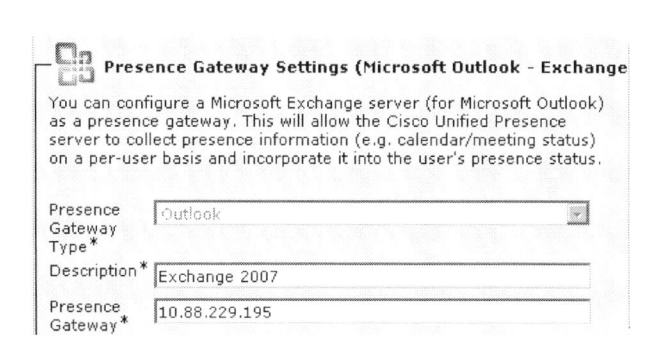

198   Chapter 5. Deploying and Troubleshooting Features

==Suggestion: In Presence Gateway configuration, use the same name as shown on the certificate.==

If you checked configuration and everything seems right, it's time to look at traces. To troubleshoot Calendar integration, we usually look at two kinds of logs:

1. CUPS Presence Engine logs (required)
2. Exchange(OWA) IIS logs (optional)

Typical log snippets

Let's take a look at some important snippets in Presence Engine logs.

Starting up

Whenever PE was restarted, you'll see following messages:

```
11/21/2008 22:30:45.465 EPE|system.pe.pa.owa.backend 84814 DEBUG Server: plano.r7.com:443
11/21/2008 22:30:45.465 EPE|system.pe.pa.owa.backend 84814 DEBUG AccountName: cupsexch
```

"plano.r7.com" is the Outlook presence gateway configured on CUPS.
"cupsexch" is the service account name configured on CUPS.

Initial attempt

When CUPC tried to retrieve calendar information, you'll see:

```
11/21/2008 22:33:10.338 EPE|system.pe.pa.owa.backend 402186 DEBUG uri: sip:htluo@r7.com@plano.r7.com:443
11/21/2008 22:33:10.338 EPE|system.pe.pa.owa.backend 402186 DEBUG -->Calendar.attach sip:htluo@r7.com@plano.r7.com:443
```

Don't be confused with the two @ signs in the SIP URI. In the URI above, htluo@r7.com is the MailID. Plano.r7.com is the OWA host FQDN.

Loading certificates

Right after that, you'll see PE tries to load certificates.

```
11/21/2008 22:33:10.515 EPE|system.pe.pa.owa.backend 410958 DEBUG Loading
certificates from: /usr/local/sip/.security/pe/trust-certs
11/21/2008 22:33:10.515 EPE|system.pe.pa.owa.backend 410958 DEBUG
ExchangeSession: loading certificate: plano.r7.com.pem
11/21/2008 22:33:10.515 EPE|system.pe.pa.owa.backend 410958 DEBUG
ExchangeSession: loading certificate: boulder.acme.com.pem
```

PE tries to load certificate from /usr/local/sip/.security/pe/trust-certs. In the example above, PE found two certificates: "plano.r7.com" and "boulder.acme.com". On CUPS server, certificate files are stored in .pem extension name.

Form Based Authentication

```
11/21/2008 22:33:10.735 EPE|system.pe.pa.owa.backend 410958 INFO received
SUBSCRIBE (initial) status: 440 Login Timeout
HTTP/1.1 440 Login Timeout
date: Sat, 22 Nov 2008 04:34:19 GMT
content-length: 54
set-cookie: sessionid=; path=/; expires=Thu, 01-Jan-1970 00:00:00 GMT,
cadata=; path=/; expires=Thu, 01-Jan-1970 00:00:00 GMT
content-type: text/html
```

The above message was received from Exchange OWA server. It's an indication that FBA (Form-Based Authentication) was enabled on OWA.

If OWA was enabled, it's normal to get this message. It is because when CUPS requests for "/exchange" URL from OWA (CAS) server, OWA will redirect that request to Mailbox server. "440 Login Timeout" is a normal message sent back to the requester.

However, if you got a 2nd "440 Login Timeout" right after the first one, it usually indicates two things:
1) FBA was enabled on "/exchange" virtual directory on *Mailbox* server. You don't have to enable FBA on mailbox server. Authentication method on mailbox server won't affect the feels and looks of the OWA logon. But it'll add complexity to troubleshooting.
2) There was an authentication issue. To get useful error messages, you should use "Standard Authentication" on "/exchange" virtual directory on mailbox server. See "FBA" section before for instructions.

IIS redirect

```
11/21/2008 22:33:10.738 EPE|system.pe.pa.owa.backend 410958 INFO received
POST status: 302 Moved Temporarily
HTTP/1.1 302 Moved Temporarily
x-powered-by: ASP.NET
location: https://plano.r7.com:443/exchange/htluo@r7.com
date: Sat, 22 Nov 2008 04:34:19 GMT
content-length: 0
set-cookie: sessionid=a583346f-ea6e-4e02-b30e-ad219d0b4600; path=/,
cadata="4C2CyPpueKW9b96BBBqaAAftixiO2IeYcs1q72NjABV+R9r5HfyJhFnDxvYw=";
HttpOnly; secure; path=/
server: Microsoft-IIS/7.0
```

This is an indication that the mailbox server was on a different server. So OWA server was doing a redirect to mailbox server.

Initial subscription response

```
11/21/2008 22:33:10.913 EPE|system.pe.pa.owa.backend 410958 INFO received
SUBSCRIBE (initial) status: 200 OK
HTTP/1.1 200 OK
x-powered-by: ASP.NET, ASP.NET
subscription-lifetime: 3600
date: Sat, 22 Nov 2008 04:34:19 GMT
notification-delay: 500
content-length: 0
content-location: https://plano.r7.com/exchange/htluo@r7.com/calendar/
set-cookie: OwaLbe={8477A0C0-A69E-441B-ADF1-64D9255C2EED}; path=/
subscription-id: 6
subscribe-group: Qg6IIJ4m90it+6ZGpVujAA==
notification-type: update
call-back: httpu://10.88.229.209:50020/501
ms-webstorage: 08.01.10240, 08.01.10240
server: Microsoft-IIS/7.0
```

This means the initial subscription was succeeded. Note the "content-location" URL. That's the URL CUPS tried to query OWA with.

Calendar search

```
11/21/2008 22:33:10.915 EPE|system.pe.pa.owa.backend 411474 INFO send
SEARCH htluo@r7.com 3600
.
.
```

```
11/21/2008 22:33:11.271 EPE|system.pe.pa.owa.backend 411474 INFO received
SEARCH status: 207 Multi-Status
HTTP/1.1 207 Multi-Status
x-powered-by: ASP.NET, ASP.NET
transfer-encoding: chunked
date: Sat, 22 Nov 2008 04:34:19 GMT
set-cookie: OwaLbe={8477A0C0-A69E-441B-ADF1-64D9255C2EED}; path=/
accept-ranges: rows
ms-webstorage: 08.01.10240, 08.01.10240
server: Microsoft-IIS/7.0
content-type: text/xml
```

PE sent search to OWA and received acknowledgement from OWA.

Calendar Status

```
11/21/2008 22:33:11.272 EPE|system.pe.pa.owa.backend 411474 DEBUG
transitionList: date: 2008-11-22T04:33:10Z status: FREE
date: 2008-11-22T05:33:10Z status: FREE
```

CUPS received FREE status from calendar server (OWA).

IIS logs

Sometimes the problem is so complicated that you might have to read IIS logs.

```
#Software: Microsoft Internet Information Services 7.0
#Version: 1.0
#Date: 2008-11-22 04:34:19
#Fields: date time s-ip cs-method cs-uri-stem cs-uri-query s-port cs-
username c-ip cs(User-Agent) sc-status sc-substatus sc-win32-status time-
taken
2008-11-22 04:34:19 10.88.229.190 SUBSCRIBE
/exchange/htluo@r7.com/calendar - 443 - 10.88.229.209 - 401 2 5 0
2008-11-22 04:34:19 10.88.229.190 POST /owa/auth/owaauth.dll - 443 -
10.88.229.209 - 302 0 0 15
2008-11-22 04:34:19 10.88.229.190 SUBSCRIBE
/exchange/htluo@r7.com/calendar - 443 cupsexch 10.88.229.209 - 200 0 0 171
2008-11-22 04:34:19 10.88.229.190 SEARCH /exchange/htluo@r7.com - 443
cupsexch 10.88.229.209 - 207 0 0 390
2008-11-22 04:34:19 10.88.229.190 POLL /exchange/htluo@r7.com - 443
cupsexch 10.88.229.209 - 207 0 0 15
2008-11-22 04:34:20 10.88.229.190 SEARCH /exchange/htluo@r7.com - 443
cupsexch 10.88.229.209 - 207 0 0 390
```

In IIS logs above, /exchange/htluo@r7.com/calendar was the URI (URL) subscribed.

This subscription was from "10.88.229.209" (CUPS server).
The account being used was "cupsexch".

Certificate issues

Certificate issues are the most common problem in calendar integration. Usually, we'll see two kinds of issues – "hostname does not match" or "CA not trusted".

Hostname does not match

In PE logs, you saw this:

```
11/22/2008 12:54:10.124 EPE|system.pe.pa.owa.backend 410782 ERROR
ExchangeSession: 0x0e4c2f48 ssl problem(s):
SESSION_HOSTNAME_DOES_NOTMATCH_CERTIFICATE_HOSTNAME - rejected
```

This message is self-explained. "Session_Hostname" (the name you configured in CUPS presence gateway) does not match the "Certificate_Hostname" (the name in certificate).

Suggestion: Go to CUPS Admin > Cisco Unified Presence > Presence Engine > Presence Gateway and enter the correct name (the name in certificate).

CA not trusted

```
11/22/2008 13:09:17.792 EPE|system.pe.pa.owa.backend 129394 ERROR
ExchangeSession: 0xffffffff91f6bec8 ssl problem(s):
CERTIFICATE_AUTHORITY_SIGNATURE_NOT_TRUSTED - rejected
```

This means CUPS server does not trust the CA (Certificate Authority) of OWA server. The message looks straight forward. However, there could be different causes for this problem.

Possible cause #1: You haven't uploaded CA certificate to CUPS server yet.

This is the simplest one. If you haven't upload CA certificate to CUPS, of course CUPS server won't trust it.

Possible cause #2: You haven't uploaded ALL CA certificates to CUPS.

Sometimes, you thought you did. But you didn't. Let's take a look at the screenshots below.

This is the Exchange certificate being viewed from Internet Explorer.

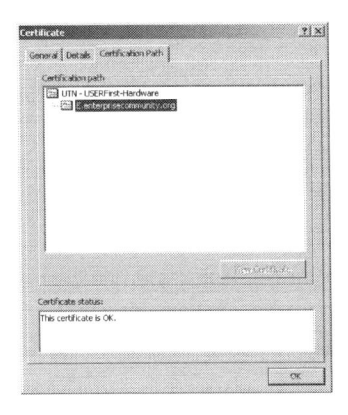

The Exchange server is E.enterprisecommunity.org. Its CA is "UTN–USERFirst-Hardware".

Since there's no further CA above "UTN–USERFirst–Hardware", it's a root CA. We double verify this by looking at the issuer of "UTN–USERFirst–Hardware". Its issuer is itself. This is normal for a root CA. (see screenshot below).

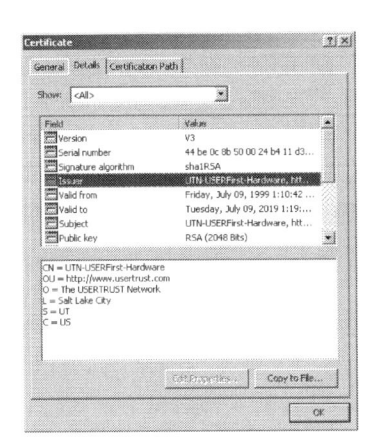

Now it *seems* that the only certificate we need to upload is this "UTN–USERFirst–Hardware" certificate. That's what I thought as well. However, it didn't work. PE logs kept give me "CERTIFICATE_AUTHORITY_SIGNATURE_NOT_TRUSTED" error.

204 Chapter 5. Deploying and Troubleshooting Features

It turned out that there WAS another CA in the chain. It just didn't show up in Internet Explorer. If we access OWA with FireFox, there's the certificate chain viewed from FireFox:

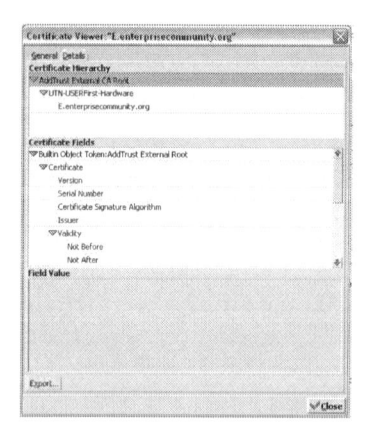

Notice that above "UTN-USERFirst-Hardware", there's another CA called "AddTrust External CA Root". Without this certificate, the chain is not completed.

Why Internet Explorer would have a different view with FireFox? I don't know. But here are some suggestions:

1. View and extract certificate on the OWA server instead of on the client computer.
2. If you have doubt, use a sniffer to capture packets between CUPS and OWA.

Sniffer capture below clearly indicates that the issuer of "UTN-USERFirst-Hardware" is "AddTrust External CA Root".

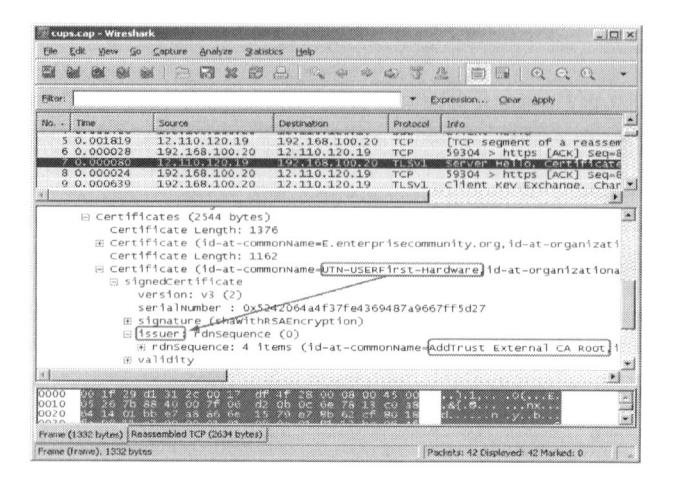

This is another reason you want to use makecert.exe to create self-signed certificate. With self-signed certificate, there's one and only one certificate to upload.

No CA bit in certificate

By default, the self-signed certificate generated by IIS does not have CA bit (because IIS server is not a CA server). CUPS won't trust any certificate without CA bit.

To generate a self-signed certificate with CA bit, you may use makecert.exe.

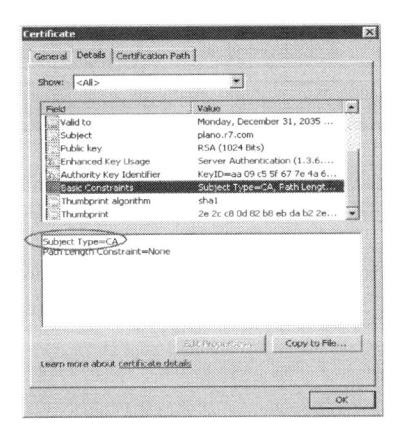

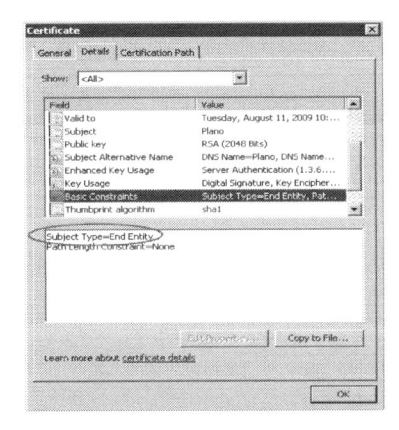

Permission issue

Remember CUPS use an Exchange service account to view other people's calendar. This service account needs to be have "Receive As" permission on people's mailboxes.

If the service account does not have sufficient permission, CUPS won't be able to use it to query calendar information.

In PE logs, you'll see

```
11/07/2008 16:15:29.756 EPE|system.pe.pa.owa.backend 381954 DEBUG --
>CalendarSubscription::doNOTIFYfail: htluo SEARCH 3 Authentication failure
on server; Could not authenticate to server: ignored NTLM challenge,
ignoring empty Negotiate continuation, rejected Basic challenge
```

There are two ways to isolate permission issues:

- Use end user account in Outlook Gateway configuration.
- Use service account to access end user's mailbox

Use end user account in Outlook Gateway configuration.

Let's assume that you're testing end user user1's calendar feature. You suspect that the service account does not have sufficient permission to access user1's mailbox.

1. Go to CUPS Admin > Cisco Unified Presence > Presence Engine > Presence Gateway > Outlook Gateway.
2. Change "Account Name" to "user1"
3. Change "Account Password" and "Confirm Password" to test1's password
4. Restart Presence Engine

Test the calendar feature of user1. If it works, it's a permission issue with the service account.

Use service account to access end user's mailbox

For Exchange 2003:

1. Open a web browser
2. Try to go to https://owa-server/exchange/<*user_id*>/calendar, where "owa-server" is the IP address/DNS name of your Exchange OWA server. <user_id> is the end user ID you want to test calendar feature on.
3. When prompted to enter username and password, enter service account name and password.

If you passed the authentication with the service account, it means the service account can open end user's mailbox.

For Exchange 2007:

You cannot use this test on Exchange 2007.

Exchange interoperability issue

When you have more than one server in your Exchange environment, things would be more complicated, especially when you have FBA enabled and in a mixed environment (Exchange 2003/2007).

For example, you have two servers in an Exchange 2003 cluster. One server is the Front End server, the other one is backend. You CANNOT enable SSL on the backend even though SSL is enabled on front end. Otherwise, WebDAV would fail while front end server doing redirect.

In a mixed environment (Exchange 2003/2007), things are more complicated. Exchange 2007 uses different URLs for OWA and WebDAV access, while Exchange 2003 uses same URL. For more details, please refer to Microsoft documentation:
http://technet.microsoft.com/en-us/library/bb885041.aspx.

If your company has different versions of Exchange in the same cluster, there's not too much you can do. But you can try to disable FBA (or add another server with FBA disabled). This will eliminate potential issues on FBA and make troubleshooting easier.

Exchange Hosted Solution

Now more and more service providers provide a solution called "Exchange Hosted", which means the Exchange servers are located at service provider's building instead of your company's server room. This is a convenient solution. However it usually causes problems with CUPS calendaring if not configured properly.

The symptom is there was no calendar status update on CUPC. However, if you disable/re-enable calendar feature from CUPC (or restart Presence Engine), calendar status will show up on CUPC. But no further updates after that.

To troubleshoot this problem, we need to know a little bit about how CUPS get calendar status from Exchange.

When calendar was enabled for a user the first time (or when Presence Engine was restarted), Presence Engine (PE) sends SUBSCRIBE to Exchange OWA via TCP protocol. There are two kinds of messages in this SUBSCRIBE:

1. I'd like to know this user's calendar status.
2. If there's any update on this user's calendar, please update me at 192.168.1.100 with UDP port 50020.

For the first one, Exchange will always respond t with TCP protocol, because the sender (CUPS) was using TCP.

The second one is called "callback" address. Something to notice:

1. Exchange will try to send update to "callback" address whenever there's an update in calendar.
2. Updates are sent from mailbox server to CUPS.
3. You cannot change the protocol. It'll be UDP. However, you may change the port number in CUPS Admin > System > Service Parameters > "Microsoft Exchange Notification Port"

Let's consider the diagram on the right.

In the diagram, Exchange OWA server was allowed to communicate with CUPS freely. Initial subscription from CUPS to OWA would succeed and get the calendar status. However, when there was an update in Calendar, Exchange mailbox server would fail to send notification to CUPS. It's because firewall does not allow any communication between mailbox servers and CUPS.

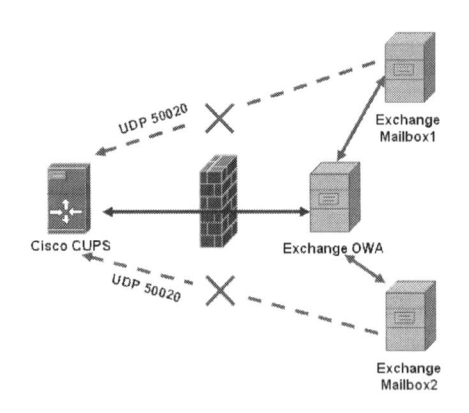

To troubleshoot this kind of problem, we need packet capture on CUPS and Exchange mailbox server. We'll see mailbox server tried to send UDP packets but CUPS server didn't receive it.

Instant Message

Prerequisites

1. You can log in to CUPC.
2. CUPC client status (availability) works fine.

Enable Instant Messaging

1. Go to CUPS Admin > Presence > Settings.
2. Make sure option "Enable Instant Messaging (cluster-wide)" is enabled (checked).

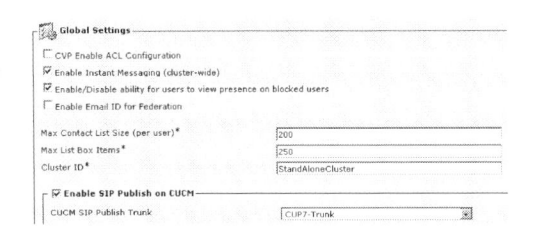

Test

1. On computer A, log in to CUPC with user A. Add user B to contact list.
2. On computer B, log in to CUPC with user B. Add user B to contact list.
3. User A and user B can see each other's status is "Available".
4. User A sends instant message to user B.
5. User B receives message from user A.
6. User B replies message to user A.
7. User A receives message from user B.

Troubleshooting

Best Practices

Instant messaging depends on availability information. If a user appears to be offline (even though he's actually online), you won't be able to send/reply messages to him. Troubleshoot client presence (availability) issue before troubleshooting instant messaging issue.

SIP domain issue

When SIP domain was configured with upper case letters (e.g. "Cisco.com" instead of "cisco.com"), it might cause problem on Instant Messaging.

This is a limitation on some old version of CUPC.

In CUPC log, we can see:

```
Presence.Domain = Cisco.com
```

This was downloaded from CUPS proxy domain configuration.

When there's an incoming instant message from user A, the SIP message reads like "sip:userA@cisco.com" (domain is lower case).

```
2007-12-05 16:07:20,619 [0x548] DEBUG LCPersonManager -
(MWMSG_PMI_PMMSESSIONCREATED) PersonMessageManager: New incoming IM
session from sip:userA@cisco.com
```

The mismatch causes CUPC to regard the IM as coming from a different entity for which it sees no presence, and therefore is presumed not to be IM-capable.

Suggestion: Change proxy domain to lower case.

Logs

CUPS SIP Proxy log

IP Phone Messenger

As mentioned before, IP Phone Messenger (or IPPM) gives you the "messenger" feature on a phone. You may receive/send messages on IP phone. You may also receive meeting notification on the phone.

However this feature is not supported on all phone models. Please refer to Cisco documentation regarding the supported models.

Prerequisites

1. You have deployed and tested CUPC logon and client status feature.
2. IP Phone is supported by IPPM

Step 1: Create IPPM application user

1.1 Go to CUCM Admin > User Management > Application User. Click "Add New".
1.2 In "User ID" field, enter a user ID for IPPM service (e.g. "PhoneMessenger")
1.3 In "Password" and "Confirm Password" field, enter a password for this account.
1.4 Save.

Step 2: Associate phones to IPPM application user

On "Application User Configuration" page, associate phone devices to the IPPM application user you created in step1. You just need to associate the phones that will use IPPM service.

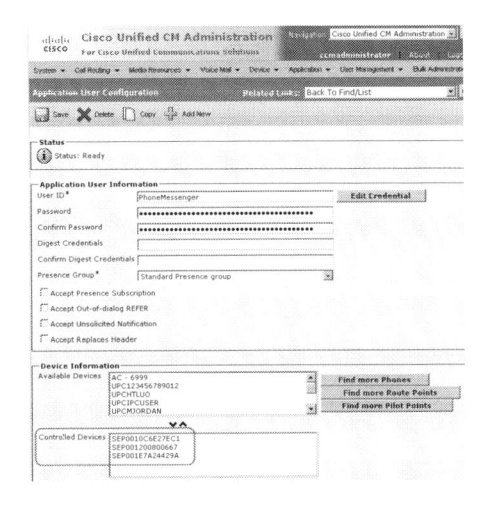

Step 3: Create IPPM phone service

3.1 Go to CUCM Admin > Device > Device Settings > Phone Services. Click "Add New".
3.2 In "Service Name" and "ASCII Service Name" fields, enter any name you want.
3.3 In Service URL field, enter "http://cups-address:8081/ippm/default?name=#DEVICENAME#", where "cups-address" is the actual IP address or FQDN of CUPS server.
3.4 Save.

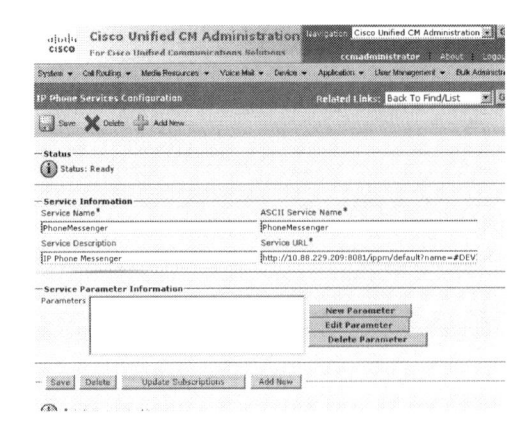

Step 4: Subscribe phone to IPPM service

4.1 Go to CUCM Admin > Device > Phone.
4.2 Find the phone you want to configure IPPM service on.
4.3 Click the search result to go to "Phone Configuration".
4.4 From "Related Links" drop-down menu, choose "Subscribe/Unsubscribe Services". Click "Go".

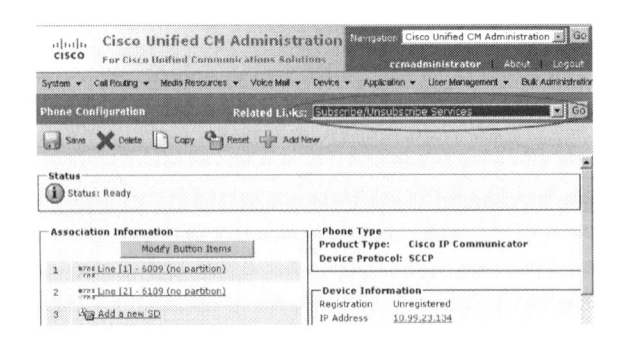

4.5 A window pops up. From "Select a Service" drop-down menu, choose IP Phone Messenger you created in step 3. Click "Next".

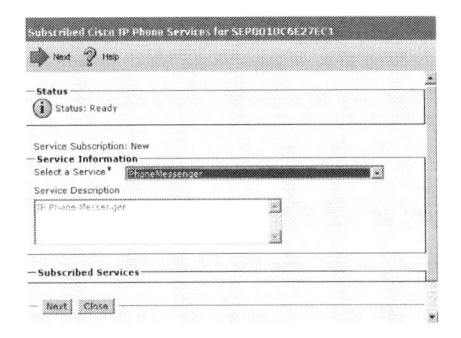

4.6 Click "Subscribe".

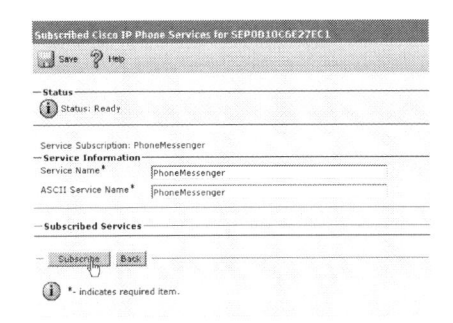

4.7 Notice IP Phone Messenger service shows up under "Subscribed Services". You may close this window.

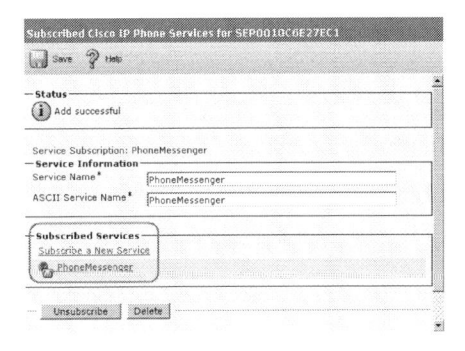

4.8 Repeat steps above for each phone you want to enable IPPM service.

Step 5: Configure IPPM on CUPS

5.1 Go to CUPS Admin > Application > IP Phone Messenger > Settings.

5.2 Set "IPPM Application Status" to "On".
5.3 In "Application Username" and "Password", enter the application username you created in step 1.
5.4 Save

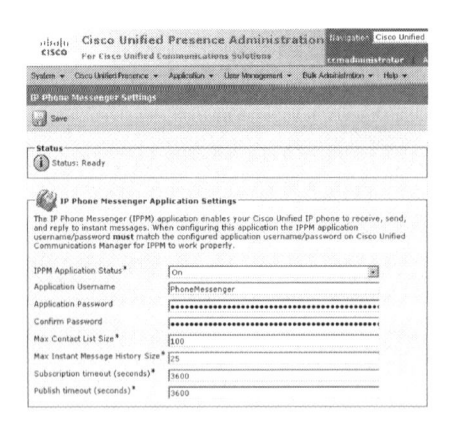

Test

1. Press "Service" button on IP phone.
2. Select "IP Phone Messenger" from service list.
3. Enter user ID (e.g. user1) and PIN number.
4. From a computer, log in to CUPC with a different user ID (e.g. user2).
5. In CUPC search for user1 and add him to contact list. User1's status should be "Available".
6. In CUPC send an instant message to user2.
7. Observe the message shows up on IP phone.

Troubleshooting

Best Practices

Before troubleshooting IPPM, make sure CUPC presence and instant message feature works fine. If not, troubleshoot those features first.

No visual or audio alerts on phone when message arrives

This was because phones were not associated with IPPM application user.

IPPM logs

There's no dedicated log for IPPM feature. You may turn on the IPPM option in SIP Proxy log. That would give us information to troubleshoot IPPM issue.

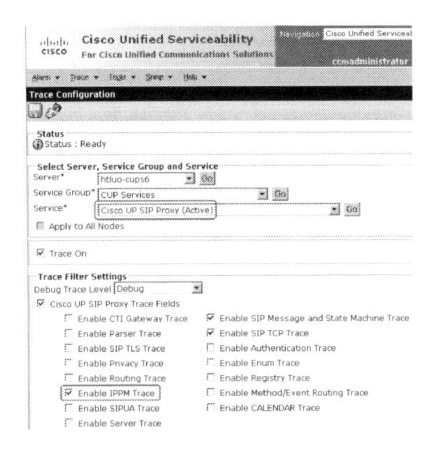

Web Conference

Prerequisites

1. You have MeetingPlace deployed.
2. You can log into CUPC.
3. You have CUPC LDAP feature deployed.

Best Practices

Web Conference here refers to Cisco MeetingPlace. Please test MeetingPlace features/functions before you integrate it with CUPC.

Step 1: CUPS: Configure Conferencing server

1.1 Go to CUPS Admin > Application > Cisco Unified Personal Communicator > Conference Server
1.2 Click "Add New"
1.3 In "Name" field, enter a name you like.
1.4 In "Hostname/IP Address" field, enter the address of your web conference server.
1.5 In "Port" and "Protocol" field, choose the right port and protocol for your web conference server. Contact your web conference engineer for details.

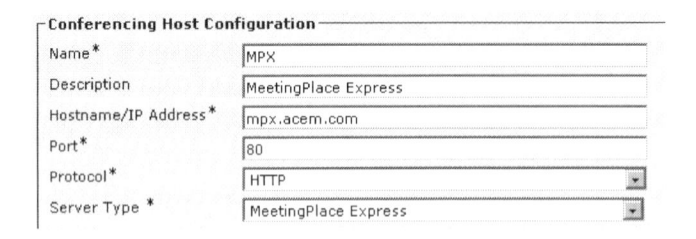

Step 2: CUPS: Configure Conferencing Profile and assign users to it

2.1 Go to CUPS Admin > Application > Cisco Unified Personal Communicator > Conferencing Profile
2.2 Click "Add New"
2.3 In "Name" field, enter a name you like.
2.4 In "Primary Conferencing Server" field, choose the server you configured on step 1.
2.5 Click "Add Users to Profile".
2.6 In the pop-up window, search for the users you want to assign. Select users. Click "Save Selected".

Step 3: CUPC: Configure MeetingPlace credential

Web Conference 217

3.1 Log in to CUPC
3.2 Go to "File > Preferences > Accounts"
3.3 Enter the username and password to access your web conference server.

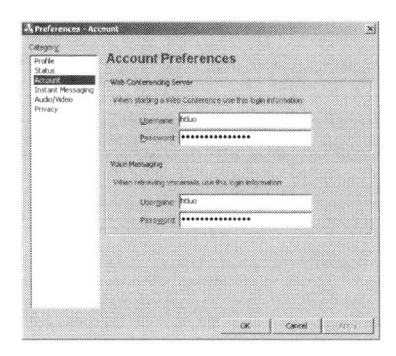

Test

1. Get user1 and user2 logged in to CUPC.
2. User1 calls user2. Call is connected.
3. In the conversation window, click "Start Web Conference" button.
4. Observe MeetingPlace launched on user1's computer and user2's computer.

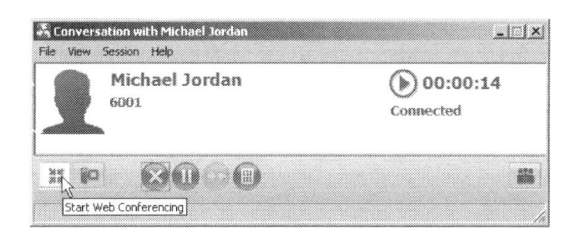

Troubleshooting

Please note, we will only cover the CUPC "integration" part in this book. For MeetingPlace issues themselves, please refer to MeetingPlace troubleshooting guides.

Before troubleshooting CUPC, please test MeetingPlace feature from the same PC. If MeetingPlace feature works fine, continue to troubleshoot CUPC.

CUPC does not launch MP automatically

When you're on a call, you may use CUPC to escalate the voice call to a web conference call. Ideally, CUPC should launch MeetinPlace on both ends. However, CUPC failed to do the job. You have to copy/paste the MeetingPlace URL to the other party.

This kind of problem is usually caused by directory lookup. In order to launch MeetingPlace on the other end, CUPC has to know the other party's user ID. CUPC looks up the directory (LDAP) by the phone number and tries to find the user ID. If the phone number in the call doesn't match with any number configured in LDAP, directory lookup would fail.

Please refer to "LDAP" and "Application Dial Rules" for details.

Password issue

You can log into MeetingPlace from web browser but not from CUPC. So it looks like a CUPC issue. Well, yes and no. This problem happens when the password is longer than 11 characters.

The reason was: MeetingPlace only takes maximum of 11 characters as password. On the web, it seems like you could enter a password longer than 11 characters (e.g. "ciscocisco12"). But MeetingPlace actually takes the first 11 characters (ie. "ciscocisco1").

If you configured "ciscocisco12" in CUPC, CUPC will try to authenticate with MeetingPlace with the full 12 characters. Unfortunately, MeetingPlace didn't trim the password in the scenario. Hence the authentication failed.

Before Cisco can make enhancement on CUPC or MeetingPlace, you'd better use passwords shorter than 12 characters.

For more MeetingPlace troubleshooting tips, please see CUPC troubleshooting guide at: http://www.cisco.com/en/US/docs/voice_ip_comm/cupc/7_0/english/troubleshooting/guide/trouble.html#wp1043866

OCS/LCS/MOC integration

You may integrate CUPS with Microsoft OCS (Office Communication Server). For CUPS 6.0.x, the only integration supported is MOC RCC (Microsoft Office Communicator Remote Call Control). Basically, it allows MOC to control the hard phone (Cisco 79xx IP phones).

Prerequisites

1. OCS/MOC has been deployed successfully
2. CUPC Desk Phone feature has been deployed successfully*

CUPC Desk Phone feature is actually NOT required in OCS integration. But it will validate lots of configuration on CUCM side (such as CTIManager, device association, etc.). So it's recommended you deploy/test CUPC desk phone feature first.

Once CUPC desk phone feature was proven to work, you may exit CUPC. It's NOT recommended that you use MOC and CUPC control the same phone at the same time. The phone might get confused and not function as expected.

Best Practices

1. Deploy CUPC desk phone feature first even though you don't plan to use it. This will validate lots of configuration on CUCM and CUPS and makes our integration easier.
2. Use IP address as much as possible. This can eliminate many issues caused by DNS.
3. Use TCP instead of TLS during initial deployment and test.
4. On MOC, use "manual configuration" instead of "automatic configuration" during testing.
5. Make sure same end user ID is used in AD and CUCM.
6. If possible, get rid of load-balancer in troubleshooting. One less piece, one less problem.
7. Use only one CTI gateway (CTIManger) during test.

Step 1: CUCM: End User Provisioning

Device association would tell CUCM which user is in control of which device(s).

220 Chapter 5. Deploying and Troubleshooting Features

1.1 Go to CUCM Admin > User Management > End User.
1.2 Find the user you want to provision and click on the search result. You will go to user configuration page.
1.3 Click "Device Association". Find the phone device (desk phone) you want MOC control. Choose it and click "Save selected". You'll see the phone device shows up on "Controlled Devices" list.

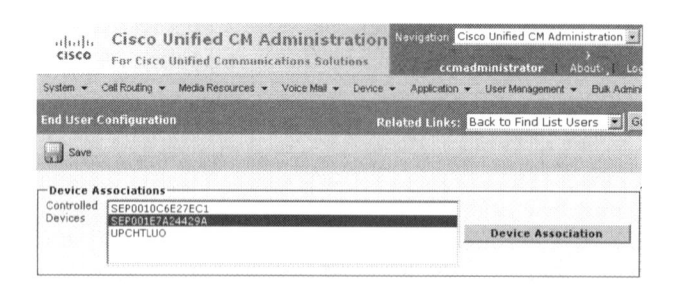

Step 2: CUCM: Application User Provisioning

2.1 Go to CUCM Admin > User Management > Application User.
2.2 Click "Add New"
2.3 Create a new user. Add this user to "Standard CTI Enabled" group and "Standard CTI Allow Control of All Devices" group.

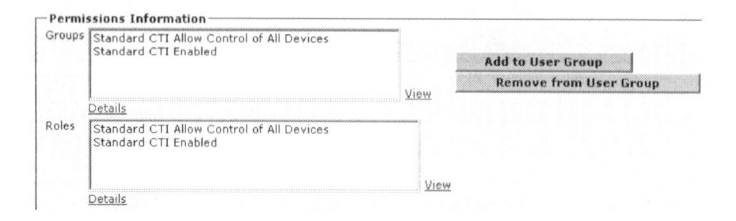

Step 3: CUPS: Configure "Deskphone Control"

3.1 Go to CUPS Admin > Application > Deskphone Control > Settings.
3.2 Set "Application Status" to "On".
3.3 In "Application Username", enter the application user you created in step 2.
3.4 In "Application Password" and "Confirm Password" field, enter the password you configured in step 2.

OCS/LCS/MOC integration

3.5 In "Cisco Unified Communication Manager" field, enter the IP address of CUCM (with CTIManager service running)
3.6 Save

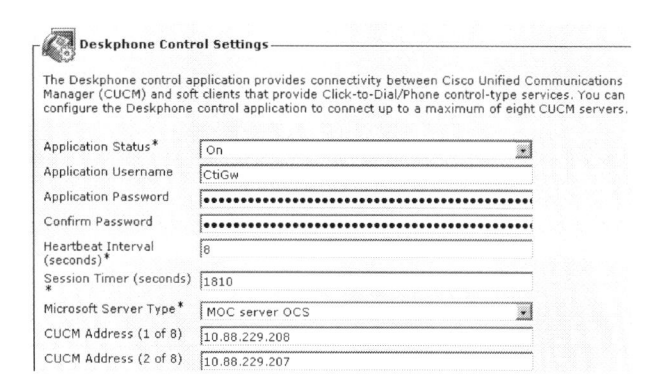

Step 4: CUPS: User assignment

4.1 Go to CUPS Admin > Application > Deskphone Control > User Assignment.
4.2 Find the user you want to configure.
4.3 Click on the search result and enable MOC for the user.

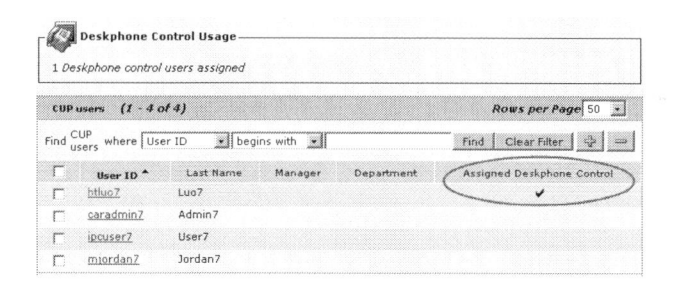

Step 5: CUPS: Incoming and Outgoing ACLs

5.1 Go to CUPS Admin > System > Security > Incoming ACL
5.2 Click "Add New"
5.3 Add a rule with address pattern "ALL"
5.4 Go to CUPS Admin > System > Security > Outgoing ACL
5.5 Click "Add New"
5.6 Add a rule with address pattern "ALL"

Note:

222 Chapter 5. Deploying and Troubleshooting Features

1. You may add the IP address of OCS as address pattern for tighter control.
2. Incoming ACL also affect digest authentication for CUPC presence feature. See "client status" section before for details.

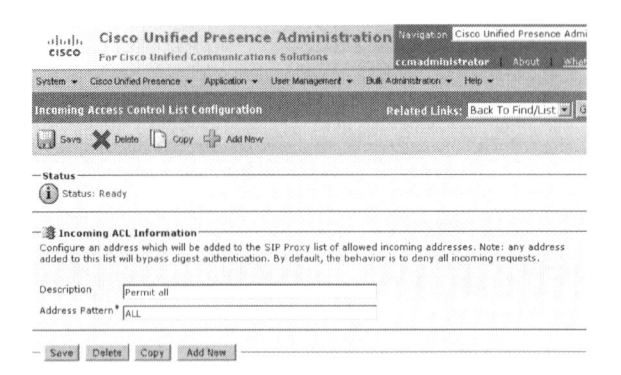

Step 6: OCS: Static Route and Host Authorization

6.1 Open "Microsoft Office Communication Server Management Console"
6.2 Expand your forest > Enterprise pools > your pool. Right-click "Front Ends". Go to "Properties".
6.3 Go to "Routing" tab and click "Add". "Add Static Route" window pops up.
6.4 In "Domain" field, enter something* (see notes below)
6.5 In "IP Address" field, enter the IP address of CUPS server. Click "OK".

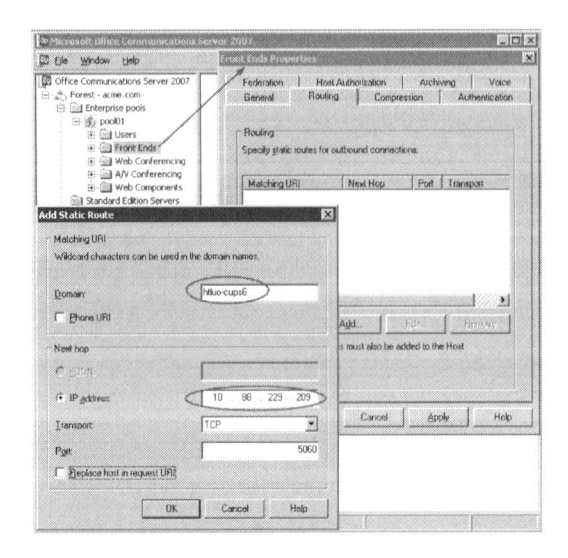

6.6 Go to "Host Authorization" tab.
6.7 Add the IP address of CUPS to the list.

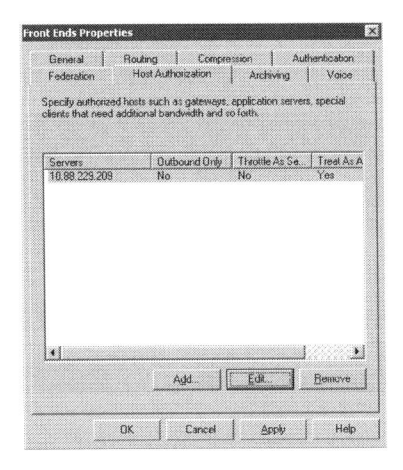

Notes:

In step 6.4, "something" can be one of the following (and nothing else):

- CUPS hostname (such as htluo-cups6).
- CUPS SIP domain (such as acme.com).
- CUPS hostname plus CUPS SIP domain (such as htluo-cups.acme.com)

Hostname and SIP domain above was configured on CUPS. The name/domain does NOT have to be configured in DNS (You could configure them in DNS if you want to. But it's not necessary.)

If you don't have preference, I'd recommend you use CUPS hostname. So you have more flexibility on SIP domain. SIP domain plays a critical role in SIP routing, especially when SRV records were used. If you don't understand that SRV record is, don't worry. Just use CUPS hostname.

Step 7: Active Directory: Server URI and Line URI

7.1 Open "Active Directory Users and Computers" (ADUC)
7.2 Open the properties of the user you want to configure. Go to "Communication" tab.
7.3 Click "Configure" in "Additional options"

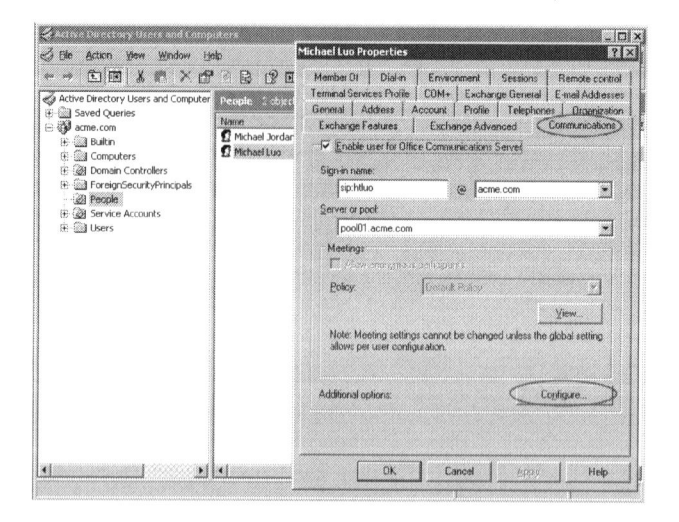

224 Chapter 5. Deploying and Troubleshooting Features

7.4 On "User Options" window, select "Enable Remote call control".
7.5 In "Server URI" field, enter "`sip:xxxx@something`". "xxxx" is the directory number of the user's phone. "something" is the value you configured in step 6.4. For example: `sip:6002@htluo-cups6`
7.6 In "Line URI" field, enter "`tel:xxxx;phone-context=dialstring;device=YYYY`". "xxxx" is the directory number of the user's phone. "YYYY" is the device name of the phone. For example: `tel:6002;phone-context=dialstring;device=SEP001E7A24429A`

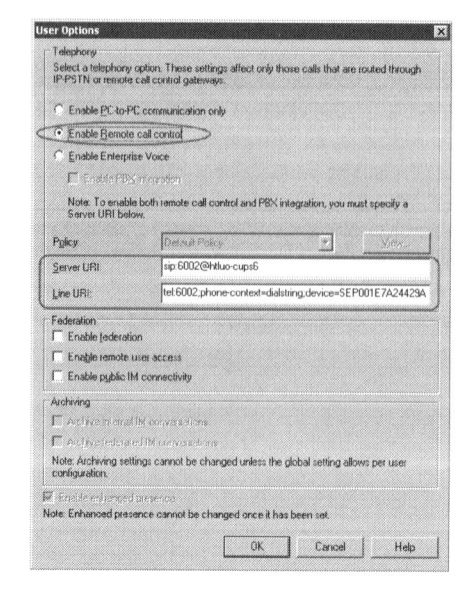

Line URI is a very important configuration in this integration. Line URI must *uniquely* indentify a line appearance of CUCM. Otherwise, integration won't work.

What does mean "uniquely"?

Scenario 1: Shared-line across multiple devices.

If you have the same directory number (DN) configured on multiple phones (devices), it is called a "shared line".

In this scenario, you should specify device in line URI:
```
tel:6002;phone-context=dialstring;device=SEP001E7A24429A
```

Scenario 2: Shared-line across multiple partitions.

If you have the same directory number (DN) configured on multiple partitions, it is still considered as a "shared line" (even if there's only one device in the picture).

For example, on the same phone, you have two lines:
Line 1: 6002 in partition "Part_A"
Line 2: 6002 in partition "Part_B"

In this scenario, you should specify partition in line URI:
```
tel:6002;phone-context=dialstring;device=SEP001E7A24429A;partition=Part_A
```

Phone Selection Plug-in

If you have shared line across multiple devices or partition, you might want make the selection on the fly instead of hard-coding it in Active Directory line URI.

If that's the case, you need to install a Cisco plug-in on MOC. This plug-in gives you the GUI to choose which line to control.

This plug-in can be downloaded from CCO > Cisco Unified Presence section. In later version of CUPS, it can also be downloaded from CUPS Admin > Application > Plug-ins menu.

226 Chapter 5. Deploying and Troubleshooting Features

Please note that you cannot just double-click to install the plug-in. To correctly install the plug-in, you'll have to supply some command parameters.

```
msiexec /I Cisco_MOC_RCC_Plug-in.msi CUPFQDN=your-cup-fqdn
```

"Cisco_MOC_RCC_Plug-in.msi" is the plug-in name. Substitute "your-cup-fqdn" with the actual fully qualified DNS name of your CUPS server.

For more details, please see URL:
http://docwiki.cisco.com/wiki/Cisco_Unified_Presence%2C_Release_7.x_--_How_to_Deploy_the_Phone_Selection_Plug-in

Test

1. Log in to MOC.
2. Enter an internal directory number and dial.
3. Observe the desk phone (Cisco IP phone) dials out the number.

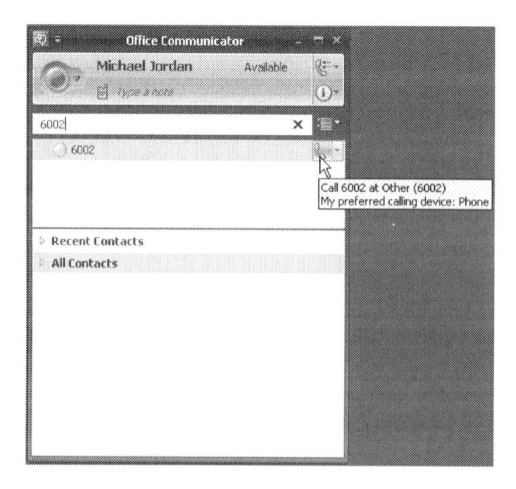

Troubleshooting

Simplify the integration

Troubleshooting integration problems is usually difficult because of too many components and interactions. The best approach is to keep things as simple as possible. As mentioned in "best practices", here's something we can do to simplify the integration. I'm not saying you have to sacrifice features to get integration done. But in troubleshooting process, you want to make it as simple as possible. After the integration is done, you may add features back, one by one. If a feature broke the integration, you would have a smaller area to look at.

- Use IP address instead of DNS name.
- Use TCP instead of TLS.
- For MOC, use manual configuration instead of automatic configuration.
- Use only one CTI gateway (CUCM).
- Avoid using shared line on multiple devices (phones)
- Avoid using traffic load balancer

Divide and conquer

Remember there are multiple segments between MOC and phone. The data flow is like below:

```
MOC -> OCS -> CUPS -> CUCM -> Phone.
```

Do not assume the problem's location. Troubleshoot the problem from the source (MOC) to destination (phone).

MOC -> OCS

Your MS engineer should have taken care of this. It is one of the "prerequisites" of CUPS/OCS integration. Normally, you don't have to troubleshoot this segment. But if you're interested, here's the MOC logging for your information.

To turn on MOC logging, go to MOC options > General > enable "Turn on logging in Communicator".

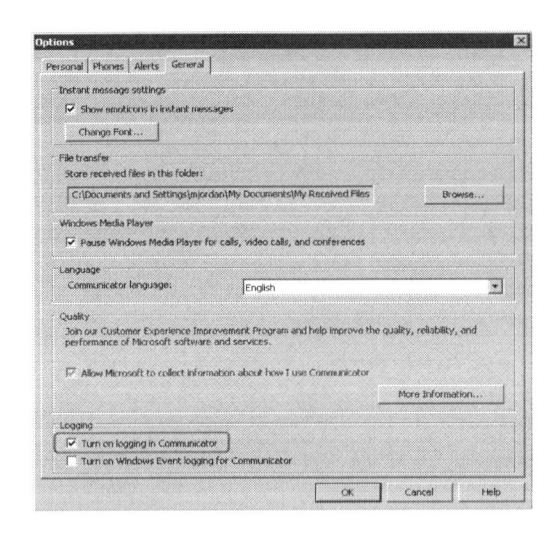

228 Chapter 5. Deploying and Troubleshooting Features

MOC log files are in C:\Documents and Settings\<*user_id*>\Tracing

You may also use OCS log analyzer to troubleshoot problems between MOC and OCS (see following section). Keep in mind that any problems between MOC and OCS should be the job of a MS engineer, which is NOT discussed in this book.

OCS -> CUPS

To troubleshoot the problem between OCS and CUPS, we can either look at OCS logs or CUPS logs.

Rule of thumb
If you know how to read OCS logs and CUP logs, that's fine. If not, you may search for the keyword "CSTA" in CUP SIP proxy logs. If you couldn't find "CSTA" in CUPS SIP proxy log, OCS wasn't configured properly and failed to send messages to CUPS. You should ask help from MS instead of Cisco.

OCS logs

1. Open "Microsoft Office Communicator Server" management interface (MMC) > Expand your forest > Expand "Enterprise Pools" > Right click your pool > Logging Tool > New Debug Session.

OCS/LCS/MOC integration 229

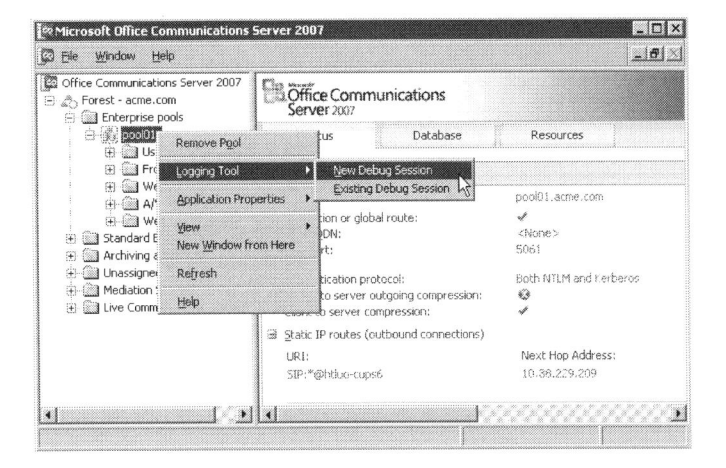

2. On the "Components" list, choose "SIPStack". Click "Start Logging"

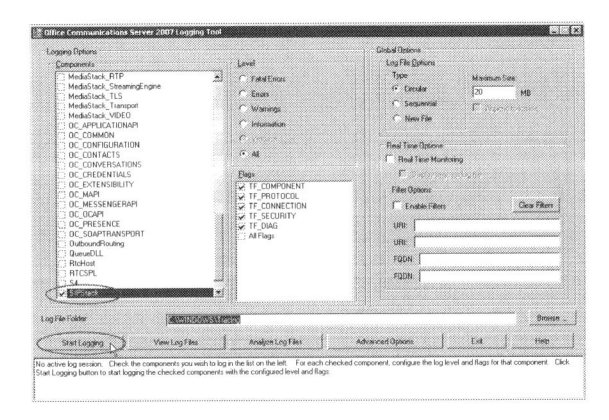

3. Start MOC (client) and wait until you see the error. Click "Stop Logging" > Click "Analyze Log Files" > Click "Analyze".

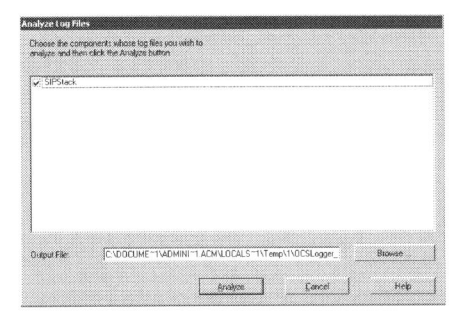

Below is the analysis result window.

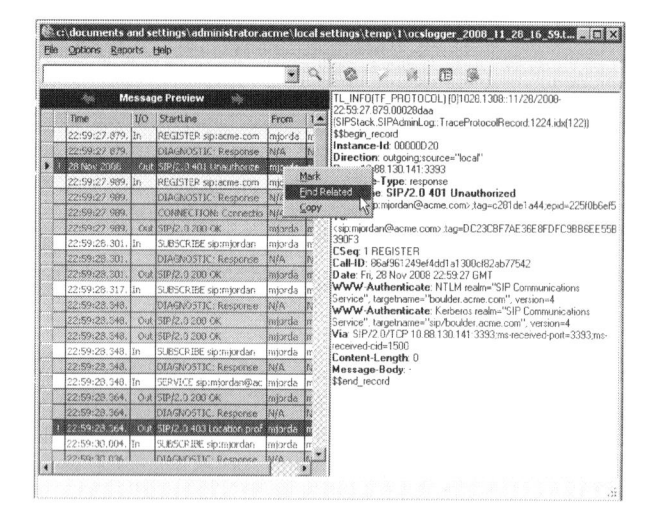

[Screenshot of OCS Logger message preview window]

Pay attention to those messages in red. You should be able to identify where the message originated from. You may right-click on one of the messages and "Find Related". It'll show you the dialogs related to that message.

Frequently Seen Errors

"482 Loop Detected"

This is usually caused by proxy domain or DNS setup. When SIP proxy receives a request, it'll check the SIP domain in the URI. If the SIP domain in the URI does not match proxy's alias name (hostname, SIP domain or hostname.sip_domain), proxy will try to route the request again, thus cause a loop.

"401 Unauthorized"

Check CUPS Incoming/Outgoing ACLs. Check OCS "Host Authorization".

Logs:
1. CUPS SIP Proxy logs (with CTIGW option turned on)
2. OCS SIP Stack logs

CUPS -> CUCM/Phone

Problems between CUPS and CUCM are usually CTI related. Here's a check list:

1. Do you have an application user on CUCM for this integration (CtiGw)?
2. Was it the same username/password you configured on CUPS side (case-sensitive)?
3. Is the application user in "Standard CTI Enabled" and "Standard CTI Allow Control of All Devices" group?
4. Has the phone device been associated with the end user (on end user configuration page)?
5. Is the phone currently registered to CUCM?
6. Does the phone allow CTI control (on device configuration page).

Logs:
1. CUPS SIP Proxy logs (with CTIGW option turned on)
2. CUCM CTIManager logs (at detailed level)

Sametime Integration

Sametime is the Instant Messaging solution from IBM Lotus. Sametime consists of Sametime server and Sametime client.

When Sametime is integrated with CUPS/CUCM, it provides phone control and phone presence information on Sametime client. So you may control your desk phone and see your buddies' phone status.

Cisco offers two kinds of integration: server integration and client integration. You may use either one. Using both is technically possible but not recommended.

There are pros and cons for each integration model. For details please see documentations on Cisco web site.

In my humble opinion, I would recommend client integration for the following reasons:

1. You don't have to make any changes on Sametime server, which usually requires an official change management.
2. You don't need a Sametime administrator while you're testing the deployment. Because of #1.

232 Chapter 5. Deploying and Troubleshooting Features

3. People are more willing to test out the solution because of #1 and #2.

We will only discuss client integration in this book.

Client integration with Sametime is usually referred as "**PCAP**" (Phone Control and Presence). For now, PCAP only works on Windows platform.

There are two types of Sametime clients:

- Standalone client – Lotus Sametime Connect
- Integrated client – Lotus Notes

Below are the screenshots of Standalone client and integrated client.

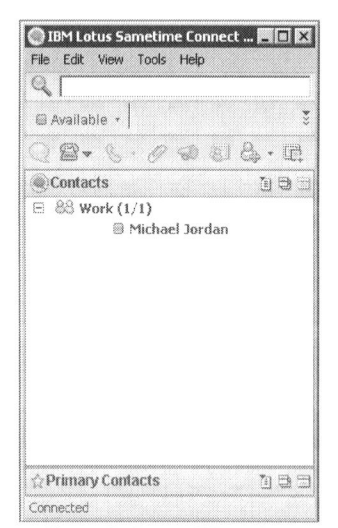

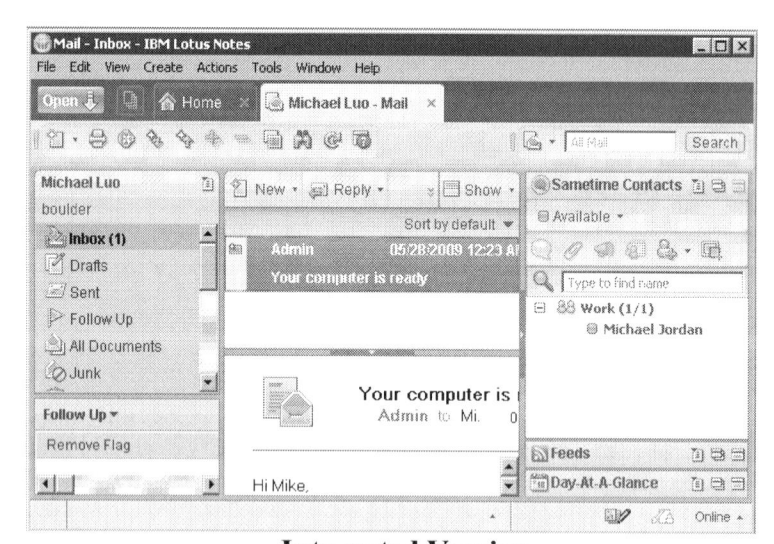

Standalone Version   **Integrated Version**

Integration procedures are pretty much the same for both types of clients.

Prerequisites

1. CUPC Desk Phone feature has been deployed successfully
2. CUPC Phone Presence has been deployed successfully

Best Practices

Though most of Sametime users don't need CUPC at all, it's recommended you use CUPC as testing tool. If you can get CUPC worked but not Sametime, you know the problem is not on CUPS. You may narrow down the troubleshooting on Sametime client.

PCAP is a plug-in installed on Sametime client. PCAP works like a "mini-CUPC". Most of the terms and concepts also apply to PCAP.

PCAP plug-in is a client-side plug-in. It was designed in such a way that you'll have to configure it first, install later. If you want to change the configuration, you need to reconfigure and reinstall.

Because of this, we'll discuss configuration first, installation later.

Configuration

PCAP configuration consists of two parts: **pre-install** configuration and **post-install** configuration.

Pre-install configuration defines system-wide parameters, such as CUCM server, CUPS server, LDAP server, etc. Pre-install configuration is done by running CiscoCfg.exe. If you'd like to change system-wide parameters after install, you need to re-run CiscoCfg.exe and re-install the plug-in.

Post-install configuration defines user-specific parameters, such as user ID/password and phone device selection. Post-install configuration is done by going to Sametime client > File > Preferences > Cisco > Phone.

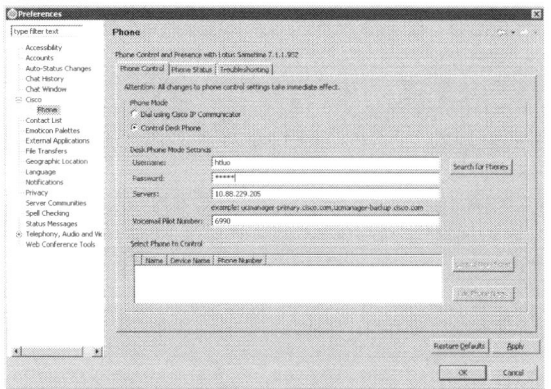

234 Chapter 5. Deploying and Troubleshooting Features

Some of the system-wide parameters may or may not be changed in post-install configuration, depending on pre-install parameters.

Pre-Install Configuration

Feature Control

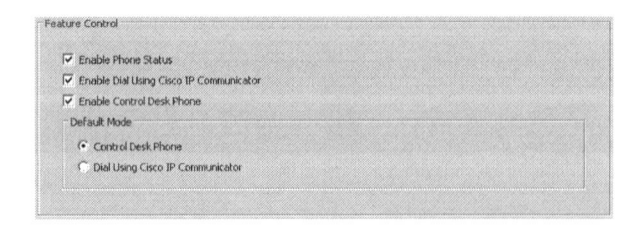

Enable Phone Status – So you can see your contact's phone status from Sametime (off-hook / on-hook).

Enable Dial Using Cisco IP Communicator – PCAP differentiates IP Communicator from 79xx IP phones. If you'd like to use IP Communicator, you need to select this option.

Enable Control Desk Phone – Allow user control 79xx IP phones.

Default Mode – If you have 79xx IP phone and IP Communicator, this option determine which device take precedence.

Control Desk Phone Settings

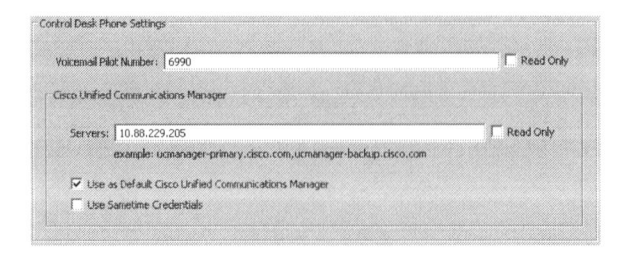

Voicemail Pilot Number – Voicemail pilot number of CUCM. When you click "Send to Voicemail" from Sametime, PCAP would send the call to this number.

Servers – Comma separated CTIManager servers (CUCM server running CTIManager service). PCAP talks to those server as a CTI client to control desk phones.

Use Sametime Credentials – Use Sametime login ID/password to authenticate with CTIManager (for phone control).

If you choose this option, you don't have to configure username/password in Post-Install configuration. But you have to make sure user ID and password match between two systems. This option is usually chosen when both Sametime and CUCM are synchronized to the same LDAP system (e.g. Active Directory). If you're not sure, don't choose this option.

Read Only – "Read Only" option prevent the parameter from being changed in Post-Install configuration. This is for security and supportability purpose.

LDAP Phone Attributes

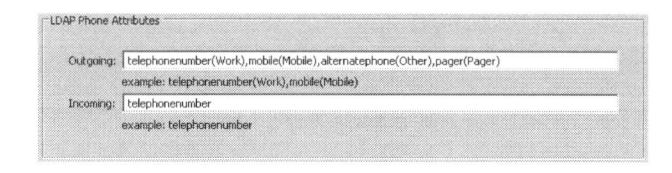

This is to tell PCAP which LDAP attribute to use for phone number related actions.

For example, when you try to dial a contact's 'Work' number, PCAP will use the "telephonenumber" attribute in LDAP for outgoing calls.

When receiving an incoming call, PCAP will use "telephonenumber" attribute in LDAP to look up the FirstName and LastName to display on the screen.

Phone Status Settings

236 Chapter 5. Deploying and Troubleshooting Features

[Screenshot of Phone Status Settings dialog showing Cisco Unified Presence Servers field with 10.88.229.209, Use Sametime Credentials checkbox, Sametime User ID Mapping options (Use LDAP Attribute, Use Business Card Attribute: MailAddress, Remove Domain), and Display Off-Hook Status Only checkbox.]

Cisco Unified Presence Server – The address of CUPS server.

Use Sametime Credentials – Use Sametime login ID/password to authenticate with CUPS (for presence).

If you choose this option, you don't have to configure username/password in Post-Install configuration. But you have to make sure user ID and password match between two systems. This option is usually chosen when both Sametime and CUPS are synchronized to the same LDAP system (e.g. Active Directory). If you're not sure, don't choose this option.

Sametime User ID Mapping – Tells PCAP how to map a Sametime User ID to a CUPS user ID.

This is a very interesting topic and is the most confusing part of PCAP. We'll discuss it in detail later.

If you do not have preferences, I'd recommend you choose "Use Business Card Attribute – MailAddress" and select "Remove Domain". Then you have to make sure the user ID part of the mail address in Sametime business card matches with CUPS user ID. For example, if CUPS user ID is johndoe, you need to make sure the mail address in Sametime business card is johndoe@domain.com. (In Sametime, it is called "Internet Address")

Display Off-Hook Status Only – If this option is checked, PCAP will only display the handset icon next to the contact when the contact is on the phone.

If this option is not selected, PCAP will display (different) icons on Sametime client to reflect different phone status. Some customers prefer this because it'll tell them if phone presence is being received or not. Below is a screenshot when this option was selected.

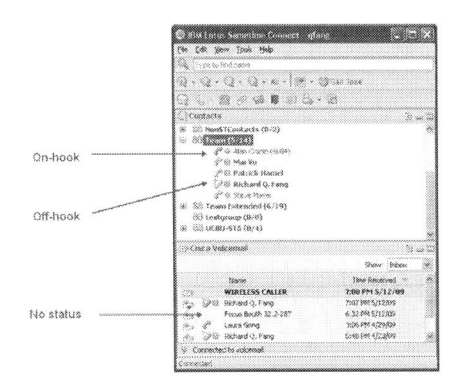

Sametime Client Version and Logging

This is to choose the Sametime client version and logging level. Please note: If you're using Notes (integrated Sametime), you need to choose "Sametime 8.x or Notes 8.x".

Directory Server Settings

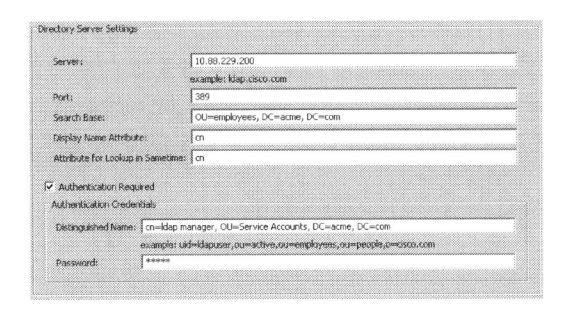

This is to configure LDAP related features. The most frequently asked question is "is this required or optional?" The answer is: "it depends". But most likely you'll need it.

LDAP is used for the following functions:
1) Look up phone numbers by user ID.
2) Look up first name, last name by phone number (reverse lookup)

3) Correlate a CUPS user ID with a Sametime contact ID (in some scenarios)

Without LDAP, the above functions won't work.

Directory Usage

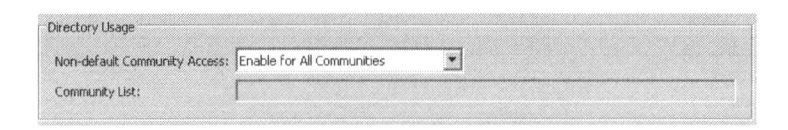

Unless you have more than one community in Sametime and you want to limit some communities from using LDAP, you may choose "Enable for All Communities".

Dialing Rules Files

PCAP use XML files to store dialing rules. You may find sample files in the "template" folder. For more information on "dialing rules" see previous chapters in this book.

*Directory Type**

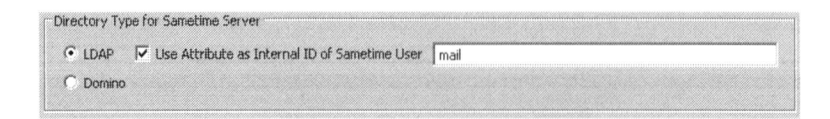

This is not something you can configure at will. This is actually a reflection of the directory configuration on Sametime server.

Due to technical limitation, PCAP was not able to retrieve this information automatically. PCAP relies on you to retrieve that information and put the information here. For detailed instructions to retrieve this information, please contact your Sametime server engineer or refer to Sametime server documentations.

Obviously, if you gave the wrong information, PCAP won't function properly. So don't guess!

User ID mapping

Sametime is an Instant-Messaging system by IBM Lotus. CUPS is a presence system by Cisco. Each of them has its own user database. They also have different syntax to identify users. For example, a person "John Doe" may be identified as "uid=jdoe, o=employees, o=acme" on Sametime. The same person was identified as "jdoe" on CUPS. PCAP won't be able to correlate those two persons unless we tell it the mapping rules.

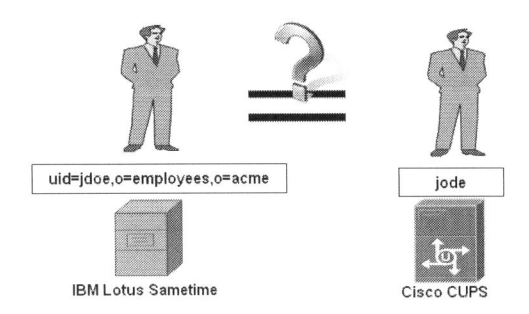

Terminologies:

Contact ID - also being referred to as the "Sametime Internal User ID", uniquely identifies Sametime users.

Contact ID could be in different formats depending on Sametime directory settings.

When directory type is Domino,
    - "Contact ID" would be in the format of "cn=John Doe/ou=people/o=acme"

When directory type is LDAP (Active Directory, Open LDAP, etc.),
    - "Contact ID" could be any attribute in LDAP (depending on Sametime Server directory settings)
        - It could be Distinguished Name (DN): uid=jdoe,ou=people,o=acme.com
        - It could be any LDAP attribute, such as email: jdoe@acme.com

How to find out a user's contact ID?

240 Chapter 5. Deploying and Troubleshooting Features

1. Hover the mouse over a contact, the "Business Card" will pop up
2. Hover the mouse over the name in the business card, a tool tip window will pop up.
3. You may find the contact ID in the tool tip window.

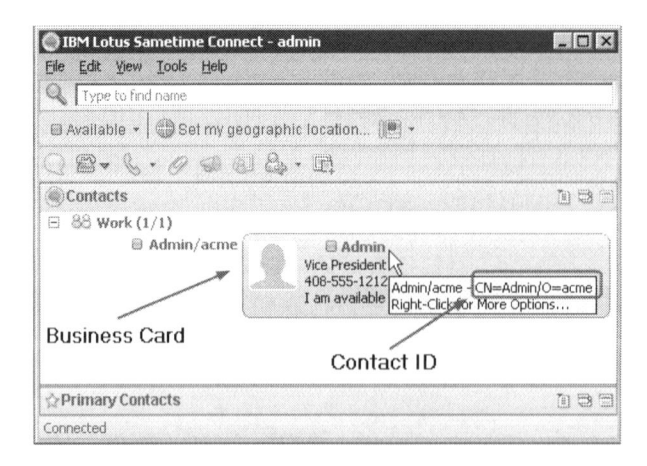

In the example above, the "Contact ID" is "CN=Admin/O=acme".

Business Card – A subset of directory attributes (such as telephone, email address, etc.) that will be displayed in the chat window and in the contact list.

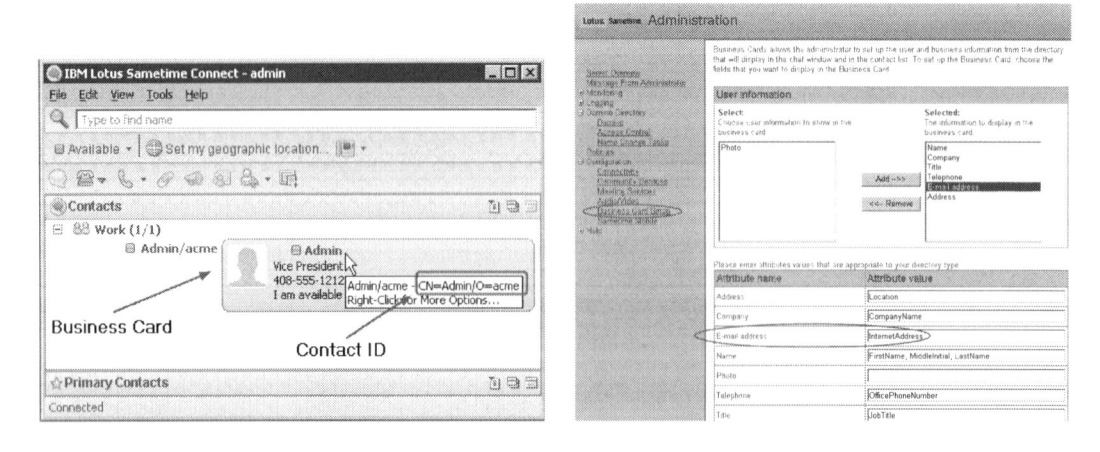

On Sametime server, you may decide what attributes to be displayed on business card.

Internet Address – A Sametime directory attribute that presents email address in SMTP format (e.g. user@domain.com).

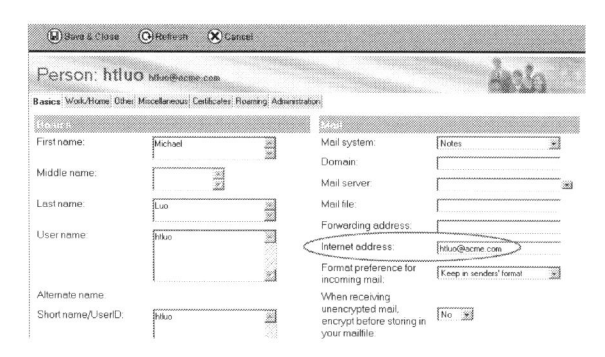

Note: In Sametime Business Card setup, "E-mail address" is by default referred to "Internet Address".

User ID – We are referring to CUPS user ID (also known as CUCM user ID, because CUPS synchronizes user database from CUCM).

ID Mapping Scenarios

The goal of user ID mapping is "*to correlate a CUPS user ID to a Sametime contact ID*".

This is done by the "Sametime User ID Mapping" configuration (configured with CiscoCfg.exe). See screenshot below:

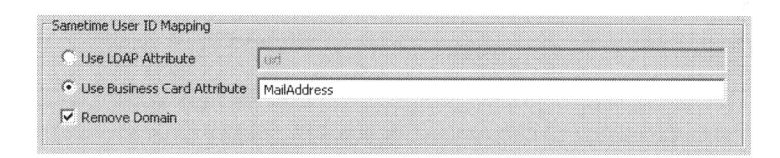

There are two options – "Use LDAP Attribute" or "Use Business Card* Attribute".

* For the concept of "Business Card", please see "terminologies" above.

For each option, you may specify an "attribute". PCAP will use this attribute to correlate user ID to contact ID.

For those attributes that have a value in "user@domain" format, you may choose the "Remove Domain" option to strip the domain part.

Please note "LDAP Attribute" does not necessarily requires a LDAP server (will explain later).

Scenario 1: Contact ID does not contain CUPS user ID. Business Card contains CUPS user ID.

When Sametime server uses Domino directory, contact ID would be usually in the format of "CN=John Doe/OU=Employees/O=Acme".

For CUPS user ID, it is usually in the format of "jdoe".

In this case, Contact ID does not contain CUPS user ID. It's difficult to correlate CUPS user ID to Sametime contact ID directly (ie. difficult to correlate "jdoe" to "CN=John Doe/OU=Employees/O=Acme").

If you're lucky, one of the Business Card attributes might contains the CUPS user ID. Let say, if the "MailAddress" is jdoe@acme.com in Business Card, it contains CUPS user ID "jdoe). You may configure user ID mapping as below.

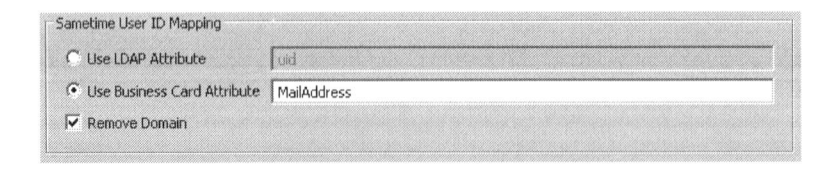

PCAP will extract "MailAddress" from Business Card and remove the domain. PCAP then compare the result with CUPS user ID. If they match, PCAP would think they are referring the same person and populate phone presence on Sametime client.

What if the "MailAddress" is johndoe@acme.com instead of jdoe@acme.com? Then you're out of luck. You have the following options:

   a) Change the "MailAddress" to jdoe@acme.com. This option might not be practical for large organizations.
   b) Use another "Business Card" attribute and populate "jdoe" in it.

c) Use LDAP (see scenario 3 below)

Scenario 2: Contact ID contains CUPS user ID

When Sametime server uses LDAP (such as Active Directory, Open LDAP, etc.) as directory server, Contact ID would be usually in the format of "uid=jdoe, OU=employees, O=acme.com"

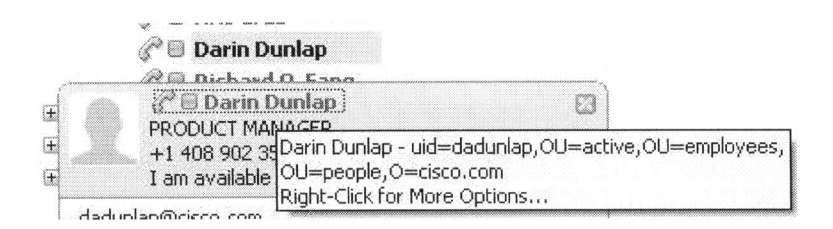

For CUPS user ID, it is usually in the format of "jdoe".

This is an ideal scenario. In this case, Contact ID contains CUPS user ID. You should configure user ID mapping as below:

Don't be fooled by the word "LDAP". No LDAP server is required here for phone presence purpose. Here's the workflow:

1) PCAP will look into Contact ID and find an attribute named "uid" (for example, "uid=jdoe")
2) PCAP will use the value of this attribute ("jdoe" in this example) to compare with CUPS user ID ("jdoe" in this example)
3) If they match, PCAP would think they are referring the same person and populate phone presence on Sametime client.

Scenario 3: Contact ID does not contain CUPS user ID. Business Card does not contain CUPS user ID.

This is the worst case scenario and should be avoided by all means. Because:

1) It has performance impact – a dedicate LDAP query needs to be performed for each contact.
2) It requires the LDAP record contains Contact ID and CUPS user ID (so PCAP can correlate them).

For example, Contact ID is the format of "CN=John Doe, OU=Employees, O=acme.com". CUPS user ID is in the format of "12345" (IP Phone Extension Number).

In this case, Contact ID does not contain the CUPS user ID. Business Card does not contain the CUPS user ID either. You should configure user ID mapping as below:

```
Sametime User ID Mapping
  ● Use LDAP Attribute          ipPhone
  ○ Use Business Card Attribute MailAddress
  □ Remove Domain
```

Please note in this case, a LDAP server needs to be configured in PCAP LDAP tab (CiscoCfg.exe).

PCAP workflow as below:

1) PCAP tried to find "ipPhone" attribute in Contact ID value ("CN=John Doe, OU=Employees, O=acme.com"). PCAP was not able to find an attribute named "ipPhone").
2) Since the attribute was not found in Contact ID, PCAP knows it has to go to LDAP to find it.
3) PCAP contacts LDAP and do a search on "CN=John Doe, OU=Employees, O=acme.com".
4) LDAP returns a record with many attributes (including "ipPhone").
5) PCAP uses the value of "ipPhone" to match CUPS user ID.

Post-Install Configuration

Depending on your pre-install configuration, you might have to do some post-install configuration. For example, if you didn't select "Use Sametime Credentials", you'll need to configure the credential after installing the plug-in.

Sametime Integration

To perform post-install configuration, you need to log into Sametime client and go to File > Preferences > Cisco > Phone.

Phone Control

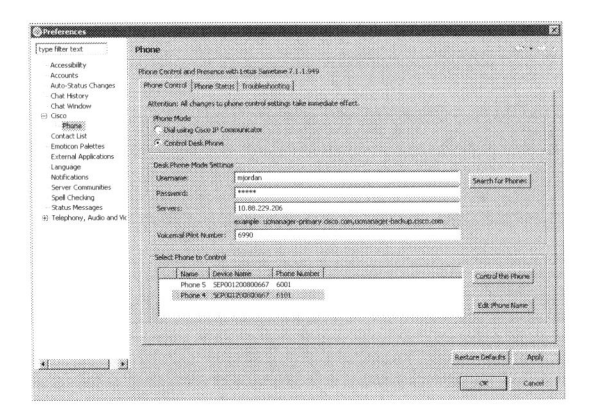

Here you configure CTIManager servers address and credential to authenticate with CTIManager. You may also choose which phone to control (or use IP Communicator).

Phone Status

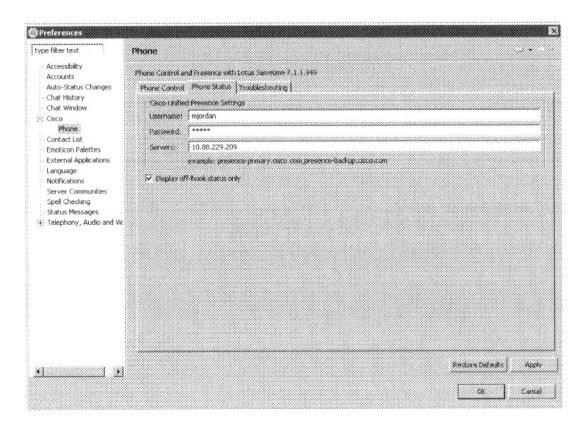

Here you configure presence (CUPS) server address and credential to authenticate with CUPS.

Installation

246 Chapter 5. Deploying and Troubleshooting Features

The installation of PCAP is different with "regular software". For "regular software" (such as CUPC), we double-click the .exe or .msi file to kick off the install. After installation, we launch the software from Windows "Start" menu and configure necessary parameters.

For PCAP, it's an "add-on" on Sametime client. In order to integrate the add-on into Sametime client, we need to follow specific procedures defined by Sametime.

Here's a summary of installation steps:

1. Download PCAP from Cisco website. Description would be like "Cisco Unified Communications with IBM Lotus – *7.1(1)*". File name would be like "*Cisco_Plugins_7.1.1*.zip".

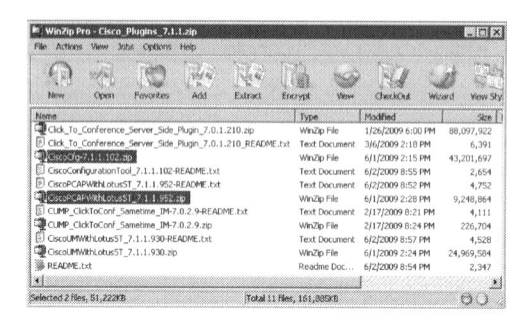

There are a couple files in the zip (for different features). The files we need are:

- **CiscoPCAPWithLotusST**_*7.1.1.952*.zip – Sametime plug-in for phone control and presence.
- **CiscoCfg**-*7.1.1.102*.zip – Configuration tool.

Please note: version numbers would be different when Cisco releases new software.

2. Extract PCAP zip and CiscoCfg zip into two different folders.

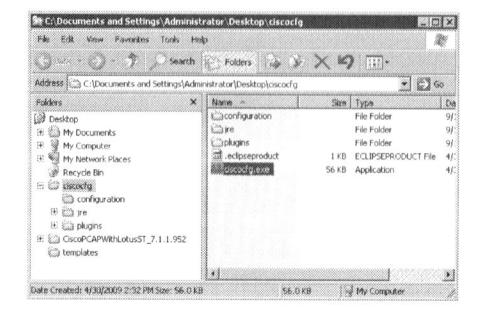

Sametime Integration 247

3. In "CiscoCfg" folder, run ciscocfg.exe. It'll prompt you to select an "Update Site". "Update Site" is an IBM Lotus term. It could be a local folder or a server URL. For simplicity, we'll use local folder in this book.

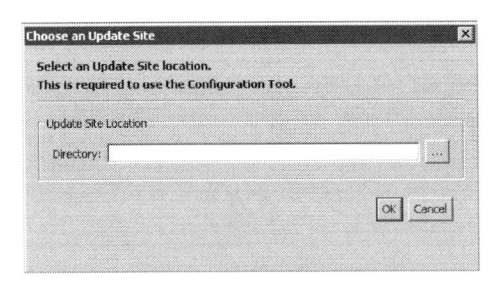

4. Click the "..." (browse) button to choose the "UpdateSite" folder. It's a subfolder in PCAP folder, which you extracted in step 1 above.

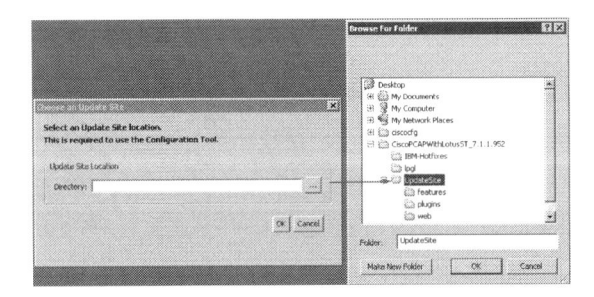

5. After you selected an update site and click OK, CiscoCfg configuration interface will come up.

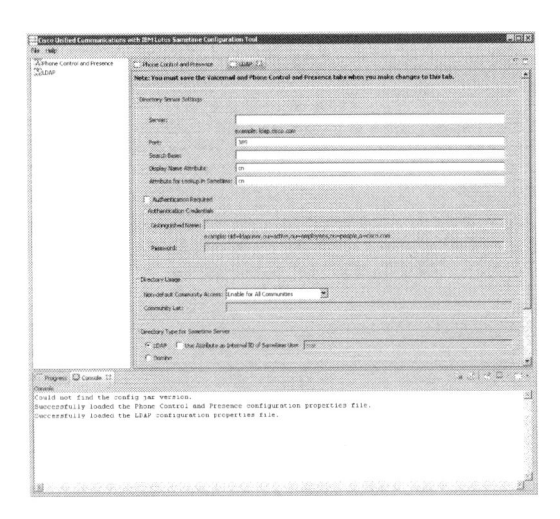

248 Chapter 5. Deploying and Troubleshooting Features

6. Go to "File > Save". You'll notice the messages at the bottom window – "`Phone Control and Presence configuration save completed successfully.`" Now we've got the plug-in configured and ready for install.

7. The installation of plug-in is initiated from Sametime. For standalone Sametime client (Sametime Connect) go to "Tools > Plug-ins". For integrated Sametime client (Lotus Notes), go to "File > Application".

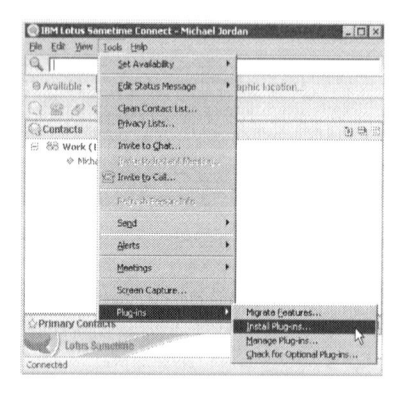

8. From the "Install" window, choose "Add Folder Location…" and select the "UpdateSite" folder we configured in step 4 above. Then click "OK" on "Edit Local Site" pop-up window.

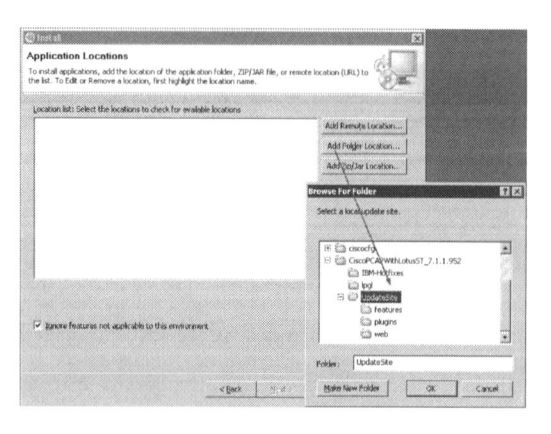

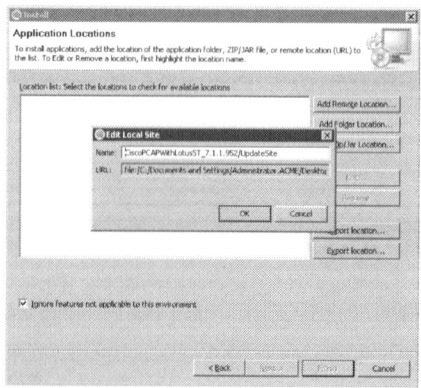

9. Click "Finish" on "Location List" screen. Expand feature set and choose your Sametime version accordingly. If you're not sure, choose both.

Sametime Integration 249

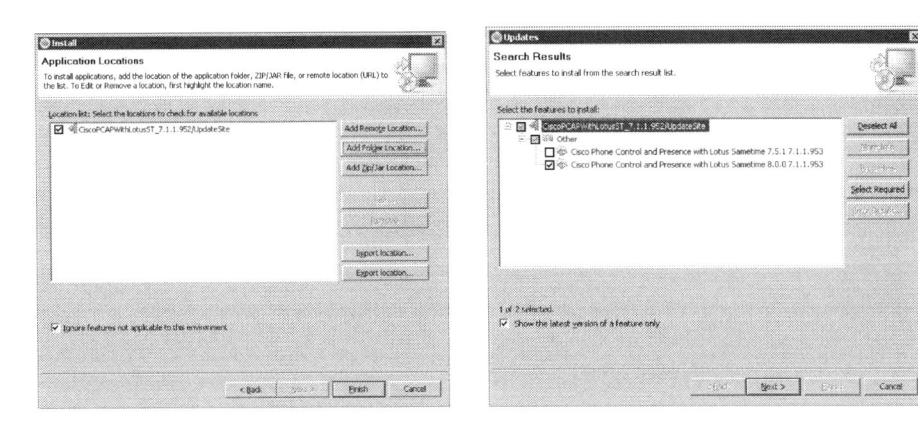

10. Accept license agreement then click "Finish" to start install.

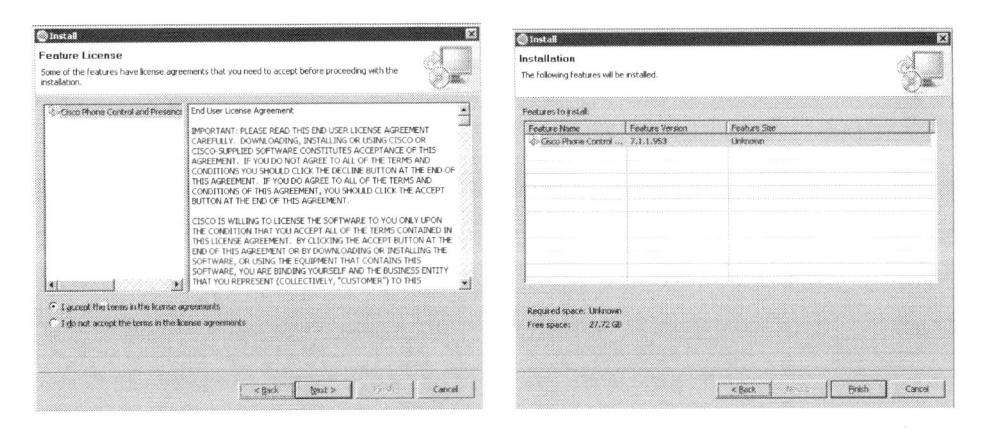

11. Sametime will prompt you to restart after finishing the install.

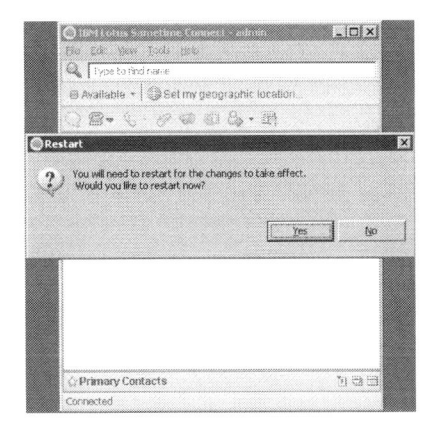

Troubleshooting

In "Troubleshooting" tab, you may see servers status (similar to CUPC "Show Server Health").

You may also "Enable detailed logging" for troubleshooting purpose.

You may also see the location of the logs and "Create Problem Report".

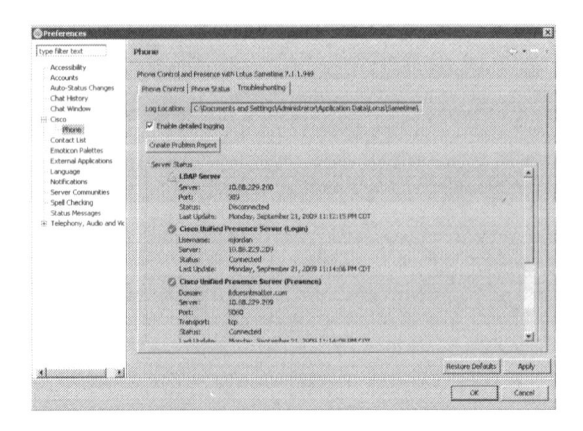

Disable Sametime built-in telephony

In Sametime 8.x and Note 8.x, there's a phone button for built-in telephony (voice chat). This causes confusion with Cisco PCAP. You may disable it from Sametime server. See screenshot below:

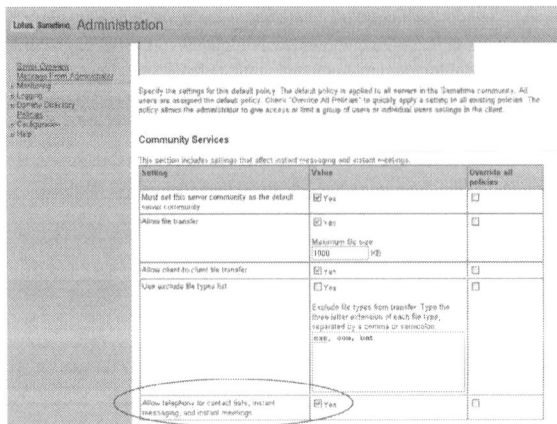

Troubleshooting

Again, CUPC is your best troubleshooting tool. Don't try to troubleshoot PCAP before you get CUPC worked (phone control and presence).

If CUPC works fine but you're having trouble with PCAP (such as no presence), it's most likely user ID mapping issue.

Logging settings

PCAP by default logs messages in XML format. I personally don't like it. Because:

1) It makes the file huge (with useless XML tags).
2) It makes WinGrep result unreadable.

To disable XML formatting, do the following:

For Sametime Connect, edit `C:\Documents and Settings\<userid>\Application Data\Lotus\Sametime\.config\rcpinstall.properties`

For Lotus Notes, edit `C:\Program Files\IBM\Lotus\Notes\Data\workspace\.config\rcpinstall.properties`

Change these two lines:

```
com.ibm.rcp.core.internal.logger.boot.RCPTraceHandler.formatter=com.ibm.rcp.core.internal.logger.cbe.CBE101Formatter
com.ibm.rcp.core.internal.logger.boot.RCPLogHandler.formatter=com.ibm.rcp.core.internal.logger.cbe.CBE101Formatter
```

to:

```
com.ibm.rcp.core.internal.logger.boot.RCPTraceHandler.formatter=com.ibm.rcp.core.internal.logger.boot.RCPFormatter
com.ibm.rcp.core.internal.logger.boot.RCPLogHandler.formatter=com.ibm.rcp.core.internal.logger.boot.RCPFormatter
```

Keywords in Logs

Configurations: *com.cisco.sametime.phone.config.ConfigManager*

General phone (phone menu): *com.cisco.sametime.phone*

Dial Using Cisco IP Communicator mode:
com.cisco.sametime.phonecontrol.CTIPhoneAgent

Control Desk Phone mode: *com.cisco.sametime.phonecontrol*

Phone Status: *com.cisco.sametime.phonestatus*

Login server/SOAP interface: *com.cisco.sametime.phonestatus.cup.CUPAgent*

Presence server/SIP interface: *com.cisco.sametime.phonestatus.cup.CUPPresenceWatcher*

Outlook Click-to-Call

Overview

Outlook click-to-call plug-in allows you to click on an Outlook item and call the relevant party (such as a contact or the sender of an email).

CUPC 7 was designed to work with Outlook contacts only. It doesn't work with GAL (Global Address List). CUPC 8 is capable to work with GAL. See "CUPS 8 and CUPC 8" chapter for details.

Outlook contacts are the contacts in your Outlook "Contacts" folder. See screenshot below.

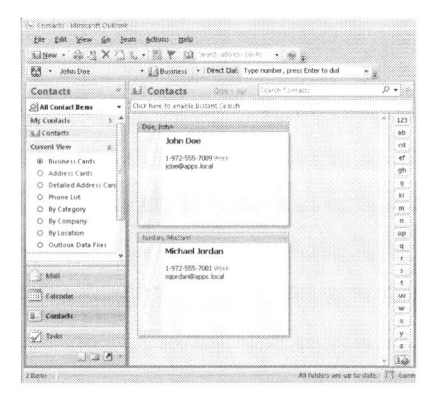

GAL (Global Address List) is the address book stored on Exchange server. See screenshot below.

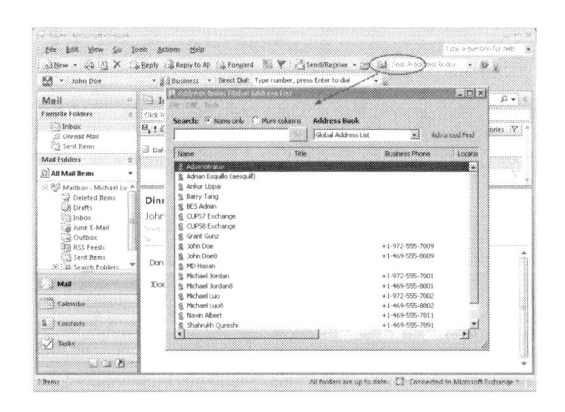

254 Chapter 5. Deploying and Troubleshooting Features

When you highlight a business card in Outlook contact, you should have the option to dial the contact's number (Business, Home, etc.) in CUPC tool bar. See screenshot below.

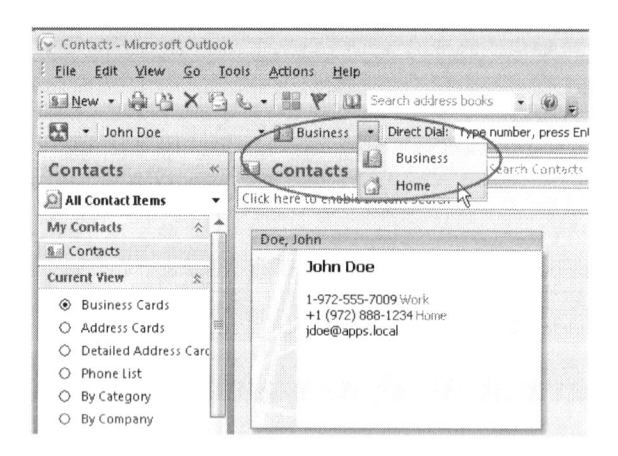

If you click on a number type (Business, Home, etc.), CUPC will dial the number configured in the contact's card.

This click-to-call feature is more useful if it can be used on emails. For example, you received an email. You click a button on the toolbar. CUPC immediately calls the sender. Unfortunately, this feature has some limitation in CUPC 7.

As mentioned before, CUPC 7 can only retrieve phone numbers from Outlook contacts. When you highlight an incoming email, the sender may or may not be in your Outlook contacts. If the sender was not in your Outlook contacts, CUPC won't be able to retrieve phone numbers. You'll see a "Call…" button instead of "Business" (or "Home", whatever). See screenshot below.

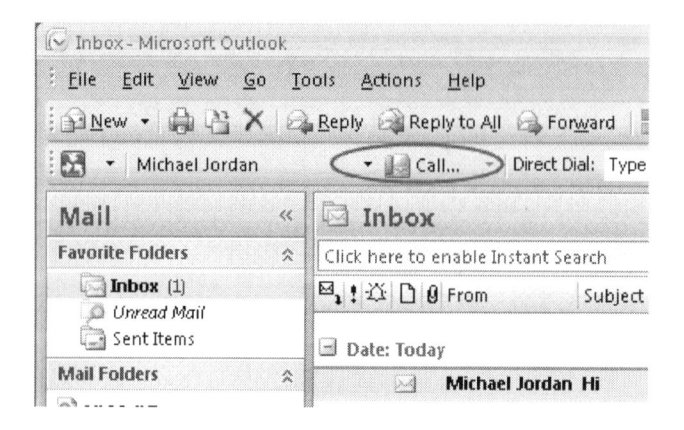

If you click on the "Call…" button, CUPC will prompt you manually enter the number you want to dial. This defeats the purpose of click-to-dial.

Even if the sender was in Outlook contacts, CUPC still needs to correlate the sender to an Outlook contact.

Searching Mechanism

CUPC Outlook plug-in follows the search mechanism below.

1. Search for email address

CUPC will try to retrieve email address of "Return-Path" from the "Internet headers" of the email. If no email address could be retrieved, continue on step 2.

If you're interested in seeing the "Return-Path" value, you may right-click an email in the INBOX and choose "Options" (or "Message Option" if you're using Outlook 2007).

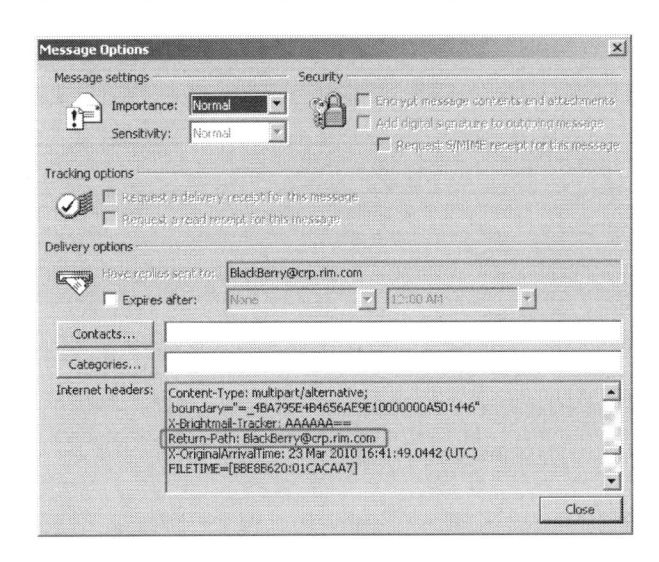

"Return-Path" might not be present if the sender and recipient are on the same Exchange server. In that case, CUPC will continue on step 2.

If an email address was retrieved, CUPC will search that email address in Outlook contacts.

If a match was found, CUPC will retrieve phone numbers from that contact.

If no match was found, continue to step 2.

2. Search for display name

CUPC will retrieve sender's display name from GAL and try to search that in Outlook contacts.

If a match was found, CUPC will retrieve phone numbers from that contact.

If no match was found, continue to step 3.

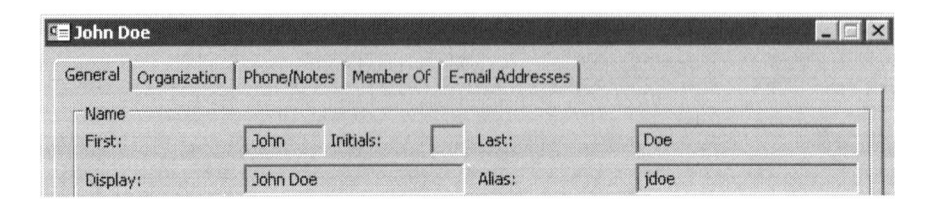

3. Search for first name and last name

CUPC will retrieve sender's first name and last name from GAL and try to search that in Outlook contacts.

If a match was found, CUPC will retrieve phone numbers from that contact.

If no match was found, CUPC will stop searching and display the "Call…" button.

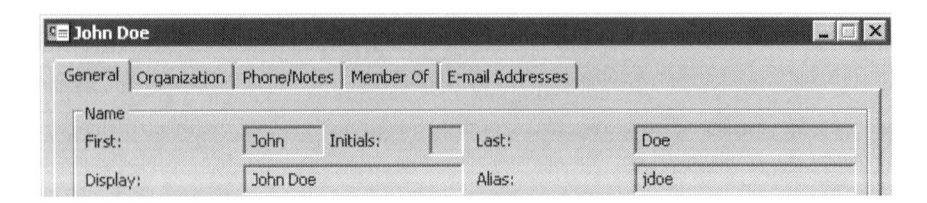

Logs

If you need to look deeper, log file would be in %userprofile%\Local Settings\Application Data\Cisco\Unified Personal Communicator\Logs\cupc_outlook_log.txt.

Chapter 6. Operation and Maintenance

In this chapter, we will talk about the daily operation and maintenance of the CUPS system. This is usually referred to as "Day 2 operation" or "MAC (Move, Add, Change)". At this point, the initial deployment should have completed.

User Management

Add a user

Step 1: CUCM: Create End User

    1.1 Go to CUCM > User Management > End User.
    1.2 Add New.
    1.3 Configure username, password.

Notes:
- If your CUCM was configured to use LDAP Synchronization, you cannot create a user. Users are synchronized from LDAP.
- If your CUCM was configured to use LDAP Authentication, you cannot configure password. Users will authenticate against LDAP

Step 2: CUCM: Provision Desk Phone

If you have not done so, follow CUCM documentation to create a desk phone (Cisco 79xx IP phone). Make sure the phone is registered and can make phone calls.

    2.1 Go to CUCM > Device > Phone.
    2.2 Search for the desk phone you want to configure.
    2.3 Click on search result to go to device configuration page.
    2.4 Click on the primary directory number on the device page to go to "Directory Number Configuration" page.
    2.5 Go to the bottom of the page. Associate the DN with the end user.

Step 3: CUCM: Provision Soft Phone

3.1 Go to CUCM > Device > Phone.
3.2 Add New
3.3 From the device type list, choose "Cisco Unified Personal Communicator"
3.4 All letters in device name has to be in upper case. Device name has to begin with UPC and in the format of UPC*USERNAME*. Where "USERNAME" is the actual user ID in CUCM.
3.5 Configure other parameters (such as calling search space, directory number, etc.).

Step 4: CUCM: Configure End User

Now we back to end user configuration again. The reason we didn't finish the configuration on step 1 is because some parameters are depending on the existence of desk phone or soft phone (step 2 and 3).

4.1 Go to CUCM > User Management > End User.
4.2 Search for the user you created on step 1.
4.3 Click search result to go to user configuration page.
4.4 In "device associations", associate the desk phone. (If the user doesn't have a desk phone, associate the soft phone)
4.5 In "Directory Number Associations", select a DN as "Primary Extension"
4.6 In "Permission Information" add the user to "Standard CTI Enabled" group.

Optional:
- Configure "Digest Credential". If you don't have ACL configured on CUPS, you need to configure a non-blank digest credential for the user. It could be any non-blank value.
- Add the user to "Standard CCM End Users" group. For troubleshooting purpose, you may add the user to "Standard CCM End Users" group.

Step 5: CUCM: License End User

5.1 Go to CUCM > System > Licensing > Capabilities Assignment.
5.2 Search for the user you want to license.
5.3 Click search result to license the user.

Step 6: CUPS: Configure End User

6.1 Go to CUPS > Application > Cisco Unified Personal Communicator > User Settings.
6.2 Search for the user you want to configure.
6.3 Choose appropriate settings from drop-down menus

Delete a user

Remove a user from CUPS

To "remove" a user from CUPS, all we need to do is to "unlicensed" him from CUCM.

1. Go to CUCM > System > Licensing > Capabilities Assignment
2. Search for the user.
3. Click on the search result.
4. Uncheck both CUP and CUPC options to unlicensed the user.

The purpose of above steps is to free up CUCM DLUs consumed by CUP and CUPC. See "licensing" chapter before for details.

Remove CUPC soft phone from CUCM

1. Go to CUCM > Device > Phone
2. Search for device with the name UPC*USERNAME*, where USERNAME is the user ID in CUCM.
3. Delete the device.

The purpose of above steps is to free up CUCM DLUs consumed by UPC device (soft phone). See "licensing" chapter before for details.

Remove a user from CUCM

Optionally, you may remove the user from CUCM.

Change a user

Usually, changes involved with a user would be:

- Directory Number change
- Phone device change

Whenever the above was changed, you want to go through the "Add User" process to make sure all configuration was updated. After that, you need to reset the phone to refresh the state.

Bulk Administration Tool (BAT)

Bulk Administrator Tool (BAT) is a powerful tool on CUCM and CUPS to help you add/change configuration in batch. BAT itself deserves a separate book (The Cisco BAT documentation is more than 500 pages long).

The basic idea of BAT is to prepare a txt file (CSV file). Then use the file as input and update the configuration.

For example, you have 1000 users in your company. For some of them, you want to enable CUP and CUPC features. For the others, you want to enable CUP feature only. Instead of manually configuring 1000 uses on the management web page, you may create a txt file in following format:

```
User ID,Enable CUP,Enable CUPC
jdoe,t,t
jsmith,t,f
```

For user 'jdoe', we want to enable CUP and CUPC feature. Both fields are set to 't' (true). For user 'jsmith', we want to enable CUP feature only. CUP field is set to 't' and CUPC field is set to 'f' (false).

1. Save this file as cupupdate.txt.
2. Go to CUCM > Bulk Administration Upload/Download files.

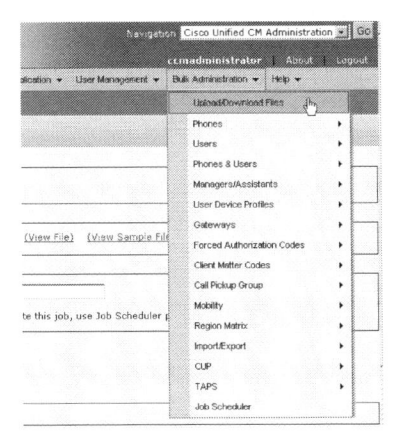

Bulk Administration Tool (BAT)

3. Click "Browse" to choose the file you created. In "Select The Target" drop-down menu, choose "CUP Users". In "Select Transaction Type" menu, choose "Update CUP Users – Customer File". Click "Save".

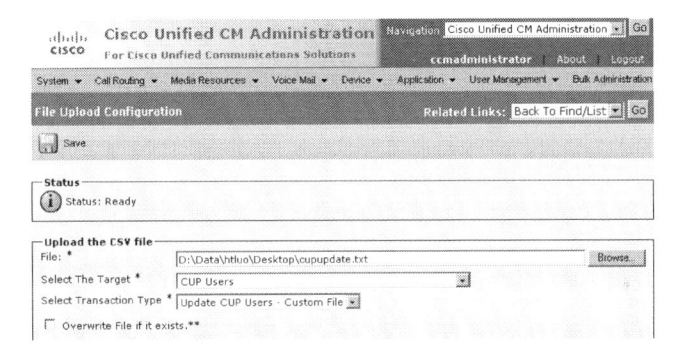

4. Go to CUCM > Bulk Administration > CUP > Update CUP/CUPC Users

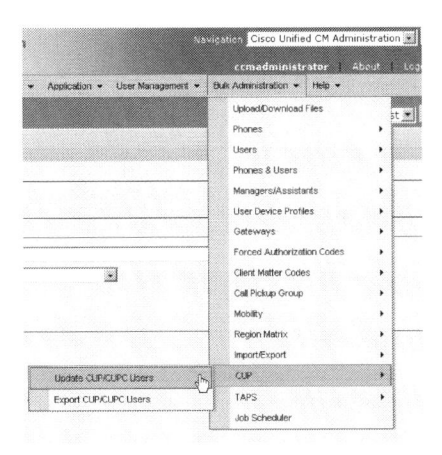

5. From "File Name" drop-down menu, choose the file you uploaded in step 3. Choose "Run Immediately". Click "Save".

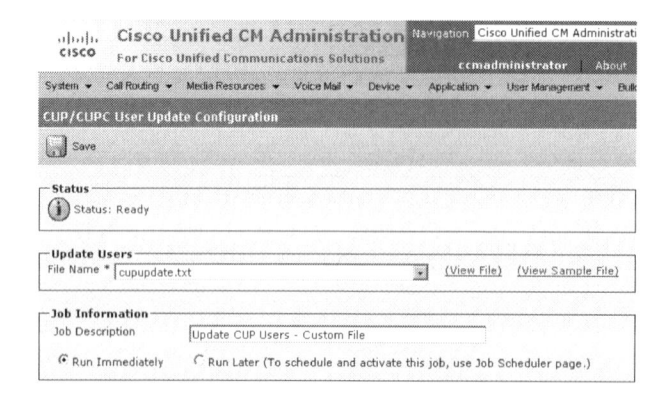

The above process updates the "Capabilities Assignment" on CUCM.

On CUPS, there's a similar tool to update user settings (Application > Cisco Unified Personal Communicator > User Settings).

For more information on how to update other configuration (such as phone association, DN association, primary extension designation, etc.), please refer to CUCM BAT documentation: http://www.cisco.com/en/US/docs/voice_ip_comm/cucm/bat/6_1_1/bat611.html

Backup and Restore

Like CUCM, CUPS has a "Disaster Recovery System" to backup/restore the system configuration.

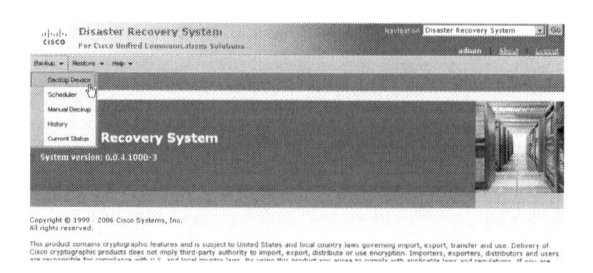

You may use a tape drive attached to the server to backup. Or more popularly, use a SFTP server to store backup files.

I recommend FreeFTPd as the SFTP server. See "Tools" section for details.

For detail instructions on back up and restore, please see:
http://www.cisco.com/en/US/docs/voice_ip_comm/cups/6_0_1/disaster_recovery/administration/guide/drsag601.html

Most frequently seen problems on backup/restore are:

- SFTP configuration issue (username, password, path)
- Network connectivity issue (port 22 was blocked by firewall)
- Version mismatch (you backup the CUPS system on version X. You try to restore the configuration on version Y).

Patch and Upgrade

To perform a system upgrade or install a patch, please go to "OS Administration" web interface.

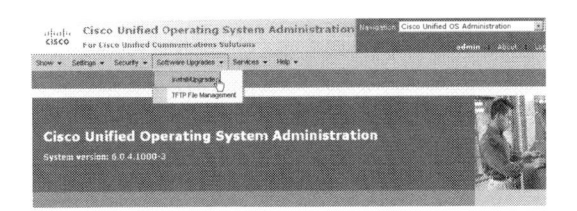

You may burn the upgrade file to a DVD or put the file on SFTP server. Then specify the file location.

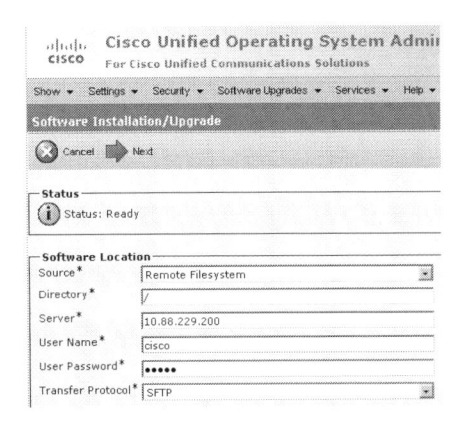

Frequently seen problems on upgrade are:

- SFTP configuration issue (username, password, path)
- Network connectivity issue (port 22 was blocked by firewall)
- You put the ISO image on DVD instead of "burn image". – if the upgrade file is an ISO file, you need to use the "burn image" function of a DVD burner software. On the DVD, you should see the content of the ISO image, instead of the ISO file itself.

Chapter 7. Advanced Topics

Multi-node

In a CUPS cluster, you could have up to two CUPS servers – one publisher and one subscriber.

During installation, you'll be asked if this is the first CUPS server in the cluster. If you answered no, the software would install the server as a subscriber and try to synchronize data from publisher.

The advantages of having a multi-node cluster are fault-tolerance and load-balancing.

However, we have different scenarios when CUPS is interfacing with clients (CUPC) and server (CUCM, OCS, etc.).

CUPC

When CUPC tries to log on to CUPS, it will contact the logon server to download configuration. Without the configuration, CUPC won't be able to register other features.

To achieve the "failover" feature, CUPC needs the awareness of a standby server (CUPS server). Based on different version of CUPC and CUPS, the failover and load-balancing feature would be different.

	CUPS 6.0.x	CUPS 7.0.x
CUPC 1.2.x	Failover: manual. Load-balancing: client.	Failover: manual. Load-balancing: client.
CUPC 7.0.x	Failover: manual. Load-balancing: client.	Failover: auto. Load-balancing: server.

Failover

Failover here refers to hot-standby server. When the primary server failed, can CUPC still be able to log in?

CUPC 1.2.x

On CUPC 1.2.x, there's no "failover" feature at all. CUPC 1.2.x has no awareness of the CUPS subscriber. In the case CUPS publisher is down, you'll have to change the logon server on CUPC logon window to the subscriber.

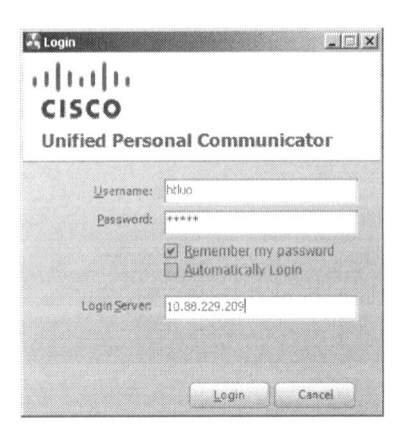

CUPC 7.0.x with CUPS 7.0.x

After CUPC 7.0.x successfully logged on the first time, it retrieves the backup server (if there's any) address and caches it in local configuration file. In case CUPS publisher is down, CUPC will use backup server to logon. This failover is automatic. No manual configuration is required.

The backup server address is stored in C:\Documents and Settings\<*user_id*>\Application Data\Cisco\Unified Personal Communicator\uclocal.xml

```
<property name="PAS.SOAP.serverAddress">10.88.229.211</property>
<property name="PAS.SOAP.backupServerAddress">10.88.229.212</property>
```

Load-balancing

CUPC 1.2.x

On CUPC 1.2.x, if you'd like to balance the load on two CUPS servers, you may specify the login server on the logon window. The server you log in to would be the server who serves you.

CUPC 7.0.x with CUPS 7.0.x

When CUPC 7.0.x works with CUPS 7.0.x, the load-balancing was configured from server.

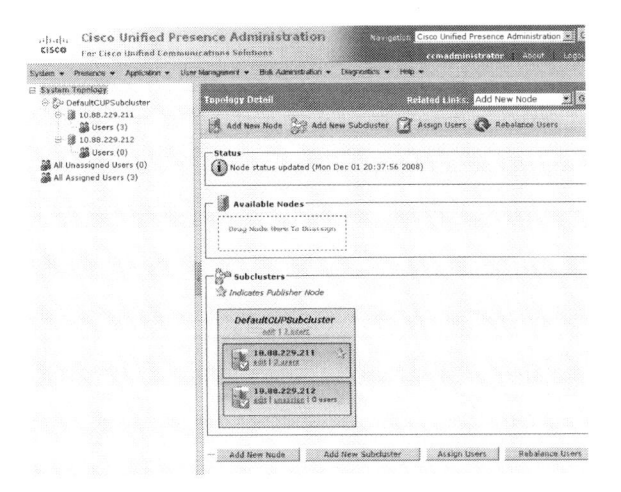

Each user can be assigned to a specific server. That server would be your "home server" regardless what server you tried to log on to.

For example, in the screenshot above, all users were assigned to server 10.88.229.211. You may try to log on to another server (10.88.229.212). After login, you'll see the logon server and presence point to your home server (10.88.229.211).

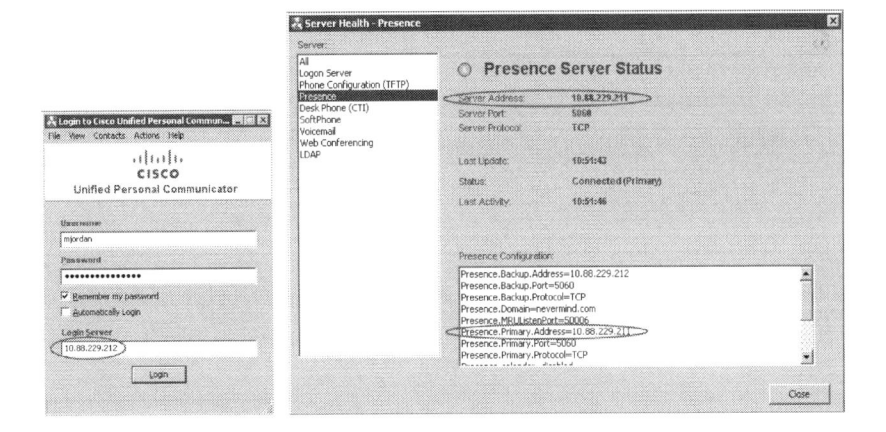

CUCM

To get phone presence, a SIP trunk has to be set up between CUCM and CUPS. You can only have one SIP trunk to a CUPS cluster regardless how many CUPS nodes you have. In case a CUPS node failed, CUCM needs a way to find its destination for the SIP trunk.

A DNS server is required to achieve this. You may either configure a DNS A record or a DNS SRV record for multiple CUPS nodes. For example, you have two CUPS nodes:

Node 1: 192.168.0.1
Node 2: 192.168.0.2

You may configure a DNS A record "cups.acme.com" and point it to 192.168.0.1 and 192.168.0.2.

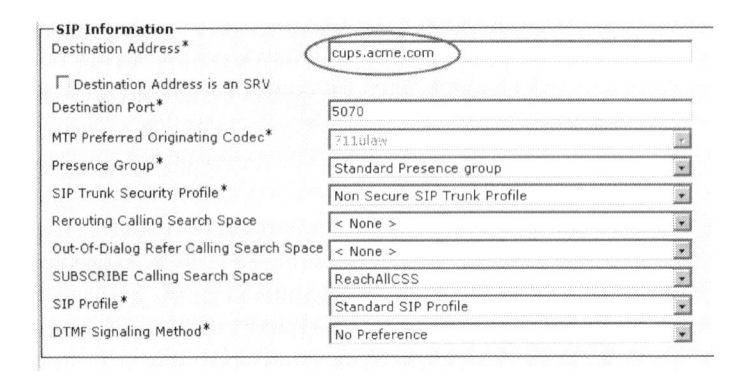

When CUCM tries to set up the SIP trunk, it'll look up the destination "cups.acme.com" in DNS. DNS will return two IP addresses – 192.168.0.1 and 192.168.0.2. CUCM will try the first one. If first one failed, CUCM will try 2nd one.

SRV record is different with A record. It not only defines the destination address, but also the port and protocol being used. For details, please refer to RFC3263 (http://www.ietf.org/rfc/rfc3263.txt).

I don't recommend you use SRV record unless you understand how it works. SRV records might affect other products such as MOC. (MOC uses SRV records for automatic login).

OCS

For OCS, CUPS server was defined as "next-hop" in front-end static routes.

When using TCP, you can only use IP address as next-hop. You cannot leverage DNS for failover. The only way to do failover is to use a load-balancer.

When using TLS, you may specify FQDN as next-hop. If multiple IP addresses were associated with the FQDN, OCS will try them one by one.

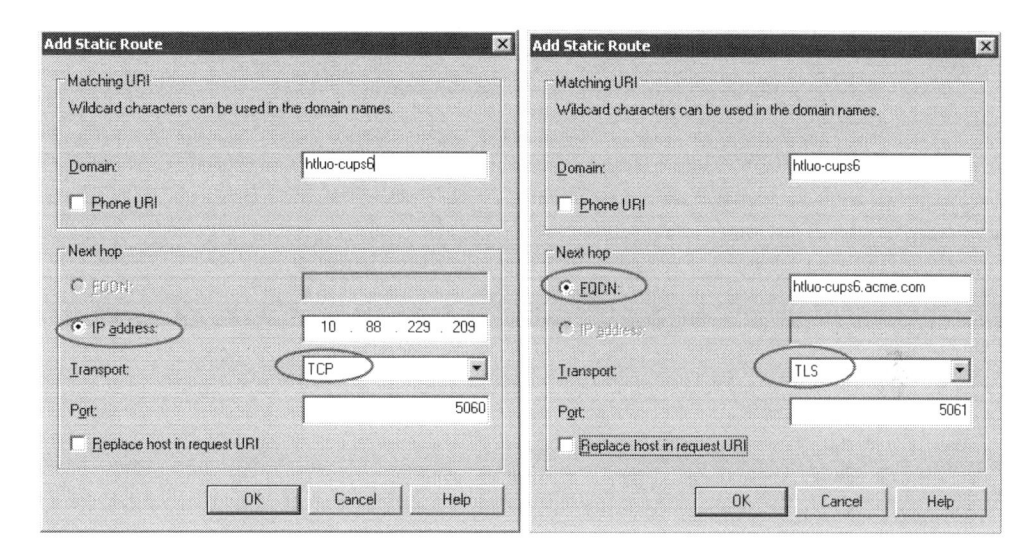

Inter-cluster

In CUCM/CUPS, a "cluster" means a group of servers that share the same set of configuration. A CUPS server can be integrated with one and only one CUCM cluster. If you have two or more CUCM clusters, you need at least one CUPS server for each cluster.

It is not uncommon that one organization has more than one CUCM cluster (due to capacity and design consideration). With appropriate configuration, a CUPS server in cluster A can communicate with another CUPS server in cluster B. This is called "inter-clustering".

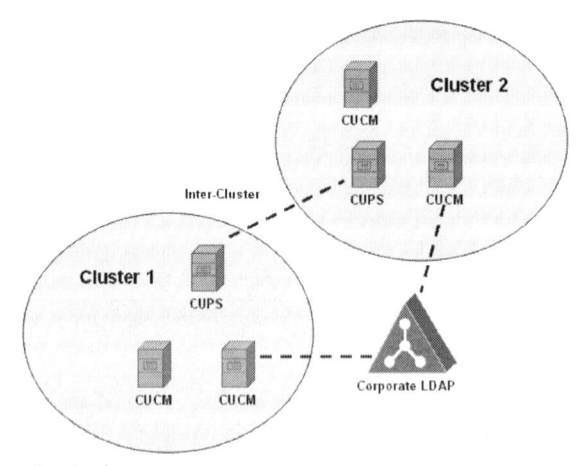

The advantages of inter-clustering are:

- CUPC users in two clusters can see each other's presence.
- CUPC users in two clusters can send instant messages to each other.

Steps to deploy inter-clustering

Step 1: CUPS: Configure same proxy domain for each cluster

1.1 Go to CUPS Admin > System > Service Parameters > Cisco UP SIP Proxy
1.2 Enter the proxy domain (e.g. acme.com). Since this is a cluster-wide parameter, you just need to configure it on one server in the same cluster.
1.3 Repeat above steps for each cluster(s).

Step 2: CUPS: Create AXL group for each cluster

2.1 Go to CUPS Admin > User Management > User Group
2.2 Add New
2.3 Enter a name for the group (e.g. "AXLGRP")
2.4 Save

Note: If you see a message "Update failed. java.sql.SQLException: Could not insert new row - duplicate value in a UNIQUE INDEX column", the group name you tried to use already exists. It might not show up on CUPS Admin page. But it is in database (synchronized from CUCM). You may verify that with CLI command "run sql select name from dirgroup".

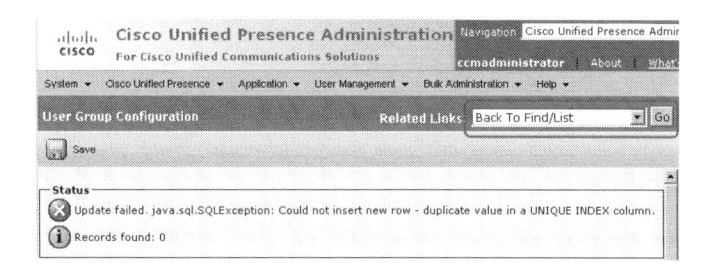

2.5 Click "Go" next to "Back To Find/List" to go back to the group list.
2.6 On the new group you created, click the "i" icon in the "Role" column.

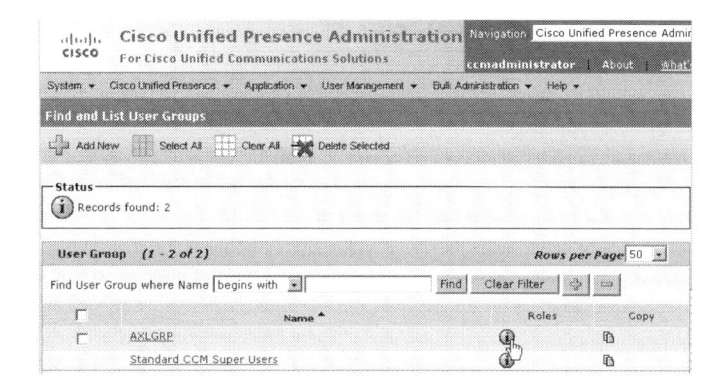

2.7 Click "Assign Role to Group"
2.8 Click "Find"
2.9 Check "Standard AXL API Access" and click "Add Selected"
2.10 Save.
2.11 Repeat above steps for each cluster.

Step 3: CUPS: Create AXL user for each cluster

3.1 Go to CUPS Admin > User Management > Application User
3.2 Add New
3.3 Configure user ID and password
3.4 Click "Add to User Group"
3.5 Check the AXL group you created in step 3. "Add Selected".
3.6 Save

3.7 Repeat above steps for each cluster.

Step 4: CUPS: Configure Inter-cluster peers

4.1 Go to CUPS Admin > Cisco Unified Presence > Inter-Clustering
4.2 Add New
4.3 In "Peer Address" field, enter the CUPS address in another cluster.
4.4 In "Username" and "Password/Confirm Password" fields, enter the AXL username and password on the remote CUPS server.
4.5 Save
4.6 Repeat above steps for each peer (if you have more than one peer).
4.7 Repeat above steps for each cluster.

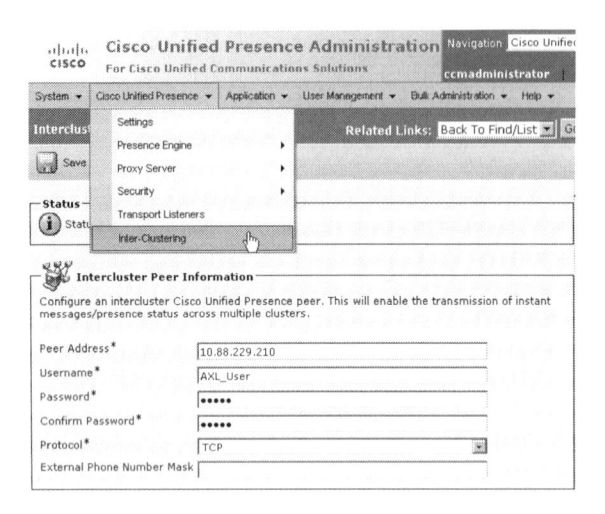

Step 5: CUPS: Activate AXL Service

5.1 Go to CUPS Serviceability > Tools > Service Activation
5.2 Activate "Cisco AXL Web Service" (if it's not already been activated)

Step 6: CUPS: Verify Services

6.1 Go to CUPS Serviceability > Tools > Control Center - Feature Services. Make sure "Cisco AXL Web Service" is running.

6.2 Go to CUPS Serviceability > Tools > Control Center - Network Services. Make sure "Cisco UP Intercluster Sync Agent" is running.

Notes:

- CUPS servers in different clusters should be configured with same proxy domain
- Inter-cluster is two-way configuration. i.e. peers should be configured on both sides.
- Make sure you don't have duplicate CUPS user ID in different clusters. This can be controlled by CUCM Admin > System > Licensing > Capabilities Assignment.

Troubleshooting

Logs:
CUPS – Intercluster Sync Agent log

Database:
cupsuserlocation. "islocal" column indicates if the user is local user or not. "t" means "true". "f" means "false". For example:

```
admin:run sql select userid, islocal from cupsuserlocation
userid             islocal
==========         ==========
htluo              t
mjordan            t
jdoe               f
```

Network Issue

Sometimes, you'll experience problems that CUPC not getting updated status (either self-status or contact status). As a side effect, when you switched phone mode (between desk phone and soft phone), the GUI didn't change until you sign off / sign on again.

This is usually an indication of network issue.

Sometime, the problem is easy to isolate. For example, problem only happens on VPN connection.

Sometimes, it's not so easy because it happens on LAN and all other applications (except for CUPC) were working fine.

To troubleshoot the problem, we need to understand the traffic pattern of client/server and common practice of firewall (or any traffic policing device / software).

Typical traffic pattern for client/server

For most of the client/server applications (like Web, Email, etc.), traffic was initiated from the client.

For example, you when you type www.cisco.com in a web browser and hit "Enter", the web browser initiate a request to web server www.cisco.com. Web browser is the "client". Web server www.cisco.com is the "server".

If you look deeper into the network layer, you'll see the famous "TCP 3-Way Handshake" like below.

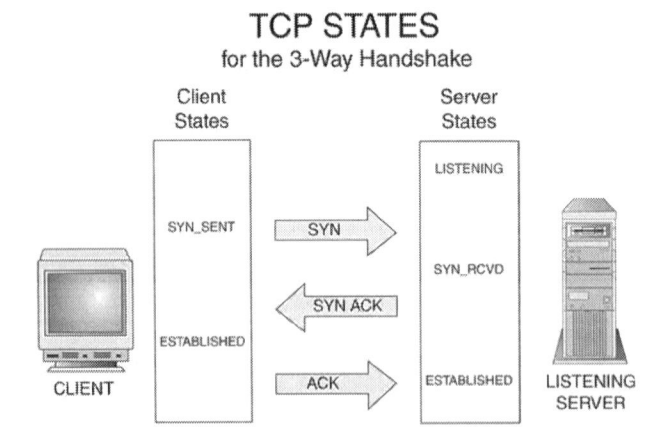

TCP STATES
for the 3-Way Handshake

Client States	Server States
SYN_SENT → SYN →	LISTENING
	SYN_RCVD
← SYN ACK
ESTABLISHED → ACK →	ESTABLISHED
CLIENT	LISTENING SERVER

The point is: the communication session is *usually* initiated from the client.

Typical firewall behavior

Most of the firewall/VPN (hardware/software/network module) has the default behavior of "adaptive mode".

In "adaptive mode", firewall will:
- Dynamically open ports for outgoing traffic from client.
- Block and incoming traffic to the client (unless it's a return traffic)

In the example of web browser, firewall will dynamically open ports in the following order.

		Outgoing-to-Server	Incoming-to-Client
1	Original state	Blocked	Blocked
2	Web browser trying to open www.cisco.com. Source port 12345. Destination port 80.	Allow Source port 12345 Destination port 80	Blocked
3	Web server trying to reply. Source port 80. Destination port 12345.	Allow Source port **12345** Destination port 80	Allow Source port 80 Destination port **12345**

Step 3 above is a key step. Firewall allows incoming traffic to client port 12345 because that matches the source port in step 2 (a return traffic). If server tried to send the traffic to a different client port (let say 56789), it would be blocked by firewall.

This makes sense if the client expected server respond instantly (which is the case for most client/server applications).

However, in presence applications, this is not the case.

Traffic Pattern of CUPC/CUPS

When you log into CUPC, you "SUBSCRIBE" to your contacts' presence. The server (CUPS) will "NOTIFY" you whenever there's a change in their presence.

In most of the cases, your contacts' presence won't change frequently (every second). If their presence didn't change, server won't send any NOTIFY to client. If server has no data to send, it's unnecessary to keep the TCP session open (opened session will consume system resource). Instead, client (CUPC) will give server its "callback" address (IP address and port number) and say *"Hey server, I'm going to drop off for now. Whenever you have news for me, please call me back at 192.168.1.101 on port 50000 – 50063. I'll be listening on those ports."*

278   Chapter 7. Advanced Topics

Unfortunately, when server "call back", the traffic is a new TCP session from server to client. Firewall won't allow this traffic because there's no pre-established session from client to server. This is where the problem happens.

How do you prove that and how do you pinpoint which socket was blocked?

To do that, you need packet capture from client and server for the same time period when the problem happens.

Drop the capture into SIP Workbench and look for missing/undelivered SIP messages. In the example below, you see that the NOTIFY was undelivered. Direction is server (Cisco-PE/7.0) to client (Cisco-UCModel01/7.0.1). Source port is 52078. Destination port is 50038.

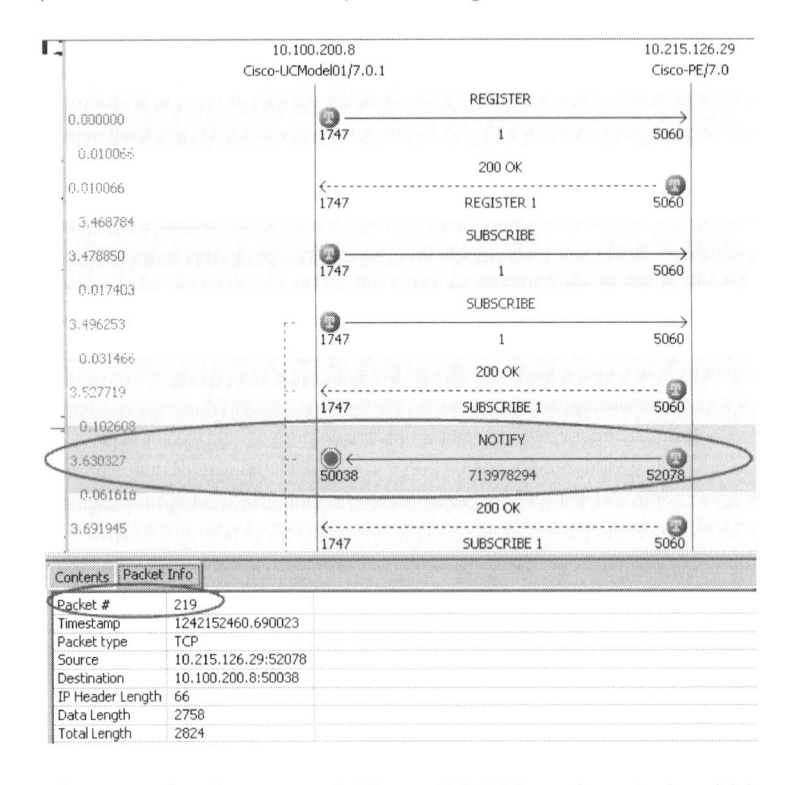

```
                        10.100.200.8                           10.215.126.29
                        Cisco-UCModel01/7.0.1                  Cisco-PE/7.0
                                         REGISTER
 0.000000               ───────────────────────────────────────▶
                        1747              1                    5060
 0.010066
                                         200 OK
 0.010066               ◀────────────────────────────────────────
                        1747              REGISTER 1           5060
 3.468784
                                         SUBSCRIBE
 3.478850               ───────────────────────────────────────▶
                        1747              1                    5060
 0.017403
                                         SUBSCRIBE
 3.496253               ───────────────────────────────────────▶
                        1747              1                    5060
 0.031466
                                         200 OK
 3.527719               ◀────────────────────────────────────────
                        1747              SUBSCRIBE 1          5060
 0.102608
                                         NOTIFY
 3.630327               ◀────────────────────────────────────────
                        50038             713978294            52078
 0.061618
                                         200 OK
 3.691945               ◀────────────────────────────────────────
                        1747              SUBSCRIBE 1          5060
```

Packet #	219
Timestamp	1242152460.690023
Packet type	TCP
Source	10.215.126.29:52078
Destination	10.100.200.8:50038
IP Header Length	66
Data Length	2758
Total Length	2824

With that information, you (or the network/firewall/VPN engineer) should be able to identify the problem quickly.

Chapter 8. CUPS 8.0 and CUPC 8.0

What's New

Whenever a new version of software is released, people usually ask "What's new in this version?"

For CUPS 8.0 and CUPC 8.0, the answer could be *"not too much"* or *"lots of changes"*, depending on your point of view.

From end user point of view, "noticeable" new features include:
- Instant Messaging (XMPP-based, server feature)
    - Group chat, offline chat, chat archiving
    - Persistent chat rooms
    - Federation with other IM system
    - Rich text and Emoticons
- Video (CSF-based, client feature)
    - HD video
    - Video with desk phone (CUVA-like)

That doesn't seem to change a lot for a major version leap, does it? Well, from development and architecture point of view, version 8.0 is the biggest change in CUPS and CUPC history (so far). You don't see too many user-facing "enhancements" because Cisco is still in the process of implementing new features based on the new architecture. CUPS 8.0 and CUPC 8.0 is the milestone of next-generation Unified Communication.

CUPS 8 Architecture Overview

When talking about the new stuffs on CUPS 8, you'll run into a couple acronyms – XMPP, Jabber, and XCP. Don't worry if you're not familiar with those words. We'll further discuss those later. For now, let's take a look at a high-level overview of CUPS 8.0 architecture. To put it simple, CUPS 8.0 is like "CUPS 7 + Jabber".

280 Chapter 8. CUPS 8.0 and CUPC 8.0

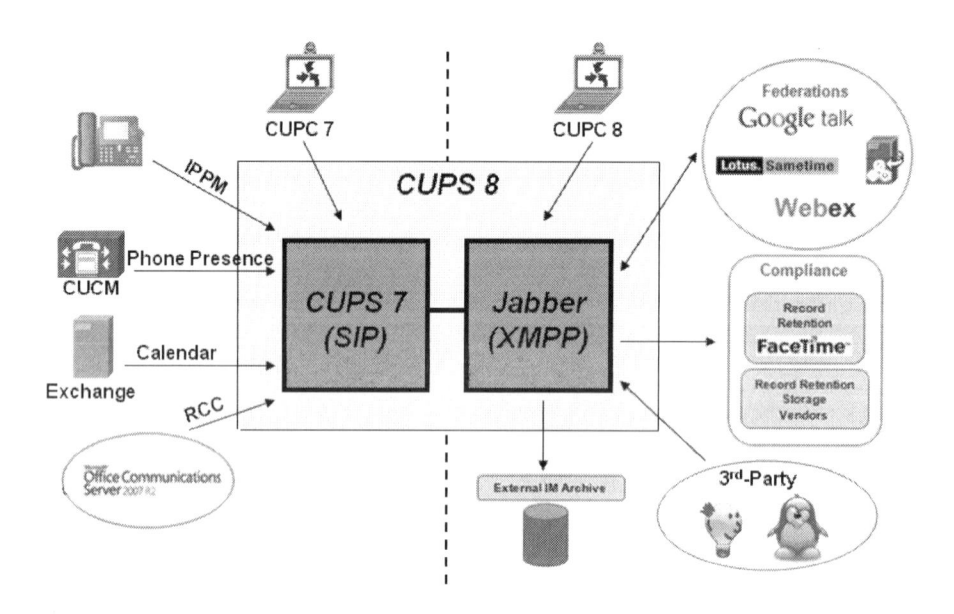

If you have read through previous chapters of this book, you should be quite familiar with the left portion of the diagram. The left portion is the functionality of CUPS 7. We call it "UC Integration (SIP)". Nothing was changed for this part on CUPS 8.

The right portion is the newly added function on CUPS 8. We called it "Jabber Integration (XMPP)".

History of Jabber/XMPP

[This history section is quoted from "XMPP: The Definitive Guide" by Peter Saint-Andre, Kevin Smith, and Remko Tronçon]

Jabber/XMPP technologies were invented by Jeremie Miller in 1998. Jeremie was tired of running four different clients for the closed IM services of the day, so in true open source fashion, he decided to scratch an itch, releasing an open source server called jabberd on January 4, 1999. Before long, a community of developers jumped in to help, writing open source clients for Linux, Macintosh, and Windows; add-on components that worked with the server; and code libraries for languages such as Perl and Java. During 1999 and early 2000, the community collaboratively worked out the details of the wire protocols we now call XMPP, culminating in the release of jabberd 1.0 in May 2000.

As the community grew larger and various companies became interested in building their own Jabber-compatible (but not necessarily open source) software, the loose collaboration evident in 1999 and 2000 became unsustainable. As a result, the community (spearheaded by a company called Jabber, Inc., **_acquired by Cisco in late 2008_**) formed the Jabber Software Foundation in August 2001. Ever since, this nonprofit membership organization, renamed the XMPP Standards Foundation in early 2007, has openly documented the protocols used in the developer community, and has defined a large number of extensions to the core protocols.

After several years of implementation and deployment experience, members of the developer community decided to seek a wider review of the core protocols by formalizing them within the IETF, which has standardized most of the core technologies for the Internet (including TCP/IP, HTTP, SMTP, POP, IMAP, and SSL/TLS). Given that most good protocols seem to be three- or four-letter acronyms ending with the letter "P," the relevant IETF working group labeled its topic the Extensible Messaging and Presence Protocol (XMPP). After less than two years of intensive work (mostly focused on tightening communications security), the IETF published the core XMPP specifications in its Request for Comments (RFC) series as [RFC 3920] and [RFC 3921] in October 2004.

Publication of these RFCs has resulted in widespread adoption of XMPP technologies. In August 2005, the Google Talk IM and Voice over Internet Protocol (VoIP) service was launched on a basis of XMPP. Thousands more services have followed. Prominent and emerging software companies use XMPP in their products, including the likes of Apple, Cisco, IBM, Nokia, and Sun. Countless businesses, universities, and government agencies have deployed XMPP-based instant messaging systems for their users. Many game developers and social networking applications are building XMPP into their services, and a number of organizations have used XMPP as the "secret sauce" behind some of their most innovative features.

In this book, we use Jabber, XMPP, XCP interchangeably. But you should know the subtle difference:

Jabber
- The very fist name of XMPP technology.
- Jabberd, the name of first XMPP server (open source)
- The name of a company (acquired by Cisco in 2008)

XMPP – Extensible Messagin and Presence Protocol (IETF RFC 3920 and 3921)

XCP - Extensible Collaboration Platform, a commercial product from Jabber Inc. to provide presence and instant messaging. It's now a Cisco property with acquisition of Jabber.

Jabber/XMPP on CUPS

After acquiring Jabber, Cisco was trying to utilize XMPP in its unified communication products. CUPS, of course, would be the first one on the list.

Ideally, CUPS should be re-built from ground with XMPP (and phase out SIP). But due to product dependencies and other considerations, Cisco decided to put Jabber and the original CUPS components (PE, Proxy, etc.) on the same box. So it looks like the diagram below.

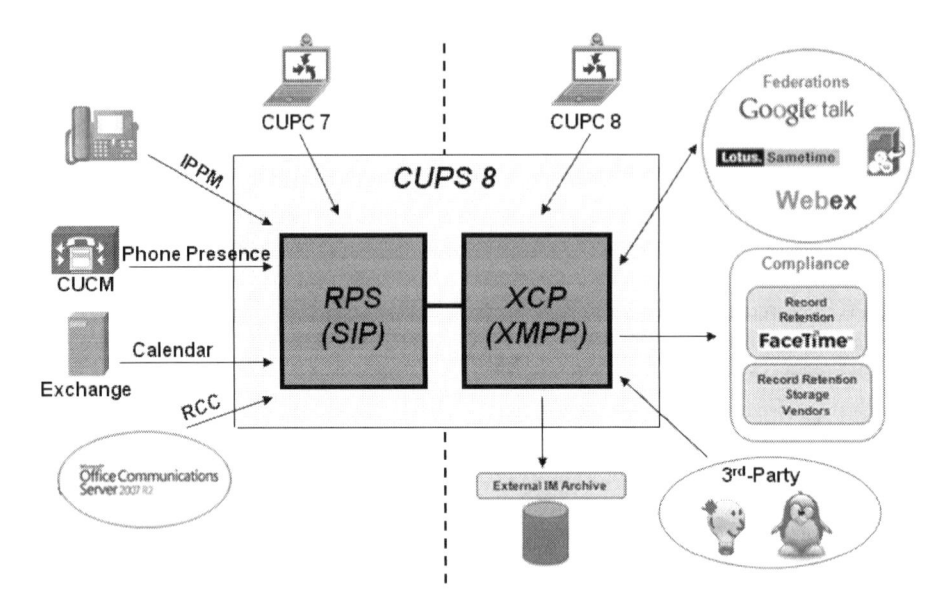

Please note there are some wording changes here. The little box on the left is called "RSP", stands for Rich Presence Service. It contains the original CUPS7 components such as PE, Proxy, etc. The little box on the right is called XCP, which is the modified XCP component from Jabber.

The "pipe" between RPS and XCP is called "Client Emulation Interface", which translates SIP messages to XMPP. Thus CUPC 7 (SIP client) can communicate with CUPC 8 (XMPP client). Also, rich presence (such as phone presence, calendar) can be translated into XMPP.

To make the transition as smooth as possible, Cisco made the translation transparent for end users. If you followed the "old" procedure (CUPC 7) to deploy a CUPC user, most of the features will work on the new version (CUPC 8).

Before we move on, let's take a look at the newly added service on CUPS:

CUP Services

	Service Name
○	Cisco UP SIP Proxy
○	Cisco UP Presence Engine
○	Cisco UP Sync Agent
○	Cisco UP XCP Text Conference Manager
○	Cisco UP XCP Web Connection Manager
○	Cisco UP XCP Connection Manager
○	Cisco UP XCP SIP Federation Connection Manager
○	Cisco UP XCP XMPP Federation Connection Manager
○	Cisco UP XCP Counter Aggregator
○	Cisco UP XCP Message Archiver
○	Cisco UP XCP Directory Service
○	Cisco UP XCP Authentication Service

Feature Service

CUP Services

	Service Name
○	Cisco UP Config Agent
○	Cisco UP OAM Agent
○	Cisco UP Client Profile Agent
○	Cisco UP Presence Engine Database
○	Cisco UP Intercluster Sync Agent
○	Cisco UP XCP Router

Network Services

You should be already familiar with the "legacy services", like "SIP Proxy", "Presence Engine" etc. The services with "XCP" on it are the newly added services. Below is a summary of XCP services.

XCP Service	Description
Router	Main router for XMPP traffic
Connection Manager	Services XMPP clients, forwards traffic to XCP router
Web Connection Manager	Services OpenAPI clients, forwards traffic to XCP router
SIP Federation Connection Mgr.	Services S2S connections for SIP federation
XMPP Federation Connection Mgr.	Services S2S connections for XMPP federation
Text Conference Mgr.	Supports persistent and ad-hoc chat services
Directory Service	Supports XMPP based directory search on LDAP server
Message Archiver	Enables compliance logging for chat and persistent chat
Authentication Service	Authentication service for XMPP client connections
Counter Aggregator	Feeds XCP performance data into VOS performance counters

We'll get into the configuration details later, because it depends on what client you're using and what feature you want to deploy.

History of CUPC

CUPC (Cisco Unified Personal Communicator) is probably the 2nd famous "communicator" Cisco built (the most famous one is CIPC – Cisco IP Communicator). CUPC was built as a multi-feature application for Unified Communication.

After CUPC, Cisco built some other desktop applications for UC (Unified Communication), such as Click-to-Call, Sametime plug-in, MOC plug-in (CUCIMOC), Webex plug-in (CUCI Connect), mobile communicator, etc.

Developers found that those applications share quite lot commonalities, such as desk phone control by CTI, soft phone by SIP, voicemail by IMAP, directory search by LDAP, etc.

Instead of reinventing the wheel every time, they start "sharing" CUPC software codes among different projects. Because of this, you'll see CUPC's shadow everywhere. For example, CUCIMOC will look for application dial rules in CUPC folder on TFTP. And the common software codes of CUPC are referred as "core" in many projects.

CSF – Client Service Framework

With more and more projects sharing CUPC codes, it's required to have a better quality control and unified interface for the "core". Hence the concept of CSF (Client Service Framework) was introduced.

You might have heard about "Microsoft .Net Framework". The word "framework" stands for a common library for different applications. With the "framework" installed, different applications can conveniently use the pre-built functional components instead of building everything from scratch. It's the same idea of Cisco CSF.

CSF is the core of Cisco client applications. There will be couple different flavors:

- CSF – For desktop applications
- ThinCSF – For mobile devices (cell phones, wireless headsets, etc.)
- WebCSF – For web applications
- OpenCSF – For 3rd-party developers

Almost everything you've seen (or not seen) will be using CSF, including but not limited to:

- CUPC – Cisco Unified Personal Communicator
- CIPC – Cisco IP Communicator

CSF Architecture

- CUCIMOC – UC Integration with MOC
- CUCI Connect – UC Integration with Webex Connect
- CUMC – Cisco Unified Personal Communicator
- Quad (a.k.a. ECP) – Enterprise Collaboration Platform

Benefits of having a common framework are obvious:

- For developers, it's easy to add features or fix bugs. Instead of fixing 20 different applications, they just need to fix one library.
- For system integrators, it's easy to design, deploy and test the system, because all applications follow the same working model of CSF.
- For support engineers, it's easy to troubleshoot the problem, because all applications have similar behavior and same log format. Experience gained on one product could be applied to another product.
- For end users, they have similar (if not same) user experience across different products.

CSF Architecture

Below is the architecture overview of CSF.

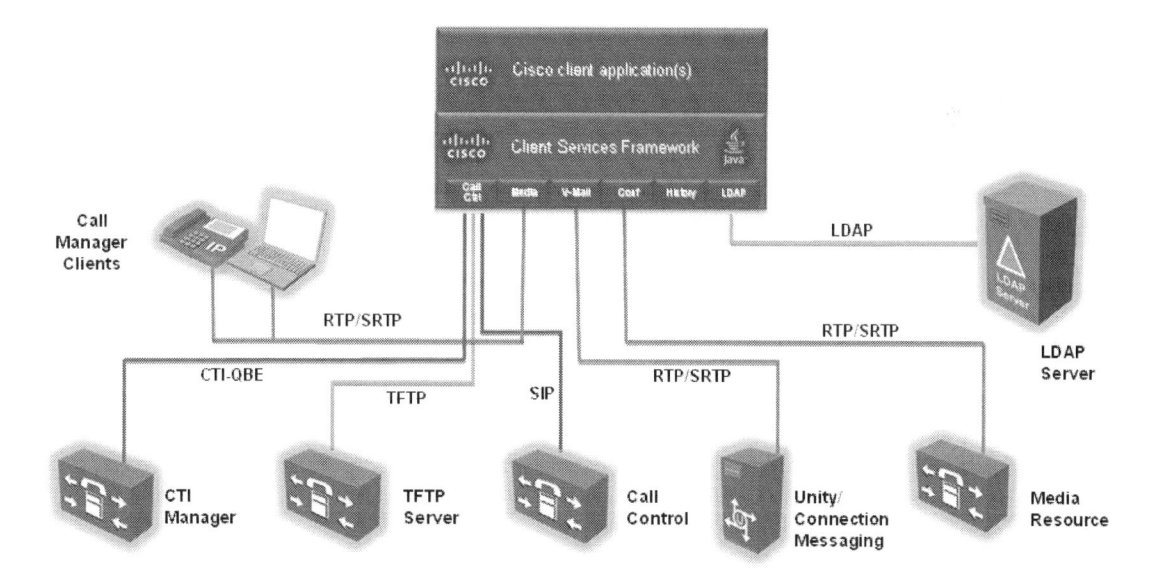

As shown in the diagram above, many "CUPC features" has been extracted and standardized, such as CTI-QBE (deskphone control), TFTP (softphone and configuration download), SIP (soft phone), LDAP (directory lookup), voicemail, web conference, etc.

Those features can be called (used) by upper layer "Cisco client applications", such as CUCIMOC, CUCI Connect, CUPC 8.0, etc.

If you'd like to know more inside CSF, you may take a look at the diagram below. In case you need to read CSF logs, it'll help you understand components.

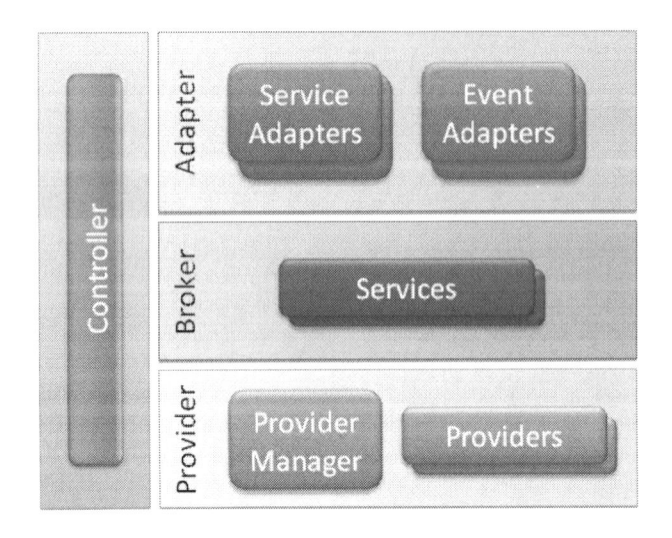

Controller's main function is making sure that another CSF isn't already running (if so, it quits).

Adapter layer is the 'northbound' CSF interface. This layer uses SOAP to abstract the internal business logic (Services) and data from the client(s), such as CUCIMOC and WebEx Connect.

Broker layer contains the various CSF Services, which house the business logic of CSF. Example Services include: Audio, Contact, Phone, Conversation, Communication History, Device.

Provider layer is the 'southbound' CSF interface. This layer abstracts the Services from the various backend servers and their protocols, as well as the platform/OS functions and resources.

In this book, we'll discuss CSF on Windows platform only, though CSF will be supported on multiple platforms (Windows, Linux, MacOS, Symbian, WinMobile, Blackberry, Andriod, etc.)

CSF itself does not have a visible user interface. It runs as a background process (cucsf.exe) on the local machine.

CSF is not a Windows "service". CSF is an application that is started by the client application (i.e. CUCIMOC or CUPC 8).

CSF configuration is stored in Windows registry. Since CSF does not have a visible user interface, it's up to the upper layer application (or human being) to populate the configuration in registry. Different applications have different approaches. For example, CUCIMOC require configuration data to be entered into registry manually. There's no application or web GUI to enter those data. For CUPC 8, you may enter those data from CUPS admin web page.

What's new in configuration?

Depends on what client or feature you're using, configuration could be the same or different from previous version (CUPS 7.x).

There's no change in applications below. Please refer to chapter 5 – "Deploy and Troubleshooting Features" for configuration instructions.

- CUPC 7.x client features (such as desk phone, soft phone, LDAP, voicemail, web conference).
- Calendar Integration
- IPPM
- MOC RCC
- Sametime Plug-in

For CUPC 8.0, configuration steps for ***Soft Phone*** were changed due to the new CSF architecture.

CUPS 8.0 also added new configuration screens for persistent chat and compliance features.

CUPS 8 New Services

As mentioned before, a couple of XCP services were added to CUPS 8. Some of them are required. Some of them are optional depending on features.

Network Services

A network service will be up and running along with the system startup. You don't have to activate it explicitly.

A newly added network service on CUPS 8.0 is "XCP Router".

Cisco UP XCP Router

XCP Router is **required**, which means, it should be up and running all the time. This applies to all clients (including CUPC 7). This is because both PE and XCP Router must be running and functional in order for presence to work.

If XCP Router is down, PE will no longer process SIP requests, a 503 response will be sent until the connection is re-established.

Time	Source	Destination	Protocol	Info
3.45	10.99.23.142	10.88.7.228	SIP	Request: REGISTER sip:apps.local;transport=tcp
3.47	10.88.7.228	10.99.23.142	SIP	Status: 200 OK (1 bindings)
3.65	10.99.23.142	10.88.7.228	SIP	Request: SUBSCRIBE sip:htluo8-contacts@apps.local
3.75	10.99.23.142	10.88.7.228	SIP	Request: SUBSCRIBE sip:htluo8@apps.local
3.75	10.99.23.142	10.88.7.228	SIP	Request: SUBSCRIBE sip:htluo8@apps.local
3.76	10.88.7.228	10.99.23.142	SIP	Status: 503 Service Unavailable
3.79	10.88.7.228	10.99.23.142	SIP	Status: 503 Service Unavailable
3.80	10.88.7.228	10.99.23.142	SIP	Status: 503 Service Unavailable
6.65	10.99.23.142	10.88.7.228	SIP/XML	Request: PUBLISH sip:htluo8@apps.local
6.68	10.88.7.228	10.99.23.142	SIP	Status: 503 Server Locked or Disabled

XCP router is also the most important service for XMPP-based clients (CUPC 8.0). Any configuration change on XMPP features requires XCP router to be restarted.

Feature Services

A feature service, as the name indicates, is for a specific feature. Since we might not need all features on a server, feature services can be activated or deactivated selectively.

You may see the list of XCP feature services in the picture below.

☑	Cisco UP SIP Proxy	Activated
☑	Cisco UP Presence Engine	Activated
☑	Cisco UP Sync Agent	Activated
☑	Cisco UP XCP Text Conference Manager	Activated
☑	Cisco UP XCP Web Connection Manager	Activated
☑	Cisco UP XCP Connection Manager	Activated
☐	Cisco UP XCP SIP Federation Connection Manager	Deactivated
☐	Cisco UP XCP XMPP Federation Connection Manager	Deactivated
☑	Cisco UP XCP Counter Aggregator	Activated
☑	Cisco UP XCP Message Archiver	Activated
☑	Cisco UP XCP Directory Service	Activated
☑	Cisco UP XCP Authentication Service	Activated

There are four services you usually want for CUPC 8. See below.

XCP Connection Manager

Connection Manager services XMPP clients, such as CUPC 8, Pidgin, MomentIM, etc. If you want to use CUPC 8, you need this service.

XCP Authentication Service

Authentication service is to authenticate XMPP clients. If you want to use CUPC 8, you need this service.

XCP Text Conference Manager (TC)

Text Conference Manager (usually referred as TC) is for text conference (group chat). If you want group chat feature, you need this service. TC service requires external database support. If you haven't configured external database, TC service will fail to start.

XCP Message Archiver (MA)

Message Archiver (usually referred as MA) is for archive instant messages. If you want archive feature for instant message, you need this service. MA service requires external database support. If you haven't configured external database, MA service will fail to start.

The above services are the frequently used service by CUPC 8. Services discussed below are not directly related with CUPC 8.

XCP Web Connection Manager

Web Connection Manager services OpenAPI clients (web clients).

XCP SIP/XMPP Federation Connection Manager

SIP Federation and XMPP Federation Connection Manager services are for domain federation. If you want to exchange presence/IM with another system (e.g. OCS, Sametime, Google Talk), you need these services.

XCP Counter Aggregator

Counter Aggregator is the service that feeds XCP performance data into VOS performance counter. So you may use VOS tools (such as RTMT) to retrieve/monitor performance.

XCP Directory Service

This service supports XMPP based directory on LDAP server. This is for 3rd-party clients only (if the client supports directory search). CUPC 8 does not use this service. CUPC 8 search LDAP server directly.

CUPS 8 New Features

Now we've discussed all the new services from technical perspective. From end users perspective, what's new on CUPS 8.0? The two major new features are persistent chat room and compliance.

Persistent Chat Room

Persistent chat room exists after all participants leave (so they can rejoin it in a later time).

Compliance

Compliance archives, audits, filters or blocks IM messages (or file transfers in IM).

There are two compliance options on CUPS 8.0 – *Message Archiving* (native built-in on CUS) and *3rd-Party Compliance* (requires 3rd-party server). You may choose either one but not both. It's because most of the 3rd-party compliance servers have message archiving feature. CUPS' native message archiving will be redundant if you use a 3rd-party compliance server.

Message Archiving

Message Archiving is a native feature built in CUPS 8.0. It archives instant messages to an external database (PostgreSQL). This is a less expensive solution because the only extra component you need is PostgreSQL, which is free. The down side is you only get raw data with this solution. There are no reporting/analyzing tools on CUPS for the archives. Though you may build your own reporting tool (or buy from 3rd-party).

3rd-Party Compliance

If you need more features such as reporting, analyzing, and content-based filtering/blocking, you may consider a 3rd-party compliance server, such as FaceTime Vantage. 3rd-party compliance servers are usually commercial products. Technical support of the compliance server is provided by 3rd-party vendor, not Cisco.

CUPS 8.0 supports different 3rd-party compliance products. In this book, we'll use FaceTime Vantage as example.

Dependencies

Due to the design of Jabber XCP, persistent chat room and messaging archiving require an external database (PostgreSQL). This may be changed in future release of CUPS, since CUPS has its own internal database (Informix).

Obviously, 3rd-party compliance depends on 3rd-party compliance server (such as FaceTime Vantage).

You may see the dependencies from the diagram below:

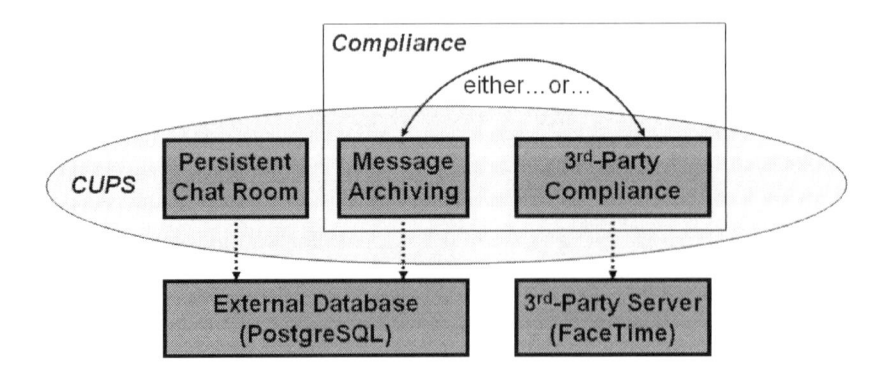

External Database

To support persistent chat room and message archiving feature you need to set up an external database.

Right now, only PostgreSQL is supported. You may install PostgreSQL on Windows or Linux. We'll use Windows as example in this book.

Download PostgreSQL

PostgreSQL is open source software. You may download it for free from www.postgresql.org.

Windows version of PostgreSQL is an exe file. Download the exe file to your Windows box.

Install PostgreSQL

Installation of PostgreSQL is pretty straightforward. The only information you need to enter is the admin user (postgre) password.

1. Double-click the downloaded exe file and you'll see a welcome window. Click "Next".
2. Unless you want to change the installation directory. Otherwise, click "Next".

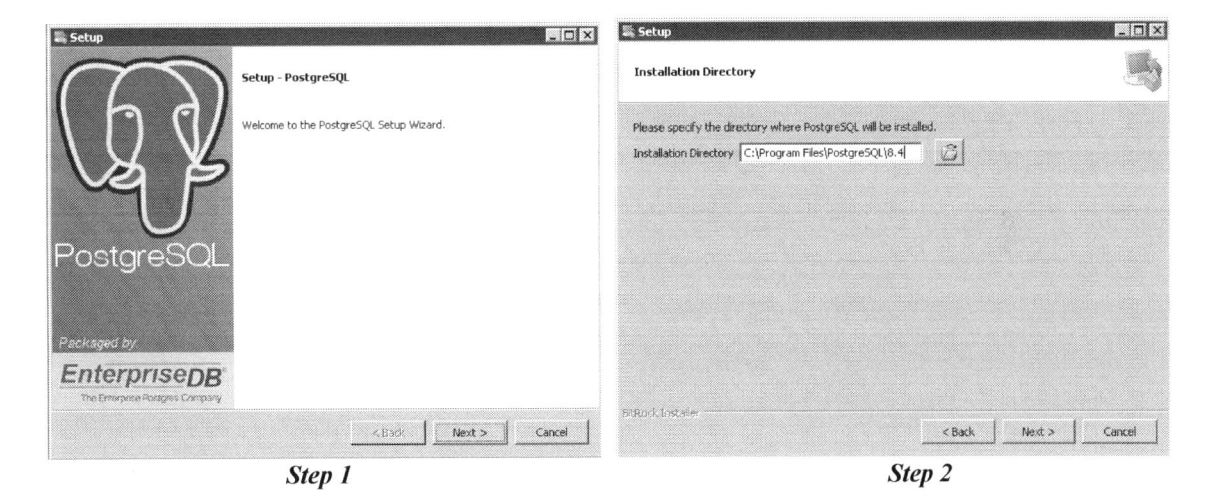

Step 1   *Step 2*

3. Unless you want to change the data directory. Otherwise, click "Next".
4. Enter an admin password. The default admin user is called "postgre".

294 Chapter 8. CUPS 8.0 and CUPC 8.0

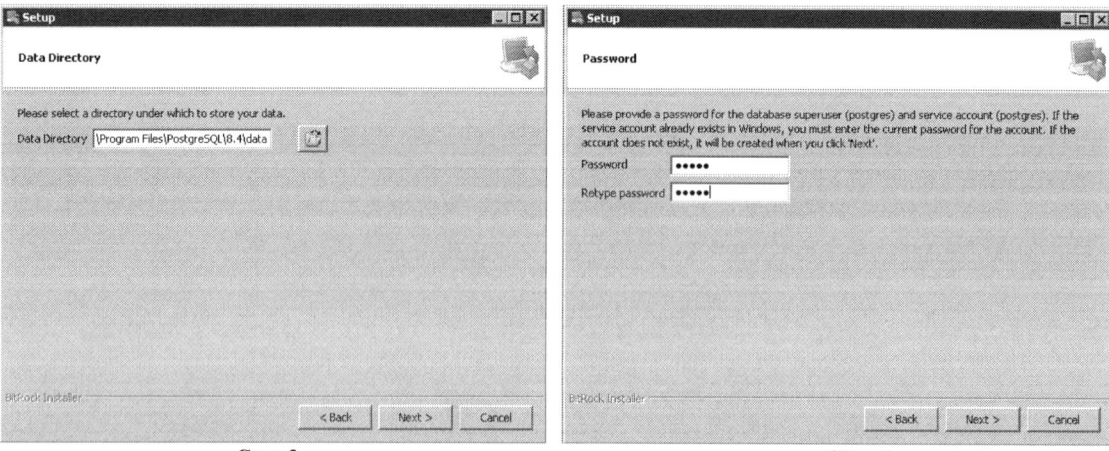

Step 3   *Step 4*

5. Accept the default port number (5432) and click "Next". If you changed the default port number, you need to match it on CUPS side.
6. Accept default setting and click "Next".

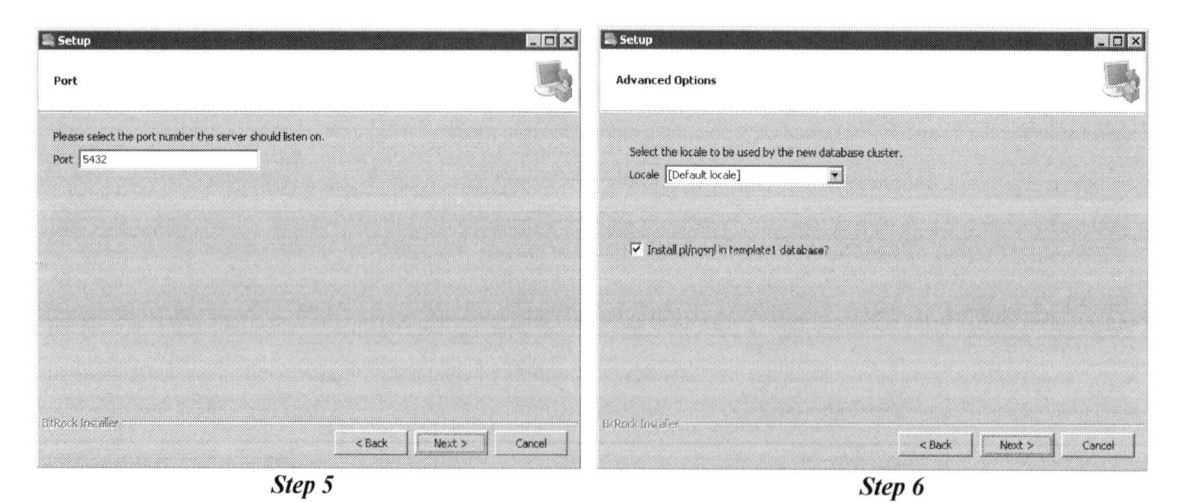

Step 5   *Step 6*

7. Click "Next" on "Ready to Install" screen. Wait for install to finish.
8. Uncheck "Launch Stack Builder" option and click "Finish".

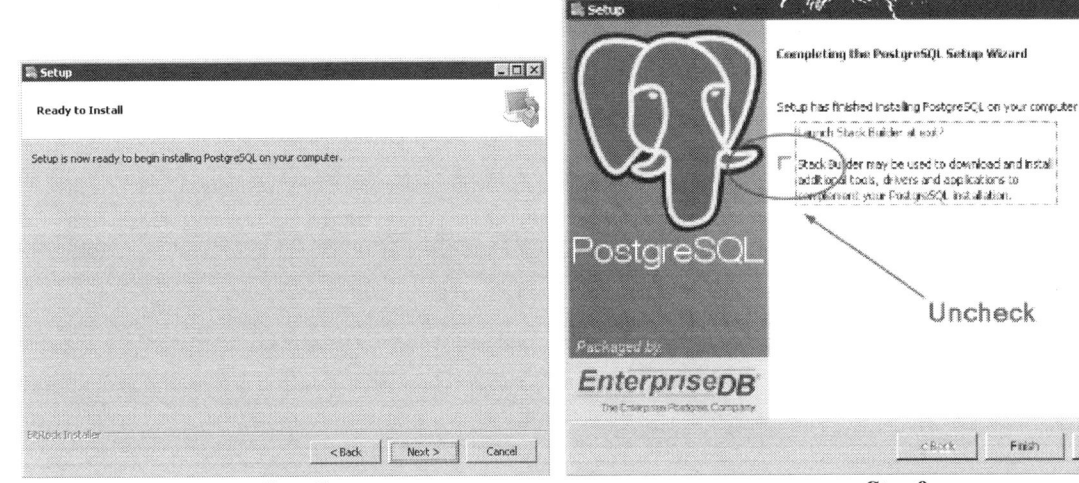

Step 7   *Step 8*

Configure PostgreSQL

It's the best practice to create dedicated database and access account for each integration. We'll create a dedicate database and account in PostgreSQL for CUPS.

1. Make sure PostgreSQL service is running (started).
2. Launch PostgreSQL admin tool from Windows start menu > PostgreSQL > pgAdmin III.

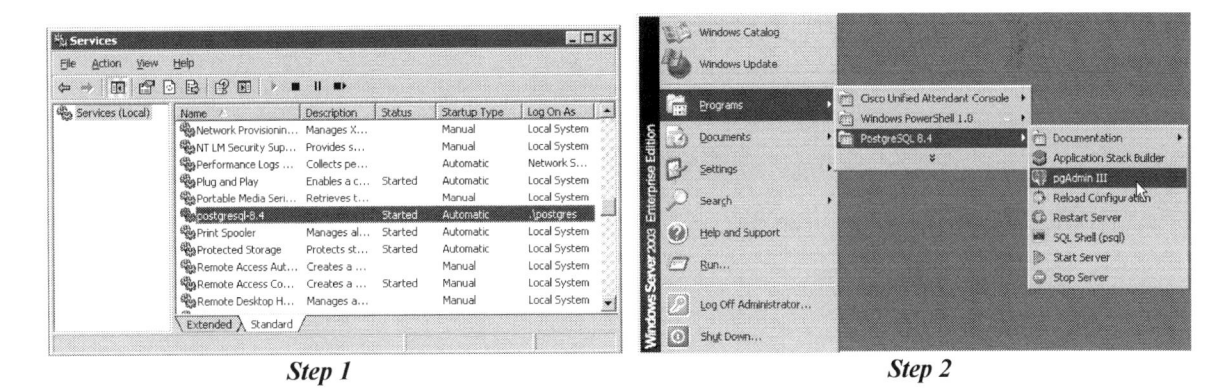

Step 1   *Step 2*

3. Right-click on the "localhost" instance and click "Connect".
4. Enter the password you configured during installation and click "OK".

Step 3

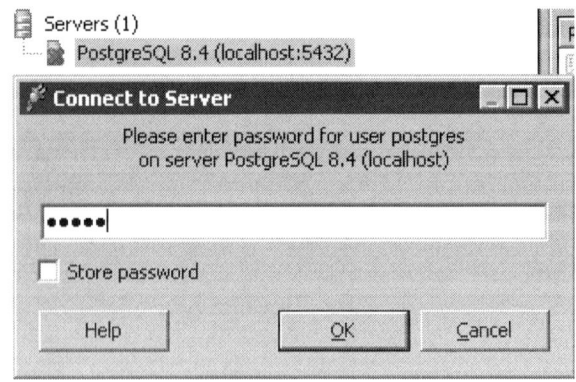

Step 4

5. Right-click "Databases" and click "New Database…"

6. Enter a name for the database (eg. "cups") then click "OK". Now we created a database called "cups".

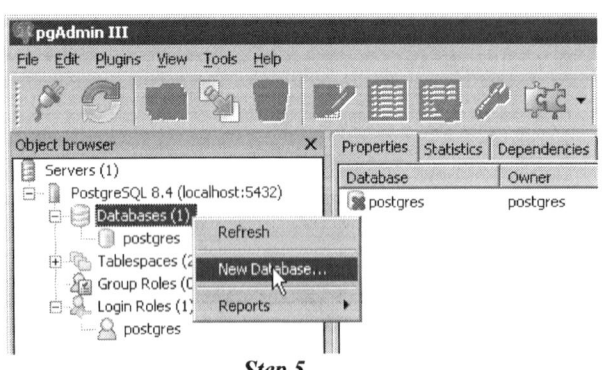

Step 5

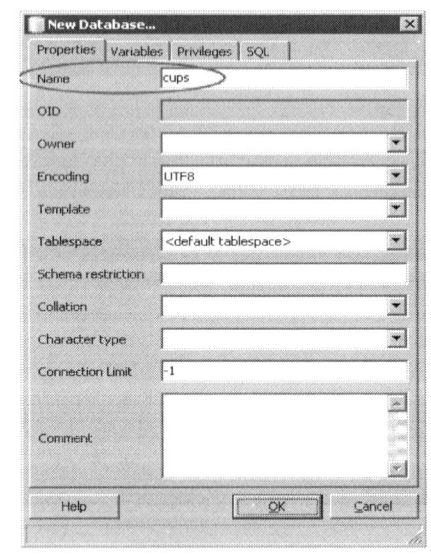

Step 6

7. Right-click "Login Roles", then click "New Login Role…"

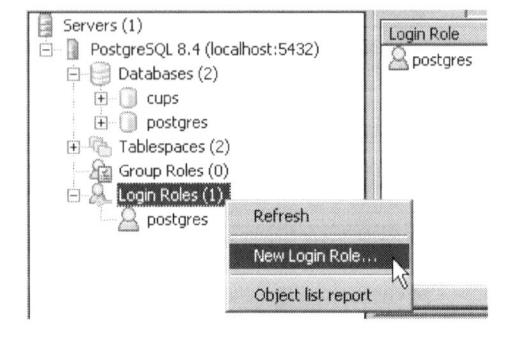

Step 7

External Database 297

8. In "Properties" tab, enter a username in the "Role name" (e.g. "cups"). Enter a password for this user (e.g. "cisco").

9. In "Role Privileges" tab, check "Superuser" checkbox. Click "OK". Now we created a database user called "cups" with password "cisco".

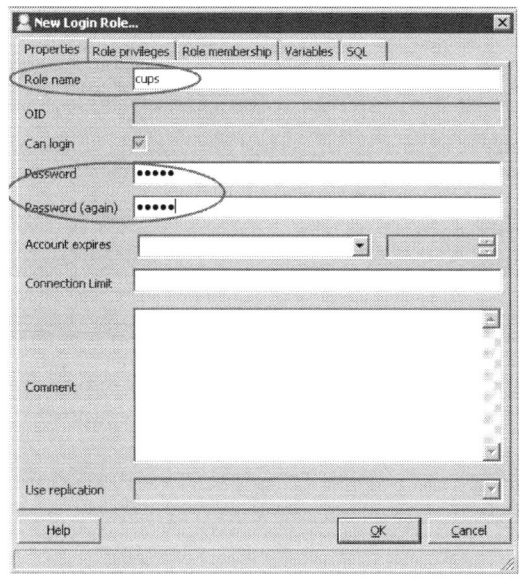

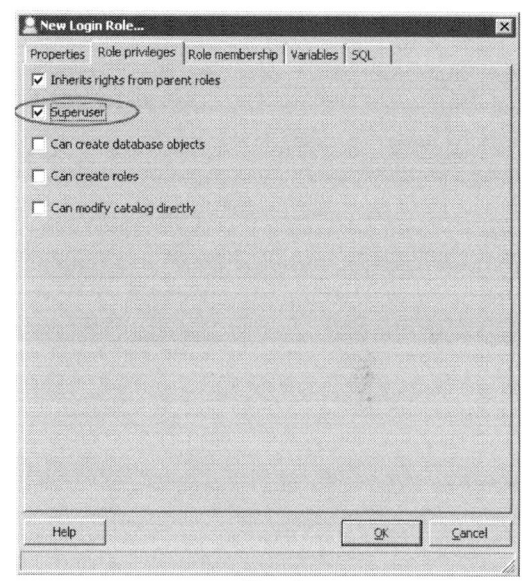

Step 8

Step 9

10. Expand database "cups" > Schemas > Public > Tables. You'll see there's zero (0) tables in this database. Since this is a newly created database, we don't have any tables in it yet.

11. With notepad, open C:\Program Files\PostgreSQL\8.4\data\pg_hba.conf. Add a new line to the end of the file:

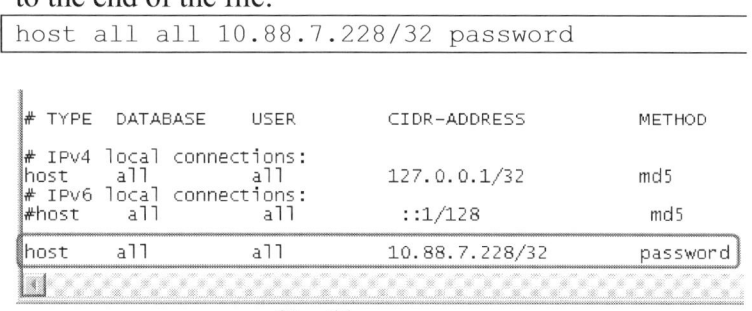

```
host    all    all    10.88.7.228/32    password
```

```
# TYPE  DATABASE        USER       CIDR-ADDRESS         METHOD
# IPv4 local connections:
host     all             all        127.0.0.1/32         md5
# IPv6 local connections:
#host    all             all        ::1/128              md5
host     all             all        10.88.7.228/32       password
```

Step 11

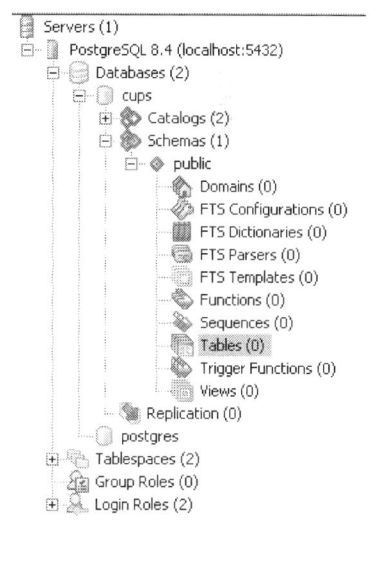

Step 10

10.88.7.228 is the IP address of your CUPS server. Without this line, PostgreSQL won't allow connection from your CUPS server. You'll have to restart PostgreSQL service to make this change take effect.

12. Now we are done configuring the PostgreSQL database. Before we go to CUPS server to configure external database let's open the PostgreSQL server status window by going to "Tools > Server Status". The server status window will show us real time messages that are useful for troubleshooting.

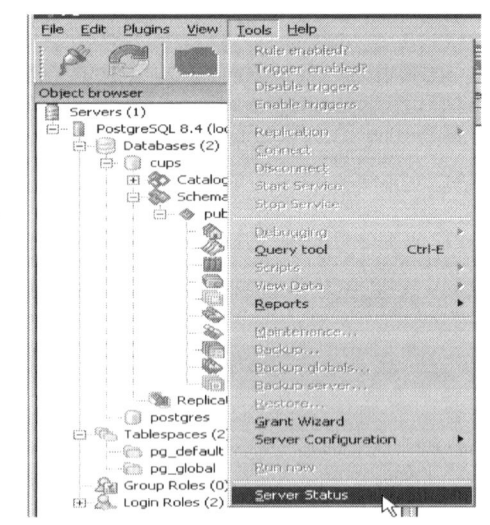

Step 12

Configure CUPS to use external DB

Now we have PostgreSQL ready for use. We need to configure CUPS to use it.

1. Go to CUPS > Messaging > External Databases. Click "Add New" to add a new reference to the external database.

"Database Name" is the database you created in PostgreSQL. In our example, it was "cups". "User Name/Password" is the user we created in PostgreSQL. In our example, it was "cups".

Configure CUPS to use external DB 299

Hostname is the address of the PostgreSQL server.
Port Number has to match the port number being used by PostgreSQL (default is 5432).

2. After entering all information, click "Save". You'll get a warning that "Unable to execute the connectivity test because this external database server is not mapped to either the Message Archiver or Persistent Chat services". This is normal. We'll associate this database to those services later.

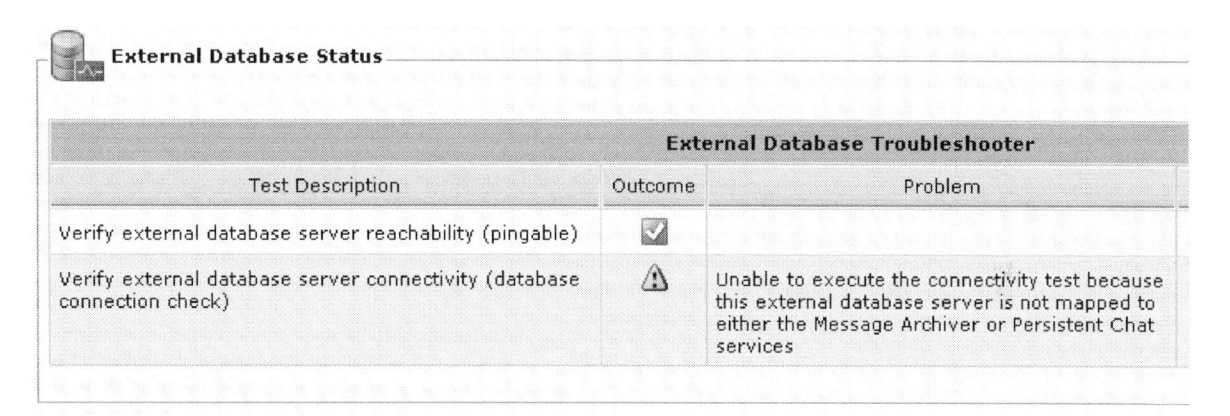

3. If the information you entered in step 1 was correct, you would get some messages on PostgreSQL server status window.

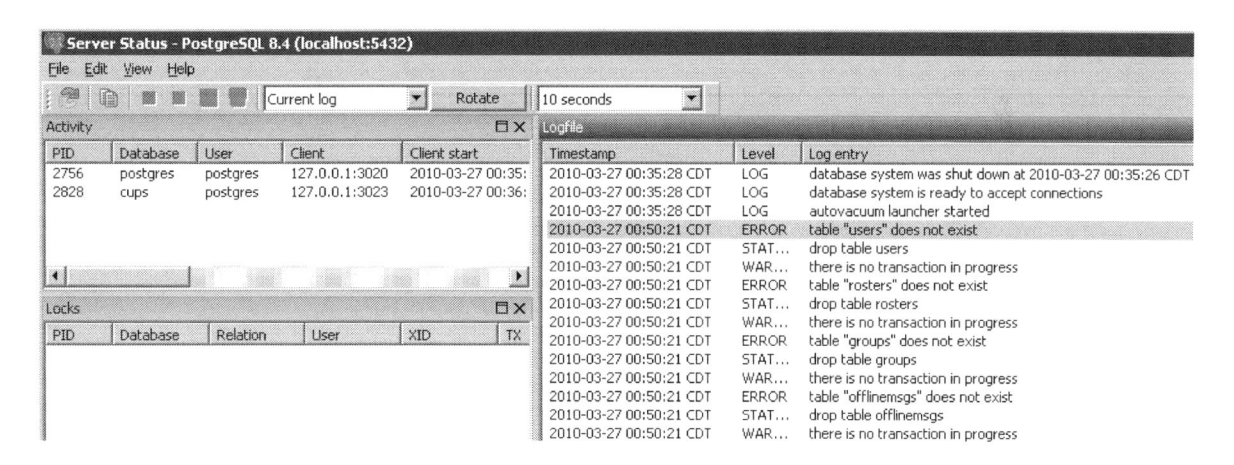

Don't panic on those "Errors" and "Warnings". It was CUPS checking if tables exist in the database already. If not, CUPS will create them.

4. You'll notice that the number of tables in "cups" database increased from 0 to 27. And you'll see the table names on the right-hand side.

For explanation of each table, please refer to CUPS documentations. For example, the "jm" table is used to store archived messages.

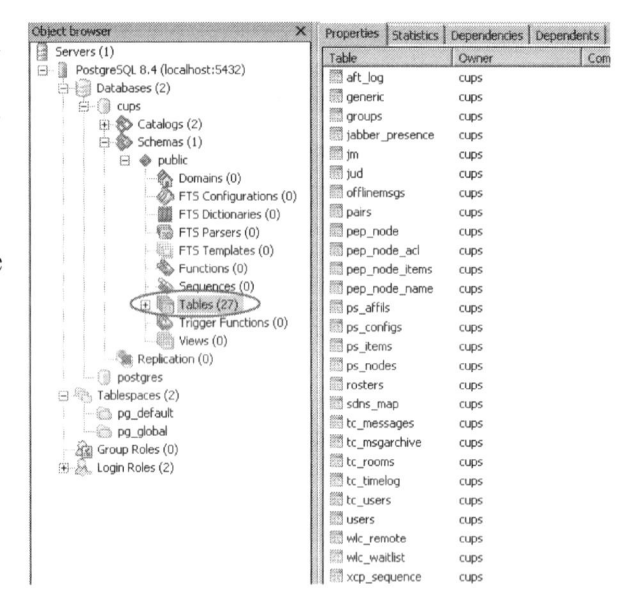

Persistent Chat Room

The biggest advantage of "persistent chat room" is you may join the chat room actively without an invitation (given that you have proper permission).

To enable persistent chat room feature, you need an external database. See earlier instructions to set up external database.

Enable Persistent Chat

Steps to enable persistent chat room:

1. Go to CUPS > Messaging > Conferencing and Persistent Chat.
2. Check "Enable Persistent Chat" checkbox.
3. From "Persistent Chat Database Assignment" drop-down menu, choose the database configured before.
4. Click "Save".

Persistent Chat Room

[Screenshot: Enable Persistent Chat settings with Archive all room messages, Number of Connections to the Database: 5, Database Connection Heartbeat Interval (seconds): 300, Persistent Chat Database Assignment with Node 10.88.7.228 and External Database cup]

5. You'll see notification warnings on the top of the screen. Follow instructions to restart XCP Router and XCP Text Conferencing services.

Test Persistent Chat

You'll need supported XMPP client to test persistent chat. In this book, we'll use CUPC 8 for testing.

1. From CUPC, go to File > New Chat Room.
2. Enter a room name (e.g. "Tech Team). Optionally, enter a subject (e.g. "Apollo Project")
3. Click "Invite" to create the chat room.

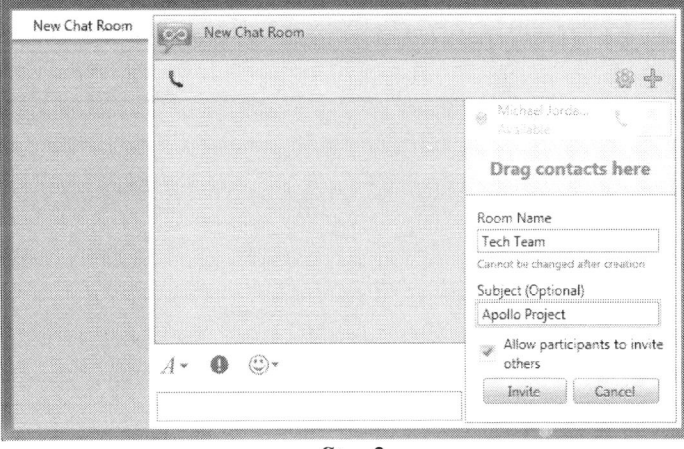

Step 1 *Step 2*

4. After chat room was created, you may click the plus (+) sign on upper-right hand corner to invite other contacts. Or just drag and drop an existing contact from your CUPC contact list to the chat room.

5. The contact being invited will receive a notification. He may click "Join" to join the chat room.

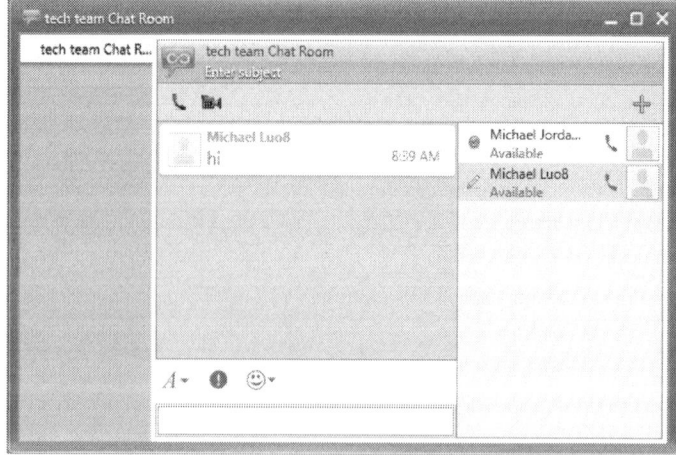

Step 5   *Step 5*

6. Please note that we have the chat room in our contact list now. You may join the chat room anytime by double-click it. You don't need invitation to join the chat room.

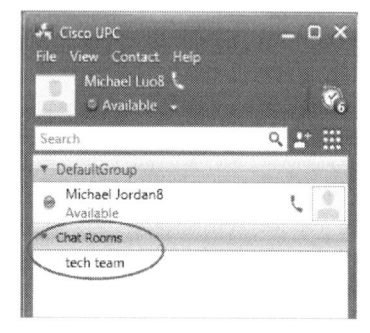

Compliance

What is compliance?

When IM (Instant Messaging) becomes a business tool, it has to compliant with corporate policies. For some organizations, instant messages need to be archived, audited. Some sensitive contents may be filtered or blocked from instant messages. This is called "compliance".

On CUPS 8.0, you may choose one (and only one) from the following three options:

- Not configured
- Message Archiver
- 3rd-Party Compliance Server

Message Archiver

Configure Message Archiver

To configure Message Archiver, we go to CUPS > Messaging > Compliance

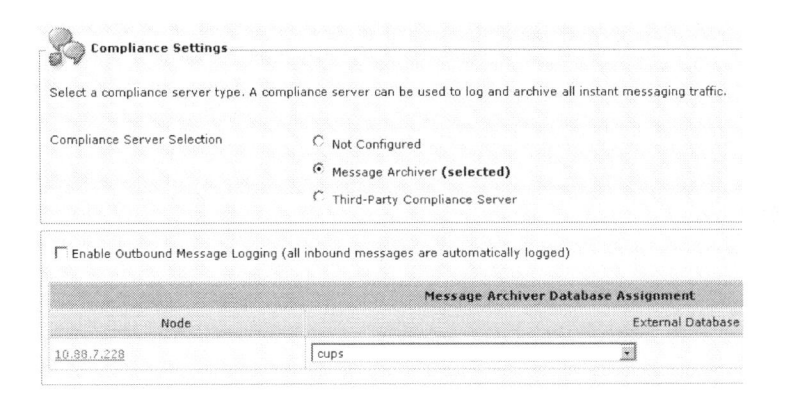

1. On "Compliance Server Selection", choose "Message Archiver".
2. From "Message Archiver Database Assignment" drop-down menu, choose the external database configured before. Then click "Save".

Normally, we don't choose "Enable Outbound Message Logging". Enable this option will duplicate every message in database.

Once you click "Save", you'll notice a notification warning on the top of the screen. Move the mouse over the warning, you'll see the details.

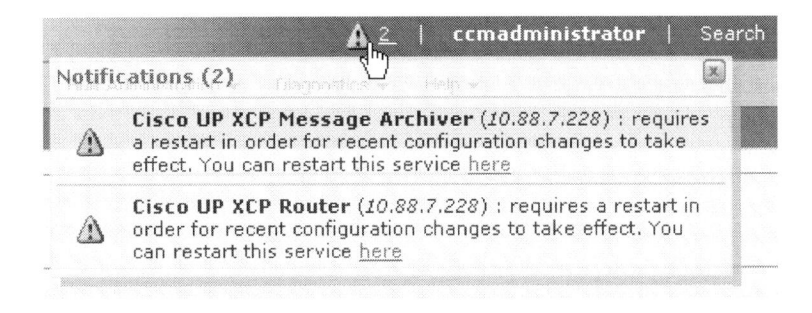

304 Chapter 8. CUPS 8.0 and CUPC 8.0

As you can see from the picture above, you'll need to restart XCP Router and Message Archiver after making changes to configuration.

There are some catches about the "restart":

- XCP Router is the "foundation" of all other XCP services.
- If you shut down XCP Router, it'll shut down all other XCP services.
- If you start XCP Router, it will not start other XCP services.
- If you restart XCP Router, it will restart other XCP services that were running.
- If you restart XCP Router, it will not start other XCP services that were not running.

Best practices:
- You should "restart" XCP Router instead of "stop and start" XCP Router.
- If a service was not running before XCP Router restart, you need to start it manually.

Test Message Archiver

How do we know message archiver was working? You may send a couple instant messages and examine the "jm" table.

1. Connect IM client (such as CUPC) to CUPS and send some test instant messages.
2. Use PostgreSQL admin tool (pgAdmin III) connect to database.
3. Navigate to "Database > cups > Schemas > Public > Tables".
4. Right-click on "jm" table > View Data > View Top 100 Rows.

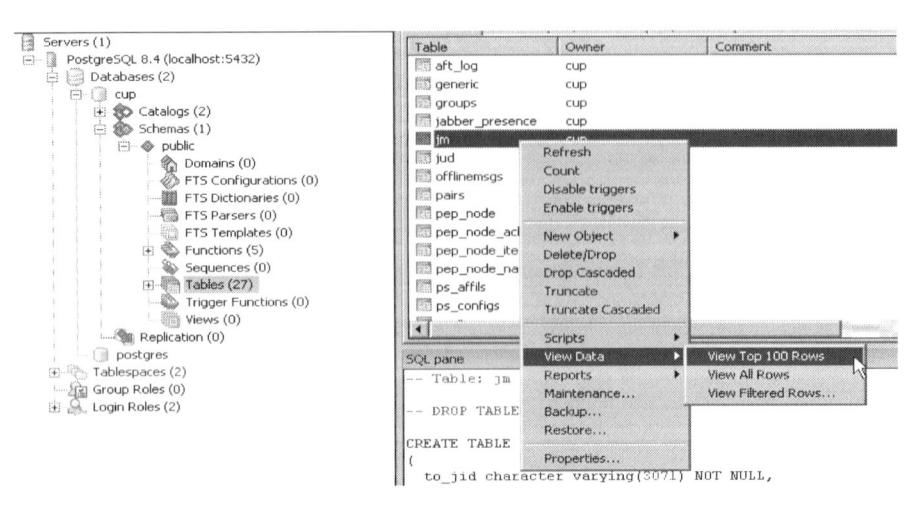

5. You'll see the message you sent in the database table.

Please note that there are no built-in tools on CUPS to do data report for archived messages. You either query the database manually or use a 3rd-party tool.

3rd-Pary Compliance Server

3rd-party compliance servers provide more features comparing with the native "Message Archiver". The workflow is as below:

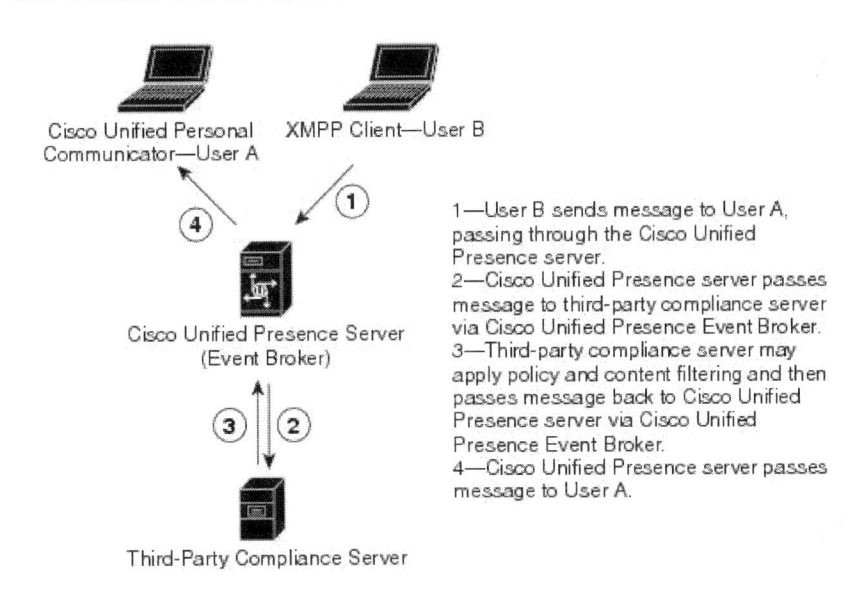

1—User B sends message to User A, passing through the Cisco Unified Presence server.
2—Cisco Unified Presence server passes message to third-party compliance server via Cisco Unified Presence Event Broker.
3—Third-party compliance server may apply policy and content filtering and then passes message back to Cisco Unified Presence server via Cisco Unified Presence Event Broker.
4—Cisco Unified Presence server passes message to User A.

Chapter 8. CUPS 8.0 and CUPC 8.0

Please note:

1. Cisco does not provide technical support on 3rd-party compliance server. Please contact the 3rd-party vender for technical support.
2. CUPS works with different compliance servers as long as they support XDB protocol. XDB is a protocol for 3rd-party to communicate with CUPS XCP components.

We'll use FaceTime Vantage as example in this book. We assume that FaceTime Vantage has been installed. We'll cover the configuration only.

FaceTime Vantage Configuration

Below is the configuration screen of FaceTime Vantage configuration page.

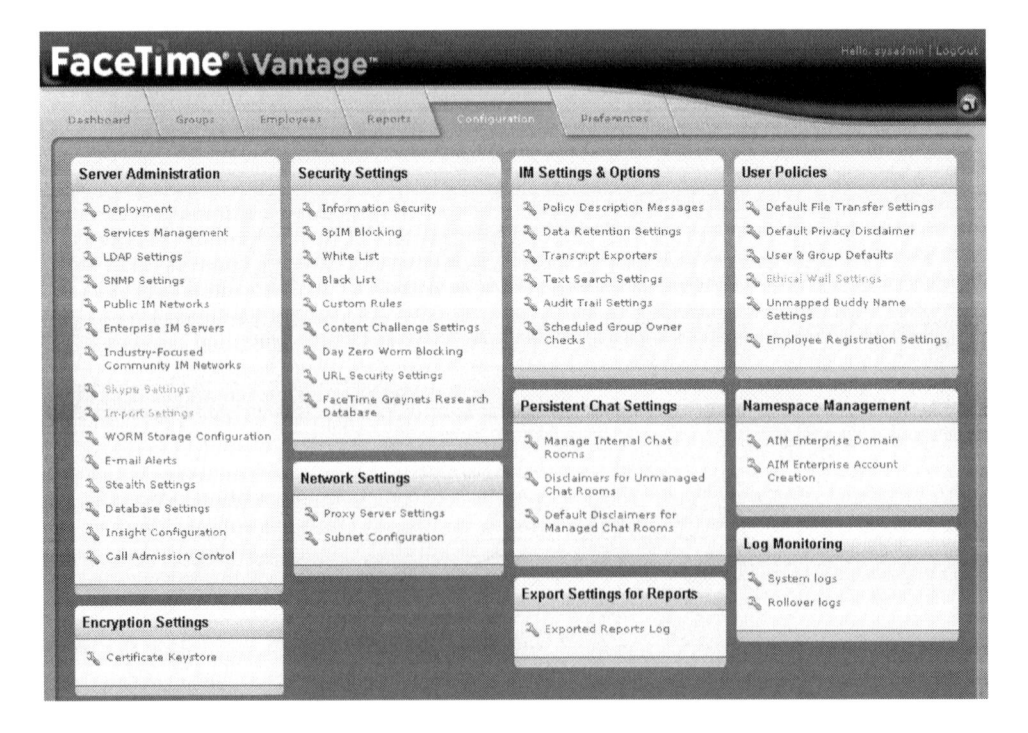

1. We go to "Configuration > Server Administration > Enterprise IM Server > Jabber/XMPP Compliant Service".
2. Choose "Connector for Jabber" and enter the following information.

[Screenshot of Jabber/XMPP Compliant Service configuration showing Connector for Jabber with fields: Connector User ID: open-compliance.10-88-, Connector Password, Connector Host: 10.88.7.209, Connector Port: 7999, Run On Server ID: 1]

Connector User ID

"Connector User ID" will be in the format of "`open-compliance.realm`".

To find out the realm of a CUPS server, you may either do it from CUPS CLI (command line) or CUPS Admin web page.

From CLI, enter the following command:

```
run sql select xcprealm from processnode where systemnode='f'
```

Screen output would be like below:

```
admin:run sql select xcprealm from processnode where systemnode='f'
xcprealm
==========
10-88-7-228
```

As shown in the screenshot above, "`10-88-7-228`" is the "realm". In "Connector User ID", you should enter "`open-compliance.10-88-7-228`".

From GUI, you go to CUPS Admin > System > Cluster Topology. You'll find the hostname/FQDN or IP address of the CUPS server. If there's any dots in the name or IP, you need to replace them with dash ("-").

For example, if it was IP address `10.88.7.228`, the realm would be `10-88-7-228`. If it was FQDN `cups.acme.local`, the realm would be `cups-acme-local`.

Connector Password

Here you configure an arbitrary password. The password configured on CUPS side needs to match with this one (see details later).

Connector Host

Here you enter the IP address of the FaceTime Vantage server.

Connector Port

Here you enter an arbitrary port for FaceTime Vantage server to listen on. It could be any unused port on the FaceTime Vantage server. The port number configured on CUPS side needs to match with this one (see details later).

After saving the configuration, you need to restart IMAuditor service.

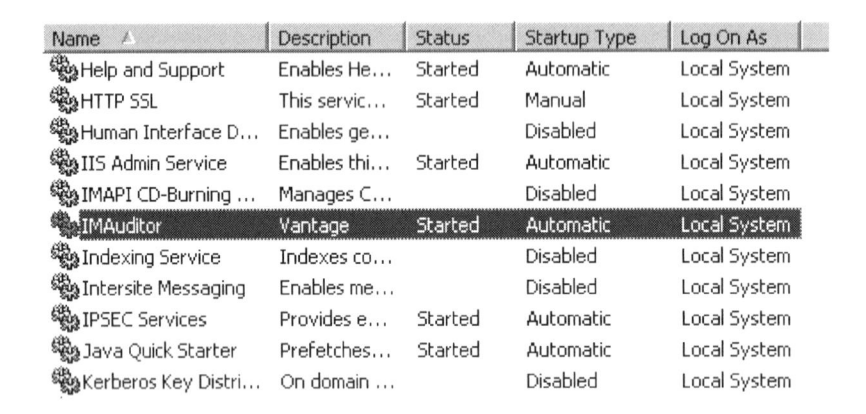

Name	Description	Status	Startup Type	Log On As
Help and Support	Enables He...	Started	Automatic	Local System
HTTP SSL	This servic...	Started	Manual	Local System
Human Interface D...	Enables ge...		Disabled	Local System
IIS Admin Service	Enables thi...	Started	Automatic	Local System
IMAPI CD-Burning ...	Manages C...		Disabled	Local System
IMAuditor	Vantage	Started	Automatic	Local System
Indexing Service	Indexes co...		Disabled	Local System
Intersite Messaging	Enables me...		Disabled	Local System
IPSEC Services	Provides e...	Started	Automatic	Local System
Java Quick Starter	Prefetches...	Started	Automatic	Local System
Kerberos Key Distri...	On domain ...		Disabled	Local System

CUPS Configuration

To configure CUPS use 3rd-party compliance, we go to CUPS Admin > Messaging > Compliance. Select "Third-Party Compliance Server" and enter the following information.

Server Address

This would be the IP address of FaceTime Vantage server.

Server Port

This would be the port number you configured on FaceTime Vantage server.

Server Password and Confirm Password

These would be the password you configured on FaceTime Vantage server.

Test 3rd-Party Compliance

Unfortunately, there's no easy way to tell if the 3rd-party integration was working or not. You either test the feature with some IM clients or you'll have to look at the logs.

On CUPS, you may look at "Cisco UP XCP Router" logs. If it was working, you'll see messages like this:

```
09:37:24.869 |Connection established to host '10.88.7.209', port 7999
09:37:24.870 |Component open-compliance.10-88-7-228 is CONNECTED
```

10.88.7.209 was the IP address of 3rd-party compliance server. 7999 was the port on the 3rd-party compliance server.

Compliance in Action

Below is a screenshot to demonstrate one of the "compliance" features – restricted phrase.

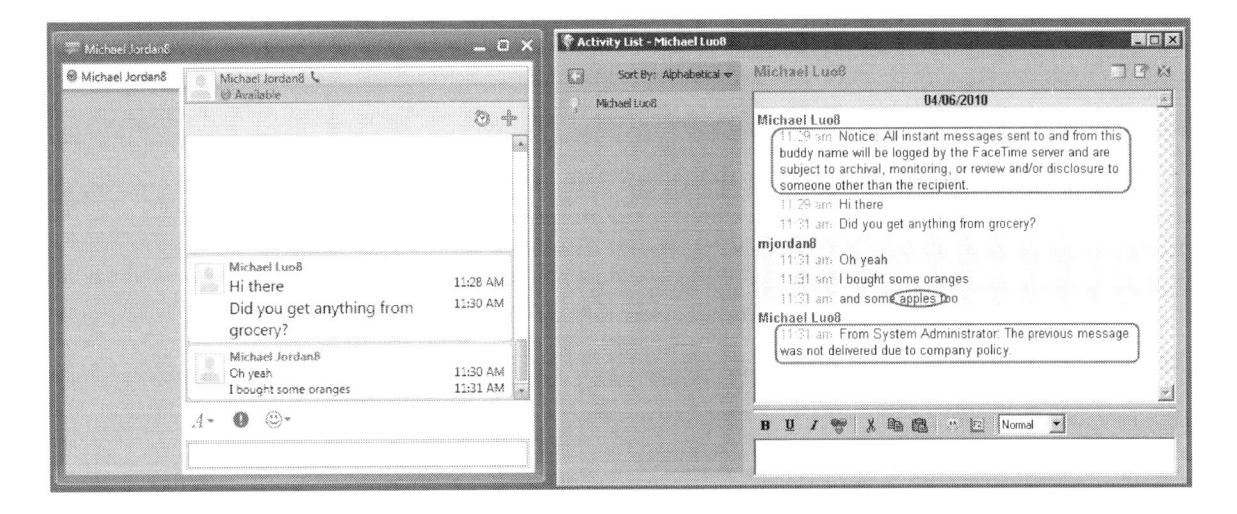

In the example above, "apple" is a restricted phrase configured on 3rd-party server. When the user on the right tried to send an instant message that contains the word "apple", the server blocked it and gave a warning.

Reviewer can use the reporting feature on 3rd-party server to review violations.

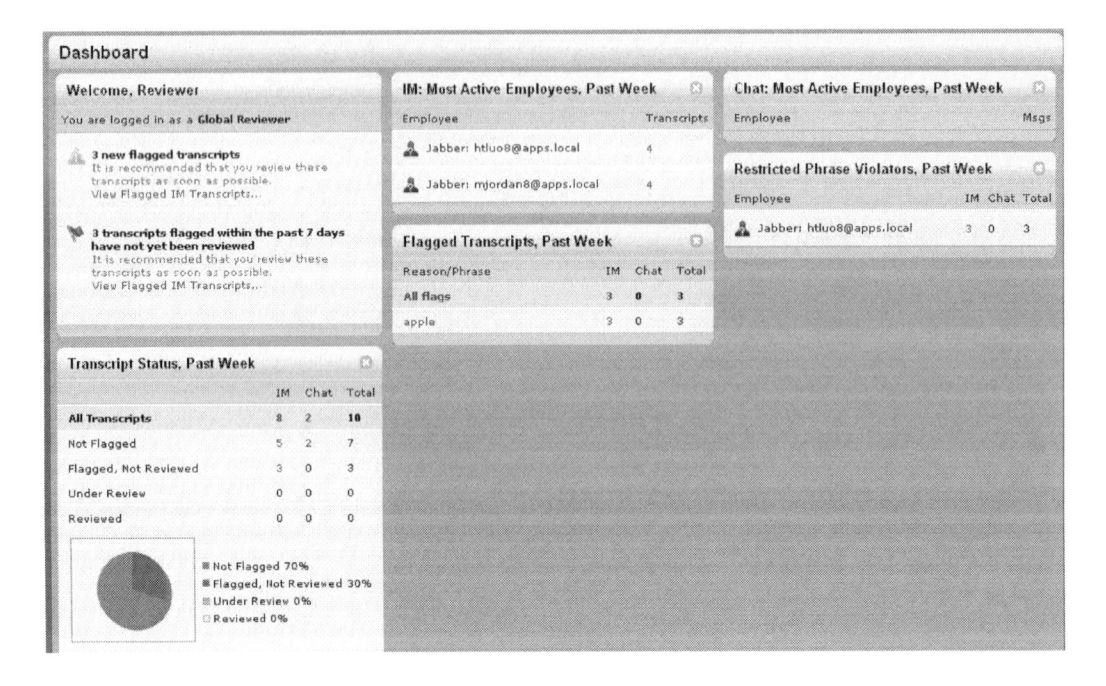

Server Configuration Changes for CUPC 8

Because CUPC 8 adopted CSF technology, there are some configuration changes on CUCM and CUPS. For now, the changes are for "**soft phone**" feature. (i.e. if you don't care about soft phone, you could probably ignore that).

CUCM

Changes on CUCM:

1. A new device type "Cisco Unified Client Service Framework" (CSF) is used for CUPC 8 soft phone mode. (The old "Cisco Unified Personal Communicator" device type still exists for CUPC 7 and earlier versions).

Server Configuration Changes for CUPC 8   311

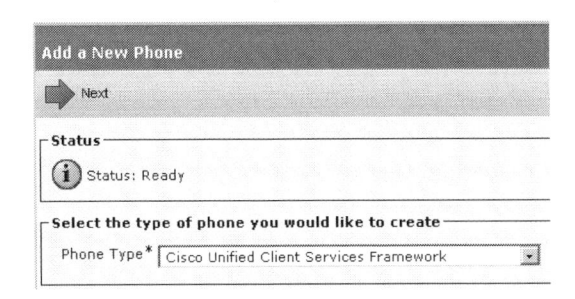

2. You may use free form name for the CSF device. The device name doesn't have to be UPC+UserID (this was required on CUPC 7 and earlier versions).

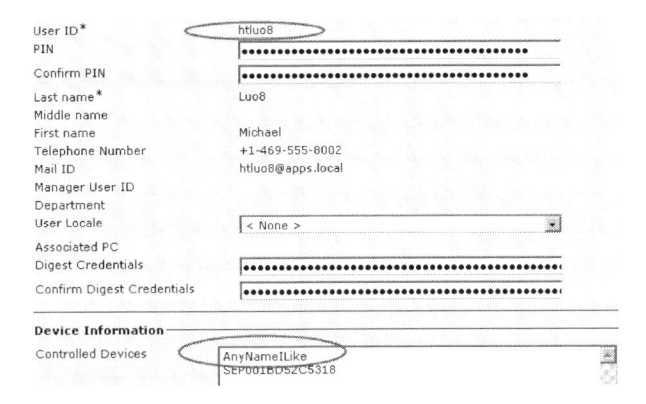

3. You need to associate the CSF device on CUCM End User configuration page. (It is not required for CUPC 7 and earlier versions).

CUPS

Changes on CUPS:

1. Audio Profile is required for soft phone. With CSF, CUPC soft phone has better audio control, such as noise suppression, echo cancellation, etc. A "Voice Profile" is to configure those parameters.

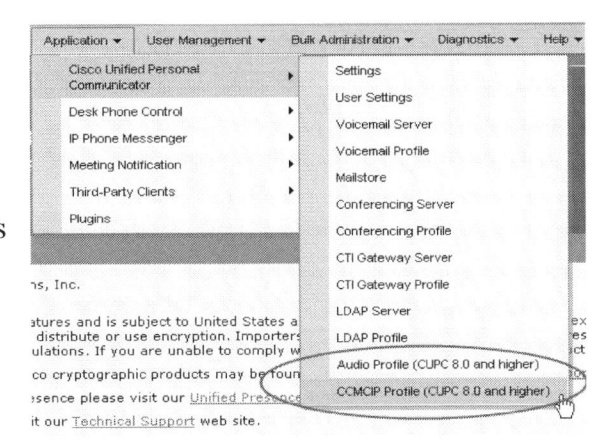

312 Chapter 8. CUPS 8.0 and CUPC 8.0

2. "CCMCIP Profile" is required. CSF uses this profile to locate CCMCIP address. CCMCIP is a network service running on CUCM servers. CSF uses CCMCIP to retrieve the device list associated to an end user. Then CSF retrieves the soft phone device name from the list by device type.

CUPC 8 Changes

Phone modes

Phone mode on CUPC 8 is less explicit comparing with CUPC 7 and earlier versions.

To use "desk phone" mode, you check the box "Use my desk phone as my phone". To use "soft phone", you uncheck that box.

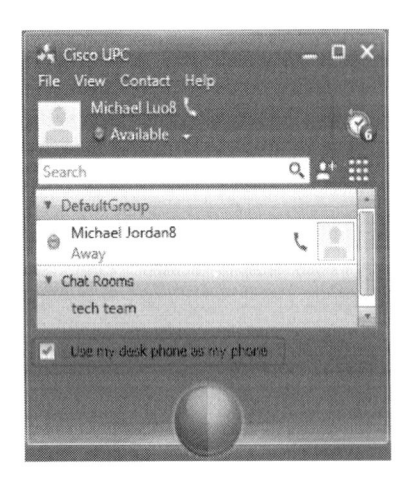

Unfortunately, unlike earlier versions, there's no way to tell if the phone mode was successful or not from the main window. To see the health of each feature, you need to go to CUPC > Help > Show Server Health.

Please note that in "Show Server Health" window, "Desk Phone (CAST)" is for video feature. "Desk Phone (CTI)" is for desk phone control (desk phone mode). They are two different features.

Video Feature with Desk Phone

CUPC 8 has a video feature when you're using desk phone. If you've ever heard of CUVA (Cisco Unified Video Advantage), you should be familiar with this feature.

To use this feature, there are some requirements:

1. The network cable on CUPC computer needs to connect to the desk phone's "PC port".
2. You need to enable the video capability of the phone from CUCM device configuration page. If the video feature was enabled, you should see a little "camera" icon on the lower-right hand corner of the phone's screen.

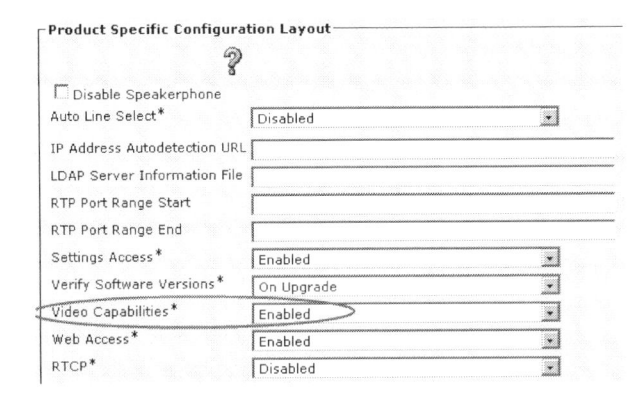

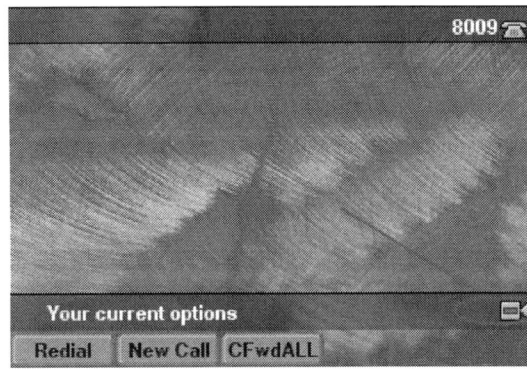

Chapter 9. CUCIMOC

Introduction

CUCIMOC (pronounced as "cookie-mok") stands for **C**isco **U**nified **C**ommunication **I**ntegration with **M**icrosoft **O**ffice **C**ommunicator.

Technically, CUCIMOC has nothing to do with CUPS. CUCIMOC does not require CUPS. It was mentioned here because some customers would treat it as an alternative for MOC RCC (which requires CUPS).

MOC/OCS is in parallel with CUPC/CUPS. OCS and CUPS actually has some functions overlap (for example, Instant Messaging, Calendar status, etc.). If a customer already chose MOC/OCS as their primary Instant Messaging system, all they want is to integrate MOC/OCS with Cisco phone system (CUCM, Unity, etc.). Before CUCIMOC, MOC RCC is their only option.

MOC RCC is server-side integration (integration between CUPS server and OCS server). To deploy MOC RCC, it requires knowledge of SIP routing, SIP URI, SRV records. OCS load-balancer would add addition complexity to the picture.

In contract, CUCIMOC is client-side solution, which means:

     1) You don't have to make changes to OCS server.
     2) No CUPS server is required.

Please note CUCIMOC is an "add-on" or "plug-in" instead of a standalone application. CUCIMOC utilizes MOC API to extend the function of MOC.

CUCIMOC talks to CUCM for phone control and phone presence. CUCIMOC then passes the information to MOC. MOC will display status accordingly (such as "On the Phone").

To successfully deploy and troubleshoot CUCIMOC, it's very important to understand the integration and interaction of different components. When a function doesn't work as desired, you need to know which component is responsible for it. For example, you drag a contact from MOC contact list and drop it to CUCIMOC tab to dial. CUCIMOC reports "No

316 Chapter 9. CUCIMOC

phone number associated with the contact". Contact information is being handled by OCS/MOC. In this case, you should open a case with Microsoft instead of Cisco.

Below are the screenshots of CUCIMOC tab on MOC:

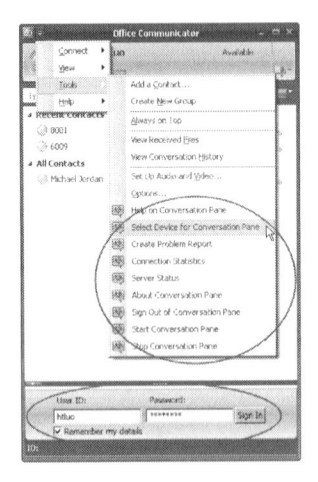

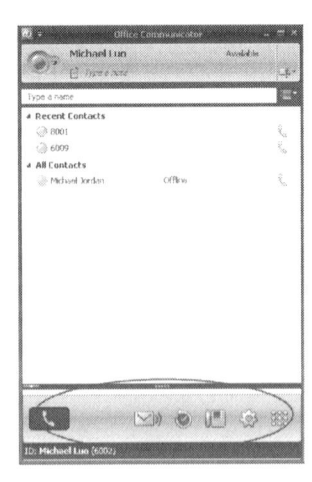

After installing CUCIMOC, there will be a tab showing up at the bottom of MOC. It is called "Conversation Pane".

After logged into MOC, you'll have to log into conversation pane to authenticate with CUCM (sorry, no single sign-on at current version of CUCIMOC).

After logged into conversation pane, you'll have a couple icons showing up. From left to right are: "drop-to-dial", voicemail, call history, phone mode, setting, dial pad.

Components

There are three Cisco components in the picture: UC Tab, CUCIMOC and CSF.

Here's a chart that displays each components' function and corresponding exe.

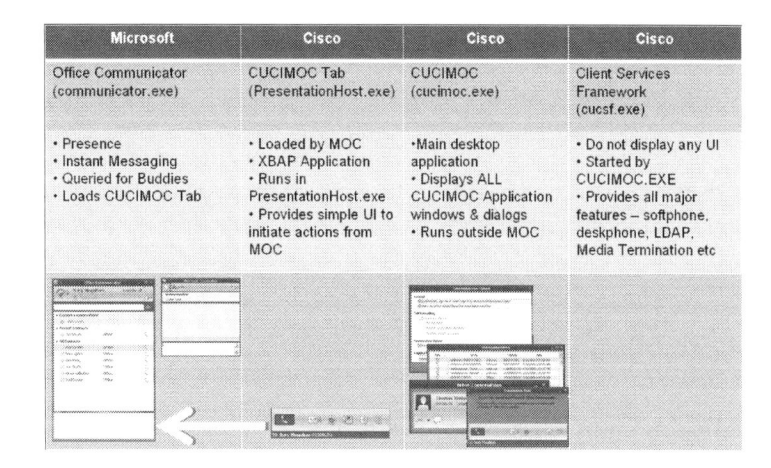

Microsoft	Cisco	Cisco	Cisco
Office Communicator (communicator.exe)	CUCIMOC Tab (PresentationHost.exe)	CUCIMOC (cucimoc.exe)	Client Services Framework (cucsf.exe)
• Presence • Instant Messaging • Queried for Buddies • Loads CUCIMOC Tab	• Loaded by MOC • XBAP Application • Runs in PresentationHost.exe • Provides simple UI to initiate actions from MOC	• Main desktop application • Displays ALL CUCIMOC Application windows & dialogs • Runs outside MOC	• Do not display any UI • Started by CUCIMOC.EXE • Provides all major features – softphone, deskphone, LDAP, Media Termination etc

Each component on the client side interacts with different services on server side.

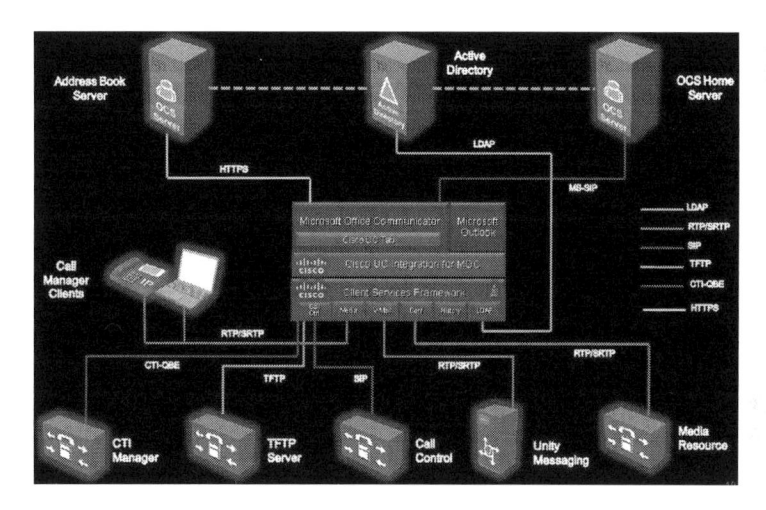

CSF – Client Service Framework

CSF (Client Service Framework) is a new component in Cisco Unified Communication products. Please note that CSF is not dedicated to CUCIMOC. CSF is just first used by CUCIMOC.

What is CSF?

If you're familiar with Cisco Unified Communication clients (such as CUPC, Sametime Integration, Webex Connect, etc.), you'll notice that they share some common features. Such as "Desk Phone Control" (CTI), Soft Phone (SIP), Voicemail, LDAP search, etc.

Before CSF, each product team has to build their software code independently. Since they share the same functionality and architecture, why don't we build a common infrastructure and share among different products? This is the idea of CSF.

CSF does not have a user interface. CSF runs at the background and provides service for different applications (such as CUCIMOC, Webex Connect, etc.).

Stop and Start

Since CSF does not have user interface, the only way to stop it is to kill it from Windows task manager (the name is cucsf.exe). When you launch MOC (CUCIMOC), CUCMOC will start CSF automatically.

Sometimes, restart CSF is required (for example, to refresh application rules).

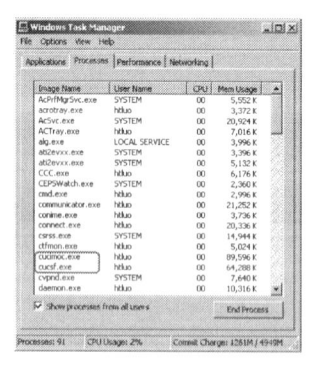

Configuration

Without a user interface, you cannot configure CSF from GUI (Graphic User Interface). CSF reads configuration from Windows registry. The registry is at "HKCU\Software\Cisco Systems, Inc.\Client Services Framework\AdminData".

In the registry, it contains the information CSF will use to perform different functions (such as login, TFTP, CTI control, LDAP, etc.).

Cisco provides a sample BAT (batch) file to update the registry. You may also use system management tools (such as Microsoft login scripts or group policies) to populate the registry to multiple client computers.

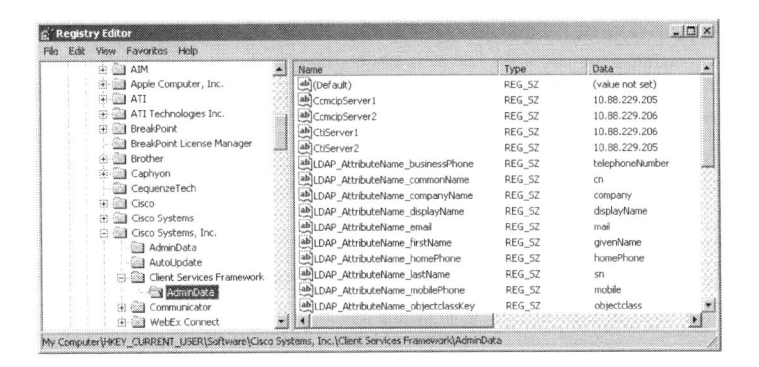

CSF – Softphone device

Soft phone is one of the services CSF provides. It terminates the medial stream on your computer (ie. you may use your computer as a telephone). It's similar to "CUPC soft phone".

The soft phone uses SIP protocol. In order for the soft phone to register with CUCM, we need to configure the device on CUCM server first (CUCM Admin > Device > Phone).

The device type on CUCM server is called "Client Service Framework" (CSF). Sometimes, it causes confusion for customers. Some customers think a CSF device on CUCM is required to use the CSF on client side. It is not true. CSF device on CUCM is just for the "soft phone" feature of CSF. If you're not going to use "soft phone" feature, you don't need to configure CSF device on CUCM. Other features of CSF will still work fine (such as desk phone, LDAP, etc.).

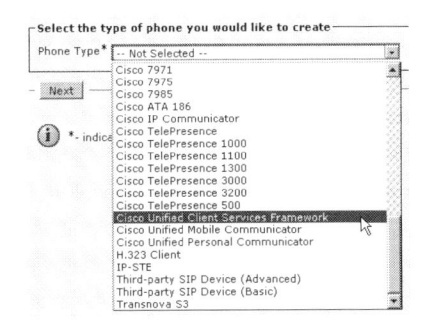

Installation

You may download installation file from www.cisco.com. There are two files in the CUCIMOC download section: cucimoc-Admin-xxx.zip and cucimoc-Install-xxx.zip. ("xxx" stands for different versions).

Cucimoc-Admin contains the files for configuration and administration (such as CUCM COP files, sample registry file, sample BAT file, etc.).

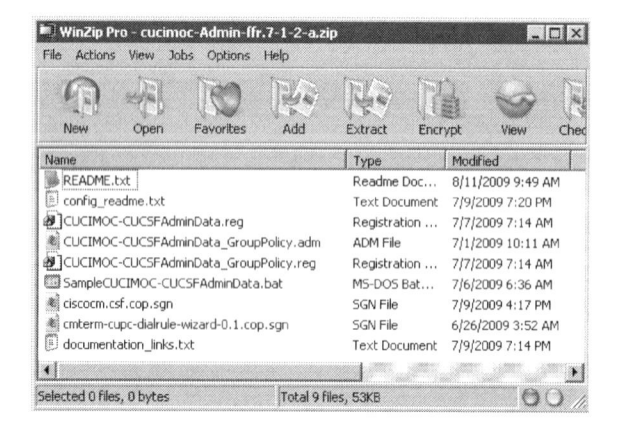

Cucimoc-Install contains the files for client installation (CUCIMOC add-on).

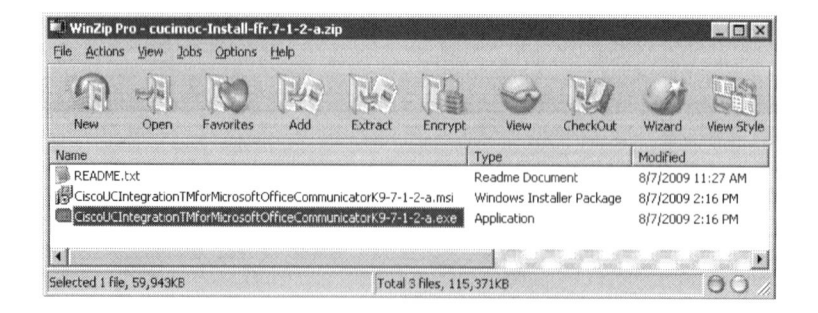

The Cucimoc-Install zip file contains an EXE and a MSI. They are pretty much the same. The only difference is: EXE would download and install .Net 3.5sp1 if needed. MSI would require .Net 3.5sp1 to be installed first.

Note: If .Net framework is not installed on the computer already, the installation EXE will try to download it and install it. This could take considerable long time and CUCIMOC installation would seem to be "not responding".

Configuration

Registry Keys

Instead of using Windows registry editor, it's recommended to use batch file to update registry.

You may find SampleCSFClientDeviceSettings.bat file in the admin package. Edit the file with notepad. Here are some of the most important parameters:

TFTP – the CUCM server address running TFTP service. This is for CUCIMOC to download the soft phone configuration and dial rules.

CTI – the CUCM server address running CTIManager service. This is for desk phone control.

CCMCIP – the CUCM server address running "Cisco CallManager Cisco IP phone" service. This is for CUCIMOC login.

VMPilot – the default voicemail pilot configured on CUCM.

LDAP – LDAP related configurations.

You should edit the BAT file with appropriate attribute. Then run it to update the registry. You may verify the update by using Windows registry editor and look at "HKCU\Software\Cisco Systems, Inc.\Client Services Framework\AdminData"

CUCM

Depending on the features you want, you'll need to configure CUCM for the following:

- CUCIMOC logon
- Soft phone
- Desk phone control
- Dial Rules

CUCIMOC Logon

CUCIMOC authenticate against CCMCIP service. To make sure CCMCIP service is running, please go to CUCM Serviceability > Tools > Control Center – Network Services. Make sure "Cisco CallManager Cisco IP Phone Services" is running.

CM Services	
Service Name	Status
○ Cisco CallManager Personal Directory	Running
○ Cisco Extension Mobility Application	Running
○ Cisco CallManager Cisco IP Phone Services	Running

Soft phone

To use soft phone feature in CUCIMOC, you need to create a CSF device.

If you're running an old version of CUCM, CSF device type might not be available. You'll need to upgrade the CUCM or install "ciscocm.csf.cop.sgn" file on CUCM. "ciscocm.csf.cop.sgn" file can be found in the admin package. You need to restart CUCM cluster after installing the file.

To create a CSF device, follow the steps below:

Step 1: Go to CUCM Admin > Device > Phone. Click "Add New".

Step 2: From the "Phone Type" drop-down menu, choose "Cisco Unified Client services Framework". Click "Next".

Step 3: Configure device name. You may use any name as "Device Name", as long as it's accepted by CUCM. Though there's no requirement on the naming conventions, it's recommended that you use a unified naming convention for ease of management. For example, it might be a good idea to contain the user ID or directory number in the device name. So you can easily identify them.

Step 4: Configure other device parameters. Configure other parameters like you configure a regular phone. If the user already has a desk phone, you may use the configuration on the desk phone for reference (such as Calling Search Space, MOH, etc.)

Step 5: Add directory number. CSF device supports only one line. If the user has multiple lines on desk phone, configure the primary line on CSF device. This line should match the "Primary Extension" on end user configuration page ("CUCM Admin > User Management > End User").

Step 6: Associate the device with end user. Go to CUCM Admin > User Management > End User. Find the end user you want to configure. Click "Device Association". Association the CSF device you just created to the end user.

Desk Phone Control

Desk phone control configuration would be the exactly the same as CUPC desk phone control. The steps would be: associate desk phone with end user, put end user in "Standard CTI Enabled" group. For details, please refer to CUPC desk phone control.

Dial Rules

The configuration of Dial Rule would be the same as CUPC. But the way to populate dial rules to CUCIMOC would be very different.

Based on current design, CUCIMOC can only download configuration from CUCM via TFTP protocol. CUCIMOC cannot query CUCM database (where ADRs are stored). In order to bridge this gap, Cisco provides a cmterm-cupc-dialrule-wizard-0.1.cop.sgn file. This file can be found in CUCIMOC admin package.

Every time you install this file on CUCM, CUCM will read the dial rules in database and put the rules in two XML files – AppDialRules.xml and DirLookupDialRules.xml. CUCM then put these two files in TFTP folder for CUCIMOC to download.

Because of this, every time you make a change in dial rules on CUCM, you need to do the following:

      1) Reinstall cmterm-cupc-dialrule-wizard-0.1.cop.sgn file.
      2) Restart TFTP

Active Directory

It is very important (and required) that all MOC users have their phone numbers in E.164 format. A phone number in E.164 format would be like +14085551234.

MOC gets the phone numbers from OCS address book. OCS gets the phone numbers from Active Directory. To make things simple, you'd better make sure phone numbers in Active Directory are in E.164 format. If not, you need to configure "Number Normalization" on OCS, which is outside the scope of this book.

Troubleshooting

Like CUPC, the most useful troubleshooting tools have been built in the client:

"Tools > Create Problem Report" will collect all logs for troubleshooting purpose.
"Tools > Server Status" will give you real-time status of the server.

I'll include more troubleshooting tips in the next edition of this book for the following reason:

1. This book is for Cisco Unified Presence (CUPS). CUCIMOC has nothing to do with CUPS. It was introduce here as an alternative of MOC RCC (which requires CUPS).
2. Most of the problems are Microsoft related (such as registry keys, permission, group policy, etc.) instead of Cisco related.
3. Most of the "tips" won't be needed in the next release of CUCIMOC when Cisco improves the interoperability between CUCIMOC and Microsoft.

Appendix

CUPS Documentations:
http://www.cisco.com/en/US/products/ps6837/tsd_products_support_series_home.html

CUPC Documentations:
http://www.cisco.com/en/US/products/ps6844/tsd_products_support_series_home.html

CUCM Documentations:
http://www.cisco.com/en/US/products/sw/voicesw/ps556/tsd_products_support_series_home.html

Session Initiation Protocol (SIP) on IETF:
http://www.ietf.org/html.charters/sip-charter.html

XMPP Standard Foundation:
http://xmpp.org/

XMPP on IETF :
http://datatracker.ietf.org/wg/xmpp/charter/

Wireshark (Packet Sniffer):
http://www.wireshark.org/

FreeFTPd (SFTP server)
http://www.freeftpd.com/

WinGrep
http://www.wingrep.com/

Made in the USA
Lexington, KY
04 May 2012